Also by Leland Stowe

NO OTHER ROAD TO FREEDOM

". . . he possesses all the qualities of the glamorous war correspondent. Among these are the gifts of vivid description and dramatization, warm emotional sympathy for the peoples whose struggles he is reporting, and a remarkable knack of being in the most exciting place at the right time."
—W. H. Chamberlin in the *Atlantic Monthly*

THEY SHALL NOT SLEEP

"One of the best of our war correspondents does one of the best pieces of reporting that has come out of the war."
—the *New Yorker*

These are Borzoi Books published by

ALFRED · A · KNOPF

While Time Remains

WHILE
TIME
REMAINS

Leland Stowe

ALFRED A. KNOPF

NEW YORK

1947

THIS IS A BORZOI BOOK,
PUBLISHED BY ALFRED A. KNOPF, INC.

Published August 22, 1946
Second Printing, October 1946
Third Printing, January 1947
Fourth Printing, January 1947

TO YOU—

If You Care

ACKNOWLEDGMENTS

Sources of information have been identified as scrupulously as possible in these pages which, I hope, may serve as a modest sort of sourcebook to our present, doubly-revolutionary world.

In the preparation of this manuscript I have been assisted enormously by the intelligent criticism and unfailing encouragement of my wife, Ruth Bernot Stowe, and of Anna Gale Seidler; also by the friendly interest and suggestions of Sonia Tomara and of Derso; in the final stages, by the perceptive recommendations offered by Blanche Knopf and Bernard Smith. To each of these friends, my sincere thanks for tightening the keel and loosing the stays of this paper boat. Bon voyage.

L. S.

BRONXVILLE, N. Y.
APRIL, 1946.

CONTENTS

xi

PART I

The Shape of Things Present

Chapter I

INVITATION TO AN INVENTORY

No doubt but ye are the People—absolute,
strong, and wise;
Whatever your heart has desired ye have not
withheld from your eyes.
On your own heads, in your own hands, the
sin and the saving lies!

Rudyard Kipling

I suppose I shall always remember Mireille because she's the only woman who ever asked if she could kiss me. Of course, Mireille was very young and also very French—which probably accounts for it. And Suzy was also very young and very French, and I have a particular reason to remember her, too.

It seemed they were as fresh and unspoiled as girls of seventeen or eighteen could possibly be; and in this newly liberated, American-occupied, and supersophisticated Paris they were like the two first tulips of spring, swaying and laughing in the March wind. They were sitting at the adjoining table in the corner café, and three GIs, who knew only about two words of French apiece, were straining themselves in strenuous pantomime that only resulted in gales of laughter from blonde Suzy and more restrained mirth from the dark Mireille. The GI, who was much taken by Suzy, and rightly so, enlisted me as interpreter as soon as he heard me speak to the waiter. After that I was kept very busy, in a very gay fashion, for the next half hour.

I translated the eloquent pleadings of Suzy's American admirer as accurately as possible, and gilded them with some of those French expressions which really put a glow on words. But it didn't make a bit of difference. These were obviously *jeunes filles*, well-brought-up as the French say. They regretted very much, but they could not go dancing. Yes, they would like to go; it would give them great pleasure, but it was not possible. "Will you explain, Monsieur, that in France *jeunes filles* well-brought-up do not go out dancing with young men whom they have not met before, not even with our gallant allies?" So I explained that several times, with Suzy and Mireille teasing and joking constantly in between; and finally the three GIs reluctantly accepted defeat and bade their regretful adieus with a sincerity that was highly justified. I think they left half-realizing that they had met something of the best of France; as I lingered understanding that some of the best of France, high-spirited and full of the joy of living, still remains and has not been dimmed.

This is how it happened that I walked Mireille and Suzy to their door, only a few blocks from our old home near the Porte Champerret. Their questions and their observations came in torrents, like persons who have wondered too much and experienced too much for too long a time. What a relief to have the Germans gone! And they told about the German officer who had almost run them down in his car, and had leapt out and struck them when he heard Suzy exclaim: "Dirty Boche!" They told about their fathers who had both been taken into Germany as slave laborers and were still there. They were both incredibly young, with a freshness that made it seem that the war and the long years of occupation had scarcely touched them at all. They were both slight and not very tall; the one, brown-eyed and more reflective; the other, golden-haired, with her fine features aglow with eagerness and vivacity. They were gay as the French are born to be gay, yet they were suddenly earnest as only the young can be earnest.

We stood by the door, still talking swiftly, and at last I started to hold out my hand to say good-bye; reluctantly, too. Then Mireille, in her suddenly serious way, and in a manner as completely inexpressible as it was utterly unexpected, said: "Will you permit us to kiss you, *Monsieur?*" In French there is somehow something uncapturable in that phrase as I heard it: *"Voulez-vous nous permettre de vous embrasser, Monsieur?"* I think I must have felt as if someone had suddenly presented me with the grand cross of the Legion of Honor or the Congressional Medal. So I kissed Mireille, and I kissed Suzy, and we said *au 'voir* and then *bonne chance;* and I walked back to the subway for the Place de l'Opéra thinking how wonderful the world is that there are still such wonderful people in it.

And on the way I thought again of what Suzy, with that same

sudden and urgent earnestness, had said: "Will the Americans stay a long time? Oh, I hope so. And how long will the Allies occupy Germany?" Then a pause, and then with even greater earnestness: *"We don't want to get married and have children, and then have to send them to another war."*

This now seems like quite a long time ago and something that happened in another world; but it wasn't really very long ago, and I feel sure that Mireille and Suzy are much the same, and I know they would ask many of the same questions, and Suzy would say the same thing. The world, too, is the same world in most ways, and yet it is an entirely different world as well. But in this changed and changing world the great consuming fear and the desperate hope of petite and lovely Suzy is the common fear and hope of women who face motherhood in every land. These are yearnings which belong to the ages. Yet since I said *au 'voir* near the Porte Champerret they have taken on a new urgency and a new meaning. I could say now: "Don't worry, Suzy, about having to send your sons to another war. If it happens, only a few will have to go to it. If it happens, Suzy, it will come to all of us—to all of us living in great cities, it will come *where we are,* and then we shall be finished. It will not be a war of soldiers, Suzy. It will be a war to annihilate civilians *en masse."*

But perhaps Suzy and Mireille are engaged or married by now, and they still have time for perhaps a great happiness in a little time; or perchance, for more happiness in the midst of many difficulties over a longer time. In any case, Suzy and Mireille will have a certain time in which to think; a certain time in which to look at our changed and changing world. And in this they will have as much as you and I and no more. Will they make more of it than we, I wonder? I wonder, too, if you and I—in our unscathed America—will make as much of it as they?

For the little time that seems sure, and the greater time which is so unsure, is all the time that any of us will have. The world that used to be exists no more. The world which they taught us about, and which they thought they had in some measure educated us to live in, has disappeared. And Mireille and Suzy have become our daughters or our sisters in a new sense, but we have always thought of them as being French and very different from ourselves. Now, suddenly, they are more our daughters or our sisters than we know; and their fears are our fears, and their desperate hope is our desperate hope; and the freshness of their faces is the freshness of this very life which has become newly dear to all mankind. It was not like this, in this intensity, in 1919 —or in 1939. The world that is still so very old has become unbelievably new, and it is this strange and tremulous and unpredictable newness which defies our comprehension, yet at the same time has made the whole world kin.

This is why we cannot shut our eyes or turn our heads. This is why the time has come when each of us must somehow strive to take an inventory of this strange new world in which all of us may live for a little while, and each of us may not remain for very long. For the fact is plain that the world we now know cannot survive for long unless it is better managed than the old world ever was. The fact is plain that neither men nor governments can safely manage what they do not understand. The fact is indisputable that those who are elected to govern for us cannot be expected to show more comprehension and more vision than we ourselves possess. We say that those whom we elect should ask the right questions and know the right answers. But this is a strange, new world. Things that are happening on the other side of it or in its farthest corners are also directly related to life or death for us. Most of this world's vital problems now come knocking at your door and mine. What we cannot be bothered with and what we pass unheeded may well determine the final, unalterable destiny of us all. This is why—

It is time for an inventory of the new world in which we live.

What has happened to our old world since 1939? What explains the new power of the Soviet Union? How does the new Europe differ from the old? How and why do the Europeans of today differ in their thinking, their desires, and their demands from what they were thinking, sought, and were satisfied with just a few short years ago? Why are the Europeans closer to Americans in a physical sense since the war, yet more removed in spirit and mentality? And what explains this rising tide of national awakening among hundreds of millions of Asiatics from India to Korea? Why are the Chinese people disillusioned and impatient? Why do they pin their hopes for a chance at self-government and democracy chiefly upon America and the American people?

Then there is the new position of the United States as the world's most powerful nation. Do we tend to take this too much for granted? Because we are so conscious of our great advantages do we ask ourselves what our disadvantages are as we assume such a fateful role? Are most of us aware that we too have disadvantages, and that certain of these could cost America dear? Would you venture to claim that we Americans are adequately prepared for world leadership? Indeed, have we even been educated for peace?

The questions which we share with all humanity multiply themselves at an amazing rate. In whatever order you may place them it's extraordinary how they overlap and are interrelated. Peace, hope, and survival for Asia's billion people and Europe's hundreds of millions can no longer be divorced from the same aspirations throughout North and South America. Survival, in truth, has now become the paramount personal problem for a vast legion of peoples everywhere. The days of one out of every two inhabitants of the British Isles may now be numbered. But so may the days of one out of every three Americans. A slight difference in percentage does not matter much when nations must estimate their possible future war casualties in scores of millions. Yet politics and politicians in other lands usually seem, at first glance, to be pretty much a repetition of the same old thing.

Why should it matter to the George Joneses of Kalamazoo or Pocatello what kind of government the Greeks have? Or the Bulgarians, or the Chinese? George Jones is not related to any of these peoples. Why should *their* problems be related to *him*? The Russians want their spheres of influence in eastern Europe and the Near East. The British want theirs in the Mediterranean and the colonial regions. Why should George Jones bother his head about all this any more than his father, back in 1919, bothered his head about similar problems? People are busy getting back to normal in Kalamazoo. But somehow the Joneses are strangely like Suzy and Mireille. They don't want to send *their* children to fight another war. It's a natural, human desire. But do we dare phrase it that way? Do we dare to ask any more for our children than we ask for other peoples' children everywhere —in this kind of world?

We begin to take stock and the questions come tumbling. Before you do more than begin to concentrate on the first two or three, something interrupts you. Sometimes everything seems too complicated anyhow; and most of the time there's plenty else that's much more fun doing. Taking inventory is kind of a drudge. You do it only when you have to—maybe once a year. Or maybe not at all, if you have the habit of floating along and letting someone else do the itemizing. But supposing they've passed a law that all those who don't take inventory get shot? Or supposing they haven't passed a law, but what's likely to happen is a million times worse than that? Well, it may be there are one or two inventories in a lifetime which it would be fatal to skip. Perhaps this is a time when taking stock could be an important investment. Otherwise our refusal might sound like the jest of a ghost in a graveyard at five seconds to midnight— and the trouble is that it could be so.

Even a fabulous world revolution frequently gets snowed under or washed out of sight by the day-to-day incidentals. Fiction, of course, is infinitely more entertaining than fact, and often it seems considerably more exciting than a momentous world revolution—*unless* you know you are in one, and unless you understand that you'll never be able to escape it as long as you live. So a great deal depends on what kind of pencils and adding machines we use for our inventory. An enormous lot depends on the kind of eyes with which we look, and whether we comprehend that right now is perhaps the most urgent Time for Inventory since the birth of Christ. But if you and I can bring reasonably accurate tools and the proper measuring rods, this stock-taking, as of 1946, might be more exciting and repay us more than we had supposed.

When you take a close, round-the-world look you see that taking stock has rather formidable dimensions. You will probably find, as I do, that it can scarcely be done off-the-cuff; in your spare time. But has there ever been a more wonderfully exciting world to explore? And is it not the more provocatively interesting because your future and mine are inextricably involved with what becomes of it? We shall find things to which we cannot go back, and other things to which we must go forward. We shall find certain things which can never be the same, and others which will always be the same. And we shall see, perhaps a little more closely, those dominant and inescapable features of the new world which make us brothers—in fear and hope and destiny—with all mankind. Perhaps we shall see a little more clearly some of those fundamental and imperative questions for which we must all strive to find answers because we cannot possibly escape the questions. Certain of these questions must some day add up to life, or add up to death, for hundreds of millions of human beings—and almost surely, in our time.

But this need not be a macabre and gloomy enterprise. It is you and I who still have the choice of a point of view, and the choice of direction. If we do not elect to voyage toward despair, then we shall set our sails toward hope. This is the great adventure; the adventure of living and facing life in an era of stupendous change. We are still men and women of free will; of minds which are or should be free. And our own personal decisions will count for one vote in the great and final decision. But to reach a personal decision that time's judges will rule as reasonably valid we must seek the widest possible range of pertinent facts. We must test our shaping conclusions with those of other searchers along the way.

For there are common denominators in our revolutionary world, and these are not beyond the reach of modest picks and shovels. To sense the new world and its unique adventure is to gain an advance assurance that we may find more than we had dared to hope. If we do not find all that we seek, we shall surely find more for the seeking. If we push back our horizons a little way we shall find others of greater skill and perception to push them back still farther. The inventory, it seems to me, is the beginning. It is an initial repudiation of doubt and fear; a first step toward hope; the reaffirmation of faith that man's greatest work is yet to be done, that human creatures are still capable of meeting a challenge more fateful than any which mankind has known in many centuries.

Chapter II

EMANCIPATED ATOMS VERSUS
UNEMANCIPATED MINDS

*And fire came down from God out of heaven
and devoured them.*
                    The Revelation of St. John

*Until we are taught what our history books do
not teach—that the fault is usually ours quite
as much as some other nation's—we have not
taken the first step to that wisdom which alone
can save us.*
                    Dr. Albert Einstein

When informed about Hiroshima, Hermann Göring blubbered: "I don't believe it." Upon being convinced, he exclaimed: "I don't want anything to do with it. I am leaving this world." Even Hitler's greatest champion of ruthless destruction from the air recognized immediately when it was time to call quits. We have since been witnessing how many militarists and ordinary civilians are far less intelligent than Air Marshal Göring.

Hiroshima was "atomized" on August 6, 1945.

With that single act the nature of the entire world was changed. All previous rules governing man's day-to-day safety and security were destroyed or radically diminished. What we had yearned for as a prelude to peace was suddenly transformed into a preface to superwar; a door opened to global annihilation. Our calendars still bore the legend: A.D. 1945. In reality humanity was now living in: Year One, A.A. (Atomic Age). After nearly two thousand years history had recorded another momentous dividing line. This dividing line is both deep and irrevocable.

Since August 6, 1945, governments and chiefs of staff have been striving desperately to juggle an atomic bomb. But when we juggle with a ball of uranium only one slip of the fingers is required. Only a single unretrieved fumble, and the game is ended. With that, the world as we know it will be gone forever. Thus our gambler's stakes for peace or war have been inflated to their highest peak of human folly. Where nations for so many centuries have shaken the dice for victory or defeat, nations must now gamble as all civilians must gamble—for survival.

This is what the multicolored mushroom of destruction spelled out ominously above the furnace of 100,000 bodies in Hiroshima. But man had created and committed what the average man's mind could scarcely begin to comprehend. Fear came—the most all-pervading fear in human history. Even so, it was many months before some slight comprehension of this new weapon of world-wide doom began to filter into public consciousness. Upon the average citizen the shock of the world's first atomic bomb was paralytic. For most of us this is still frighteningly true today. Like a whirling circus performer, catapulted out of a cannon at tremendous speed, we have been rocketed end over end into a terrifying new world. We are dizzy and our eardrums are still numb. Through the walls of our numbness and dizziness the atomic scientists have been trying to reach us. How much have we heard? How much have we understood?

Let's begin by attempting to put the facts in order. In these months of confusion the elite among some fifteen hundred atomic scientists have told us everything that any intelligent person needs to know. But they had to tell it piecemeal. Their indispensable information came here a little, there a little, as the unprecedented revolt of the scientists grew in scope and in boldness. Now their urgent warnings can be summarized.

What are the warnings of the atomic scientists?

"The atomic bomb is something against which no defense is possible, the 'secret' of which is *no secret at all* . . . the production of which by other nations is only a matter of time . . . not more than a few years, probably, for some of them." On all these counts Dr. R. J. Oppenheimer, director of Los Alamos, has the unanimous agreement of his fellow-scientists. He added: "From the armament race that would almost certainly follow, the United States might, or might not, emerge the winner—nor would it greatly matter."

The scientists have told us that "permanent security for the United States from the tremendous destructive power of the atomic bomb can be obtained *only* by means of *international control.*" [1] They have warned us that "lack of decision *within even a few months* will be preparing the world for unprecedented destruction, not only of other countries but our own as well." [2] They have declared that "a World Security Council must be made the *only custodian* of nuclear power in the world"; that "in a few years" America's bargaining power will have vanished, for many nations will have atomic bombs.[3] Their overwhelming conclusion has been that the United States must "initiate immediately steps to achieve effective world cooperation *for the prevention of war.*" [4] The final emphasis, let us note, is that the *abolition* of war—any kind of war—constitutes the only safe goal for humankind hereafter.

Interviewed by a *New York Herald Tribune* reporter,[5] Professor Albert Einstein stated: "I believe if the statesmen of the world will understand what is at stake they will not ask if it is possible to form a world government. They will realize *it is absolutely necessary, or a great part of humanity will be killed without need.*"

These are the principal findings of those foremost world authorities who split the atom and made the bomb. They have assured us that Armageddon and Doomsday are now suspended over the heads of our generation. That from 25,000,000 to 50,000,000 Americans can be—and *may* be—burned to nothing before 1970, or even before 1955. That the atomic bomb puts a premium upon starting a war *first*. That any smaller nation, such as Spain or Argentina, can be as aggressively powerful as the United States—once it accumulates a few hundred or few thousand bombs, and uses them first.

Thus, if we read and analyzed what we read, we learned that

1 Declaration by the Association of Manhattan District Scientists, October 29, 1945.

2 Statement of 400 members of the Association of Los Alamos Scientists, October 13, 1945.

3 Statement by the Association of Oak Ridge Scientists, September 1945.

4 Statement by 515 war research scientists of Harvard and Massachusetts Institute of Technology, October 30, 1945.

5 October 26, 1945.

war has now become so terrible it cannot be tolerated any longer. If we listened and if we thought, we learned that the huge armies and navies of 1944 belong, in large measure, to the age of Napoleon or of the Spanish Armada. We learned, too, that the same atomic energy—if employed solely for peaceful purposes—might lift the standards of living of hundreds of millions of people to an incredible level within this century. We were also shown— if we cared to learn—that all the world's peoples are in the same shaky, menaced, wobbling boat; that the Bulgar and the Bolivian, the Peruvian and the Pole, the Chinese and the Canadian, the Russian and the Briton, the American and the African—that all the members of our modern Tower of Babel have only one world and only one fate.

It was this realization which prompted Anthony Eden to declare in the House of Commons: [6] "Every succeeding scientific discovery makes greater nonsense of old-time conceptions of sovereignty. . . . For the life of me I am unable to see any final solution that will make the world safe from atomic power other than that we all abate our present ideas of sovereignty. We have got somehow to take the sting out of nationalism. . . . I want to go to a world where relations between nations can be transformed in a given period of time as the relations between England, Scotland and Wales have been transformed."

Anthony Eden spoke with a Damoclean sense of the shadow of doom and the shortness of time. He spoke a new language for a new atomic world. But this was not the kind of language or of thought which emerged from the White House during those first crucial months after Hiroshima. Looking back now we can see how America's voice became tragically lost in the very midst of one of the greatest, most perilous crises in history. With the passage of these many months it becomes painfully clear—

How Washington blundered in handling the atomic crisis of 1945.

Historians, I am convinced, cannot fail to place responsibility for the following serious errors in international and domestic

[6] November 22, 1945.

atomic policy squarely upon the United States government and the Truman administration:

1. The first grave and irreparable mistake was for the United States Army to use the bomb offensively, thereby killing 100,000 persons—all but a few, civilians. This was done over the appeal and protest of an important proportion of American atomic scientists who urged President Truman that a test demonstration of the bomb's destructiveness, without needless infliction of death, should be made. That, they insisted, should be sufficient to make Japan sue for peace. But the President listened to certain U.S. Army generals. The bomb was used against Japanese cities instead of Japanese wastelands or forests. The United States became morally guilty of being the first nation to inflict mass murder, on a scale of horror hitherto unknown, through an atomic weapon. It cannot be contended today that a "test demonstration" would have failed to precipitate an early surrender of Japan. History's stark record simply reads that America's leaders were not humane enough to make the attempt. The terrible indictment of Hiroshima and Nagasaki defied and shocked the men who made the bomb. But the indictment now stands against us, written indelibly in human anguish and some 150,000 snuffed-out human lives.

2. Washington's second atomic blunder was almost as disastrous and short-sighted politically as its first was morally. By using the atomic bomb our government immediately enveloped the world in a fog of acute fear. Having created this unprecedented worldwide apprehension, this new terror of potential annihilation, the first obligation of the United States government was to take some swift and reassuring action to relieve anxiety in every world capital—and especially in Moscow. Yet for nearly *three months* after August 6 President Truman made no gesture toward any of our wartime allies. In late October Prime Minister Attlee had to invite himself to Washington for an atomic conference, with Canada included. Not until late November was any American move made toward consultation with the Soviet Union—and in this period of wasted opportunity Russian-American relations sank to an all-time low.

How this could have been permitted to happen defies all common sense and reveals the most elementary grasp of human psychology. Whatever our differences or complaints against Soviet Russia, she had fought loyally as an ally throughout the war. Her losses in soldier and civilian dead had been from twenty to fifty times greater than those suffered by Americans. Even comparative newcomers to international politics, like the President and Secretary of State Byrnes, should have understood the Soviets' long-harbored suspicions of the long-term intentions of the capitalist governments toward their Marxist state. When we had kept secret, used, and were still manufacturing atomic bombs —and when we made no move to discuss the future status of this frightful new weapon with them—what could the Russians help concluding? They could only conceive that Washington was deliberately holding the atomic bomb over their heads "to make them toe the line" according to Western and capitalistic prescriptions. Living in such diverse circumstances no human beings could be expected to react in any other way. But America's spokesmen remained silent. For the Russians, the French, or any others outside the tight Anglo-American orbit they had no word of reassurance; no statesmanlike promise of some immediate common cooperation against a common peril.

If there had been imagination or psychological awareness in Washington (speaking only of top levels), President Truman would have called a Big Three atomic conference within three weeks after Hiroshima. Instead, Marshal Stalin was left in foreboding seclusion in his Crimean retreat, nursing apprehensions and counterbalancing actions which can only be imagined— where that degree of obvious imagination exists. The essential facts are plain. The United States *created* the atomic crisis. In those initial months when a demonstration of American goodwill was most essential, Washington's leaders, internationally, demonstrated nothing but—tongue-tiedness, paralysis and lack of vision. In foreign eyes these, in turn, frequently boiled down to lack of American good faith. In the opinion of many of these alarmed people the United States was "keeping the secret" to dominate or dictate to the rest of the world.

3. The consequence of Washington's failure at once to call in the Russians may prove to be an error of inestimable costliness for most of Europe, Asia, and all of North America. It may have launched a race in atomic armaments which the United

Nations Organization is incapable of stopping or curbing. The hard fact is that the United States government, by failing to make a gesture toward Moscow for nearly four months, actually *invited* the Russians to start an atomic arms competition with the Anglo-American powers. It is already clear that the first stage of such an extremely dangerous armaments race was well under way before 1945 ended. The Soviets could not afford to wait indefinitely for President Truman, Secretary Byrnes, and a few others to make up and speak their minds. The Russians reacted just as our American generals would have reacted, had the bomb been in the other's pocket. Historically, the Truman administration's share of responsibility for this unhappy development can scarcely be glossed over. Once again, having made and used the bombs—and steadily making more of them—it was chiefly America's responsibility to take an immediate international initiative to prevent an armaments race.

The Soviets did not conceal the practical nature of their re-actions. On November 6, 1945, Foreign Commissar Molotov declared to a vast 28th-anniversary audience's pronounced applause: "We will have atomic energy, and many other things, too." And when Joseph Stalin at last spoke out, months later, he stated pointedly: "We are building on a large scale scientific research institutes to enable science to develop. I have no doubt that if we help our scientists, they will not only catch up with but surpass those abroad." [7]

Generalissimo Stalin, I have noticed, has a habit of making many of his most significant declarations in a single, unadorned sentence. He rivals the British in his gift for understatement. In this case the implications behind Stalin's few words were enormous. . . . What Washington had so heedlessly asked for in the way of an atomic arms race, the world had now got. Again and again the scientists had warned that this ominous thing would happen if our government wasted those first decisive months. But when prompt action to prevent such a race was imperative, our American leaders offered the world nothing—and did nothing co-operatively.

4. What the U.S. Army was doing meanwhile, however, consti-

[7] Stalin's important Five-Year Plan speech of February 9, 1946.

tuted Washington's fourth major atomic blunder. Our Army continued to manufacture atomic bombs. The more bombs we made, the more frightened foreign governments and peoples became. The United States was using its "sacred trust" (self-appointed) apparently to stock-pile enough bombs to destroy almost every major city in Europe and Asia. Many other people besides the Russians asked—why? The United States of America could cripple any single industrial power in the world with a few score atomic bombs. Why, they asked, are Americans making hundreds of such bombs? Does Washington actually want peace? Or does it really want to boss the world?

Nearly one year after Hiroshima the U.S. Army was still producing more and more bombs—and reputedly far more destructive bombs. This was heaping fear upon fear. It was equally senseless because the United States—with its biggest air force, incomparably largest navy, and the bomb—was already a super-Goliath astride the globe. In the next two years no other nation could conceivably produce an atomic bomb. What possible good would hundreds and hundreds of more bombs do the U.S. Army, or the American people? For the immediate short period both were utterly unassailable from any quarter on earth. When the UN Assembly held its first meeting in London in January 1946, the Truman administration missed another unique opportunity. The U.S. delegation could—and should—have announced a one-year's recess on bomb manufacturing. That would have demonstrated American goodwill to the other nations. It would also have been a spur toward reaching an international atomic agreement.

But the American atomic generals were very much in the saddle in Washington. At a press conference, CBS Correspondent Tris Coffin asked Secretary Byrnes: "Were you or the State Department consulted on the decision to continue manufacture of atomic bombs?" [8] Mr. Byrnes seemed surprised, even startled. After a thoughtful pause he answered: "No. We were not." This is a very sobering and damaging admission. For the U.S. Army to continue making atomic bombs month after month, with complete secrecy as to their number and location, was inevitably an action which must profoundly affect American diplomacy

[8] See Tris Coffin: "Washington's Atomic War," the *Nation*, February 16, 1946.

and peace-making negotiations with every major nation. It had
already helped to poison our relations with Russia for many
months. Yet the Secretary of State had never so much as been
consulted about the advisability of the Army's action.

These first four atomic errors, originating in the United States
government, are all international in their disruptive and distrust-
sowing repercussions. In our domestic field at least two related
matters must be classified as serious mistakes. The first of these
was the May-Johnson bill, which Professor Einstein has described
as "a measure of such reactionary tendency as has never been
thought of by any modern state." This Army-sponsored measure
provided such rigid censorship and dictatorial control over all
atomic research and developments that it forced the scientists
into open revolt. Its antidemocratic extremism killed its chances.
But the charge stands that the generals behind the May-Johnson
bill made strong efforts to get it railroaded through Congress.
Dr. Leo Szilard, one of the leading atomic scientists, has said:
"On the 9th of October, however, it transpired that the [Army's]
earlier request for exercising discretion [in the scientists' public
expressions] arose from a desire of having the May-Johnson bill
passed—I quote—'*without unnecessary discussions in Congress.*'"

The menace of the flagrantly iron-handed May-Johnson bill
plainly was permitted to arise from another and closely related
atomic blunder in Washington's high places. President Truman
and his civilian advisers were taking most of their advice from
a few Army and Navy officers—and were seeking almost no guidance from those eminent scientific authorities who solved nuclear
fission and made the bomb. In the course of the first months it
was demonstrated that a few Army generals, in particular, dominated almost every key White House decision in regard to the
atomic crisis, both domestic and international. Analyze each of
the six major atomic blunders I have just enumerated and you
will find that either the military mind or a lack of imagination
(if the two can often be separated) was chiefly responsible for
them. Mostly, in the first critical months, President Truman
leaned upon the advice of Major General Leslie R. Groves, military chief of the Manhattan Project, and a few others.

What seemed incredible to me at the time was complete lack
of indication from Washington that President Truman and

Secretary of State Byrnes were consulting a truly wide and representative group of the nation's topmost atomic scientists. It's true that Dr. Vannevar Bush and Dr. James B. Conant, president of Harvard University, served as advisers closely associated with General Groves. But these two outstanding citizens were not primarily nuclear physicists. They had not worked on the key research and they had not made the bomb. What about the 1,500 atomic scientists who were intimately concerned with various phases of this revolutionary development? Among them there were certainly a score or more physicists to be ranked as world authorities on atomic energy. Why did the President not call in the most prominent of these men who had lived with the bomb and who had pondered longest and most seriously on how its terrible destructiveness might be controlled?

At this writing, many months after Hiroshima, there has never been any evidence that such a step was ever taken by Washington's policy-makers—not before a few of the real atomic authorities began to appear before the Senate's McMahon Committee. It would have seemed elementary common sense to call to the White House immediately after August 6 such pre-eminent scientists as Dr. Harold C. Urey, Dr. Enrico Fermi, Dr. Henry DeWolf Smyth, Dr. Leo Szilard, Dr. Albert Einstein, and a score of others. Instead of this a handful of Washington's military minds largely monopolized the attention of our government's chief policy-makers—even where the policies being decided were social, political, and scientific. With the most brilliant collection of atomic-fission brains in the world readily available the record stands, throughout those decisive first months, that the Truman administration did not begin to make use of them.

If our most authoritative nuclear scientists had been called in at the outset, several of the six serious atomic errors which I have been compelled to enumerate here might certainly have been avoided. Instead of this, the United States government fumbled and floundered around, and in large part because it was not beginning to utilize America's superb scientific brain power. But the paralysis and the lack of imagination displayed by Washington's key policy-makers were merely a reflection of the confusion or indifference being then displayed by a majority of American citizens. We must confess frankly that we, as a people, revealed extremely little awareness of the stupendous world crisis which the U.S. Army precipitated by bombing Hiroshima. The emancipated atom had collided head-on with the general public's unemancipated minds. If the bomb itself could blast a large city into nothingness, it still could not make more than a slight dent on tens of millions of unemancipated minds.

With a stargazer's delightful whimsy Dr. Harlow Shapley, director of Harvard University Observatory, remarked that the atomic crisis "has been sudden for slow thinkers." In the United States, much more noticeably than in countries which have known repeated bombings, the advent of the Atomic Age has been marked to an alarming degree by slow thinking. It is time that we turned our concerned attention to—

The menace of our unemancipated minds.

Even in the spring of 1946, as I have had too strikingly confirmed during a recent interlude of lecturing, the majority of Americans are amazingly ill-informed or frighteningly unconcerned about the dimensions of the atomic peril under which we now live. Although the scientists have been talking their heads into weariness, and even though the newspapers have printed a certain amount of their testimony and speeches, it's clear that the average American has read little more than the headlines about the atomic crisis. Because this is a very unpleasant subject, people steer away from it. In this Year One, Atomic Age, our press, radio, and motion pictures have definitely not distinguished themselves by any intelligent and consistent efforts at atomic education. For these and other reasons it seems almost certain that the first anniversary of Hiroshima will find 85 or 90 percent of American adults and students lamentably and dangerously uninformed about our extremely risky future in an era of atomic weapons.

After several months of the scientists' persistent warnings, the Gallup poll indicated that possibly 73 percent of American citizens favored keeping "secret" what the makers of the bomb had been repeatedly declaring was no secret at all. That is a revealing measuring rod of the illusions and self-deceptions which a great many among us are nourishing in a kind of perverse blindness.

Either it is "slow thinking," or it is an incredible ostrichism. What couldn't an atomic bomb do to a nation with its head in the sands? Yet for all their magnificent battle to reach the American people with the most compelling atomic facts, the scientists, long after Hiroshima, seemed usually to be plunging themselves heroically against a frustrating wall of feathers—ostrich feathers at that! When your child's life is known to be threatened with infantile paralysis, or your own life is imperiled by any dread disease, do you hire a renowned specialist—and then disregard most of what he tells you must be done? This is the last folly any of us would think of committing. But the atomic scientists are equally great specialists. They have been telling us again and again what we must do—and most of us have paid little or no attention to their prescriptions. This, in truth, is the fantastic folly of the unemancipated mind.

In your lifetime and in mine—at any time after another four or five years—it is now conceivable that atomic rockets and similar missiles may destroy between 100,000,000 and 500,000,000 human beings; a large percentage of them Americans. The atomic ultimatum, therefore, is unescapable. It is one world—or none. It is control and abolition of atomic weapons—or a world perpetually dominated by the anarchy of a fearful race in suicidal armaments of mass destruction. But we are still a long way from a Government of the World's Peoples. We are still sadly unfit for a Brotherhood of Man. Mentally, spiritually, and morally most of humanity, like most Americans, must be recorded as unemancipated and, consequently, gravely unprepared.

Through their technical and scientific brilliance a few hundred physicists have created a new world, fraught with the mixed potentialities of immeasurable death or immeasurable life. In atomic energy technology has fashioned either a Supreme Dictator or a Supreme Liberator of mankind—and the average citizens and voters of the western democracies will largely decide which of these it is to be. If the government and Congress in Washington have revealed themselves predominantly as slow-thinkers about the atomic crisis—and this became a recorded fact in Year One, A.A.—then the thinking and awareness of a great number of the American people's representatives must be speeded up, or they must be replaced by men of greater understanding and vision. Of course, this cannot be done without an American electorate which clearly comprehends the perilous years of decision and the nature of the atomic menace which now confront the peoples of earth.

In the next decade or two we can emancipate the world from the likelihood of atomic war. Or we can ape the infuriated ancient gods and duplicate—in reality, far exceed—their supremest wrath. A tiny fraction of earth's inhabitants, thanks to this fearful discovery, can decimate the white race and therewith subjugate and enslave the rest of the world. Or nations and peoples may unite to make these same smashed atoms serve all of humanity, and so provide scores or hundreds of millions of earth's impoverished with food, clothing, and opportunities such as they never knew. But we can never make atomic energy serve mankind if we use its presently limited supply chiefly to keep each other in a state of unrelaxed and increasing fear and dread. Admittedly, in these next few years, the menace of eventual global terror and worldwide annihilation must remain forever present and stupendously great. But the time-limited opportunity to transform atomic energy into a boon and blessing for all mankind is equally stupendous.

How can we achieve this transformation to high humanitarian purposes save through a far greater social and political awareness? How hope that other nations will dedicate their efforts to the spirit of peace unless we, the American people, become spiritually conscious of the great contribution we ourselves must make? How can we master the formidable machines we have created unless it be through a great broadening of our sense of brotherhood and community with humanity at large?

We have shaped a new world which is far too small to live in—and survive in—unless we understand that the fate of every other people is the fate of ourselves. For one hundred and seventy years we, the Americans, have lived in the prevailing conviction that American nationalism was sufficient safety in itself. Now we have inaugurated a weapon which, within a few years, will be able—from any remote corner of the earth—to obliterate New York or Chicago together with virtually all of their inhabitants. Thus, to be nothing more today than a nationalist—American or otherwise—is to choose to attempt to live alone, endlessly beneath the shadow of doom, for the remainder of your days. To be a nationalist in this Atomic Age is to be ever-ready and alerted for war—to invite war by imposing terrible fears upon your neighbors—to make war finally inevitable—and thus to condemn twenty or forty or more of our greatest American cities to sudden oblivion.

These, too, are facts which the atomic scientists have been trying to tell us throughout Year One of the Atomic Age. For the atomic crisis is far more than the unprecedented military and political crisis which is its most obvious manifestation. The atomic crisis is also a spiritual crisis, as much a crisis of public and private morality as a crisis of mass intelligence in every land. If we fail spiritually and intellectually—if we fail in our individual atomic *self-education*—it is hopeless to assume that our worldwide political crisis can be solved, or solved in time to prevent an eventual atomic war. In short, one thing must become clear to every man or woman who desires to survive and to exist in a livable world in this century: *We cannot conceivably emancipate the world until we emancipate ourselves.* That is the dictatorial, unalterable decree of the emancipated atom.

We yearned for the end of this last world war and before it had yet concluded we gained an instrument which threatens a war that would be a thousand or ten thousand times more horrible. Where 20,000,000 or 30,000,000 people died yesterday, perhaps one-fifth of humanity could be killed wantonly the day after tomorrow. In reality, then—and in severest restraint—one fact is clear. No nation's people can hereafter hope to save themselves from war without striving to save the entire world.

But this fear-ridden new world, this world with its paramount gamble in atomic existence, is also torn with social dissensions and complicated by many rival ambitions and greeds and contests for power. In such a world of rampant revolutionary forces the technological revolution of atomic energy has made its debut, superimposing a tremendous scientific revolution upon political and social revolutions already seething and unpredictable. In this same world the United States of America, for a fleeting period in history, exercises a physical power supreme above all others.

But how are the American government and the American people going to use the gigantic power which is theirs for the moment? In strict realism and honesty our record during Year One of the Atomic Age has been far from reassuring. We have not yet made a beginning upon which any serious optimism for survival, or for a tolerable chance at any protracted avoidance of catastrophe, can be based. Perhaps we need to weigh much more closely and accurately the relationship between American responsibilities and America's presently all-predominant but probably transitory power. From the Persians and the Pharaohs, through the Roman emperors and Genghis Khan, on into the undecipherable future the world's supremely powerful nations have had or can hope to exercise their opportunity of unchallengeable power only for an interval in the womb of time. Today we live in the superacceleration of *atomic time*. By comparison the Romans had centuries in which to learn what they could or could not do.*

---

* The State Department's "report on the international control of atomic energy" was released in April 1946, some weeks after this manuscript was completed. The report was prepared by a Board of Consultants under the chairmanship of David E. Lilienthal, appointed on January 23, 1946. It has become generally known as the Acheson Report or the Acheson-Lilienthal Report.

This statesmanlike and definitely encouraging document proposes an international "Atomic Development Authority" with two tasks: (1) to aid peaceful uses of atomic energy; (2) to create machinery to prevent its military use. The ADA itself would prospect, mine, and refine uranium and thorium. It would produce plutonium in plants equitably distributed throughout the world. But no nation or individual would be permitted to engage in any of these activities. In other fields of nuclear physics the report proposes that independent work by nations and individuals should be encouraged and the ADA would make available radioactive materials for scientific, technological, and medical works.

The Acheson-Lilienthal Report thus offers a broad and constructive basis for international negotiations toward the control and abolition of atomic weapons. The scientists hailed it as a forward step of much promise.

Chapter III

U.S. RESPONSIBILITIES VERSUS U.S. POWER

What made the strong man join the circus? I doubt very much that it started as an idea of an easy way to earn a living. It began on the back lots or in the neighborhood playground. It began with an adolescent, animalistic pleasure in showing off one's strength. The exceptionally muscled strong boy, especially if not overbright, simply graduates into the sawdust ring. There he continues to drink adulation—and actually gets paid for it. Of course, you and I admire his superb physique; in considerable part because it's perfectly safe for us to admire it. We know the strong man isn't going to whirl suddenly around and crack us on the jaw.

But with extremely strong nations things are entirely different. Different for the neighbors and the onlookers, I mean. For them it's like Mr. Five-feet-four standing at a frontier bar alongside two-gun Mr. Six-feet-three. So long as you're in that room, being Five-feet-four, you're pretty careful not to raise your voice above a certain pitch. It's two-gun Six-feet-three who usually makes the emphatic gestures, and obviously feels he can afford to do so. Sometimes, however, the Big Guy walks right into trouble with someone several inches smaller than he is. The big fellows often seem totally unconscious of how their words sound or their actions look to their smaller, less robust associates. Being big is frequently, in itself, an invitation to overestimate one's punch —and privileges.

Perhaps something of this was in President Truman's mind when, on August 9, 1945, he said: "We tell ourselves that we have emerged from this war the most powerful nation in the world—the most powerful nation, perhaps, in all history. That is true, but not in the sense some of us believe it to be true."

I read on hopefully, but the President failed to make specific the important truth he had touched upon. He did not nail it down with illustrations. The appeal to prudence, humility, and common sense on the part of the American people somehow got lost in a vague allusion. What remained was a familiar awareness; the recapitulation of—

The well-known American might.

Between the fall of France in June 1940 and the surrender of Japan in August 1945, the measure and extent of American power developed to fabulous, almost Gargantuan dimensions. Not an American lives today who is unconscious of this epoch-making transformation. If the present physical force of the United States is unpredictable in its future long-term influences, we are none the less vividly aware of possessing it. In their hours in the sun the Greeks and the Romans and each of their successors must have been equally conscious of the nature of their ascendancy.

So the self-confidence of the American of the waning 1940's is tinged, in varying degrees, by the knowledge of his country's foremost position in the world. He can join with the President in saying: "We are the most powerful nation militarily on earth; with the largest Navy and Air Force." He may reflect with self-congratulation—or with some trepidation—that his is the only truly solvent government among the larger nations; that his country possesses an overwhelming monopoly of the world's available gold. He may survey with pride a gigantic industrial plant, worth many billions of dollars, which has been doubled or trebled in relatively few years—which now exceeds by far the productive capacity of any other nation, or of a whole series of nations lumped together. Within the brief space of five years the United States of America became incomparably the Strong Man of twentieth-century earth; if not for this century's duration, surely for this generation.

These are tremendous facts. But they are so tremendous as to be a danger as well as a comfort to the American people. If they provide a vast amount of temporary security, if they are flattering to patriotic instinct and a natural New World egoism, they are equally capable of blurring our collective judgment and of perverting that American idealism which has offered greatest hope to humanity. *For power is what power does.* It is not what the strong man can lift, but what he does with what he lifts. It is not brawn alone that makes an All-American halfback. It is not smashing the atom, of itself, that can assure a great advance in human progress. It is what the atom-smashers do with the liberated atom. For the United States to be paramount in physical power does not in itself spell security; does not of itself imply any increased understanding of this revolutionary world; is not necessarily an ultimate good.

When the component parts of all American power have been added up one fearfully uncertain element remains: commensurate American responsibility.

This is why I wonder whether George Jones has taken into serious consideration—

Our widely neglected American weaknesses.

There has never been an empire or a world power which did not have within its armor the crevices of its eventual defeat or its ultimate failure. Cracks in any wall grow progressively from lack of attention. They are seldom repaired adequately at the last moment, in time of crisis. If we Americans were able to see ourselves as others see us, obviously we should make far fewer mistakes in the use of our enormous power; we should make fewer potential enemies, and a great many more friends.

Perhaps we are so well aware of America's power and unique advantages, as we fumble toward building peace, that we largely overlook the existence or importance of America's inevitable handicaps and disadvantages. Our credit column meets the eye in arresting capital letters. But for every nation, as for every man, there also exists a debit column. Supposing we were to call in almost any expert in human behavior, perhaps a psychologist who has specialized in the conduct of national entities as well as of individuals; a professor who has studied various nations' foreign policies in relation to the character and habits of their citizens.

What would such a professor find in the debit column of the United States as of today? While considering Uncle Sam as the world's greatest power, what weaknesses would he write down, coldly and objectively? This, too, could be a provocative, instructive, and constructive game on our national radio. And with a moderate amount of concentration I suspect almost any thoughtful American could anticipate some of the most obvious of the professor's findings. Some of them would surely fall into some such pattern as this.

The United States is handicapped in its avowed intention to play a leading role in building world peace by the following:

1. Lack of experience in handling world affairs; lack of a wide choice of citizens long trained in international politics; lack of an adequate number of diplomats, career men, and others with a broad grasp of contemporary revolutionary trends, in economics as in politics; a State Department, saddled with nineteenth-century habits and ingrown bureaucratic inefficiency, which is still far from renovated or modernized.

2. By the long-established inclination of American voters to leave foreign affairs to the President and the Secretary of State; the failure of American citizens to keep themselves informed on developments in foreign countries and foreign relations; the general tendency of Americans to exert no persistent influence upon the makers of American foreign policies, or to become genuinely concerned about Washington's disputable actions only when war, or the threat of war, is upon us.

3. In general a lack of active civic responsibility on the part of Americans. (The percentage of those qualified who actually vote in our average local or national elections is sufficient confirmation of this fact.)

4. The widespread American assumption that technological and material progress automatically constitutes political progress; that superrefrigerators or the newest thing in television in themselves imply that American democracy is marching forward and leading the world.

5. The pretty general tendency to believe that what the all-wise founding fathers shaped in 1787 is sufficiently all-embracing to meet the formidable industrial, economic, and social strains of the U.S.A. in 1946 or 1947—without constant adjustments and rather frequent amendments or revisions. The American public's lack of comprehension that the struggle to find a balance between social controls and individual freedom is as ever-present in the United States today as in Europe and Asia.

6. The curious aversion of a majority of Americans to political ideas. (Our professor insists that the prevalent fear of "foreign isms" in the United States is not merely a healthy skepticism about Marxism or Fascism. In his analysis the American people have lost a great deal of their keen, intelligent interest in political trends and political meanings which characterized so many of our national leaders between 1776 and 1865. The professor maintains that Americans have tended to become self-satisfied or timid and indifferent in their political thinking while becoming engrossed in technical skills and mechanical progress; that we have become increasingly less interested in the functionings of democracy while becoming more and more interested in the functioning of turbines and physical production. In technology and the sciences, so the professor says, we experiment constantly and boldly; but in regard to the political system, which must somehow carry the frightening weight of all this technical experimentation, most of us cling desperately to the political machinery that was "good enough" fifty or one hundred years ago. The professor declares flatly that a nation cannot be supermodernized technically and industrially—not with safety—without some proportionate modernizing of its political democracy; that this is necessary to make certain that the *reality* of democracy is not crushed beneath the fearfully unbalanced weight of man-made machines.

"If the conservative British people are adopting a considerable degree of socialism," says the professor, "it is not because they are radical by nature. Something is pushing them toward partial socialism, and this is true everywhere outside the American continents. Economic conditions are compelling *political* change. Can we Americans escape the worldwide pressures of political change? Certainly we can never safely meet political change—or devise practical measures to stave it off, or tone it down—without a consuming and new American awareness of political ideas. Does it really make sense to blame it all on the big corporations, or the labor unions, and leave it at that?"

7. Another disadvantage for Americans in a world of revolutionary change lies in the nature of certain predominant American characteristics. Throughout our history American energy, audacity, self-reliance, and mechanical ingenuity (to mention

the most obvious) have contributed vastly to the nation's progress.
Yet throughout our history Americans have revealed the faults
of their qualities. We have always been an impatient people and
a people of disconcerting extremes. The American way has been
"to live for today and worry about tomorrow when it comes."
Our enthusiasms froth up and die as quickly away. National elections swing wildly from Republican sweeps to Democratic land-
slides, and back again. In one year Ginger Rogers or Frank
Sinatra is the rage; in the next, it's anybody's guess. It is American to build the world's tallest skyscraper in two years, more or
less. It is unheard-of for a Washington administration to present
a four-year plan—even for taxes. The Columbia, the Missouri,
and several other of our greatest river valleys could be made to
enrich inestimably the American people, many millions of Americans, through the enactment of a twenty-year plan. The Russians
do things like that, but this is one of the last things our Congress
would ever think of doing.

We are too impatient and changeable, too susceptible to
extremism according to the political or economic weather of the
moment, to commit ourselves nationally to a long-term program
—if any short, vote-catching alternative presents itself. We indicate this constantly by our conduct. One tragic and recent example was the American public's pressure to bring our boys home
from Germany and Japan at the utmost possible speed, regardless of the fact that we may well have lost the war with both
Germany and Japan in large measure through this incredibly
shortsighted action. We set out to lay the foundations of peace
by crippling our occupation forces—by making the task of "de-
mocratizing" Germans and Japanese dangerously difficult, if not
impossible. This is merely a classic example of American impatience and extremism at its worst. Yet you and I and George
Jones have got to do a twenty- or thirty-year job in Germany
and Japan, or there will surely be another war. As for building
a peace that is capable of lasting until 1975 or beyond, how can
this conceivably be hoped for without the unceasing interest and
leadership of the American people as well as their government?

8. American power is likewise undermined by a popular American assumption that it is unassailable and unalterable. Quite

humanly, we do not look ahead to assess where—quite possibly—
we may rate in one or two generations. We do not think of the
world's mightiest nation as merely an incidental upwash on the
evolutionary sands of humanity's vast ocean. Perhaps we should
be wiser and safer—and so, more earnest in our efforts—to think
of our country in this way.

Natural resources and population are two of the fundamental
criteria of any nation's power. To think in terms of industrial
strength alone would give an utterly false picture. In regard to
raw materials—such as iron, coal, copper, oil, manganese, gold,
and pitchblende (the source of uranium)—the Soviet Union is
already known to equal or surpass the United States in several
vital items. Tomorrow the Soviet Union's reserves in some of
the most essential materials may surpass our own—and, quite
conceivably, by a wide margin in gold and the source of atomic
energy. Tomorrow the physical wealth of China, Brazil, and
Africa may be found to have moved far closer to our own, even
surpassing it in some important particulars. Thus, it is self-deception of the most dangerous kind for any American to think of
our present advantage in natural resources as something permanent, beyond the probability of serious revision. For where the
earth's riches are concerned the present proportions or balances
will surely be greatly altered within this century. And the U.S.A.
happens to be an industrialized dragon which is eating up many
of its favorite foods (coal, copper, iron, or what-have-you) much
faster than many other countries.

But the demographers, those chilly and professorial experts
on population trends, provide us with another variety of food
for reflection. They try to remind us—if we would listen—that
the relative population strength of the United States, compared
with Asia and the Soviet Union, is heading straight into a marked
diminution.[1] The experts foresee that the population of the
U.S.A. will probably become stationary in less than thirty years.
In 1970 it is expected that America's population will not be
much more than 135,000,000. Yet in this same period the Soviet
Union—with a gain of approximately 65,000,000 lusty young

1 See "World Populations," charts and text, in *Life*, September 3, 1945.

citizens—is expected to increase its population to a total of 250,-
000,000. Roughly one third of that huge man power will be
between the ages of twenty and forty. If you hear someone talking
about its being necessary for us to fight Russia some day, you
might ask for further particulars on this aspect of the prospectus.

There is another very pertinent angle to the facts which the
population experts consulted by *Life* magazine provided graphically. They report that in 1970 the Soviet Union will have
32,000,000 men of military age between the ages of twenty and
thirty-five, whereas the United States will have 18,000,000 in
these same brackets. But the demographers are unintentionally
misleading because they evidently kept strictly to their own field.
These two totals are by no means an accurate indication of the
relative military-age man-power strength of the two nations. They
do not take into consideration what percentage of the Soviet
Union's 32,000,000 might probably be rejected for military
service, or what percentage we may safely estimate would be
rejected in the United States.

As far as I know the Soviet percentage of rejections for physical disabilities in the Second World War have never been published. But from personal observation of the physique of the
Soviet peoples and of the soldiers in the Red Army it seems to
me highly probable that Soviet rejections were less than 10 percent; perhaps no more than 5 percent. Consider, in contrast, the
shockingly high percentage of physical unfitness revealed in
American men by the records of the Selective Service System between September, 1940, and the end of the war. Major General
Lewis B. Hershey reports: "We knew that nearly half of those
sent for examination would be rejected for either physical, mental
or moral reasons. . . . Of the 17,000,000 registrants between 18
and 37 years of age who were physically examined, about 5,000,-
000 were rejected for military service. Roughly *30 percent of*
American young manhood, then, has been found physically unfit
to bear arms in the national defense." [2] This ought to be a matter for nationwide concern and for governmental action through
a program to improve systematically the health of America's
youth. I do not hear of any popular concern, or any demand for

2 (From "We must Improve Our Youth"; *New York Times Magazine*, Feb. 10,
1946.)

such action. It is easier for those who are more emotional and most prejudiced—and usually safely nearing or past middle age— to remark knowingly: "Of course, we'll have to fight the Russians sooner or later."

Nor do many of us pause to consider what the populations of Japan, China, and India are likely to be by 1970. Nor how much the industrial strength of the U.S.S.R., China, and India will have increased in the next twenty-five years. Nor whether the long-suppressed and freedom-demanding eight hundred millions in China and India are likely to be on our side, if the calamity of a war with Russia or someone else should come upon us. For if an atomic war should come, we can count with certainty upon one thing: the hundreds of millions who would or might survive would *not* be Americans, nor would they belong chiefly to the white race. The only race that can be reduced to a weak and shattered fraction of itself through atomic war is, obviously, the white race. The geographical disposition of peoples, and the increasing population preponderances of certain races and peoples, make this conclusion irrefutable. Quite possibly, this is worth five or ten minutes of your thought and mine.

But these observations are merely a by-product of what I was trying to point out. Right here we are concerned with certain outstanding disadvantages of American power. So far as world population trends go—and they go a very long way—I think the average American today gives little or no consideration to the fact that the man power of the United States will shortly become stationary; that what has already happened to the British and the French will begin to happen to us before very many years. In certain essential respects what the United States has today, or in 1950, is an enormous *transitory* power. We can exercise it to its *fullest* degree, for peace and toward a world government, only for a few limited decades. If we waste or dissipate this tremendous moral and physical authority during the next two decades, we may never have another opportunity to use it so persuasively or effectively again.

But have we Americans as yet learned to speak with great persuasion to foreign governments and foreign peoples? Do we show a tact and a tolerance which immediately incline Englishmen or Hungarians, Frenchmen or Russians or Latin Americans to lend receptive ears to what we propose? Do our representatives speak, as a rule, thinking of the sensitiveness and the mentality and the cultural backgrounds of our brother nations? Or do our representatives more often speak with an eye to winning the American public's applause, and with an ear plainly cocked for the rustle of votes in the ballot-boxes of Oshkosh and Kalamazoo?

9. I would add one more handicap for the U.S.A. as the foremost world power—and make it brief. In the past twenty years as a global reporter I have often come home to be struck by one thing in the attitude of many of our politicians and many of our plain citizens. This is an unspoken assumption that America does not necessarily need friends abroad. It is implicit in our impatience with "those quarreling Europeans." It underlies the tone of unconscious self-righteousness which often crops out in the speeches of some of our presidents and many of our politicians.

I think I know the warm-heartedness and fair intentions of my own people well enough to know that most of us do not mean to sound or act "holier than thou." So I wonder if perhaps this explains it. Perhaps we have been so long self-sufficient and so long renewed by vigorous new blood from abroad that, subconsciously, we tend to convince ourselves that we do not need the goodwill of foreign peoples. Perhaps we have had for so many generations the esteem and admiration and affection of others—given unsought and freely by countless millions of Europeans and Asiatics—that we incline to take their warmth and confidence for granted. Behind our broad protective oceans we have seldom, if ever, thought that the day might come "when America needs a friend."

That day, I believe, is swiftly approaching—if indeed it is not already here. The trust and amazing affection which the little Greek people hold for America and Americans is something which no gold—or mere physical power—could ever buy. The hope of all Europeans, and of Chinese and Indonesians and Indians and countless others—their long-nourished faith in American democracy—constitutes the most important letter-of-credit that the American people have ever had. So long as we do not despise or betray this immeasurable goodwill, this hope and faith of a majority of the world's peoples, American power will be measurable in something far greater than the size of its Navy and air force. But that kind of freely offered trust and friendship can be retained only by a nation, and particularly by a great nation, which is wise enough to want friends—which is sufficiently clear-sighted and tolerant to know how to make friends; above all, to *keep* friends.

This is not something that we Americans have ever felt it necessary to make a conscious effort to do. Like most other people we have thought of foreign people as "foreigners"; and even of many among ourselves in the same way. We have not thought of the United States and the Western democracies as a small minority among the world's two billions of humanity. We have seldom, if ever, thought that an industrialized Russia and Asia—now marching irresistibly toward their goal—must inevitably reduce America to a much smaller minority in the world scheme. We have rarely considered that every decade in the next two centuries must tend to even the competitive stands of East and West; that the days when Americans and Englishmen hold the muskets and the majority of mankind holds the arrows are inevitably numbered—because neither the automobiles, the airplanes, the movies, the industrial plants, nor even the secret of atomic energy can conceivably be kept in reserve for ourselves alone.

We have thought of peoples living outside our borders as "foreigners." But there are no "foreigners" to the mysteries of science and technology. There are no "foreigners" to the right to higher standards of living, or to the rights of man. There are no "foreigners" in a world that shrinks as recklessly as we ourselves are making this world shrink. *There are only people.* It is a fortunate man and a fortunate nation that has many people as friends. In an atomic world the peoples will become better friends—or those who cast their greatest and most decisive influence toward refusal must surely be among the first to be destroyed. The chief survivors must be those peoples whose lands presented the fewest, the most scattered, and the least attractive industrial targets.

Thus we, who have greatest responsibility for world leadership, have most to lose—and most to learn. But—

What we learn must be learned so terribly fast.

The psychological and educational unpreparedness of the
American people for supreme world leadership is a frightening
thing—almost as frightening as the menace of the atomic bomb.
In one respect it is possibly more dangerous. We can all sense and
see the peril of the bomb. But can we see, do we understand, the
menace which lies in ourselves? In our inexperience, in our indifference to becoming self-informed, in the average citizen's assumption that we are not seriously unprepared?

Surely no nation in all history has been catapulted so swiftly
into the undisputed position of the world's greatest power. Rome
was not built in a day, nor any of the empires which preceded or
followed it. Yet the upward surge of the United States has occurred between 1917 and 1945; little more than a day in the
sands of time. And it is only in the past few years, since 1940, that
the growth of U.S. power has shot head and shoulders above all
others. With this startling suddenness the hour of greatness, the
day of Supreme Responsibility, has been thrust upon us. In the
perceptive phrase of Anne O'Hare McCormick: "Standing as
the victor over dying systems in two continents, neither of which
is her own, America assumes a world leadership without parallel
in the annals of the rise and fall of empires."

Who can measure the tragedy, for ourselves and humankind,
if Americans should prove inadequate to meet the stupendous
opportunities now imposed upon them? What failure could be
more fateful and more devastating if the final historical descend-
ing curve of American leadership should become as sharp and
sudden as its ascent?

Raymond Swing once said: "There never was a democratic
society that could get up early in the morning without an alarm
clock." As Manchuria and Ethiopia fell, as Spanish democracy
was bludgeoned to impotence, as the Czechs were sold down the
river, there were alarm clocks which sounded—yet rang insistently
with slight success—in America. Today, when as chief victor we
may still tear our victory into tattered ribbons, the democracy of
America is surely in need of thousands of clanging alarm clocks.
We must see our responsibilities as clearly as our might. We must

gauge our handicaps and our unpreparedness as realistically as we understand the nature of our easily apparent assets.

The war has red-lettered—indeed, has written in blood—the great and fearful unbalance in modern society. The yawning gap between physical plant and technological ability, on one hand, and political awareness and spiritual comprehension on the other, has been underscored for all who are able to think. The barbaric uprisings and practices of Nazism, Fascism, and Shintoism were merely volcanic expressions of a time and systems which are disastrously "out of joint." France became the sad epitome of self-divided capitalist society in general; torn by conflicting greeds and prejudices, rotted by political corruption, paralyzed by the irresponsibility and self-seeking of a majority of its citizens, riven by uncurbed war between one class and another—and fatally drugged by a widespread false conviction that French democracy, simply because it had existed so long, could survive persistently mounting abuses and public indifference without fundamental reforms. There were parallels to all this in pre-Fascist Italy and in pre-Nazi Germany. There were sufficient parallels in Great Britain to keep Baldwin and Neville Chamberlain in office until disaster was assured. There are important parallels in present-day China. There are many of these parallels in the United States today.

For we cannot pretend to have achieved as yet any safe balance in our own American society. We have now built such unprecedentedly huge industrial equipment that our internal security is dominated by the necessity to produce. To prevent grave unemployment and accompanying social disorders, we must produce—and sell—several times more goods than most of us dreamed possible in 1936. The machines we created have become our masters. Industrial management and labor are to a serious degree fiercely antagonistic. Our government struggles incessantly to placate the great American industrial Frankenstein monster, while countless voices cry out against planning or governmental controls. Has the increase in the American citizen's interest in political and social problems been one tenth of the increase of our productive capacity in the past decade? Have we made any really consequential progress in diminishing racial discriminations and class divisions in American society? Is there any marked improvement in the average American's realization of his moral responsibility for the strengthening and betterment of the functioning of our democracy, if it is not to become the victim of its abuses?

Answer these questions honestly and you must decide that the Achilles heel of American power is still dangerously large. For the scope of our internal disunity—not to mention frequent indifference—lays a crippling hand on those who would formulate and practice an American foreign policy which enjoys united support at home and can be truly effective for world co-operation abroad. If the American people cannot put their own house in reasonable order, with a reasonable show of tolerance and goodwill, how can we expect an American government to be of brilliant help in putting the world's house in order? Thus, even when we face this tremendous dual task—and how relatively few of us really face it!—our thinking is almost crushed by our enormous American responsibilities. We have so very little time, and we shall need the collective wisdom of many centuries to do what *must* be done passably well.

Even in June 1945 we had very little time. Then came the atomic bomb, the all-powerful alarm clock that rings for all humanity and against the deadline of Doomsday. While yet we have our Bilbos and Rankins, while yet some 13,000,000 darker Americans are still deprived of many freedoms and anti-Semitism in the United States is more rampant than at any time in our history—in summation, while yet American democracy is but a caricature of what it ought to be, the American people are called upon to champion and promote democratic freedoms for hundreds of millions of oppressed throughout the world. While yet we have not succeeded in establishing a tolerable brotherhood among our own citizens or an American society which is securely at peace within itself, destiny has elected us to exert decisive leadership toward a brotherhood of mankind and a peace capable of saving the world's foremost nations from destruction.

In June 1945 you and I and George Jones might have had the soothing luxury of thinking of these staggering obligations in terms of several decades. Now, after the atomic bomb, we have no escape. We must think of them in terms of years and months. We must deal with these life-or-death ultimatums even as we are striving to learn how to deal with them. We cannot possibly know enough to act with any guarantee of safety for our present civilization. Because we cannot possibly know enough to forestall an atomic war with certainty, for you and I to act "normalcy" as we knew it in 1938, and to think with no more clarity than we thought in the pre-atomic age cannot logically lead to anything less than mass suicide.

We must see with new eyes the society in which we live, and the world in which we live. Somehow we must make this part of our daily business. We must understand that the fate of a Welsh coalminer, a French or Hungarian shopkeeper, a Greek or a Chinese peasant, a Russian collective farmer, and a Mississippi Negro without a vote—all this is the fate of you and me. We may turn our backs upon this fate, but we shall never escape it. What the people of Britain learned from buzz bombs and rockets in this war American survivors will learn from atomic missiles in the next—provided only that we learn in time, before the dreadful alternative becomes unescapable. For the Dreadful Alternative will not wait for the "slow thinkers" and the non-thinkers of our generation. If the extroverts in our society win, the swiftness of their extermination will merely equal the unpardonable magnitude of their blindness and indifference.

But the Loreleis of a dead and irretrievable past still sing their alluring songs of normalcy and ephemeral postwar profits. The American people are still lured by—

The sirens of prejudice and emotionalism.

This way the escapist citizen may find a scapegoat for his own mental and spiritual shortcomings or inadequacies. This way we may be tempted, once our top-heavy gigantic productive plant falls frighteningly into low gear, to seek the easy "outs" offered by a Fascist-flavored American nationalism or a self-aggrandizing American imperialism. This way future Mussolinis or Hitlers of our own may eventually find their open door to power, denouncing and blaming other nations or other classes for all our mounting woes. This way American democracy can be maneuvered out of control, from one extreme or the other. For totalitarian dictatorship springs from the stricken soil of widespread unemployment and flourishes on all the class divisions and hatreds of minorities which it finds at hand to exploit.

There is a higher and nobler road which is worthy of the American people. It is a road which has served us well in the past, and along it the signposts bear the names of Washington, Jefferson, Lincoln, Wilson, and many others—and now, in the eyes of our contemporary world, the name of Franklin D. Roosevelt. The signposts are a reminder, it seems to me, that a nation's physical power is not nearly enough; that "the American way" was built solidly upon a foundation of great humanitarian principles applicable to all mankind; that the vision which created the United States was far more than a narrow conception of self-interest and immeasurably exceeded the limitations of national prosperity. It seems to me that the most imperishable signposts in America's history are written not merely in the American language but in Esperanto—in the hopes and aspirations of human beings in every clime, of every race and every creed.

But the alarm clock rings from the desert of New Mexico and the ruins of Hiroshima and Nagasaki. It rings in a new and enormously different world, where social revolution rumbles and the minute hands race with the superspeed of a portentous new era. In this new world America will be great—in leadership or in failure. The responsibilities of Americans are as stupendous as our power. If we do not clearly and accurately comprehend this new world, and how it has changed from the old, what possibility is there that we—the American people—shall measure up to an opportunity never faced by humankind before? While the minute hands of the atomic age race madly we have only a bare minimum of time in which to analyze and try to understand the role of Americans in a doubly revolutionary world.

PART II

Tour of Our Revolutionary World

Chapter IV

THE NEW SOVIET POWER

Let's begin with Soviet Russia. And let's begin, so far as humanly possible, with the detached spirit of a presumed reporter from the *Neptune Beacon* or the *Mars Morning Gazette*. As such a reporter we are not involved in World politics. We are simply trying to analyze one of the great new forces in world affairs of today, as related to other forces. We do not come to champion the Soviet system, or to prove it impractical or intolerable. We come merely to try to evaluate its present power and some of its present tendencies, and their bearing upon other earthly nations. To do this we are equally interested in the prewar Soviet Union, where the postwar Union may differ, and how it has grown.

What we are primarily interested in is not in proving either the merits or the faults of the Soviet system; nor whether or no the liquidation of the kulaks or the later purges were justified. We want, first of all, to get some grasp of what the U.S.S.R. *is* today. We want some basis for judging where the Soviet Union is going. We are even more interested in what it *may be* in 1965 or 1975. What with rockets and fantastically powerful emancipated atoms, the Neptunians and Martians are becoming definitely concerned lest their timeless, taken-for-granted isolation should be ended by one of these colossal upstarts from Earth. So you and I, as interplanetary investigators, are chiefly interested in some of the outstanding facts about the new Soviet Union. At the very outset we want something concrete about—

The nature and scope of Soviet power.

It bears repeating that the Soviet Union is nearly three times larger in area than the United States; that it covers one sixth of the earth's surface and includes almost one tenth of the world's total population. From Russia's Polish frontier to her closest Siberian promontories on the Bering Straits, opposite Alaska, is a direct-line distance of more than 5,000 miles. In north-south width the Soviet Union averages close to 2,000 miles. In this vast, irregular rectangle something more than 180,000,000 Soviet citizens live today, although some place the figure nearer to 200,000,000. In his enlightening book, *The Basis of Soviet Strength,* Professor George B. Cressey says the "key word in Soviet geography is *continentality*. Within the Union is room for all of the United States, Alaska, Canada and Mexico."

We can best get a clear picture of the "power fundamentals" in the U.S.S.R. by listing certain of Professor Cressey's authoritative facts.

Perhaps the most important of all, politically and socially, is the fact that the Soviet Union is a federation of very numerous and contrasting races, tongues, and creeds. Its population includes no fewer than fifty different nationalities of considerable size, but 169 distinct ethnic groups have been charted within its borders. Thus, in its own one sixth of the earth, the U.S.S.R. constitutes a kind of a "league of nations" of its own. There are no "color lines" or similar distinctions in citizenship. In fact, I never saw or heard of any racial discrimination whatever while I served as a war correspondent in the Soviet Union. The Red Army could not be described as the kind of cross-bred melting pot which was exemplified by our more assimilated American Army. But the Red Army contained a far greater number of national groups, with promotions quite apparently open to all. The lack of racial antagonisms, or racial barriers as such, is one of the most impressive and thought-provoking things about the Soviet Union. In actual practice and psychology it seems much more international than any other political entity on the globe. For the yellow and brown and black races—for the underdogs of the earth—this common citizenship and racial equality undoubtedly constitute, in Owen Lattimore's beautifully apt phrase, an inestimable "power of attraction." And in a world where at least four fifths of humanity are needy, shabby, hungering, and exploited, the power of attraction is a terribly real power.

A breakdown of nationalities in the Soviet Union, again crediting Professor Cressey, discloses the following chief entities:

Great Russians	99,000,000	*or* 50 percent
Ukrainians or Little Russians	28,000,000	17 percent
White Russians	5,267,000	3 percent
Uzbeks	4,844,000	3 percent
Tatars	4,300,000	3 percent
Kazakhs	3,098,000	2 percent
Hebrews	3,020,000	2 percent
Azerbaijanians	2,274,000	1 percent
Georgians	2,248,000	1 percent
Armenians	2,151,000	1 percent
Tadzhiks	1,228,000	1 percent

But from here on, the roll-call of Soviet nationalities brings a long list of names, most of which are beyond the ken or any precise conception of Westerners like ourselves: Kirghiz, Bashkir, Turkmenians; Udmurts, Komi, Ossetians, and Moldavians; Chechentsi, Kalmuks, and Bolgars; Unarigani, Inuits, Nanai, and Eveni; Selkupi, Mariitsi, Karelians, and Khanty. Even today it seems almost incredible that a revolution, which began in Moscow and Leningrad in 1917, should have swept successfully eastward across the Urals and the reaches of Siberia until it touched the Pacific at Kamchatka and has embraced a modern Tower of Babel so variegated in racial hues, traditions, and religions as this. We are also compelled to remember that, within the lifetime of most of us, the population of this Soviet house of many nations will total 250,000,000 or more; perhaps 80 percent of it white.

In mineral resources the U.S.S.R. possesses a fabulous assortment, as yet scarcely tapped in many important items. A brief summary of a few will provide a broad, if inadequate, conception.

Soviet coal reserves	2nd to the U.S.A.
Oil and gas	2nd to the U.S.A. in production, but her reserves may exceed ours
Manganese, most essential of ferrometals	U.S.S.R. 1st in reserves 1st in production
Lead	11 percent of world total
Zinc	19 percent of world total
Gold	2nd to South Africa in production Reserves: possibly 1st

| Platinum | More than 35 percent of the world's supply |
| Pitchblende, source of uranium | ? (Amount unknown) |

After a more comprehensive survey than this Professor Cressey concludes: "No other country has so great a variety of minerals, and only the United States is richer." There remains one further fact. In the past twenty-five years hundreds of Soviet geologists have located hitherto undreamed-of deposits of coal, iron, gold, oil, and other minerals in the vast hinterlands of the Soviet Union. These geological experts are still at work, and probably some of their most important discoveries have not yet been disclosed. Thus it remains possible that Soviet reserves in certain key minerals may already equal or surpass, or may shortly come to surpass, the equivalent reserves in the United States. Between the two world wars Professor Cressey reports that the Soviets' reserves of coal increased sevenfold, of petroleum sevenfold, of zinc tenfold, of iron ore (including ferriferous quartzites) one hundred and thirty times, and of copper twenty-eight times. In terms of a nation's potential power these figures are sufficiently eloquent.

With the German invasion, Russia had a major proportion of her finest industrial plants destroyed or gutted in the Ukraine and the west. But four years of war brought an extraordinary transplantation of industries: in the Urals, throughout central and southern Siberia, and beyond. The record of the five-year plans astonished the world's skeptics as evidence of Soviet capacity for industrial growth. The record of the Soviets' wartime industrial recovery and expansion, under excruciating difficulties, made a profound impression upon Americans like Wendell Willkie, Eric Johnston, and Donald Nelson, who were given every facility to judge for themselves. In view of the colossal obstacles involved, Russia's wartime industrial recovery must be rated as at least as remarkable as America's industrial expansion. This means that her postwar growth, during the next two decades, is certain to break all previous records by a wide and probably a surprising margin.

In the Ukraine, Leningrad, and Stalingrad the Soviet Union lost to Nazi devastation more than the Detroit-Cleveland-Pittsburgh triangle in the United States. She lost a major proportion of her prewar key mines and industries. Yet by V-E Day, nearly four years later, it seems likely that Soviet production had recovered not far from its 1940 peak. Consequently, although reconstruction in Soviet devastated regions is unquestionably an enormous long-term task, we may be sure that Russia's postwar industrial plan will vastly exceed anything attempted or accomplished between the 1920's and 1940. The Soviet goal is not to make the U.S.S.R. the world's second industrial power. It is to make the Soviet Union at least the industrial equal of the United States well within the life expectancy of those who fought this war. The Kremlin's master minds are in a hurry, and so are the Soviet people. It is a fact that no nation in history has ever started from rock-bottom and registered such extraordinary industrial development as the U.S.S.R. achieved, through "blood, sweat, and tears," between 1917 and 1940. But the Soviets' leaders now see even more urgent need for accelerated industrial expansion. In part the need undoubtedly springs from lingering distrust of the intentions of the Western capitalist powers and from the instinct for self-protection. But in part the demand for continued and greater acceleration comes from the demands and material desires of 200,000,000 Soviet citizens. After all that they have sacrificed and suffered in the Second World War the Soviet government is compelled to concentrate upon giving this vast federation of nationalities an increasingly higher standard of living; more of the necessities and something more of the luxuries of life. To fail to do this would be for the Soviet government (as for our own or any government) to invite increasing internal troubles and possibly serious disorders.

Thus, while we in America are striving somehow to keep most of our fantastically overbuilt plant producing, we can safely assume—we can be confident—that the Soviet Union will be working with even greater intensity to build a far-flung industrial kingdom designed to rival our own to the highest attainable degree. In plain fact the Soviets already have a five-year plan for postwar reconstruction and expansion. This was being perfected by Soviet specialists while German armies still held Kiev and the Dnieper line late in 1943. As in everything, the Soviets plan far into the future; and the men with a plan more often than not get where they set out to go.

In 1943, while half of the rich industrial Ukraine was still in German hands and Anglo-American landings in Normandy were still hidden in the uncertain future, Russians in Moscow already talked about their vast program for recovery and expansion after the war. Edgar Snow [1] made a detailed study of its possibilities. Where foreign observers granted that Russia would well surpass her prewar industrial highs in anywhere from fifteen to thirty years, Snow found Russian Communists who confidently insisted this would be accomplished within five years. One of them said to him: "Our problems won't be nearly as difficult as they were at the end of the civil war. At that time we had almost complete paralysis of production and complete disorganization of distribution. We had little industrial plant. We had few technicians and skilled workers. . . . It took us about seven years to create order out of chaos."

Today we must also measure Soviet power by factors which citizens of a long-established governmental system, like our own, tend to overlook. We must include in our reckoning of new Soviet power tens of millions of skilled factory workers where only a relative handful existed in 1917, or even in 1925. We must take into account an experienced administrative and management machine whose members have demonstrated their ability, and streamlined their methods, through four years of invasion and all of the disruptions of a seesawing fifteen-hundred-mile battlefront on home soil. It is also pertinent to consider that even in 1942, after months of war, Soviet spokesmen stated that 75,000 new industrial and communication engineers, physicians, agronomists, and similar specialists were graduated from Soviet schools.

Talking with a Russian who had lived for some years in the United States, Edgar Snow asked in what way he considered the Soviet Union better prepared for the future than America. The Russian's reply certainly merits some thought. He said: "The unquestioned acceptance here of national economic planning. This is the main factor which will help us recover from the war in a few years. One must stress that again and again, because it means there are no contradictory interests which can interfere with the logical development of postwar economy."

[1] "How Fast Can Russia Rebuild?", the *Saturday Evening Post*, February 12, 1944.

It seems to me that this observation likewise has an important relation to present and future Soviet power. Of course, this is what any convinced Marxist could be expected to say. But 200,000,000 people who will unhesitatingly accept the restraints and enforced discipline of a national economic plan may well be capable of astonishing the rest of the world in the next two or three decades. Nor do I see any reason why national economic planning should be considered a monopoly of Marxist philosophy. Could we not do with more planning, and more long-term planning, in our own capitalist economy?

In any case the Soviet Union's industrial might is indubitably a small fraction of what it will be in another twenty or twenty-five years. It has almost everything that it needs to feed upon: enormous raw materials; a vast man power which is hardworking and energetic and now includes unprecedented numbers of skilled labor; a large body of able and gifted scientists; a strong administrative machinery—and planned direction toward long-term goals.

But the new Soviet power also rests firmly upon—

The new strategic security of the U.S.S.R.

A glance at postwar maps makes it clear that the Soviet Union now probably enjoys greater geographical insurance against successful foreign invasion than any other nation on earth. In Europe the following changes are of great importance. From the revised Finnish frontier Leningrad has gained notably in protection. Estonia and Latvia—which had never existed as independent states until the treaty-makers of 1919 began their alterations—have returned to Russia. This is also true of Lithuania, which had also been a province of Russia for several centuries. But the Baltic corner of East Prussia, including the fortress of Königsberg, has likewise gone under Soviet control. These readjustments combine into a strategically solid "Baltic shield" for the Union's north-central area.

The new Soviet-Polish border returns to Russia the strongly defensive Pripet Marshes. By Prague's cession of Ruthenia the Soviets now hold the Carpathian passes into Hungary. Farther south, with the return of Bessarabia, they possess a natural line of defense along the Prut River down to the mouth of the Danube.

With new rights assured to Russia in regard to the Dardanelles, her entire position facing Europe is more secure than at any period under the Czars.

In eastern Asia Russia has recovered Port Arthur and Dairen. While recognizing Chinese sovereignty in Manchuria she has also recovered joint control of the Manchurian railroads, formerly built and owned by the Russians. In addition the Soviets obtained the southern half of strategic Sakhalin Island (of great protective value for Vladivostok) and defensive bases in the Kurile Islands near Kamchatka. Thus everything that Japan took from Russia in previous aggressions and expansions has been returned, with additional advantages to the U.S.S.R. Even in an age of atomic bombs these strategic gains are highly important. Soviet industries, scattered across some 5,000 miles of the earth's girdle and naturally dispersed in many different regions, would seem more difficult for crippling destruction by atomic bombs than any other nation's industrial strength—very much more difficult, in fact. But aside from this Soviet good fortune, it would be a hardy coalition of enemy powers which would hope to gain a decisive victory by successfully invading the Soviet Union from either Europe or Asia. The war has unquestionably brought the U.S.S.R. a tremendously increased strategic security and strength.

Most of us are conscious of this change, and far less conscious of other aspects of Soviet Russia's newly emerging assets as a world power. Perhaps we would get a more accurate picture, if we were to consider—

Soviet education as a weapon, and a reward.

In October 1942 I was accompanied to the Rzhev front by a young correspondent of the Red Army's newspaper, *Red Star*. Major Arapov, blond and in his early thirties, was a trained artillery officer as well as a military reporter. I learned that he came from Voronezh, where the Red Army had held fast on the upper Don well north of Rostov. His family had been peasants in this black-earth region for many generations. Few if any of them had ever known how to read and write. Because of the revolution Arapov had received a free high school and college education, and later had graduated as an officer from the Red Army Artillery

School. I used to think about Arapov's family as I watched the keenness and intelligence with which he worked. None of his forebears had surely been anything more than clumsy foot-soldiers in the armies of the Czars. But in the space of a few years Soviet education had remarkably developed Arapov's natural abilities. Suddenly I understood why Arapov and millions of other Red Army men had a great personal stake in this war. Among other things they were fighting for something they had which neither their parents nor their grandparents had ever had.

This Red Army, as I saw on every hand, was the first Russian Army in history which really knew how to read. This was the first Russian Army in which *all* the soldiers had gone to school; had received at least an elementary education. When I talked with twenty-year-old Shura from far-away Kamchatka he spoke with enthusiasm about the studies he had begun—he a son of a railroad worker—in theatrical decoration. I noticed the way the soldiers read their Army and divisional newspapers everywhere. I saw that the Red Army fought much better because the Soviets had made it into a literate army; and that this great step away from illiteracy was one of the real sources of Soviet power.

It is stated that in the Czar's armies of 1914 perhaps as much as 50 percent of the soldiers were able to read and write—this being the lowest measuring rod of "literacy" in a strict sense. To many this figure appears dubiously high. But before that war ended there were surely many Russian peasant units whose percentage of exposure to the "three R's" was much lower than that. In the Red Army, by contrast, even the soldiers of more backward races —such as the Uzbeks, Tadzhiks, and Mongols—had averaged a considerably larger degree of schooling. In the Samarkand region of Uzbekistan, for instance, it was claimed that a 90-percent illiteracy condition had been exactly reversed. Probably the "able to read and write" type of literacy had risen to from 60 to 85 percent in every part of the Soviet Union, despite racial handicaps.

Some authorities say that literacy of Soviet children of school age had become virtually 100 percent before Hitler's invasion, while illiteracy among adults had been very greatly decreased. In any case certain figures are very striking. In 1915 there were only 8,147,000 pupils in Russia's elementary schools. By 1940 the Soviet Union had approximately 40,000,000 pupils and students in schools of every type.[2] The great forward stride in colleges, universities, and technical institutes was in proportion. Where Russia had 137,000 of such students in 1912, they had increased to nearly 2,000,000 by 1940. Approximately one out of every four persons in the Soviet Union was attending some sort of educational institution.[3]

We can scarcely imagine what this enormous increase in the wealth of trained intelligence, achieved so suddenly and universally, means to a dynamic nation. Perhaps it is simplest to consider the family of Masha Dikareva Scott, wife of *Time* Correspondent John Scott. She was one of eight children born to a peasant family in north central Russia. They were born without a doctor or midwife because her mother was too poor to travel forty miles to the nearest clinic; and there were far fewer clinics in Russia just after the revolution than at present. Today two of Mrs. Scott's sisters are doctors; one is an economist; one, a dean of history at Magnitogorsk college; one, a graduate engineer from Moscow Univer-

[2] See Professor Pitirim A. Sorokin: *Russia and the United States,* Chapter VII.

[3] The Information Bulletin of the Soviet Embassy, in its issue of December 27, 1945, included the following statistics on the expansion of education and literacy: In 1939 the total enrollment in Soviet schools and higher institutions, including all age groups, had risen to 47,400,000. . . . Kindergartens were reported to have increased from 275 in 1919 to 55,102 in 1940—with 2,331,000 children in their care. . . . In 1940 there existed 3,695 vocational and technical schools. . . . Higher educational institutions had grown from 91 to 782 in twenty years. In the non-Russian republics Georgia had 21 colleges and universities; Armenia, 9; Kazakhstan, 20; Azerbaijan, 15; and Uzbekistan, 27. . . .

Growth of higher educational institutions in the U.S.S.R. were reported as follows:

	1917	1940
Universities and single-faculty institutes for the arts	45	398
Medical institutes	9	78
Agricultural institutes	10	86
Technical and transport institutes	14	152
Economic institutes	6	43
Art institutes	7	25
Total	91	782

Increases in literacy were illustrated by:

	1926 percent	1939 percent
Russian S.F.S. Republic	55	81.9
Ukrainian " "	57.5	85.3
Azerbaijan " "	25.2	75.3
Turkmen " "	12.5	67.2
Uzbek " "	10.6	67.8

sity; and Masha Scott herself is a teacher of mathematics. Thus, six out of eight of these children of peasants have received a higher education—and this is not unusual in Soviet Russia today. It should be added that Mrs. Scott's mother learned to write when she was past fifty.

In this one family you can perceive the tremendous new stake which the average young Soviet citizen (with many of his elders) now holds in the future of his country. Universal education has been a foremost weapon in the building of the Soviet Union. But it has also become an inestimable reward. Many millions of Russia's youth have benefited by educational opportunities which their parents never dreamed could become available to people such as they. But because a classroom barrier which had stood for centuries has suddenly been removed, these same millions of youth—like others who found unimagined opportunities in the United States—look upon remaining obstacles to progress and modernization as purely secondary. For them the future is a flaming beacon. They have become inspired with the idea that almost nothing is impossible—provided only that they work hard enough.

In America, Masha Scott says, "I miss the friendliness and stimulus of collective work toward a common goal." This is something which we Americans, in evaluating Soviet society, rarely pause to consider. Yet in this widespread attitude of Soviet youth, there lies another significant factor in the new Soviet power. We must recognize at their full value—

The Soviet peoples' incentive, and their
capacity to serve.

In wartime Russia, foreign correspondents naturally saw Soviet patriotism and devotion at an abnormally high peak. If ever a people had to rise to heights of service and self-sacrifice, these people had to do it. But it was equally true that the Soviet five-year plans, the entire period between the wars, had required far more than a normal peacetime effort. In fact, the Soviet people had been living and working all along on a kind of emergency level not much removed from the pressures of war. Collectivization and industrialization had been a very real war against Russia's feudalistic backwardness. Regardless of the famines and the purges, a majority of Soviet citizens had supported this gigantic effort to such an extent that the outside world was astonished by the results.

This is why the difference in the Soviet peoples' peacetime spirit and their wartime morale was considerably less than the differences in Britain and the United States. Even before the German invasion, as most experienced foreign observers testify, the newly educated youth of the Soviet Union was kindled by the élan of a national crusade; and a great many adults felt this almost as keenly. The October Revolution had declared war on ignorance, on póverty and mass disease, and on economic lags which belonged in the nineteenth or the eighteenth century. Thus the average Soviet citizen found that new kind of incentive. Given the very different fundamental conditions, it spelled opportunity quite as much as opportunity beckoned to the newly arrived Greek or Polish immigrant at Ellis Island.

So an entire generation has grown up in Soviet Russia in an atmosphere teeming with the idea, and ideal, of service to the nation. As the Soviet Union progressed and eventually prospered, so would Ivan Ivanovich progress and prosper. The real rewards could not come in two or three years, as in America. The greatest rewards could come only through many years of sustained effort— but some would come as they went along. On the collective farms and in the factories, in the schools and colleges, in the free clinics and libraries and public health institutions, the Soviet people have unquestionably already found sufficient remuneration to have great faith in other advantages which must come later on. I think these things go far to explain the enthusiasm of youth and the confidence in a much better postwar tomorrow which you encounter on every hand in Russia today.

One could cite many examples of the young Soviet spirit. Somehow I always remember a conversation with Nila Magidov, the Russian wife of NBC's Robert Magidov. When she arrived in America during the war she spoke only a few words of English. In an incredibly short time she was addressing large audiences, from coast to coast, as an outstandingly successful speaker for the National War Fund.

"But how did you learn English so quickly and so well?" I asked.

Nila Magidov laughed gaily. "People always say it must be because Russians are natural linguists," she said. "But I don't think that's true. Certainly, I am not. What they don't know is how terribly hard I worked when I first reached America. Do you know what I did? I made a phonetic system of my own for English —I just invented a way to understand English pronunciation. For the first months I studied English twelve or fourteen hours every day—sometimes I studied even sixteen hours. I *had* to do it. It was for my country."

I wondered what I would do, if I knew that I must learn to speak Russian in three months in order to serve my country—in order to tell Russians what Americans were doing in the war. Would I start right in, alone, at a pace of fourteen hours of study a day? Yet this kind of patriotic devotion was not at all uncommon among Soviet youth. They had not only grown up almost without a capacity to recognize physical or mental obstacles; millions of them had grown up with a readiness to make extreme sacrifices so long as these were regarded as essential to the advancement of their nation. In the younger Soviet citizens like Nila Magidov this spirit was highly contagious. But she was saying something else.

"If I am told that I must make a pearl," Nila said with her burningly vigorous enthusiasm, "then I will make a pearl. For a Russian nothing is impossible."

In our much more privileged land such sentiments might sound melodramatic. But they are accurately descriptive of the mental attitude of a very large number who are the spark-plugs and leaders in the postrevolutionary generation in the Soviet Union. Any analysis of Russia's present and future power cannot neglect this development. In the intensity of its conception of patriotic service and of the "stimulus of collective work toward a common goal" it is a tremendous force: a new kind of idealism linked to a great pioneering spirit. Such a youth dreams of a Soviet Russia as highly industrialized, as modernized, and as rich in consumer goods as the United States. With these young people's capacity to work and to serve, and with the incentives which are kept unceasingly aroused in their minds, it would be rather surprising if they do not achieve most of their objectives within this century. It seems to me far more practical and pertinent to understand these sources of Russia's present strength than to argue the pros and cons of her Bolshevik past. For the sources of new Soviet power are not subject to argument. They exist—and they will have their influence upon more than one billion more backward peoples in the next twenty-five years. This is inescapably true because there also exists now—

The magnetism of Soviet success.

The war has made the whole world newly conscious of the magnitude and the possibilities of the Soviet experiment. Even here in the United States we have been greatly stirred by the emergence of the U.S.S.R. as a great world power, second only to ourselves. The transformation of relative strength has certainly been as unprecedented in Russia as in our own country. The achievements of the Red Army became a constant reminder of the changing balances in world affairs. Americans looked toward Moscow with new respect and a new personal interest; and sometimes with highly sharpened but familiar suspicions and fears. If this awareness of new Soviet might was true of us, in our universally admitted greatest citadel on earth, what must have been the reaction in Englishmen, Frenchmen, and Italians; and in Chinese, Hindus, Persians, and many others?

For those peoples who are much less strong than ourselves, and especially for those who have never had real independence, the Soviets' new stature marks the beginning of a new period in their existence. Where once the world's "have-nots"—constituting much more than half of humanity, and perhaps three fourths—looked to Britain and the United States, they now look as searchingly and inquiringly toward the huge land mass of the U.S.S.R. There they see a new success story, built upon a different ideology. And Soviet success is on such a scale, with such power behind it, that they can never erase it from their minds. Thus, one of the important fruits of victory has become the magnetism of Soviet success. In the United States we have benefited prodigiously for many generations by a similar kind of magnetic appeal which our prosperity and technical progress have had for foreign peoples everywhere—and still have. But did we not also benefit from the fact that in many ways our American magnetism had no serious rival among the other great powers? Now this is changed. There is another magnetism which now competes for the admiration, emulation, and sympathies of the unprivileged and exploited throughout the world.

In reality, then, we must recognize another intangible force in present-day Soviet Russia; an asset which is capable of exceptional human appeal and political power. The far-sighted leaders of the Kremlin are far too astute to underestimate the potentialities of the Soviets' remarkable success in these years of trial. This is a magnetism which any alert regime could not fail to exploit, especially after having struggled so long to attain it and after having often been humiliated by the scoffing of skeptics from abroad. This newly created magnetism was also earned and paid for the hardest way. Therefore, Moscow will not make one mistake so often made in recent years by the policy-shapers of the U.S.A. They will not fail to capitalize on a magnetism which has been so dearly won.

Owen Lattimore has developed the meaning of this in masterly fashion in his eye-opening and indispensable guide to tomorrow, *Solution in Asia*. He speaks of the "politics of Soviet attraction" and he brings that down to earth, in practical ABC language, in the following terms:

If this Uighur learns . . . that among his near kinsmen the Soviet Uzbeks, a poor man's children may attend, free, a school at which they are taught in their own language and taught to take pride in their own history and culture; that they may go on to the university and become doctors, engineers, anything in the world; that they may be elected to powerful positions in which they can give orders even to Russians, because Uzbeks and Russians are equal and it depends on a man's position, not his race, whether he gives orders—then he is going to think that the Uzbeks are free and have democracy.

This, of course, might also be said of the peoples in India, the Burmese, the Malayans, the Tibetans, the Indo-Chinese, and a great proportion of the Chinese—and of many people in eastern Europe, the Balkans, and the Near East. Add them all up and the total would not be far from 1,250,000,000 people. For all these economically subjugated peoples—some partially exploited, some almost totally so—the Soviet magnet is much nearer than the

Anglo-American magnet. And unlike the colonial nations of western Europe, and the U.S.A. on its home grounds, the Soviet Union has the enormous advantage that it does not practice and never has practiced racial discrimination within its borders. For all of the vast brown and yellow populations of Asia this alone constitutes a tremendous initial attraction. There is a kind of democracy in human relations which the great white colonizing powers have seldom practiced and have usually flagrantly abused. If the Western nations do not correct this swiftly and completely, they can never hope to compete with Soviet magnetism where it touches closest upon a definite majority of humankind.

You will agree with me, I think, that this is also an important factor in the new Soviet power. You will agree, too, that this psychological and political weapon—this magnetism of racial equality—is not, by nature, a peculiar Soviet monopoly. For it is as open to the Western democracies as to anyone else. It is ours if we are wise enough and big enough to use it. For us, as Americans, it is merely an acid test of how truly democratic we are; whether we really mean it when we repeat: "We hold these truths to be self-evident: that all men are created equal . . ." Yes, the "power of attraction" of Soviet Russia has indeed become a fatefully challenging thing in our revolutionary world. The magnetism of Soviet success differs from our American magnetism in many ways, but in some of these it may prove even more potent.

Undoubtedly Foreign Commissar Molotov had these things in mind on November 6, 1945, when he told his vast audience: "Our multinational state, with its differences of language, customs, culture, and history, has grown still more united. . . . No other multinational state could have held out under the ordeal through which we passed in the years of war. Only our state, in which there is no room for exploitation of man by man, in which there are no exploiting classes . . . could have withstood the German invasion in the hard years of 1941 and 1942." A little later Molotov added another reminder: "According to the Soviet Constitution it is a crime to preach animosities among races and nations—anti-Semitism and so on—just as it is not permitted in our press to exalt murder, robbery, and acts of violence against human rights."

I record these quotations here because it is so clear that Molo-

tov was exalting certain aspects of what the Soviets regard as
"democracy." It is equally clear that Molotov was not addressing
himself to citizens of the Soviet Union only but to any foreign
peoples who, by their own experience, might "be concerned," and
also interested. If some Western critics remained unimpressed,
that would not upset Mr. Molotov. He was more alive to the
advantage of speaking directly to a majority of the earth's population; and he was not so short-sighted as to waste any of the magnetism which the Soviets had amassed in their political arsenal.
Even so, it is interesting that Molotov took pains to state his
government's appeal in its broadest terms. It was another indication that the new Soviet power, of every category, will not be
dissipated by its leaders in the postwar era.

By way of summation.

As reporters from Mars we have limited ourselves here to certain dominant characteristics of the power-assets in postwar Soviet
Russia. Germany's invasion in 1941 certainly marked the end of
the great initial phase of the Soviet Revolution. But even in the
thirties the early Bolshevik conceptions and practices had changed
notably in many respects. Aggressive revolution slowly gave way
to an evolutionary process in which religion was treated with
greater tolerance, the emphasis on family was sharply revived, and
other important shifts in emphasis became apparent. The war
itself brought a tremendous rise in nationalism, new prestige to
the Red Army, the re-establishment of Russia's past heroes in
popular affections, and other innovations.

Without devoting space to these important changes we may
still note that the Soviet Union is quite the opposite of a static
society. With its constant pressure for internal growth it is also in
a constant state of evolution. It has evolved a long way from
orthodox Communist. As a new world power it will evolve still
more energetically—on what ultimate guiding "beam" few would
now be so rash as to predict. But the present great sources of Soviet power—whether physical, intellectual or psychological—are
positive and discernible, and their future influence will be increasingly great. If we keep these factors in mind, I believe post-

war Russia will be considerably less of an enigma; and the new Europe, which has so much meaning for Americans and Britishers alike, will become considerably more understandable. For the new Europe bears a strong imprint of Soviet example; and as such, it is a fateful middle ground—or conceivably, a bridge—between Russia and the American system.

Chapter V

THE NEW EUROPE

I believe we are moving into an era when the relations of property must be defined in the interest of the masses; and I believe that the alternative in every organized society is violent conflict which will not be resolved until the redefinition . . . has been made in the popular interest.

Harold J. Laski

Leaving Athens that January morning in 1945, I hopped into the front seat of the British army truck so as to have the chance to talk with its driver. The scars of the recent fierce street battles were still fresh. The tragedy of the so-called Greek "civil war," the unnecessary and immeasurably costly war in which Britons had fought Greeks, still poisoned the air and poisoned the hearts and darkened the faces on every side. The British Tommy beside me, so I soon learned, had now served overseas for four full years without once seeing his wife and children. We were driving out to Kalamaki airfield and traversing the streets which skirt the great stadium. Little groups of shabby Athenians walked toward us. For the most part they pointedly avoided looking at our truck, a glaring symbol of the conquerors; but a few of them shot black glances of undisguised hatred in our direction.

"All these people through here are bloody Communists," said the Tommy bitterly. "They'd fight us now, if they had a chance."

I made no reply. I had been in Athens long enough to know that in the eyes of the winners every Greek laborer was a Communist. It was interesting, though, that the typical British soldier —from relatively the same kind of home and same social level— should have swallowed this so quickly. I thought I'd learn more by letting the Tommy do most of the talking, and he obliged. Soon he was telling me how the officers of his company, three of them, had left their men cut off by the "Reds" for three days without coming near them.

"It's the same 'old-school tie' stuff, in the army like in England," said the Tommy. "Before the war our captain was a clerk, earning two and a half pounds a week. Now he's getting twelve pounds, and has his own mess and a batman. He's got no use for plain soldiers. One of our blokes wrote a letter to his wife. It was published in the *Daily Worker.*"

I was tempted to exclaim: "But that's a Communist paper! I thought you hated Communists." Instead, I waited for whatever strangely contradictory revelation might be coming. The Tommy went right on.

"He wrote: 'When we get this war won, don't think it's all over, Mary. We've got to fight another war when we get home.' . . . And that bloke is bloody well right. I'd say nine out of ten of our soldiers feel the same way. We know we've got a fight on our hands when we get home. It won't be with guns—but with fists." (The Tommy swung his own clenched fist suddenly upward from the steering wheel, as un-Britishly emotional and angry as very few Englishmen I had encountered anywhere under wartime stresses.)

"'There'll be plenty of that," growled the Tommy, his jaw set and his voice stern with decision. "That's what we're going home to."

The Tommy was speaking the new language of the British people. Although he had not the foggiest realization, he was also speaking Greek—the language of the common Greek workers whom he called "bloody Communists." He was really speaking the language of the new Europe; a language which has since echoed around the world. Appropriately enough its first mighty chorus rang forth in—

Great Britain's ballot-box Revolution.

Early in July 1945, while Prime Minister Churchill was participating in the crucial Big Three negotiations at Potsdam—while the war against Japan still seemed far from won—the cautious, moderation-loving British people did the most revolutionary thing they had ever done since the days of Oliver Cromwell.

Deliberately and without a trace of violence they wrote *finis* to the old order of prewar Tory privilege and laissez-faire capitalism. The British people voted British Socialists, the Labor Party, into office by an overwhelming and unprecedented majority. Gratitude for Winston Churchill's great talents and incomparable services as a war leader, although still universally felt and remembered, was swamped in an avalanche of British practicality—and honesty. From their lessons through nearly six years of suffering and sacrifice, hunger and hardship, the British people drew their own conclusions—unemotionally, realistically, and with a sharp intelligence. The verdict of their ballot-box revolution was clear-cut, self-chosen, and unafraid. In a world of change the old Britain must be changed. In the transforming of this new Europe the British people and British government must lead in hewing out the instruments of change.

To say that the 1945 British elections electrified most of humanity from Calais to China and from Oslo to Oregon is no exaggeration. The world had been wondering what the war had done to the citizens of Europe's oldest democracy, and the world found out with a ringing, clarion decisiveness which proclaimed the dawning of a new day and a new deal in that "tight little island," so long regarded as the citadel of conservatism. It was not surprising that the *Christian Science Monitor* should comment: "The nature of this change in Britain, always Europe's great democratic stabilizer, must stir thoughtful men into recognition that social and political currents set in motion by this war's upheavals run deep and swift." Deeply, swiftly, and emphatically the British people had chosen the path of socialization.

But this right-about-face, in reality, was a most natural outcome of the war. It could not astonish those who had had some real contact with the people in wartime Britain. The changes in their habits, in their outlook and mental exposures, had been revolutionary and profound. The merciless surgical knife of war had cut to the bone. It had carved away a great flabby mass of class distinctions and privileges. It had slashed out tumors of senseless traditions and irritating formalities. It had chopped away many of the barriers between city-dwellers and country-dwellers; and many of the differences between rich and poor. When I returned to England in the autumn of 1944 it was vastly changed from the England, and the London, I had known in the early months of the "phony" war five years previously. Even among the ruins it was remarkable how much of the best, of England and of the British, had survived and grown; how much of the old resigna- tion and the old "it just isn't done" had been blown away.

"People have been living on their nerves," said Doris Hoskins, office secretary for the ABC. "We can't remember what it's like to live in normal times. But some people have been better off with the war. They didn't have jobs before. Now, if they don't have jobs in peacetime, it will be bad. It's rather crazy, isn't it, that you have to have a war to have a chance to make a decent living?"

An enormous number of habitually unaggressive British citi- zens were thinking and saying things like that. To say such things in the old England was—well, "rather revolutionary." In the areas just hit by buzz bombs and rockets people didn't have any time, right then, to talk about tomorrow. But sometimes, if you studied their faces, you could see them thinking about tomorrow. Sometimes you caught a remark, like this one from a Bond Street manicurist: "It may seem strange to say, but I'm glad we've had the bombings. If we all know what war is, maybe we'll really do something to stop another one." And when you asked Londoners what kind of government they wanted after the war, they were often not too clear in their minds. But the words they used most were "something better"; "different—it's got to be different."

A Tory spokesman like Lord Astor, for all his traditional Tory viewpoint, could discuss the inevitability of rather drastic post- war curbs on industry with a lack of emotion rarely to be found among many American conservatives. "We have one big ad- vantage over the United States," said Lord Astor quietly. "Here in England we have adopted a considerable measure of state control in a free enterprise system. Our conservatives are not rigid, and they know how to compromise. They do not think that all our enterprises can be divorced from governmental con- trol; at best, only a part of them."

I went out to a factory on the outskirts of London. I wanted to see one of Britain's wartime Joint Production Committees in action. They had been a tremendous success in ironing out shop troubles and increasing production, as our own labor-management committees were designed to do. I talked with various members of this plant's J.P.C.; but especially with Mr. Blodgett, the manager and an outspoken little cockney named Minty, who was the chief representative of the workers. I heard some amazing things that day. I saw an utterly new independence and understanding on the part of labor; a new kind of confidence and teamwork between management and labor—and frankly admitted to be such on both sides. But I also heard a British industrial manager talk the most revolutionary language I had heard anywhere in England. Mr. Blodgett and Minty were all for keeping the Joint Production Committees after the war. They got into a keen discussion of Britain's postwar industry and its problems—as a common concern.

"You're on the brink of that national planning which your party has always demanded," said Blodgett to Minty, an ardent Socialist. "The change to postwar peacetime operation in Britain has got to be on a national and controlled basis. We've got to have a balanced success of all the country's industry. This is one of the few occasions when we've got a chance to put the country on a balanced basis."

"As one of the organizers," interjected Minty, "as a representative of Labor, I must agree with what Mr. Blodgett has just said. If it can be done on a national basis, that's what we want."

"It can only be done through national planning," resumed plant manager Blodgett. "Russia had its troubles and traitors and all that. We don't need to do that—*if* we have national planning."

"Again I agree with you, Mr. Blodgett," declared the unabashed Minty. "That's what we Socialists have always wanted, and that's what we need."

"The basis of exports is whole production," continued Blodgett, "and against intense international competition. About half of our industrialists have taken a defeatist attitude. They say—look at America; look at Russia. But we British can only compete if we put our production in order. We must work more efficiently. Before the war the American worker was using five horsepower per day; the British and German worker, three and one-half per day. Unless we get greater efficiency we can't compete."

"We could work forty hours a week—and get more production," insisted Minty.

"That's true," admitted the voice of shop management.

A moment later Mr. Blodgett touched off his amazing bomb.

"To carry on this war we've sold the shirt off our backs," he said. "We haven't got a single dollar abroad now. We haven't any national wealth left to call on. We've got to operate in a closed economy. We are not assured of success yet. We've got to work with one mind, labor and management together. *We've got to adopt what amounts to national Communism.*"

I was listening to a *plant manager*, an executive in British industry, and I could scarcely believe my ears. Undoubtedly he represented a minority among British industrialists. Nevertheless he was British, and a representative of British *management*, saying: "We've got to adopt what amounts to national Communism." Coming from a land where the great majority of industrialists and management executives passionately denounce "national planning" or any suggestion of co-ordinated governmental controls over production, this was something for any American to think about. After an exposure to the wartime evolution in British industries—to the evolution in thinking in both management and labor circles—the results of the British elections could only come as a public confirmation of a deep-seated historical trend.

It was not surprising that the Bishop of Birmingham, in the industrial heart of Britain, should have declared on election eve: "We cannot continue a system bound up with large-scale unemployment. Christianity must sympathize with people who with bitter memories turn thoughtfully to Russia to see whether that land has solved the problems which are a menace to all."

In the United States there are still very few bishops who speak in these terms. But the Right Reverend Dr. Ernest William Barnes, so speaking, spoke for the great majority of the new Europe's more than 350,000,000 inhabitants. For it is now clear, beyond all possibility of make-believe or wishful thinking, what the Second World War has done to the political thinking and the social and economic aspirations of all European peoples. We can now see, in all its revolutionary baldness,

The common pattern of Europe's swing toward Socialism.

If you have closely followed the wartime trends and developments of Europe, you have not been surprised or shocked by the emergence of this socialistic pattern. It was something in the very nature of things. It had to happen. It was not unusual foresight but merely a factual adding of two-plus-two when, in the summer of 1943, I wrote:

With its extreme ruthlessness Nazism has merely been a gigantic scythe slashing European society down to a single common level. As a consequence there will be no way for Europe to survive and restore itself except through a greater degree of collective economy—more socialism—than it has known in the past.[1]

After the war, European peoples, I reported then,

will be determined not to be enslaved by the system, whether the system is chiefly feudalism as in Spain and Hungary, or feudal-capitalism as in the Balkans, or simply a virtually uncontrolled capitalism as it previously existed in France and elsewhere.

In reality this was a conclusion widely shared by most experienced observers of Europe in its prewar and warring years.

But as one European country after another was liberated in 1944 and 1945 the "community" pattern which gradually emerged from confusion and social upheaval proved amazingly consistent. Everywhere the parties of the Left (Communists and Socialists), the peoples' parties, were foremost in the leadership of resistance movements. Everywhere the Left and left-of-center organizations were champions of national restoration, of patriotic service and of vigorous domestic reforms. This was as true in Poland and Czechoslovakia as in France and Belgium; as true in Yugoslavia and Greece as in Italy. Middle-class parties and groups were also active everywhere in the resistance movements. But leaders of the Left were almost universally more energetic

[1] Leland Stowe: *They Shall Not Sleep*, p. 387.

and more numerous. And in almost every liberated country the former Rightist and ultraconservative parties were least prominent, or had simply gone somewhere. Where a great many of their members had "gone" is the shameful side of the story.

In liberated Italy the main political parties immediately emerged as Communist, Socialist, and a central Catholic party. In France precisely the same thing occurred. Under Marshal Tito's strong hand in Yugoslavia, Communist control was never veiled, yet at least so long as hostilities against the Germans continued Tito's coalition was so broad as to include many moderate groups and many patriotic churchmen. In Poland, Rumania, Bulgaria, and Hungary the Red Armies promptly placed native Communists in control of the police and gendarmerie, as ministers of the interior; and others in charge of propaganda and some other key governmental posts. In these countries Soviet control, if indirect, became automatic from the outset. Yet, curiously enough, the chief political and economic reforms put forward in the Soviet-controlled countries had many striking similarities to the reforms demanded by Frenchmen and Italians, where there was no Red Army—and no indirect Soviet control. With or without Moscow's advice or prodding it became apparent that most Europeans have many common ideas about what was wrong with their prewar system and what should be done to prevent a recurrence of these abuses.

So we find in the new Europe a common pattern of political and social reforms. In some countries, like Britain and France, they are now in process of adoption. In other countries, such as Italy and Belgium and the Netherlands, reforms are developing more gradually, but their general direction and intent has long been clear enough. In eastern Europe and the Balkans, where Soviet impact has been strongest, an extraordinary amount of fundamental reform has been carried out at high speed. We can make due allowances for these differences of emphasis and of tempo. With all that, however, the dimensions of the "common denominators" in this newly shaping European society are remarkable—and the popular impetus behind them is extraordinarily strong.

What are the most important "community" characteristics of Europe's reforms? In Britain the people voted overwhelmingly in favor of nationalization of mines, of public utilities and transport systems, of the Bank of England, and of the land. In France the October 1945 elections were equally dramatic and equally emphatic in their repudiation of the past. With astonishing unity and agreement on fundamentals French voters (including millions of women voting for their first time) telescoped some fifteen hybrid prewar parties and groups into three powerful main parties. In blazing contrast to their chaotic prewar politics the vast majority of Frenchmen demonstrated marked agreement on a broad and bold program of reform. They not only demanded a new and Fourth Republic, but a strongly *socialistic* republic—with public ownership of certain big industries, of banks and insurance and other keys to economic control. The minimum reforms advocated by the Communists and Socialists were accepted by the third great party to emerge from the elections—the new M.P.R. (Popular Republican Movement), which is overwhelmingly Catholic in composition. Thus we find that French Catholics, now supporting socialistic reforms, have moved markedly toward the Left.

In Italy the popular currents for socialistic reforms are also running very strongly. The six parties which came forth from the national resistance movement included the Christian Democrats and the Action (predominantly Catholic) party. But even the Italian Communists threw their weight toward a program of national unity. Togliatti, their leader, told *PM's* foreign editor, Alexander H. Uhl: "We are in good relations with the Church. There are many Italians who are Catholic. We respect them and will do nothing against their religious convictions. . . . We want Italy to have whatever regime the people desire through normal processes of democracy." Of course, this might be regarded as realistic political maneuvering; but it also seemed to indicate that Italian Communists were fairly confident about the *kind* of reforms the Italian people would want after twenty-odd years of Fascism.

Czechoslovakia still remains the most democratic and freest nation in eastern Europe. Its government-in-exile was far more democratic in composition than the controversial Polish government-in-exile. Under the able leadership of President Beneš the Czech government came home from London and went to work on its own program. The Czech leaders had wisely cultivated friendly relations with Russia. They had the memory of Munich and of unkept Western promises as a reminder. But they set about governing their own domain, and of their own free will they chose a sweeping nationalization. In October 1945, the Prague government decreed public ownership of commercial banks, insurance companies, and twenty-seven industries. Included in this vast change were coal mines, defense industries, utilities, porcelain and glass factories, cement and textile plants, the great Bata shoe factories, steel plants, and others. Concerns employing fewer than 500 workers were exempt. Even so, about 70 percent of Czech industries will be nationalized. This, as Maurice Hindus reported in the *New York Herald Tribune,* makes Czechoslovakia the most socialistic country in the world next to Russia: "a balance between the gradualism of the British Labor Party and Russian Sovietism."

In the Danubian-Balkan countries nationalization of industries has progressed rapidly, as was to have been expected. Yet this cannot be ascribed uniquely to the predominance of Soviet influence. From what I observed in these countries in 1940 it seemed most probable that—if ever the Rumanians or Bulgarians or Hungarians could have free elections, a virtually unknown luxury—a majority of their citizens would prefer to have their larger industries publicly owned. After all, the only way that Socialist governments were prevented in these lands, at various times in the twenties and thirties, was by "fixed" elections or violent suppression of popular, mass-based parties.

When we survey the strikingly similar pattern of reform in the new Europe we cannot escape the meaning of the common denominator which rules from Birmingham to Bucharest, from the Arctic tip of Sweden to the southernmost tip of Italy and the Peloponnesus. There is a far greater sociopolitical unity in this ravaged Europe than ever before. The thinking and the demands of most of 350,000,000 Europeans have changed radically. Even at a recognized risk to personal initiative, and at a seriously increased curtailment of free enterprise, these new Europeans have opted for a much greater degree of governmental control. They, who lost all freedom, are somehow convinced that the twentieth-century individual can and must find sufficient free-

doin—perhaps more of freedom for the many—within the limitations of *much more* State regulation. It is the same risk and
the same problem which confront us as Americans, whether we
choose to face the dilemma posed by King Machine or whether
we do not face it.

To find a safe balance between free personal initiative and
governmental controls is the key problem beneath the revolutionary cross-currents which are now agitating all industrialized
nations. A British authority, Professor Vincent Harlow, is not
alarmed by the prospect of an increasingly Socialist Britain. He
observes with justice that "the fact remains that this balance is
being achieved within a resilient yet stable democratic framework. That has been possible in the western democracies because
the mass of the people are steeped in the discipline which comes
from a respect for one's neighbor's rights, and are also in basic
agreement about the State as an instrument of the community.
It follows, then, that democracy as we understand it will *not*
work in European countries, which have hitherto rejected it,
*unless and until they are convinced it can provide a more satis-
fying solution to their economic needs than any other system."*

In the 1919 peacemaking, we Americans assumed that self-
determination would be sufficient to make democracies out of
most or all European countries. We left the economic needs of
Austrians, Hungarians, Greeks, and others pretty thoroughly out
of calculation. The nice new lines on the map of Europe did
not do much to improve the lot of these peoples; in some cases
they even made a decent livelihood impossible. Now the Europeans are thinking and acting in terms of their economic needs;
and concentrating on those precautions which they believe are
necessary if they are to achieve them. To them, in their plight
and disillusionment, Socialism is no bugaboo. It is hope. Thus,
if democracy does not mean *economic* democracy—a greater public control of how their needs shall be satisfied—then a vast
number of Europeans will not be much interested in democracy,
purely political.

As true as this is, it seems abundantly evident that all of western Europe—and perhaps most of central and Balkanic Europe—
would prefer to have economic democracy, if possible. In the
eyes of these new Europeans socialistic reform and a considerable

degree of government ownership is not incompatible with democracy. Rather, with their long political experience and their
much more intimate acquaintance with Marxist theory, they
appear to conceive that economic democracy is the only kind
that is adequate in an age of machines where overproduction
and underdistribution are a constant menace.

But it is one thing to state accurately that this is how Europe's
masses are thinking and that this is the kind of socialistic experimentation which they have elected as their choice. It is another
thing for *us*, Americans who have never been truly exposed to
socialistic theory or to a strong nationwide Socialist party in our
political life, to understand how they got that way. That is another facet of the new Europe which we cannot afford to neglect—
and can no longer afford to misunderstand. For *Socialism,
whether we like it or not, has become the last strong defender—
and perhaps the last effective champion—of political democracy
in Europe.* In the immediate future, if we cannot co-operate
with Socialist democracies in the Old World, we shall find
pre cious little democracy with which to co-operate.

Chapter VI

THE FRUITS OF COLLABORATION,
AND OF RESISTANCE

It could be terribly cold in Paris; especially at 5:30 in the morning and in January 1945. Even at this hour the little news-woman was at her stand outside the Passage de Choiseul. She had once refused to let me pay her for her last half-box of matches. I paused to say good-bye and wish her a good year. As we talked I noticed her thin coat, and how her hands were purple with cold.

"Oh this war! That it may finish soon!" she said. Then, out of her misery, the words came in a torrent. "That vile wretch, that monster of a Hitler, that ——!"

Her stream of French nouns was all that the subject required. But suddenly she broke off with the cry: "What they have done to our youth, Monsieur!" She rubbed the tears from her eyes with her purple fist, and her face twitched as her voice broke. In a moment she resumed: "Our best and our cleanest, Monsieur—they have killed them. And there has been no purge. There's a man, right in this street. Every night he used to be with the Boches. . . . Well, he is still here. Why doesn't someone get him?"

This was my farewell to Paris; and as I carried my kit toward the Army bus station I knew that the little old news vender, with tears in her eyes, had spoken for all the decent and ordinary people of Europe. I also knew that, months after liberation, tens of thousands of traitors and collaborators were still doing very nicely in various European countries. Once they had explained glibly why they felt obliged to "co-operate" with the Germans and the "New Order" of Fascism. Now they were equally suave in explaining how they had only slept with the Germans the better to push them out of bed. Or perhaps they did not bother to offer any explanations at all.

What did "collaboration" mean? If you hadn't lived in these countries when it was going on, it's difficult to grasp it with sufficient emphasis. If *your* country has never been occupied by foreign armies, propagandists, and Gestapo, you can scarcely imagine what people, apparently respectable, can be persuaded to sell their nation's freedom for cash or titles or political position. The Judas strain is a human weakness common to all races and nationalities. Had the United States been conquered and occupied by the Nazis, you and I would have been shocked to see persons in our own circle of acquaintance—perhaps even near neighbors or close friends—emerge as co-workers and champions of Hitler's "New Order." Some would have done so, here in America, because they had swallowed anti-Semitic propaganda; others because they hated the Russians, or feared Communism. Others would have "co-operated" for prestige or political power. Others would have become Quislings for "practical" business reasons, for war profits—for the tinkle of thirty pieces of silver. But somehow it's always difficult to imagine until you actually see people whom you know turn traitors.

While covering the League of Nations' sessions in the early 1930's I became acquainted with two very able French journalists —Fernand de Brinon and Jean Luchaire. They later became two of the most notorious and despicable among French collaborators. De Brinon was very intelligent, well-informed, and gifted with an acid wit. He seemed like many other capable and sardonic Paris journalists. When Pierre Laval was negotiating with Mussolini and Hitler in 1934–35, De Brinon became Laval's behind-the-scenes go-between. I heard that De Brinon got along very well with the Germans. Laval himself had a peculiar kind of political halitosis. We left France. After Paris fell, the next I knew was that Fernand de Brinon and Otto Abetz (the Hitler agent whose bribes undermined the French Republic) were bosom pals. Later on De Brinon became Vichy's "ambassador" in Paris, betraying thousands of his countrymen to death or torture at the hands of the Gestapo. When I rode in the same automobile with him, from Paris to Geneva in 1932, I could never have dreamed that this same journalist of reputation and ability would shortly be revealed as one of the most vicious rats and traitors that modern France has ever known.

Jean Luchaire, in those days, was an exceptionally good mixer for a Frenchman. He had much energy and a quick political sense and was very ingratiating. He would have been a well-liked, respected member in the correspondents' corps in Washington, or anywhere. He was ambitious, and he had a rather large family. Maybe those things account for it. Anyway, Luchaire also was bought by Otto Abetz long before Paris fell; and soon after that he blossomed forth as publisher of his own collaborationist newspaper. Meanwhile Luchaire's screen-actress daughter blossomed richly as mistress of German Ambassador Abetz. And to make everything chummy, Frau Abetz became Luchaire's secretary! With such a *combinaison* as that, Jean Luchaire couldn't fail to make millions—so long as the "New Order" lasted. But who, while enjoying a pleasant chat with him on a Geneva café terrace only a few years before, would ever have dreamed what Luchaire would turn out to be?

I mention these two cases merely as a reminder that there is no advance method of detecting traitors, any more than we have any device for detecting murderers before they commit murder. The seeds of collaboration are hidden deep inside personal psychologies and personal appetites. But the most uneducated street-cleaner can quickly discern—

The fruits of collaboration.

During nine years of journalistic pursuits in Paris I came to know personally a great many politicians, including many whose names are now covered with shame and dishonor. I also became acquainted with highly respected industrialists, bankers, businessmen, exporters, and the like. Today I wonder why I ever had any confidence in some of them—and so do the French people. But this is just as true in Belgium, Holland, Italy, and other countries. Everywhere there was a too large percentage of supposedly respectable and patriotic citizens who collaborated; for profits, for prestige, or some other personal gain. They sold themselves and sold their country. In doing this they tore the foundations from under the social system which they pretended to defend. Yet most of these future traitors, as I recall them, were well-educated and well-dressed; gentlemen with whom you were pleased to converse. Already most of them enjoyed the community's regard as "successful men." Were they so successful, I wonder, that they could not endure hard times for the sake of their country? Were they so successful that money was more important to them than anything else?

I remember the brief meeting which Warren Irvin and I had with Vidkun Quisling on the night that the Nazis took over Oslo. Quisling, too, was well dressed and obviously well educated. But his German masters kept him in sight. He dared only mutter a few hesitating phrases. It was perfectly clear that the only thing Quisling could give to Norway or the world was the undying ignominy of his name.

I remember watching Hitler's political and economic conspirators take over the Balkan countries in 1940. They wormed their way into parliaments, general staffs, and the boards of directors of powerful banks and important industries. They gave fabulous dinners and parties. They dispensed great bundles of banknotes with lavish hands. In Hungary, Rumania, Bulgaria, or Yugoslavia these Nazi "emissaries" always found influential ministers, bankers, businessmen, and editors who had their eyes most calculatingly upon their own appraisal of "the wave of the future." A few days in Bucharest, and Dr. Guido Schmidt, the Austrian Quisling, had Rumania's $50,000,000 steel corporation, Resita, in his pocket for the Nazis. Money talked! All over Europe money talked, and especially with many outstanding citizens who enjoyed the esteem and confidence of their fellow countrymen.

This was not true in France alone. It happened everywhere. Even in Norway—with its exceptional traditions of personal integrity and honesty in business and politics—several thousand were transformed into Quislings by Nazi propaganda or Nazi gold. It was demonstrated that every society has its quota of weaklings and potential traitors. Whether in occupied nations or in the Axis "puppet" countries of the Balkans, the same thing happened. And the bulk of collaborators came, uniformly, from the better privileged—either from the wealthy and aristocratic upper class, or from the professional ranks of the upper middle class. Much of the time the results offered a classic confirmation of the Mexican peasants' saying: "The rich have only one eye.

The other is in their pocketbook." If the European masses perhaps had never heard this saying, nevertheless they could recognize it when they saw it.

But the Quislings and collaborators of Europe were not concerned with the social dynamite they were strewing all about them. They were concerned only with their immediate prosperity, privileges, and prestige—as servitors and henchmen of the German conquerors. Some reaped political positions. For others there were busy factories, cheap labor, and large war profits. Others obtained jobs as spies and fixers, at salaries several times larger than they had ever been paid. Many became owners of business enterprises, of newspapers or magazines—full-fledged capitalists for the first time in their lives. Most collaborators reaped luxuries, income, or profits in excess of anything they had previously known. It paid well to sell your country—and your countrymen.

In Paris it paid a certain French nonentity, André Marquer, extremely well. He and his German wife made many millions producing textiles for the Nazis. Then they invested their swollen profits in real estate, jewelry, and automobiles—all perfectly regular business enterprises, you understand. Undoubtedly, André Marquer regarded himself as simply a good businessman, without any romantic exaggerated patriotism about him. *"Eh, bien.* France has fallen, so why should one spend his life weeping?" By the time liberation came Monsieur Marquer was a multimillionaire, who owned many race horses as a sporting sideline. He was doing very well indeed—except that he had become an enemy of the people. There are periods in history when it is downright careless to let yourself become branded as an enemy of the people.

Collaborators, by their very nature, had to be about the slickest citizens in their respective societies. No postoccupation government could hope to catch up with all of them. But the De Gaulle government in France proved more able and determined than most. Its investigators of war profiteers and other enriched collaborationists netted a considerable number of wall-eyed pike. When they landed Monsieur Marquer his jewelry collection alone was auctioned off for 10,000,000 francs. The French courts imposed fines on Marquer totaling 1,247,000,000 francs. At the existing rate of exchange that was nearly $25,000,000. Which raises a very pertinent question: If someone in your city or town had made that much swag as a Quisling for the German conquerors of your country, how would *you* feel? Marquer and his wife were sentenced to twenty years at hard labor. If *your* husband, wife, or child had died in the Resistance, defending your country's freedom, probably a sentence like that would not strike you as unduly severe.

This is what the collaborators did to public opinion in all the liberated lands of Europe. This is why the little news-woman cried out with such bitterness: "Why doesn't someone get him?" In every country the great mass of common people, the George Joneses, burned with a feeling of outraged justice. Completely helpless, they had watched the betrayers of their country wax fat on the corpse of their freedom. Like the conquerors, the traitors and war profiteers gorged themselves on the best food, while they starved. While honest and patriotic people could not buy a coat or a pair of shoes, the collaborators dressed in the best clothes and indulged in every pleasure. In Paris alone the authorities found *fifty* collaborators who had accumulated fortunes of more than $1,000,000 apiece. It had paid well indeed to sell your country. All over Europe there were new millionaires, in addition to those others who had long ago become rich serving the Fascists in Italy and Germany.[1]

1 On January 10, 1946, the French Ministry of Justice announced that 111,000 cases of war criminals, collaborators, and war profiteers had been officially investigated during 1945. Out of these, 36,904 were so serious as to be assigned to the justice courts, and another 17,000 were sent to ordinary civil tribunals. Death sentences were imposed upon 3,122 French citizens. There were 1,249 sentenced to life imprisonment at hard labor; 1,434 sentenced to solitary imprisonment; 7,942 lesser terms and 14,919 ordinary prison terms. Acquittals numbered 5,087. . . . In civil tribunals 31,537 persons were branded with national unworthiness; 7,155 were acquitted. Out of the 111,000 cases investigated, 32,432 were dropped. After November 1, 1945, no new cases could be registered, but 25,262 indictments were still waiting to be heard. (See *New York Times*, January 11, 1946.)

These official statistics show that France has done a far more thorough job of bringing war criminals and collaborators to justice than any other country. Even so, it seems certain that scores of thousands succeeded in eluding the law. In contrast to 3,122 death sentences to French collaborators, only eight persons in British-controlled Greece had been executed for collaboration more than one year after liberation. This fact may go far to explain many of the "atrocity" stories circulated against the Greek Resistance Movement.

But the magnitude of the crime of the collaborators cannot conceivably be estimated in dollars and cents alone. It can be seen only if we understand—

The background of collaboration.

Out of hundreds of thousands of human strands here is a single bright, brief thread in the backdrop to collaboration. My friend Jean, a leader in the French Resistance, told me about Hermine. Her name will never be known beyond the immediate circle of a few of her comrades. If any of her family survived, they will never receive a government pension. She will be unsung, and her grave will pass unnoticed. She is but one of a legion of incorruptibles, who died that freedom might live.

"I shall never forget Hermine," Jean said—and he had already told about Robert and Suzanne and many others. "She worked in a store which was one of our underground 'letter boxes.' Her brother had been one of our best radio-post operators to England. The Germans caught and shot him. Then Hermine's fiancé took his place. The very first time he started to send, the Boche seized him—and killed him, too. Her father had been taken to Germany. After all this her mother lost her mind.

"Hermine was not yet eighteen. She was slight and blonde, with large blue eyes. She was pretty. Such a freshness in her face. She looked like paintings you see of virgins. And she was like that—*then*. . . . One day one of our men talked with her boss in the store. He said the Gestapo colonel at Blois was a terrible beast, but unapproachable. An extraordinarily careful beast. But he was so efficient he must be killed.

" 'Let me do it,' interrupted Hermine.

" 'You're only a child. It's impossible,' said her boss.

"But they couldn't find any of our sector members who had a chance of getting anywhere near the Gestapo chief. Hermine pleaded again and again: 'Why don't you trust me? My fiancé and my brother have been killed by the Gestapo; my father has been deported to Germany. My mother has lost her mind. I have lost everything. What other credentials can I offer? It is I who should be charged with this mission.'

"They could find no one else. So Hermine went to Blois. In a few weeks she became the mistress of the Gestapo colonel. He was a brute—a gorilla. And she, only seventeen. She lived with him at his hotel for about six weeks. One night they dined in a popular restaurant, as they often did. As they were leaving the Gestapo chief and Hermine fell to the floor—dead.

"The customers had seen Hermine laughing and flirting with the Boche colonel through the dinner. They said she was so gay, so ravishingly young, everyone noticed her. A good many clients uttered ugly remarks about young Frenchwomen who sell themselves to the Boches. They saw her lifting her glass, so that the colonel would drink his liqueur. The German said something—and handed her his glass to drink from first. Hermine drank half of it—and handed it back to him gaily. The colonel then drained his glass."

This may be an exceptionally dramatic incident out of the remarkable saga of Europe's underground. Nevertheless, it is true. In the tragedy of Hermine lies all the heroism, self-sacrifice, and nobility of the Resistance Movements in every part of Europe. The heroes and heroines were mostly humble people. They were chiefly from workers' families or the bourgeoisie. Their leaders were sometimes Communists or Socialists, but often they were from the white-collar class; sometimes lawyers, doctors, or professors; sometimes former army officers. But the aristocrats and well-to-do were everywhere a minority in the Resistance. Like Washington's Continentals, the mass of these ununiformed soldiers was made up of the people. In France, Belgium, Holland, Norway—in Czechoslovakia, Greece, Italy, or Denmark—everywhere the *people* were the strength of the Resistance. It could not exist without them. Those who had least gave most.

Thus Collaboration stood out, stark and black and revolting, against a backdrop woven out of countless acts of magnificent courage—and shining scarlet with the martyrdom of tens of thousands of anonymous patriots who gave their lives, as they risked them daily, without reservation and without thought of personal gain. All over Europe—in every city, town, and village—people knew what neighbors and friends had given their lives as one more strand in the glowing and imperishable tapestry of Resistance. In every city, town, and village, people knew what men and women and boys and girls had died or had vanished while in the ranks of the underground. And in every community, people also knew who had betrayed them. Some had betrayed their fellows directly—for Nazi money. Some had betrayed them by currying favor with the Germans. Some had betrayed them by turning their backs—and rolling up war profits in service of Hitler's "New Order." Others still had betrayed the Hermines and Roberts of every land by lifting no finger for freedom; by playing it safe and living very well.

But in your city or mine many citizens cannot be dying heroic deaths, and others luxuriating in the role of traitors, without people in every street and house taking due account. Such contrasts between devotion and perfidy, between integrity and shamelessness, cannot be witnessed month after month without profound mental and spiritual reactions among all decent, self-respecting citizens. People are bound to ask themselves why such injustices can be tolerated; they are bound to ask what produced the collaborators—to take note of where they came from, and where they are likely to be found tomorrow. Thus, rather than agents of the Germans and Fascism, the traitors and war-profiteers become agents of *social revolution*. Since a majority of the collaborators in every land came from the upper class or the bureaucracy—corrupt politicians, industrialists or others who were wealthy reactionaries—the people became determined that these individuals of past privilege must never be permitted to resume their old favored positions after liberation. State ownership of heavy industries, of mines or electrical utilities, of banks and such, would take care of that. The ultimate price of collaboration became nationwide demands for nationalization of those key enterprises and industries which had produced far too high a percentage of collaborators. Europe's masses went politically to the Left, among other reasons, because collaboration much too often came from the Right. This reflex was as inevitable as it was natural.

Shortly after leaving Paris I arrived in Greece in the midst of its civil war. There I found that the same kind of people had collaborated with the Nazis, or had resignedly accepted them,

as in western Europe. I was struck by the fact that the Greeks'
only effective Resistance Movement, the E.A.M., consisted overwhelmingly of Greek workers, villagers, and peasants. Curiously,
I did not hear of many upper-class Greeks who had become
prominent in the E.A.M. guerrilla forces. Finally, I sought the
testimony of an Athenian friend in whose integrity I had great
confidence. "Were there many in the Greek upper classes who
were active in the Resistance?" I asked. "People whose sons or
husbands died while fighting with the underground?" My friend
paused for a long moment. At last, looking me in the eyes, he
replied slowly: "Yes, there were several." Out of hundreds of
such families in Athens he could only recall "several" individuals
who had died in the Resistance.

In Italy the picture was similar, but more extreme. Two
decades of Fascism had contaminated all levels of society; especially in the middle and at the top. The vast majority of Italy's
well-to-do—aristocrats, industrialists, bankers, feudal landlords
and such—had either become Fascists or gone along with Fascism.
They had been "collaborators" for so long that it had become
second nature for most of them. A great many white-collar and
professional people were no better. So the real Italian Resistance
came from trade unionists, villagers, and humble folk. In the
north the patriots became a strong and gallant force. They were
led by a professor, Ferruccio Parri, who later became Prime
Minister. In France another professor, Georges Bidault, had
stepped from the Resistance into the post of foreign minister.
Behind such leaders the rank-and-file in cities and towns rallied.
You could call them the masses, but in the U. S. A. you would
call such people the Joneses—and there are more people in
factories and farms than anywhere else. As for those Europeans
who had more or most to lose, they usually performed according to Hoyle—they took care of their pocketbooks, and themselves.

So the collaborators and the sit-tighters, in reality, spent the
years of German occupation doing the one thing of which they
were most frightened. By their betrayals, their greed and lack of
patriotism they promoted a revolutionary popular reaction. Un-
wittingly they were promoting Socialism. Hitler was doing this

by leveling down the middle class, the balance weight of society, through robbery, expropriation, and impoverishment. The traitors and war profiteers served the same ends by inflaming public resentment. Collaboration, in fact, was nothing less than excitation for radical reforms. On the part of the wealthy and privileged upper-class citizens it was shortsightedness and political folly of the highest order. But it proved to be just as costly for—

Those who collaborated with the collaborators.

This, unfortunately, is where the American and British liberators came in. The Darlan "deal" in North Africa marked the beginning of Allied collaboration with collaborators. But in Italy Anglo-American representatives first displayed their political adolescence to a disastrous degree. They supported the Fascist-smeared and cordially despised Italian monarchy. With this, Anglo-Americans revealed a great weakness for people of social rank and "importance." They preferred the company of the "best-educated" people; and were mostly indifferent to the fact that perhaps 90 percent of the "best-educated" Italians had been notoriously collaborationist. These Italian aristocrats or businessmen owned superb apartments or villas. They spoke English fluently. Their manners were charming; their foods and wines were amazingly plentiful; their women were the best-dressed and most ingratiating. The majority of American and British officers never looked behind this seductive façade. They snapped up the collaborators' bait with boyish relish. Very few of them paused to consider that their best entertainment and most agreeable pleasures came from those who had the most questionable motives for offering them. In a very short time the enemies of the Italian patriots, and those who secretly most despised democracy, became the best friends of Allied officers. Naturally, the democratic cause became suspect to the Italian people.

"They see former Fascists basking in the sunlight of Allied companionship," reported Edward P. Morgan of the *Chicago Daily News*. "And they see people who had the courage to resist when the price was highest—people who are at a loss now for leadership—wondering if their efforts were worth the risk. Who are these patriots? *They are mostly the little people.* A lot are Communists, but they include aristocrats as well. . . . Bartenders, tailors, and tradesmen of the middle class, and members of the clergy. They are people who, as one person put it, 'are still clinging to the battered but desirable ideals of decency.' " While ignoring such people as these, the hope of Italy, a large proportion of American and British officers judged the birds about them by their fine feathers. Later they did much the same thing in France; and in Germany the "educated" Nazis and their attractive, uninhibited women had a field day. In this fashion the upper hierarchy of the western democracies repeatedly dashed the peoples' faith in the motives and reliability of the democracies.

The result was a serious accentuation of political confusion and division in Italy. Again and again the Allies failed to support the truly democratic elements in the Resistance. They also maintained crippling military controls many months after these were necessary. The promising Parri government was doomed to failure and resignation in large measure because of Anglo-American policies. Although the Resistance emerged with an unquestionable democratic majority behind it, the Allies neither trusted nor attempted to build up and encourage the proven Italian patriots. Early in 1946 the forces of pro-Fascist reaction were reported to be gaining ground steadily. Observers warned that civil war might yet break out in Italy. These were the dangerous Allied fruits of collaborating with collaborators—including Italy's royalty!

Anglo-American representatives had not been able to cause nearly so much damage in France, and chiefly for two reasons. First, because of the remarkable prestige of General de Gaulle. Second, because the French Resistance was better organized and much stronger, and because the French people have a much more developed democratic instinct. No liberators could hold down a lid over the French public and sit on it. And the French also had a much clearer idea of the changes they wanted, and how they proposed to get them. In France collaboration proved most costly in the end; and in France the Resistance proved to be of greatest importance. For these reasons it is necessary for us to understand—

The exceptional importance of the 1945 French elections.

Nearly a year earlier I had a memorable conversation with a very intelligent young Frenchwoman. She belonged to an old family of the Norman nobility, a strongly Catholic family with a magnificent fifteenth-century château near Mont-St.-Michel. She had eight or nine brothers and sisters, and she represented the privileged in Normandy's aristocracy. This was why what she said surprised me so much.

"But nationalization is bound to come," exclaimed Mlle Rouselle de La Pereire. "People will have to compromise, because that is the shape of tomorrow. There is no way to prevent a great deal of socialistic reform. My mother would say that I talk like a Communist. After all, *it is I who will have to live in this different world.* I have a right to adjust myself to it. I tell my father that he was born too soon *in a century that is too old.*"

There was also a young French aristocrat who said: "I know the de Wendels and the Schneiders [leading industrialists in the great French steel combine known as the Comité des Forges]. These people accept the idea of nationalization of their great steel and armaments factories. They have their huge fortunes anyway. I think most of them are resigned to saving as much as they can of what they've got. It's the medium businessmen who really fight the idea of government ownership."

After hearing opinions like these expressed in French upper-class circles, the citadel of prewar conservatism, I went to the workers' districts of Paris. In a café off the Boulevard de Sebastopol I spent more than an hour talking with a group of typical Parisian laborers. Finally I asked how the French elections would go. A big, curly-haired fellow named Gaston boomed out immediately *"Bien à gauche!"* The others all chimed in affirmatively. And "well to the Left" was the general verdict in all such districts. If you had studied the history of collaboration and Resistance, you could not doubt the accuracy of this reaction. The fruits of collaboration could not be clipped or curbed in

France. The revolutionary and socialistic tide was the inevitable consequence of a series of enormous betrayals dating far back before the surrender of Bordeaux. In his book, *The Gravediggers of France,* Pertinax has documented with accuracy and brilliance all those actions which made the 1945 electoral revolution a necessity.

The October elections were revolutionary in at least two respects. First, because 80 percent of 20,000,000 voters cast their ballots for only three parties—rather than for more than a dozen, as in prewar years. Second, because the Socialist and the Communist parties alone elected more than half of the total number of delegates to the National Assembly. For the first time in French history the two Left parties won a powerful preponderance in a national election. Where the Communists had elected 71 deputies in 1936 (an all-time high at that time), they now won 152 seats. The Socialists, with 142, remained as strong as before. But in addition the formerly powerful French Right, the conservatives, had been drastically reduced. In its place emerged a new party, Georges Bidault's Popular Republican Movement—and it was markedly progressive, almost left of center. The MPR, as it is called, was born out of the Resistance. It is a Catholic party which is also radical and in favor of socialistic reforms. Thus the middle ground in French politics is no longer strictly anti-Marxist, but well left of center in terms of habitual American political thinking. This is the great historical change which defeat, occupation, collaboration, and Resistance achieved.

If I seem here to lay particular stress on what has changed in France, it is because the pattern of the French Resistance faithfully reflects the transformed political thinking in almost every liberated European country. Italy's popular reaction was headed in exactly the same direction until Allied and internal conservative forces combined to throttle the trend as much as possible. Whether the Italian people can yet shake themselves free of their pro-Fascist and reactionary elements remains to be seen, but that they will struggle bitterly to do so is a certainty. From Belgium through the Balkans to Greece the same general postwar shift, toward the Left and greater socialistic reform, has already been recorded or continues to develop. In Britain the choice has been emphatic.

But the common pattern has not been confined to Europe. The nationalist movements in Burma, Indonesia, and Indo-China are actuated by the same popular demand for the peoples' greater representation and voice in their form of government. The Resistance guerrillas in the Philippines consisted chiefly of the lowliest classes, especially the workers and the long-exploited tenant farmers. The Filipino collaborators came principally from the same upper-class stratum as in France, Italy, or anywhere else: the corrupt politicos, the aristocrats, the wealthy businessmen, and big landowners. And in the Philippines, as in Italy, American officers have usually been far more friendly with the collaborators than with the people. Serious trouble is also reported brewing in the Philippines; and unless our representatives are careful the United States may emerge supporting (perhaps even by force of arms) the most antidemocratic elements in the islands. To collaborate with the collaborators can only mean to sell America's professions of democracy down the river.

So it may be of great importance for all of us in America and Britain to understand what the Resistance Movements, throughout all the war-torn lands, really represent. They have not only been patriotic. They are also great popular manifestations demanding a greater opportunity for the many and a fairer share of their nation's economic benefits. In reality, although they ask for it in different terms and by more socialistic methods, what are all these people demanding? If we analyze it, we will usually find that these Europeans and Asiatics are merely asking for something more nearly approaching what the average American has had all his life. Because they have waited a long time they want these things done quickly and in a rather radical fashion. But a great deal of what they want is really not much different from what we fortunate Americans, most of us, have always had.

I was lunching in Paris with my friend Geraud Jouvre, a French journalist of exceptional ability. We had worked together in the Balkans years before and I knew he had been right about France all through the darkest days. Among his country's journalists he had been one of the distinguished incorruptibles. Geraud had been saying that De Gaulle and the Communists were then (as of December 1944) the only two real political forces in France.

"But if De Gaulle doesn't make radical reforms, he will make more Communists instead," Geraud said. "The choice for France, after all, is very simple. *If we do not dare to be revolutionary, we shall make revolution inevitable.*"

That is one of the clearest definitions that I have ever heard of the only existing choice in most of our new world. It reminded me again of the penetrating remark of that intelligent Mademoiselle from Normandy's aristocracy:

"People will have to compromise, because that is the shape of tomorrow. . . . After all, it is I who will have to live in this different world."

And so shall we all, even we who are Americans.

Chapter VII

THE CLEAN-UP OF EUROPEAN FEUDALISM

Once you hear crashing as never there was crashing in the world's history before, then realize: German thunder has at last reached the goal. . . . In Germany a play will be enacted which will make the French Revolution appear a mere harmless idyll. . . . You have more to fear from a liberated Germany than from the entire Holy Alliance combined with all the Croats and Cossacks.

Heinrich Heine, in his remarkable warning to the French; written in 1833–34.

The Budapest which American and British tourists fell in love with between the great wars was the same lovely, beguiling city I last saw in October 1940. By then the Nazi octopus was tightening its death grip upon Hungary, but you never would have guessed this from the intoxicating atmosphere of the queen of Danubian cities. Here were the same beauties and pleasures, the same refinements and civilized joy in living, which had won the hearts of so many visiting Americans. "Budapest!" they used to exclaim, when homeward-bound in Paris. "What a marvelous city—and what beautiful women!"

Now, in this glorious autumn of 1940, Budapest wore her same immaculate gowns and the same roses in the sheen of her dark hair. (The Budapest, I mean, that the holiday-makers always saw.) From the broad terrace near the Ritz her silhouette at night was a thing of rare symmetry and enchantment. Here there was a mysterious aura of ease and sophistication; something which had grown and mellowed with the centuries, and this too accounted for much of the charm of the kind of Hungarians whom visitors met. Budapest, like Bucharest, was a city playing a wonderful game of make-believe while Europe blazed. Her cabarets

and garden restaurants were jammed with merrymakers, while
Nazis ferreted their way into government offices, industries,
banks, and every mechanism of ultimate control. If you did not
examine beneath the alluring and feverish surface immediately
about you, you would never dream that continental Europe's
complete subjugation was at this moment entering its final stage
from Austria to the Black Sea.

Now all Europe was doomed to the blackest night in several
centuries, but Hungary's incurable playboys sang and flirted and
danced unheedingly. The restaurants which they thronged provided menus fit for princes and for kings. Their ladies were glittering, alluring creatures of a world without a care. There was
provocation in their eyes and the glitter of diamonds on their
perfectly manicured fingers; and the gypsies' violins poured into
every ear those mad and melancholy melodies which are at once
the height of joyous abandonment and the sudden distillation of
love forever lost. Here laughter lilted on a teardrop's edge. Reality was drowned in the magic flood which burst from bows sweeping on catgut. Time was lost and romance reigned and life was
ringed with pleasure. Everything was now.

And when the Ox-blood wine and the Tokay had been drained,
Budapest still offered the gaiety and amnesia of the continent's
most de luxe night-clubs. Some of these rivaled, or perhaps sur-
passed, anything to be found in London, Paris, or New York. The
"Arizona" was the empress of them all, cut from the predominantly Hungarian pattern of profligacy, yet ultramodern in its
well-calculated devices for surprise and merriment. Here the dash-
ing cavalier might push a hidden button, whereupon his private
booth simply descended out of view to the mystification of his
guests, to the delight of the prewarned, and to the golden advantage of those suitors whose reflexes responded promptly to the
sudden gift of quasi-privacy. In the center of the dance floor a
sinking circular space, accommodating two couples but no more,
would isolate a pair of partners in an artificial well of six-foot
depth; such sport as no seeker of merriment could resist. And
gentlemen had no excuse for remaining without companionship
at the Arizona, for here were hostesses to rival Hollywood's most
luscious, both in their graces and in their attire. Budapest? Buda-

pest was music and laughter and beauty and forgetfulness shaken into a Magyar cocktail of its own. Budapest was a gypsy dance— at a graveyard's fringe. Budapest was a mask of melody and heart's delight; a carnival, it seemed, without a season or a finale. So it was all too easy and all too human not to look behind the mask. For the Budapest of the tourists and the Hungarian playboys was only the last fling of a dying Danubian tradition; a carnival in which the Hungarian people had never shared. All this, in truth, was but the multicolored frosting on a little cake which the majority of Budapest citizens had never tasted and would never know.

You could drain the Tokay and eat the cake of Budapest and depart knowing no more about Hungary than when you came. You could talk with Hungary's aristocrats, as with the aristocrats in Madrid or in prewar Poland, and remember them as people of exceptional graces and charms. You could yield yourself to the marijuana of the gypsy maestros and plunge with them from ecstasy to sudden sorrow, yet the meaning of that ever-recurrent mood of melancholy might remain no more than the chance expression of some nameless composer's anguish and despair. Did such music spring from a single vanquished heart? Was it so universally loved without relationship to villagers and peasants, to past and present? Or was there also in it a voice echoing out of many generations? Was there also in it the vibrant hope, the soaring passion, and the dark despair of an entire people? I think, perhaps, you and I would listen with new ears to Hungarian music if we made sure to get the answer to one of Hungary's oldest questions:

What is feudalism?

It is very difficult for Americans to comprehend what feudalism really is. Nothing in school or college had prepared me to understand until I went to Spain—the Spain of Alfonso XIII, between 1929 and 1931. Yet Spanish feudalism was merely a faithful replica of long-entrenched feudalism in Hungary, Poland, East Prussia, and much of the Balkans. In all these lands, between the two wars, feudalism held on with a deathlike grip on the stifled

existence of a majority of the people. Under this feudalism a few
thousand wealthy aristocrats owned huge estates. They worked
only a portion of the land, and paid the peasants who cultivated
their land as little as absolute necessity required. For generations
the peasants in these feudal countries had barely kept body and
soul together, in a maximum of misery and a conveniently per-
petuated illiteracy.

After the last war the cry of the masses for land and more bread
became insistent on a new scale. But the postwar "democratic"
governments, on whom Woodrow Wilson had pinned such hopes,
either were quickly submerged by the old forces of privilege or
never obtained a firm foothold at all. The peace of 1919 actually
gave the Hungarian, Polish, and other conservatives a great opportunity to redistribute land and thus win millions of peasants
to the support of a solidly based democracy—a democracy with the
kind of a base which Americans had enjoyed for a long time. But
in most countries the feudal landlords had "one eye in their
pocketbooks." They refused to compromise and they fought
agrarian reform all down the line. Since they still held political
power, or soon won it back with the aid of industrialists, bankers,
and other aristocrats, the proposed land reforms were blocked or
watered down seriously in most countries. Most progress was
achieved in Czechoslovakia; some in Rumania, but in Hungary
and Poland only an ineffective minority of land was wrung from
the powerful landowners.

In Spain nothing could be done until the monarchy was overthrown in 1931. Then the Spanish Republic launched a modest
beginning at redistributing a few great estates—with moderation
to a surprising degree and with fair remuneration to the owners.
Even this gradual and restrained effort was more than Spanish
dukes and grandees, with their medieval mentality and pronounced lack of social conscience, would tolerate. The great
feudal landlords, the army, the monarchists, and the Church
united, as throughout a long past, and joined the counterrevolu-
tion—headed by Franco and backed by Hitler and Mussolini.
They won again. As far as landed privileges are concerned
Franco's Spain is still the Spain of Ferdinand and Isabella.

But facts are far more eloquent than words when considering

Europe's anachronistic feudalism. It is more enlightening to take specific cases. Between the two world wars, then,

What was feudalism in Hungary like?

For more than twenty-five years M. W. Fodor, now of the *Chicago Sun,* has been the most authoritative American correspondent in the Danubian-Balkan countries. Born in Hungary, he knows that country intimately; but his reputation as a conscientious reporter has been built through many years of experience. Fodor's *Plot and Counterplot in Central Europe,* published in 1937, still ranks as one of the ablest books on prewar conditions in this complicated, multinationed area. He describes a Hungary in which "the feudal noblemen constituted the supreme power for ages." Out of 60,000,000 acres of available land in Hungary, 19,000,000 acres were in the hands of about 2,500,000 small holders—peasants who owned less than fifty acres as a maximum. But there were nearly 19,000,000 more acres—that is *31 percent* of the total—owned by about 4,000 estates (all larger than 2,500 acres). These were in the hands of some 9,000 big owners, Mr. Fodor records.

When I was last in Budapest I obtained an official copy of a report on the largest estates in Hungary from one of the important foreign embassies, representing the Western World. Only the three hundred and fifty-four largest Hungarian estates are listed. From a list of the first twenty-five you can get an idea of the nature of feudalism in Hungary.

	Estate Owner	No. of acres
1.	Prince Paul Eszterházy	298,777
2.	Debrecen Municipality	129,736
3.	Roman Catholic Culture Fund	119,933
4.	Roman Catholic Archbishopric of Eger	113,773
5.	Prince George Festetich	105,274
6.	Szeged Municipality	97,659
7.	Roman Catholic Archbishopric of Kalocsa	88,403
8.	Count Maurice Eszterházy	78,645
9.	Marquis Pallavicini, Alfonz Charles	75,885

10. Roman Catholic Bishopric of Veszprem   73,274
11. Royal Hungarian Crown Estate   70,271
12. Roman Catholic Chapter at Veszprem   69,915
13. Royal Hungarian Stud Farms   67,695
14. Count Thomas Eszterházy   66,651
15. Municipality of Kecskemet   66,357
16. Royal Hungarian Forestry Department   66,525
17. Count Ladislas Karolyi   63,961
18. Archduke Frederick Frigyes   59,997
19. Prince Coburg of Saxony, Philip J.   57,447
20. Roman Catholic Archbishopric of Eger *   54,440
21. Roman Catholic Archbishopric of Esztergem   51,140
22. Imperial and Royal Family Estate   51,784
23. Benedictine Order at Pannonhalma   47,562
24. Trustees for the Count Gy. Karolyi Estate   46,908
25. Hungarian Catholic Culture Fund   45,035

  * Presumably a second parcel.

The smallest of these twenty-five estates totaled more than 45,000 acres. Sixteen of these largest Hungarian estates, up to 1945, were owned by Hungarian noble families and the unoccupied throne. The nine others were owned by Roman Catholic orders. The remainder of the three hundred and fifty top estates, on the official list in my possession, continue in roughly the same general divisions among aristocrats, the royal family, the princes, and the Church. In November 1945, just before the remarkable Hungarian elections, it was perhaps not surprising that Archbishop Joseph Mindszenthy issued a pastoral letter in regard to the elections. The pastoral letter included a warning against "the vindictive nature" of Hungary's new land reform legislation.[1]

But what did the feudalistic land monopoly in Hungary really mean? To conceive this we must remember certain indisputable facts. About three thousand estates totaled some 9,000,000 acres, and fully one third of tillable Hungarian soil was held in parcels ranging from 2,500 acres to nearly 300,000 acres. In American terms this would mean that approximately one third of the agricultural land in the United States was in the hands of only three or four thousand owners. Transplanted proportionately to our

1 *New York Times,* November 6, 1945; dispatch by John MacCormac.

country, it would mean that one out of every five Americans was ragged, undernourished, and illiterate—for lack of land to live upon. Such was Hungary's feudalism until 1945.

When the Red Army drove out the Germans in 1944 a genuine Hungarian land reform was bound to result. If the prewar Hungarian governments had acted to improve the livelihood of the majority of the people; if these supposedly "democratic" governments had given several million peasants the first democratic essential that had real meaning in their lives—land to call their own—this far-reaching sponsorship would not have fallen to the Soviet Union. Between the two wars, in Hungary, Poland, Spain, and elsewhere, the conservative ruling classes had a unique opportunity to buttress their future against revolutionary pressures, simply by inaugurating a long-overdue land reform. In their own long-term self-interest this would have been the smartest thing they could do. But conservatives usually seem congenitally blind and in direct proportion to the size of their properties. So the Russians became more than the liberators in Hungary. They became the champions of a chance for a decent living for the masses, an opportunity handed to them on a platter of medieval, feudalistic short-sightedness.

The new Hungarian land reforms, as everywhere else in eastern Europe, were immediate and thorough.[2] It was decided that all private estates above 1,000 acres (certainly not an excessively low dividing line) would be confiscated. Church properties, for centuries extremely large and valuable, were limited to one hundred acres. Under this reform about 3,000,000 landless peasants—or one out of five Hungarians—would be settled on small plots of soil, and would be allowed to work out the payments for the land over a considerable period of years. Unlike the Soviet system Hungary's land was *not* collectivized. On the contrary, this reform vastly increased the number of private property owners. Simultaneously Hungary's aristocrats and other wealthiest elements were shorn of their centuried basis of power. All this was part of a fundamental agrarian revolution throughout eastern Europe which, curiously enough, attracted very little attention in the United States. After outlasting its proper historical time-setting

2 For a factual survey of this whole question see the Foreign Policy Association's report, "Political Currents in Liberated Europe."

by many generations, European feudalism was being washed up and done away with, definitely and irrevocably. Undoubtedly future historians would cite this deep social change as one of the far-reaching gains resulting from the Second World War.

One of the immediate consequences of Hungary's land reform must not be overlooked. For the first time in Hungary's history several million peasants suddenly became a great political force. Although they obtained their title to land through the sponsorship of Soviet Russia, they became less open to Communist ideas than ever before. Once again private ownership reacted against the Communist ideology, as Moscow must have understood it was likely to do. It was soon apparent that distribution of Hungary's huge estates was producing no swing to the Left among the peasants.[3] On the contrary the modest new independent farmers flocked politically to join other small property owners. They greatly increased the ranks of the Small Land Holders party, and when they went to the polls the result amounted to a political revolution for Hungary.

What did Hungary's November 1945 elections mean?

Hungary's first postwar elections were remarkable both for the circumstances in which they were held and for their outcome. The Red Army, under direct command of Marshal Voroshilov, was still in complete military control of Hungary. Yet Correspondent John MacCormac of the *New York Times,* with his many years of Danubian background, reported that these were "the first wholly free national and municipal elections in Hungary's history." This was an astonishing fact to those who had most sharply criticized Soviet domination of the Polish, Rumanian, and Bulgarian regimes. At Hungarian polling places foreign observers found no trace whatever of Russian interference or pressure. Mr. MacCormac contrasted this with what he had seen at a series of Hungarian by-elections in 1932. At that time, he wrote, "electioneering candidates of the Small Holders party were run out of contested constituencies by the police. Those who wished to vote for the Small Landholders party—then rated

3 See *New York Herald Tribune,* August 23, 1945; dispatch by Seymour Frieden.

as a young and radical organization—were kept penned up to the last minute by Hungarian soldiery armed with machine guns, hand grenades, and rifles with fixed bayonets. But there were no soldiers in evidence yesterday."

The Small Landholders elected 58 percent of Hungary's first postwar deputies, out of more than 4,000,000 votes being cast. The combined Communist-Socialist opposition won only 25 percent of the parliamentary seats. The Communists, who had never been granted an opportunity to vote throughout the between-the-wars period, totaled only about 12 percent of the popular vote. Thus, in Hungary a conservative bourgeois party won a smashing majority—the only conservative victory as yet scored in any postwar European election—and on top of a radical and sweeping land reform which had been promoted by the Soviets and had benefited these very people! But these same Small Landholders had been suppressed as "young and radical" under the Horthy regime just before this war. This, unquestionably, is another measure of the profound shift in Europe's political thinking. What was radical and intolerable in Hungary in the thirties now represents sane middle ground. For those who fear Communism the "young and radical" Small Holders even represent a last bulwark against Sovietism. What the feudal landlords and aristocrats fought bitterly only yesterday they are compelled to regard as their last hope of salvation today. Decidedly, this is a new Europe. Indisputably, the meaning of Hungary's 1945 "first free" elections is clear.

Let us next consider

The fate of feudalism in Poland.

In Poland in 1921 there were 3,262,000 farms. Of these, 65 percent consisted of less than twelve acres, and twelve acres were regarded as the *minimum* necessary to support a family. Thus 65 percent of all Poland's farms were not large enough to provide a decent or adequate living for their owners. In addition some 4,000,000 Polish peasants possessed no land whatever. This was because 43 percent of the total farm area—*area* as distinguished from farms—was held by only 19,000 owners.[4] As Raymond Leslie

[4] See Raymond Leslie Buell's authoritative *Poland: Key To Europe*, Chapter VII.

Buell remarked: "Such a system of land tenure—which prevailed in Russia before Soviet collectivization, and in England more than a hundred and fifty years ago—makes efficient farming impossible." But it also made life for the majority of Polish citizens intolerable and almost impossible.[5]

The young Polish Republic set forth bravely to break up the nation's great feudal estates. But the initial thoroughgoing reform proposals were considerably diluted by 1925. In 1926 the Pilsudski dictatorship placed the Polish reactionaries back into the saddle and from that time on agrarian reform was steadily sabotaged. Even so, some improvement was registered between 1919 and 1937. About 2,500,000 hectares of land were divided into small farms. In one way and another approximately 1,500,000 peasants received some relief. But in 1937, and until the outbreak of war, much important land remained in the possession of the feudal landlords, the state, and the Church. Between six and nine million peasants, as Mr. Buell and others have reported, still could not earn a living from agriculture. It is well to remember that 9,000,000 peasants represent more than one out of every six prewar Poles.

What the Polish democratic republic, betrayed and suppressed by Pilsudski and his feudalistic colonels, failed to accomplish in land reform was therefore adjourned until 1945. Under Wicenty

[5] Mrs. Sharon Boatman of Louisville, Kentucky, has given me the following graphic picture of feudal Poland: "My parents came to this country in 1905. I was brought up an American and never bothered much about my background. In 1930 I visited Poland with my father, one of whose brothers lived in Warsaw. He was much interested in the New Poland. My father was an educated, 'high-born' gentleman. Two of his friends were large land-owners—and I mean large; regular feudal estates comprising hundreds of thousands of acres. . . . I am telling you all this to show how it looked through my eyes. Life on these estates was very enjoyable, and we were guests for some time. Such jolly fun: horseback riding, tennis on private courts, swimming, kayaks on the Vistula, servants at our beck and call.

"And the Polish aristocrats? The most charming people in the world! Afternoon tea and chocolate in lovely gardens; interesting discussions on Chopin, Mickiewicz, Reymont, Matejko, Copernicus, etc. One day I said to my father: 'My American girl friends should see me now; this is the life!' My father answered, a little sadly: 'The same brutal class system. I thought all that would be changed—that the New Poland was really democratic.' Being a real thinker, he was now disillusioned—although he came of these privileged people. When I told my father how kind and lovely all these people were, he answered that the individuals were all right—the system was wrong. I was only nineteen then, but I observed all I could. The poor peasants; and their humility which always embarrassed me, an American. Servility in others isn't a pretty sight. Ever since I have thought about these things."

Witos the Peasant Party, far from Communist, had been the out-standing champion of such reform. Since they lost out with the suppression of the republic, it was left for Polish Communists—supported by Moscow—to become the postwar leaders for the eradication of Polish feudalism. In July 1944 the Polish Commit-tee of National Liberation began to confiscate and parcel out all estates larger than 124 acres. This land went to peasants who possessed less than the "existence standard" of 12½ acres. It was estimated that this would liberate economically nearly 2,000,000 peasant families. In Poland—as in all other feudal countries, in-cluding Spain—*economic* liberation is regarded by the peasant masses as the indivisible Siamese twin of political liberation. This is so basically natural and basically imperative that any demo-cratic American must understand it at once.

Maurice Hindus summed this up accurately when he reported to the *New York Herald Tribune:* "Public opinion in America and England must recognize that this reform means more than the redistribution of the large estates. It augurs the end of the landed gentry. It spells death to feudalism, at least in its coarsest forms. The hat-doffing, hand-kissing peasant is bowing his way off the stage of Polish history, even as the French and Czechoslo-vakian peasants bowed their way from the respective stages of their feudal history."

But the chances of future peace for Americans and Britishers were also being directly affected by this same agrarian reform in another part of eastern Europe. The traditional spawning ground of aggressive Prussianism was being liquidated—again, and in-comprehensibly, with almost no attention in our daily press. For a tremendous historical change was consolidated in the final half of 1945 by the—

Liquidation of Junker feudalism in East Prussia, in
prewar German Silesia and Pomerania,
and in Saxony.

The huge Junker estates in East Prussia had been for centuries the stronghold of the Prussian marauders and war-makers. The Teutonic Knights, of forgotten infamy, laid the foundations sav-agely but thoroughly. From the twelfth through the fifteenth centuries they ravaged and plundered their way eastward, as barbaric and murderous in their day as the Nazis have been in ours.[6] It required the Napoleonic wars to liberate the southeastern Baltic triangle from the horrors of the Teutonic Knights, whose secret Order was at last dissolved in 1809. But the Junkers merely replaced the Knights in East Prussia, much of Pomerania, and Silesia. The Junkers had grabbed the land in great hunks, making the local peasants their slaves, and soon they became the new backbone of Prussian militarism.

After 1919 the hesitant and timid Weimar Republic never waxed bold enough to undertake a serious division of the vast Junker estates. Hindenburg, after all, was a great war hero as well as a Junker. The German republic finally even rewarded him with an ancient East Prussian castle and wide areas of land, all tax-free. The Junkers carried on, virtually unmolested, and eventually became ardent supporters of Hitler, of the Nazis—and of another Prussian attempt at world conquest. They had changed in no fundamentals. They had learned nothing new. They were still the spiritual—one should say, the antispiritual—descendants of the Teutonic Knights.

But the Red Army fought its long way back from Stalingrad and at last inflicted a supervengeance for the Battle of Tannenberg, so disgracefully lost by the Czar's armies in 1914. Königsberg, for centuries the heart of East Prussia and the citadel of Junkerdom, was conquered by the Russians. They swept on finally, through Danzig to Stettin and the mouth of the Oder. They are still there, and concerning what has gone on back in vanished East Prussia we have had limited information. But as to the practical results now achieved under Russians and Poles, there cannot be a shadow of a doubt.

All of East Prussia has become Russian and Polish territory. All the estates of the powerful Junker class have been divided up among the peasants, or collectivized in Soviet areas. The arrogant and medieval-minded Junkers have been utterly dispossessed. Let those mourn who can point to any humanitarian or truly social function fulfilled by the Junker barons through their generations of domination. The long-despised and exploited peasants at last

[6] See Paul Winkler: *The Thousand-Year Conspiracy*, Chapter II.

have land on which to live. The economic foundations of the
Junker class have been swept away. In these harsh facts, given the
inhuman and antisocial actions of the Junkers and the Teutonic
Knights throughout centuries, there is certainly a pronounced
justice; but also a most significant *insurance* for all people who
have reason to desire that German militarism shall not have another opportunity to wage aggressive war in this century. With
the Junkers' liquidation—and the disappearance of Germany's
stronghold of feudalism—one of the chief pillars of Prussianistic
aggression has been destroyed. The dissolution of the ancient
feudal estates in East Prussia means that this corner of the Baltic
shores will never be the same again. All of us in the United
Nations can breathe easier for that.

Under Soviet military occupation similar land distribution
has proceeded in the prewar German provinces of Pomerania and
Silesia, and inside present occupied Germany in Saxony and
parts of Brandenburg provinces. Mecklenburg, north of Berlin,
should likewise be included. Take Saxony, with its normal population of 3,000,000, as an example. The Soviet-sponsored German
Provincial government issued orders in September 1945 that
special committees would be elected before mid-December. They
would then make inventories of estates to be redistributed, and
of farmers in need of land. Here, too, any family with less than
12½ acres of land would be eligible. Payments were fixed on the
rate of one year's production for each 2½ acres. Livestock would
be divided proportionately. Machinery would be put in a community pool. This was not collectivization, as in the U.S.S.R.,
but conformed to the general pattern in all eastern European
countries.

In Saxony all land owned by the National Socialist Party or
by active Nazis was first confiscated. After that, Junker estates
of more than 250 acres were divided up, along with some 200,000
acres of Junker-owned forest land. At the end of 1945 it was reported that 7,000 estates, totaling approximately 4,000,000 acres,
had been partitioned. Some 270,000 landless or land-poor peasants and refugees received parcels of this land.[7] In this fashion
the ground was literally cut out from under Germany's long-

7 See *New York Times*, dispatch by Gladwin Hill, December 30, 1945.

powerful Junkers. They were liquidated economically. Throughout East Prussia and Germany the Junkers had been reported to own about 25 percent of all German farm land—perhaps amounting to 37,000,000 acres. Of this huge acreage it was estimated that the Junkers had not used much more than one third for productive purposes. It now seemed probable that almost all of the former Junker lands would be put to work.

On a varying scale feudalism was also being abolished in neighboring countries. This was the direct outcome of—

Land reforms in Czechoslovakia, Rumania, Bulgaria and Yugoslavia.

In regard to these last two countries adequate documentation has not been available to provide precise details. Great feudal estates did not exist in such large proportion in Bulgaria and Yugoslavia, but they were sufficient to inspire reforms similar to those elsewhere. The prewar Czechoslovakian republic, this being the only vigorously democratic country in all of eastern Europe and the Balkans, had already made very considerable agrarian reforms. The Czechs, by instinct, were so modern as to believe that economics and democracy are interrelated—and we must remember that the great Thomas Masaryk built his little country's democracy, after 1919, on frankly copied American lines.

Consequently, the Czechs after this war did not have a large feudal remnant of which to dispose. Even so, there still remained some big estates, and also farms owned by Germans and Hungarian collaborationists. These latter were confiscated and distributed to needy peasants. But instead of anything remotely resembling collectivization, the Prague government adopted a program to promote farmers' co-operatives—a strikingly democratic movement in any country. These now include a membership of more than 2,000,000 in Czechoslovakia.[8]

In Rumania there was considerably less to be done than in Hungary or Poland or East Prussia, but considerably more than

[8] See *Time*, October 22, 1945.

in progressive and enlightened Czechoslovakia. Of course, a program of nationalization of important industries and other socialistic measures accompanied land reform in all eastern European and Balkan countries. In Rumania the Groza government also first confiscated the property of war criminals and German subjects. These lands included those previously held for generations by a sizable German minority. I visited the centers of these German-descended Swabians and Saxons in 1940. Although they had lived in Rumania for many generations they were still so overwhelmingly *Deutsch* in their allegiance that their sons were openly drilling in Hitler Youth formations. We watched them click their heels and give the Nazi salute. That these people, so predominantly disloyal to Rumania, should now be dispossessed must be regarded, then, as elemental justice. Their farms were transferred to landless Rumanian peasants, and all large estates of whatever ownership have been reduced to a maximum size of 125 acres. But even in Rumania, close to the Soviet Union, private ownership and broader distribution of land have been preserved. Instead of establishing collective farms in the Communist tradition, the Rumanians will pool their tractors and farm machinery—in co-operative organizations—so that peasant landowners can lease modern machinery to boost their production.

By making a survey of all countries east and southeast of the Stettin-Berlin-Vienna line, we see much more clearly one of the outstanding revolutionary results of the Second World War. In all this long-troubled region, stretching from the Baltic down to the Black Sea, the outdated feudal foundations have been thoroughly liquidated. Many millions of peasants, whose forebears labored for generations as slaves or at barely subsistence and land-starved levels, have finally obtained a fair amount of land to cultivate and to call their own. This great historical change has not followed Communist precepts, even though it has been carried out uniquely through powerful Soviet inspiration and support. But strangely enough, there have been no Communist revolutions. If the overwhelming electoral triumph of the Hungarian Small Landholders is any criterion, then these millions of newly landed peasants regard themselves as anything but Communists. They have accepted the agrarian reforms as the beginning of economic democracy—even though achievement of a completely free political democracy in much of eastern Europe appears considerably more remote or problematical.

There remains the highly important question—

Will the redistribution of land fulfill the hopes of the peasants? Will it work out in practice?

It is by no means certain that the agrarian reforms can begin to meet the needs of so many millions of peasants. First of all, this sweeping and revolutionary experiment had to be launched under the most unfavorable conditions imaginable; in countries whose economy was completely chaotic; with serious shortages of livestock, seed, and agricultural implements and machinery; and under weak and inexperienced governments in sharply divided societies. These are very grave handicaps indeed.

There are other difficulties also. In some of these countries, such as Poland, it is believed there is not enough available land to provide each peasant with the minimum acreage which he requires for his family. If peasants must strive to exist on eight-acre parcels when no less than twelve acres is required for an acceptable subsistence level, disillusionment may be one of the first crops harvested. In addition the Russians have removed great quantities of industrial machinery from Poland, Hungary, and other countries. Whether they also removed agricultural machinery, or to what degree, is not known. To have done this would have placed a great burden upon the new independent farmers. And there is an important related fact. With their industries crippled where can the surplus farm labor go? The surplus of peasants in Poland, Rumania, and elsewhere is probably large today and will become increasingly so. Until industries can be rebuilt and restored, eastern Europe will be the prey of accentuated economic crises, which can create discontent and disorder. Thus millions of new peasant landowners must strike out on their own under the most appalling and unfavorable circumstances—and their deceptions may prove to be correspondingly great.

Some observers ask whether the Russians expect this experiment in operation of small-landed farms to work out successfully;

or whether they anticipate that most of the peasant owners will fail in the end? If the latter proves to be the case, they say the only remaining alternative would be widespread collectivization of the land. This, of course, is what happened in the Soviet Union. First the peasants received the land in their own names; then collectivization was adopted. The same evolution may prove virtually inevitable in Poland and some other countries, especially if they remain in the grip of severe economic crises for several years. At any rate, that possible outcome cannot be overlooked. Yet despite the enormous disadvantages under which the new peasant landowners must labor, it at least remains true that this is the one opportunity for which they have hungered all their lives. For them to be freed at last from near-slavery under oppressive feudal landlords certainly spells hope for the peasants, whatever their new trials and problems may prove to be.

Whatever may happen millions of European peasants must feel that the liquidation of feudalism liberates them from chains which have held their families hopeless for centuries. If it should bring them to collectivization later on, most of them probably would prefer it to the past from which they have just escaped. Under feudalism they had no hope for a decent livelihood. Now it is an established economic and historical fact that that system is finished. Throughout all of eastern Europe the clean-up of feudalism is virtually complete. As a result there remains but one last stronghold of medieval feudalism on the European continent, save for a few remnant islands in parts of Italy, Austria, or western Germany.

What is feudalism like in Spain?

Of course, it is the story of Hungary and Poland all over again. In Spain (before the 1931 republic) the ruling class, in every sense, was that of the great landowners. As I came to know this Spain and these landed aristocrats from recurrent personal contacts, I saw what I later saw in Hungary and eastern Europe. As an average there were no more charming people anywhere than the Spanish nobility; and no people in contemporary Europe more feudally blind or more socially callous. It was quite typical of most of our fashion-plate American diplomats to become conscious solely of their charm. After all, a Spanish duke and duchess do not play host to everyone. And why should an American ambassador or *chargé d'affaires* concern himself with dry statistics about the ownership of land in Alfonso's Spain? Or in Franco's Spain? Nevertheless the amazingly swift and successful Spanish revolution—achieved without bloodshed—sprang directly from those feudal statistics which have so long been ignored in the United States, as well as by most of our diplomatic corps in Madrid.

Before the republic—as is still true under the Franco-Falangist counterrevolutionary regime, and will be true under any conceivably restored monarchy—about 50,000 large landowners held a monopoly on more than half of Spain's land, including all of its richest portions. Some estimates numbered the big land-monopolists at not many more than 20,000. Thus the Spanish aristocrats, constituting one five-hundredth or less of the total population of some 24,000,000 people, owned about 51 per cent of the land; and wealthy farmers another 35 percent. About 1,000,000 small farmers, with parcels of some 12 acres, held another 11 percent of the land. This left 1,250,000 peasants, with barely one acre apiece, and representing 2.2 percent. And it left more than 2,000,000 Spanish laborers, landless and at the mercy of whatever the grandees and other propertied landlords chose to pay them for working from one third to two thirds of the year. Unemployment among these farm laborers sometimes rose to 60 percent. Without consideration of industrial conditions this, in Spain, would be the equivalent of some 6,000,000 unemployed in the United States—save that these 6,000,000 (for Spain) had to exist in unceasing hunger in the most primitive and unsanitary kind of abodes. Meanwhile large sections of many huge estates, owned by the indifferent nobility, went uncultivated. Spain was indeed a romantic and glamorous and charming country—*if* you knew the "right people," and took no pains to investigate the others who really *are* the Spanish people.

This is Spanish feudalism, with the aristocracy and the Church in the same dominant roles as in Hungary—until now. The facts about this feudalism are readily available, and corroborated by many authorities. Because the Spanish republic, for all its small beginnings toward agrarian reform, carried the long-term threat of fundamental action, the feudal-privileged of Spain rallied around Franco, the Fascist, and became willing allies of Hitler and Mussolini. Whatever Bourbon camouflage they may still choose, to save their big lands while pulling wool over policy-makers' eyes in London and Washington, the reactionaries of Spain remain Fascists at heart. They want no democracy; least of all, an American type of democracy. Their chief enemy is the twentieth century—and they still contrive to exist in an archaic prolongation of Spain's own eighteenth century.

How much longer will the New Europe tolerate the Old Spain, feudal and unrepentant? Not for so many more years, I should suspect. But so long as this feudalistic Spain—with or without the Fascist *Falangistas* in actual control, and with or without an un-wanted Spanish king—so long as this Spanish feudalism governs and dominates Madrid's government, the future peace of the United States will be undermined and menaced by Spain's strongly antidemocratic influence throughout Latin America.

In Spain, as everywhere else, the feudal reactionaries present themselves as a "bulwark against Bolshevism." This too was the foremost excuse of the Hungarian feudal landlords; and in Hungary a strong, new class of small landowners (whom the conservatives could have created years ago) has now revealed itself as the only effective barrier to Communism. But in all these lands the feudal aristocrats—through their refusal to compromise intelligently while yet there was time—have certainly driven a noteworthy percentage of the oppressed masses into the arms of the Communists.

What the Hungarian noblemen never saw and never learned is what the Spanish grandees and their chief partners in feudalism still do not see and still have not learned. It is really quite simple, and there lies in it plenty of food for reflection for all of us who want democracy to survive and expand:

There can be no safe bulwark against Communism in any country, unless it is based upon an improved standard of living for the majority of the common people. You do not need to fight or promote counterrevolutions to prevent Communism. All that any far-sighted and perceptive government needs to do is to clean house; to provide a fair standard of living, some chance and more hope, for the majority of its citizens. This is what every new national administration in the United States pledges itself to do, and strives to do. That alone is recognition that *more economic democracy* is what the American people want. In this, at a much more advanced industrial stage of development, we Americans are merely motivated by the same primary aspirations which motivate people today in every part of the world.

But before leaving the area of this newly defeudalized eastern Europe I think there is one coincidental development which should be noted particularly. It concerns

The long-term repercussions of the Red Army's occupation of eastern European countries.

I am not thinking about what almost everyone was thinking about *before* the Soviet armies' liberation of Poland, Czechoslovakia, Hungary, and the Balkans. Before the event many in Western lands were fearful that the very demonstration of Soviet military success might serve to communize a large proportion of the population in these countries. But somehow most of us were so preoccupied in estimating the possible effects of Russian presence in the liberated Eastern lands that we completely overlooked the equally important consequences upon the victorious Soviet soldiers themselves. With the passage of time we have had numerous indications that perhaps we neglected a highly pertinent side of the matter. The whetstone may be dented, but it also does something to the knife.

Beginning in the early autumn of 1945 reports from numerous sources stated that Soviet soldiers had got out of hand in many parts of their occupied areas. From Warsaw, Correspondent Irving Brant of *PM* reported that the Poles were none too happy under Red Army occupation, or the constant passage of large formations of homeward-bound Soviet troops. From Czechoslovakia, Hungary, and elsewhere came similar testimony. Brant was informed by one Pole that "the Red soldiers have been uncivilized to a degree. There have been robberies and rape and people have been shot by marauders. But compared with life under the Germans, this is a paradise." He was also informed (at Kraków in October 1945) that there had been considerable disorder in the Russian Army two or three months previously; that the greatest trouble occurred when wounded Soviet soldiers in convalescent hospitals were ordered home. "The Bolshies liked the better living conditions in Poland," this person said.

Reports from Czechoslovakia and Hungary were much the same. Czechs told of Soviet soldiers taking money and watches from civilians. They added that the Russian command made strong efforts to correct this situation and that their troops had since been better disciplined. But one Czech citizen went so far as to tell Richard Hottelet of CBS that "in his opinion the Red Army was the most powerful instrument of anti-Soviet propaganda."

Before we, as Americans, begin to feel self-righteous certain observations are in order. There has probably never been an army of occupation, of any nationality, which proved to be an instrument of favorable propaganda for its own country. Soldiers of every nationality—including those of the U.S.A—always indulge in a certain amount of looting, robbery, and rape. Certainly those observers who have traveled around France, since liberation and especially since V-E Day, know that the misbehavior of American troops often put a serious strain upon Franco-American friendship; that robbery and physical violence by our soldiers with French civilians as their victims were one of the U.S. Army's constant problems; that some men in our uniform had to be court-martialed and executed in Britain and in Continental countries; and that criminal offenses increased after hostilities because nerve-taut troops, bored with nothing much to do while waiting to get home, became much more difficult to keep within bounds. In France a few months after liberation I heard from French men and women many incidents about American soldiers' misbehavior which filled me with shame as an American. Every war correspondent saw and heard enough of this sort of thing. But while our armies were fighting magnificently, how could you sit down and inform their home folks about the blacker side of the record of an unruly minority? Because we wanted to be fair to the majority of American soldiers, we actually painted the composite GI as considerably more of a noble knight than Composite Joe ever was. Discuss this subject with the long-suffering citizens of Rheims, Le Havre, and some other French cities today and you might almost conclude that the United States forces in France had been a rather potent "instrument of anti-American propaganda."

The inescapable and only fair conclusion is that soldiers are soldiers, and that every war brings its quota of robbery, rape, and other crimes in *every nation's army*.

It was perfectly natural, then, and probably inevitable, that General Eisenhower found it necessary to officially recognize (on November 10, 1945) that "a relatively small minority can give us [the U.S. Army and the American people] a bad reputation that will take our country a long time to overcome. It is an unfortunate fact that any group is judged not only on the good behavior of the majority, but on the misbehavior of the few. It is a universal tendency to remember the bad and forget the good." We may be sure that General Eisenhower would not have circulated an appeal of this kind to all his unit commanders if there had not been some pretty serious abuses of conduct among American troops and such as to provoke severe steps to correct matters. This great American commander once more showed his wisdom and understanding when he said to his men: "Each day we are building up an impression upon Allied peoples, and this impression is largely founded upon the character of our personnel and official contacts with them."

When some thoughtless Americans became jubilant at the news that Red Army troops had been making themselves unpopular in eastern Europe, they were ignoring or ignorant of the fact that some of our own soldiers had been doing the same thing in much the same way. But if educational opportunity and general background over many years mean anything, we must admit there was considerably less excuse (although still some degree of extenuating circumstance) for American soldiers' misconduct abroad than for that of Soviet soldiers. The fact remained that the American GI did not come from a land where watches, fountain pens, jewelry, and many similar things had been unobtainable for years. Nor did he face the prospect of returning home to wait a good many years before he could hope for the chance to buy a wrist watch or other little luxuries of that kind. And to the Americans the shops of Rheims or Nancy were by no means a discovery of amazing luxury—really the opening-up of a new world of plenty. On the contrary, such capitals as Warsaw, Prague, Bucharest, Sofia, Budapest, Vienna—and even the remnants of Berlin— inevitably came as a disconcerting and attractive revelation to former peasants and workers from many parts of central Siberia and Mongolia. Their government had had to concentrate upon building vast industrial projects, tractors, and weapons instead of watches, cameras, and silk stockings. Although the common level of existence had been raised, these Red Army men were still sons of privation to whom the ordinary European luxuries were unknown. And to keep them hard at their long task of building a new Russia almost from the ground up, their government had told them little about living conditions in Hungary or Germany and had permitted only a very few of its citizens to travel abroad.

So, as we now can see plainly, the Red Army of the Soviet Union could be sent into the Balkans and central Europe only at a definite risk which might almost be called a counterrevolutionary risk. Perhaps that is not quite accurate. It could also be called a risk which could result in postwar demands for swifter and greater revolutionary progress inside the U.S.S.R. For the effect of the occupied countries upon the Red Army men was certainly as powerful psychologically as anything they could do in Rumania, Czechoslovakia, or elsewhere. Whether in Bucharest, Budapest, or Prague the Soviet soldier saw shop windows such as he had never seen before. Suddenly he became conscious that the gap between the Soviet Union's unquestionable achievements and its standard of living and the general economic conditions and the standard of living in these neighboring countries still remained quite wide—or very wide—in certain respects. This realization could not fail to be perhaps the most revolutionary thing that had happened to the average Soviet soldier since he was born, or at any rate since the October Revolution. Several millions of Red Army men must return home in the mood to demand many goods and near-necessities and a good many luxuries, of whose lack they had scarcely been conscious before they became troops of occupation.

For these reasons it would seem quite certain that the Soviet occupation of eastern Europe will have a considerable repercussion upon economic thinking and upon government policies inside the U.S.S.R. in the coming years. Edgar Ansel Mowrer went so far as to say [9] that he was willing to bet "that within five years the visit of millions of young Soviet citizens to lands of more abundant life will make itself felt within the Soviet Union." Human nature and politics being what they are, I do not see how this can fail to happen. The governors of a one-party system and a dictatorship are also acutely conscious of mass demands and popular desires. The realists in the Kremlin are no exception. One of their great postwar problems is certain to be the problem of increased production of consumers' goods, so that the Soviet masses and the mighty Red Army may be increasingly satisfied with their lot and their prospects for tomorrow.

Nor must we hereafter forget that something utterly new in the history of the Soviet system has happened. Perhaps five or six million young Soviet citizens have received the beginning of a European education during the period of their occupation service. This was a first exposure to another kind of political economy and to a different concept of national life. Because several million Soviet citizens were so exposed, a new ferment of social thinking must result inside the Union in due time. If we cannot now accurately divine just what the final consequences may be, we can be confident that they will not be entirely negligible and that some of them will be reflected in high Moscow actions and policies.

On the 28th anniversary of the Soviet Revolution, Foreign Commissar Molotov frankly recognized this fact. "Of course," he said, "the acquaintance with the life and customs of other nations will be of benefit to our people and will widen their outlook." And Molotov laid especial emphasis upon early postwar betterment of living conditions for the Soviet people. "Now *at once*," he told citizens from the Polish frontier to Kamchatka, "we must think about solving the fundamental problems of an advancing national economy, so that *within a few* years we may *considerably surpass* the prewar standard of the country's economic development—and *secure a considerable improvement in the living standards of the entire population*." (Italics mine.)

Those who distrust the Soviet desire for peace, and disregard the Soviet necessity for a prolonged peace, should weigh these words well. For the one sure way, in any land and under any form

[9] *New York Post*, November 10, 1945.

of government, to avoid the possibility of internal social disorders is to make certain that the people obtain more of the good things of life which they hunger for—and have a just right to expect. If any people in the Second World War fully earned the just right to this expectation, it is the Soviet people—and they justly expect that their hopes will be fulfilled—not for the next generation, but well within the compass of their own lifetime. Even so, the Soviet Union cannot begin to fulfill this great and just popular expectation with anything less than a long peace.

In this sense, oddly enough, the liquidation of feudalism in eastern Europe—even by making little capitalists out of formerly landless peasants—has greatly increased the social and security insurance of Soviet Russia all along its western frontiers. In the defeudalized eastern European countries a moderate and much more equitable and fairly balanced democracy may yet emerge. But such a "little man's" democracy as seems emerging in postwar Hungary could never be expected to gang up against the Soviet Union. If the lessons of the Red Army's occupation in this part of the world are well learned, they indicate that a freely democratic Danubian valley could be both friendly and an asset to Moscow. But for some time the answer to this possibility will not become final.

Chapter VIII

THE RATTLING OF ASIA'S CHAINS

*Men are freest when they are most uncon-
scious of freedom. The shout is a rattling
of chains.*

David Herbert Lawrence

George Jones and you and I are now very much involved in the future of Japan and China; and what is happening in these key Asiatic countries is directly linked with the powerful new nationalism which is flaming higher in every land and island from Korea to Karachi, India. When we reach Asia from Europe, Wendell Willkie's "one world" takes on a new meaning.

In Europe today the struggle of the masses for greater economic independence is in an advanced stage. In colonial Asia the peoples' struggle for national recognition and for liberation from exploitation is in its first stages. Yet the revolutionary undercurrents of West and East are very much the same. There are common threads of outraged justice, of self-respect and wakened pride, and of insistence upon the fundamental rights of man. If we recognize this community of aspirations, we shall understand how truly and fatefully twentieth-century mankind is on the march. Surely, by now, we have received ample warnings from every side.

Japan's vast empire of conquest crumbled overnight. But there were no wild scenes of liberation in Saigon, Singapore, Batavia, and Rangoon. The hated Jap was merely being replaced by something equally detested, because endured so much longer. In Saigon British and French lend-lease guns blasted back the pitiful, tatterdemalion Annamite forces. The Annamites were fighting hopelessly for freedom from a French rule which had often been oppressive and had held them under bayonets for many years. Revolts broke out in the Malay States, but the British had returned well prepared. Indian troops swiftly put the Malayans back in their place once more. From Burma came no news at all; there the British had returned in great force. But on the island of Java the Dutch had nothing for persuasion but their 350-year-old record. Its backfire was heard around the world.

In 1941–42 I had seen and felt the rumbling rise of Asiatic nationalisms, first in Malaya and Indo-China; later on in China, Burma, and India. Some observers assured me it was different in the Dutch East Indies. They said the Dutch had been more clever and they drew no color line for marriages there. Moreover, they insisted, the Indonesians were a docile island people; much too easy-going ever to resort to force in a serious manner. Yet now, in the autumn of 1945, the whole of Java was aflame with popular uprisings. A free Indonesian Republic had been declared. What had happened to the "easy-going," nonbelligerent Javanese people? Why was it that people who had formed no resistance movement to oppose the Japanese now forged an impressive national resistance to keep out the Dutch and the British?

Gradually the dispatches made the truth apparent. Batavia's buildings blazoned great democratic quotations from Washington, Lincoln, and Franklin Roosevelt. Street-car slogans proclaimed: "Better live in hell than be colonists again." These remote island people also had heard of the Atlantic Charter. For them radio was indeed a revolutionary weapon. Dr. Soekarno, president of the Indonesian republic, and his ardent followers had not been living in a vacuum—even under the brutal Japanese. Nor was it accidental that Dr. Soekarno had been thrice arrested by the Dutch and finally exiled. While the British were holding their forces back, trying to avoid bloodshed, Soekarno said to Homer Bigart, of the *New York Herald Tribune:* "We accepted limited independence under the Japanese because that was the best we could get. Now we demand full independence and the right of self-determination, as promised by the United Nations. . . . It is ridiculous for a nation of seven million Dutchmen to attempt to control the government of seventy million Indonesians. . . . This is not a racial movement against the whites, nor do we have anything against the Dutch as a people. We are only fighting the Dutch colonial system." [1]

But the Dutch government, like the British in India, had

[1] *New York Herald Tribune*, October 2, 1945.

offered too little, too late. Amsterdam's suggestion of dominion status for the Dutch East Indies failed to make it plain that "self-government" would be real, or that a local parliament would have full powers. Lieutenant General Sir Alexander Christison, British commander of forces landed at Batavia, told the Dutch representative: "You must meet with these chaps and give them a clear-cut statement of future status." Instead, the Netherlands home government hedged and dodged, hoping Dutch troops could arrive in time to suppress the Nationalists' forces. But the more fiery Indonesians would not wait. Soon British warships and RAF planes were shelling and bombing Surabaya, a crowded city of 500,000 population. Washington and London had had a full six weeks in which to prevent this and succeeding tragedies throughout Java.

The democracies "liberated" Surabaya with shells, bombs, and bloodshed. Yet for the previous two weeks, at least, Indonesian leaders had been appealing for—

American mediation and an Allied mission
of inquiry.

On October 25, 1945, the "Free Indonesian Republic" announced it would negotiate with the Dutch, provided the United States would arbitrate. Dr. Soekarno addressed a direct appeal to Washington by radio. Later he said: "We have appealed to the American government for mediation, but we have had no reply. . . . We feel we are entitled to a world hearing. . . . We would welcome a visit by an impartial mission of inquiry."

Seventy million Indonesians were asking the world's most powerful nation—the supposed champion of democracy—for a hearing, nothing more. Yet for months, while poorly armed patriots and helpless civilians died, Washington did not lift a finger. Indonesians had painted Lincoln's "government of the people, by the people, for the people" on their cities' walls. But the land which prides itself on those great humanitarian words betrayed no interest in their meaning for a much less fortunate people. Washington was silent. Where was this "world co-operation for peace" which President Truman and many other Americans talked so eloquently about? Where was "American leadership"?

. . . In the mocking silence Indonesian spokesmen turned their appeals, significantly, to Moscow. Whatever happened, they would remember what had *not* happened.

In India some 400,000,000 foreign-ruled peoples watched, and drew their own conclusions. They too have been kept in colonial restraint for too many centuries. They too are stirred by a profound hunger for self-government and independence. They also sense that their hour of freedom must strike within a few years at the most. Reflecting the Indian peoples' bitterness the *Hindustan Times,* published by Gandhi's son, flared out against the United States for its "utter moral cowardice" in regard to Indonesia. The Indian people, it stated, were sharply disappointed in their hope "that American democracy would use its vast resources and influence in upholding the cause of freedom and democracy in Asia." Then came a pointed statement of the supreme fact that we Americans continue to disregard at our own peril. "The people of Asia," said the *Hindustan Times,* "will increasingly turn away, not only from Europe, but also from America."

You do not need to ask a colonial Asiatic where else it is that he may choose to turn.

Like the peoples of continental Europe, the peoples of Asia have a clear choice between the Anglo-American type of democracy and Soviet Russia's conception of democracy. If most of them would probably prefer our kind today, they will not necessarily prefer it tomorrow. For they are impatient from centuries of exploitation and colonial bondage. Inevitably, in their insistent demands for a better life now, they will take friendship and support where they find most of it. Let India or China become a reasonably functioning democracy, and democracy's power and prestige throughout the world will be increased enormously. Let either India or China become a new *Soviet* Republic—then the future balance of the Western democracies will be lost for the next century or for several centuries. Either the United States and Britain will lead in the emancipation of Asia's peoples, or Soviet Russia will become their guiding star. If the second alternative becomes a reality, the English-speaking nations will become an isolated "white minority" in an utterly new sense of the phrase.

For several thousand years Asia has been the past. Now the world revolution makes it plain—to all who will weigh the facts and think about them—that Asia is on the road toward becoming the *future*. All the vast Asiatic peoples need is a measure of freedom, education and modern industrial techniques. Does the achievement of these things obviously require a century or more? Not necessarily, I should think. After all, were not the Soviet peoples hopelessly backward and ignorant less than thirty years ago? The Indians and the Chinese are no less intelligent than they —and they have the stirring example of the Soviet peoples (some 20 percent Asiatic) to spur them on.

Perhaps, then, we should re-examine some of the fundamental facts of the new East. Perhaps we should reacquaint ourselves with—

The dimensions of awakening Asia.

In the great band which sweeps from western India and the Dutch East Indies up to Korea and Japan there live more than half of humanity: some 1,150,000,000 people, to be exact. This vast area, inhabited by many shades of brown and yellow races, is more than three times as large as the United States. Together with the Soviet Union it constitutes one third of the earth's surface. But the 9,750,000 square miles included in the Asiatic band is of minor importance compared with the gigantic natural resources and riches which it contains. The combined wealth of raw materials, from India to Korea, is enormous and largely undeveloped. When these Asiatic lands have modern transportation systems and modern industries the relative living standards of the world will be revolutionized. This will not be in our time, but it may be much nearer than we think. For the important thing is that the Western colonial powers at last have roused a sleeping giant; and the Second World War—with the Japanese—taught them that they need not wait much longer.

Only a blind man could travel through the Orient today and fail to see that the white man's colonialism is doomed; that the era of Western imperialism is drawing to its close. The disparities between ruler and ruled have been too shockingly apparent to the colonial peoples. The division of the riches obtained from their own native lands has been much too one-sided for too many generations. The voice of Indonesia is by no means a lone voice. It is, in reality, the voice of some 600,000,000 forcibly "colonized" peoples—and the voice of revolutionary China is the same in its essence.

It is true, of course, that the western colonizers have brought certain important benefits to the oriental lands. To exploit native raw materials they had to build railroads and highways; comfortable homes and office buildings for themselves to live in; ports and docks; enough hospitals and schools to provide for the white colonists, and a much smaller proportion for the natives. Eventually the British, Dutch, and French brought automobiles and telephones and radios, of which the native aristocrats and small merchant class soon got their share. Motion pictures and cheap consumer goods came within the partial reach of that section of the masses which had fairly regular employment, but only in the larger cities and towns. On the eve of Japan's conquest Calcutta, Singapore, Batavia, and Saigon wore a deceptive front of modern progress—and so did Hongkong, Shanghai, and Manila. Yet in all these thriving port cities of the East the majority of the native inhabitants still existed in terribly unsanitary dwellings, and in such squalor and poverty as the average occidental visitor—if he paid any attention and looked behind the façade erected by the colonizers—had never dreamed could exist.

Asia's great port cities were the western businessman's oriental show-windows, but beyond their central macadamized highways and glittering lights the "lure of the Orient" dropped swiftly into the semi-cesspool existence which millions of natives still had to endure. Servants, of course, were dirt cheap and a $100-a-month bank clerk could often live as luxuriously as a $10,000-a-year executive at home. In places like Calcutta, Singapore, and Shanghai, Americans and Britishers rarely learned to take much interest in the living conditions of the "natives" whose lands paid them such high royalties, both social and monetary. It was easy to say you were bringing numerous modern advantages to the East. It was much less usual to note where these advantages went, and what a tiny native minority ever got more than a sniff of them. But the profits—to the colonizers and the traders—bore up wonderfully well. The East had always been like this—the lucky few;

and the ignorant, dirty, disease-ridden millions. Why shouldn't it always remain the same?

In the months just before Pearl Harbor I saw all this. In reality, I saw much more because I left the "pearls of the Orient" behind; traveled inland across Malaya, Siam, and Indo-China; up the Burma Road into those towns and villages of China's interior which very few white travelers had ever visited before the war. There the window-dressing of Rangoon or Hong Kong vanished utterly. The smells of the Orient lost all trace of Coty or Guerlain. Rats and vermin were often nightly visitors, even in the best available hostelry. You saw such poverty as the worst American slums could not rival. Yet years before this, Western prospectors had bought up the mines in these regions. Here, not far from Kunming, thousands of children had worked themselves to death in narrow tunnels which were too small even for adult Chinese to labor in. There were many other mines; of silver and lead in northern Burma; gold and silver, tin, copper, and tungsten in India; tin in Malaya and Indo-China; coal and iron mines in many different countries.

When the Japanese tide rolled southwestward it engulfed the riches of the Indies; the world's greatest supply of natural rubber; the fabulous oil fields of Sumatra, Java, and Borneo; 86 percent of the world's pepper; 72 percent of its kapok; 19 percent of its tea, and many other products. In Burma, where I was then, for a few months the Allies retained their only source of oil east of the Persian Gulf. Burma's oil was perhaps the purest natural oil in the world, and its reserves were sufficient to guarantee fine dividends for many years to come. Up and down the Mandalay road we drove past rice fields which produced large export totals yearly. Farther north we saw great teakwood forests which were square miles of green gold, waiting only for the ax and saw of the alchemist.

Thus the wealth of the East, paradoxically, was almost as apparent to an impromptu vagabond as its filth and mass poverty were revoltingly abundant. For more than three hundred years the Portuguese, Danes, Dutch, British, and French had concentrated on the appropriation and removal of these mineral and agricultural riches. Vast fortunes had been made and taken away. Great companies had been organized, and the superficial face of

Asia had been changed in many places as generations of ships carried their products westward. Yet there were still many mines that had not been opened. There were still hidden riches that had been unknown but a few years ago. There was still great untapped wealth in most of these lands and climes. But the strange thing was that you would seldom have guessed this *if* you judged by what the natives had, what they wore, or how they lived. The contradiction was so glaring that even some Westerners had to see it and think about it. When you did that you could see quite clearly—

Why the old imperialism cannot survive in Asia.

It is probably anybody's guess exactly how much profit British firms have reaped from Burma in nearly one hundred years of colonial domination. Certainly the figure runs into many scores, if not hundreds of millions, of dollars. This very sizable wealth came from Burma's natural resources, aided by Western techniques and development. It was quite natural that the people with the "know-how" should claim a fair profit for their initiative —and of course, the Americans have also taken a very fair profit from the Philippines. But when you ride up and down Burma by jeep for many weeks, as I did, some of the scenery begins to look painfully disproportioned. There was precious little that was modern or "improved" in important Burmese cities like Prome and Mandalay. They were shabby and ugly places where most of the population lived in corrugated-iron-roofed huts. Burma's 15,000,000 people were reported to have some 7,000 schools of various sorts—and one university in Rangoon. But I cannot remember seeing many buildings, outside the capital, that looked like schools; and the number of fairly adequate hospitals proved to be decidedly scarce as the British and Indian wounded began to become numerous. Even the number of trained Burmese nurses was pitifully small. The ordinary Burmese people were obviously in need of far more clinical and dietary attention than they had ever received.

You could observe these things just as clearly in French Indo-China, Malaya, and the Dutch East Indies. Since I had a longer opportunity to observe them in Burma I mention it here merely as one example of a common phenomenon. Supposing 25 percent of all the colonizers' profits in Burma had been devoted to public health, education, and other social improvements for the past fifty years. What difference would that have made? Well, for one thing, the only native nurses in northern Burma and the only hospital in a wide region above Lashio would not have been established through the self-sacrificing devotion of an American missionary, Dr. Gordon S. Seagrave. Nor would there have been any need for Indian laborers, imported by the British, to sleep nightly on the sidewalks and in the doorways of Rangoon office buildings.

But this is the East, many people remarked resignedly. The fact remained that the people who had "opened up" the East had usually been content to provide a minimum—or less—of improvement in the living conditions of the people whose lands they exploited. The great majority of improvements which you find in colonial Asia, even today, were made primarily for the benefit of the white colonizers. Railroads and roads were naturally constructed where they spelled profits for the white rulers. Decent buildings were constructed chiefly for white men, where white men needed them. Sanitation began for the protection of occidentals and was pushed much less strenuously in native quarters and the villages. Because the British, French, and Dutch made only the slightest effort to educate the mass of their brown or yellow subjects, these subjects' preparedness for self-government was conveniently delayed, generation after generation. White governors retained many of the powers and privileges of an emperor. The governors' "advisory councils" were usually hand-picked by the governors themselves. Thus there were few or no elected native-born members on them; and a gubernatorial veto power controlled most important phases of administration.

In this fashion the colonial empires, while continuing to pay their masters handsomely, really blundered along through a fatal series of neglected and lost opportunities. By their blind policies the Western governments and parliaments sowed the seeds for amazingly strong nationalistic movements in their respective Asiatic colonies. Then the Japanese came along with their alluring propaganda about an "All-Asia Co-Prosperity Sphere." That was the final match which lit the fuse to the Orient's vast powder magazine. It didn't matter very much that the Japs' fine phrases were merely a disguise for their own rapacious kind of imperialism. What mattered greatly was the greatly accelerated hunger of Annamites, Malayans, Indonesians, Burmese and Indians for a new deal and independence. They had learned at last that outsiders, white or yellow, were bound to dominate them unless they rose up and demanded the right to govern themselves.

To say that the Western imperialists promoted Asia's colonial crisis far more than the Japanese did is by no means an exaggeration. I think the best way to judge the accuracy of this is to consider—

Certain key facts behind the failure of the old colonial systems in Asia.

First, take the notorious illiteracy in the Eastern colonies. After more than three hundred years of British rule, 86 percent of India's 400,000,000 people are still illiterate. After nearly three hundred and fifty years of Dutch rule, 92 percent of 70,000,000 Indonesians are illiterate. In British Malaya illiteracy is as high or higher than in India; in Burma it is certainly almost as high. Although I do not have the statistics for French Indo-China, they unquestionably run in similar vein. In this entire great region the Philippines alone are a progressive exception; and even there illiteracy totals 49 percent.

In India there were only 47,398,000 persons in 1941 who could read and write—or 14 percent of those above five years of age. Only 9,230,000 of these were women. Yet the number of all literate Indians had almost doubled over the previous twenty years. In these respects British India was a shade better than the feudal Indian states. Yet a total of about 15,000 graduates from nineteen universities in all India was pitifully small in proportion to the total population; and completely dwarfed by the yearly number of graduates from Soviet universities and colleges where a majority of students came from illiterate families.

Educational appropriations are another testing rod of Western colonial rule and policies. British India has a population of 295,000,000, yet the budget of its central government is approximately $400,000,000. This expenditure may be contrasted with prewar annual expenditures of some $4,000,000,000 in Great Britain for the benefit of its 45,000,000 people. Even in wartime Britain was spending more than half as much (approximately $265,000,000 per year) on education as the total of British India's governmental expenditures—on behalf of nearly seven times as many people. British India's expenditures on education, in fact, have been placed at approximately four cents per year, per capita; on public health between five and fifteen cents per capita.[2]

In the Dutch East Indies, Brigadier Carlos P. Romulo reminds us,[3] the Dutch a generation ago spent $250,000,000 in campaigns to subjugate northern Sumatra, yet in the same thirty-year period their educational budget for all of Sumatra amounted to less than one tenth of that amount. In the same article he points out the singular indifference toward education in Britain's Federated Malay States. "In 1940," General Romulo reports on the basis of his personal investigation, "government revenues in those abundant lands were at an all-time high, so high that a present of 10,000,000 Straits dollars was sent off to the home government in London, and still revenues were left with a comfortable 20,500,000 Straits dollars surplus. Yet that same year less than 2,000,000 Straits dollars were spent on education. Actually it came to about 1¾ percent of the total revenue. Exactly fifty-eight pupils were learning agriculture in high school in 1938. That same year in the Philippines there were 4,600 students in agricultural schools, and another 9,000 in trade schools." To equal the Philippine record proportionately, the Malay States would have had to be training about 575 agricultural students.

I have mentioned the approximately 7,000 schools of all categories in Burma. But when you consider that the populations of Burma and the Philippines are almost identical in size, the educational lag in British Burma becomes more striking. General Romulo points out that the United States, almost immediately after taking over the Philippines, dispatched one thousand school-teachers there to open schools and start training native teachers. "In the ensuing forty-two years those Filipino teachers have grown to a force of 40,000 in some 11,000 schools; the American teaching force has dwindled to eighty; there are 5,000 public

2 See T. A. Raman: *Report on India*, p. 77.
3 "Asia Must Be Free," *Collier's*, October 29, 1945.

libraries and more than 4,000,000 books. For the three years preceding the war educational appropriations varied between 33 and 37 percent of the national budget." It is only fair to the British in Burma to add that the Filipinos already had a fairly broad foundation in a European language, Spanish, before the Americans came in. Even so, the Burmese people, quite as naturally intelligent as the Filipinos, have never been exposed to anything like 11,000 schools—although British rule existed there since the 1850's.

Burma is also a predominantly agricultural country with 85 percent of its people living on the land. When the Japanese thrust the British out of Burma it still had only one advanced school teaching scientific farming; one or two missionary farm schools of note; and the northern hill tribes were living just about as primitively as when the colonizers first arrived. General Romulo, who was a newspaper editor in those days, learned that a Burmese political party had a plank in its platform labeled: "Two acres of land and a cow for every person." He reports that the leaders of this party were jailed.

The French had been in Indo-China in a dominant way since 1862. Indo-China's present population tops that of the Philippines by about 8,000,000—i.e., a total of roughly 25,000,000 people. When the Japanese took over, the French, after seventy-nine years, had provided fewer than 5,000 schools for the natives. In 1924 only 225,000 children were attending native and missionary schools combined in Indo-China. The discrepancy—and lack of opportunity—was still startlingly great in 1941. Yet French trade and fortunes made in Indo-China in these years remained impressively large.

In most of the Asiatic colonies a certain improvement in public health was achieved, primarily because white residents had to be protected against a multitude of tropical diseases. Sanitary and other reforms brought some relief to a minor proportion of the natives. But when the great majority of natives were left in a state of complete illiteracy important progress in health conditions remained impossible. Only a small percentage of the riches taken from the land ever went into local governmental expenditures. Natural resources were exploited chiefly for the benefit of the imperial colonizers and their distant stockholders. Inevitably this system of exploitation gradually created nationalism among the people. Inevitably the old colonial systems failed because they paid white men too well, and the natives of each land far too little.

On the credit side certain benefits brought by the Western imperialists must be recognized. The British, French, and Dutch alike have built networks of communications; have laid the foundations for improved public health; have made Asia conscious of the benefits of industrialization, and have made Asia's masses aware of modern techniques and, especially, of the possibility of much higher standards of living. In such ways, however accidentally, the oriental peoples were goaded into new dreams and indirectly prepared for political action. To India the British actually brought a political unity such as that caste-ridden continent of Hindus and Moslems had never known. British courts brought a new conception of justice. British administration, despite lapses of undue police severity and the like, maintained a relative peace and order from which many Indians benefited.

Even so, the lion's share of advantages always fell to the British Raj. Between 1914 and 1941 British capital investments in India doubled, from an approximate $2,000,000,000 to some $4,000,-000,000. Meanwhile the Simon Commission placed the average Indian's income, at a most optimistic estimate, as scarcely $32 a year; and Indian economists stated that an accurate figure would be nearer $24 per year. The average Indian's annual income therefore was only half as much as the lowest average incomes in Balkan countries. As British firms boosted their capital and expanded their earnings the enormous gap between the lot of ruler and ruled in India became embarrassingly apparent. One British commentator felt compelled, in fairness, to remark: "After all, a debtor can hardly feel that his interests are entirely safe when exclusively in his creditor's hands. Yet this is India's position so long as her financial and exchange policy is in British hands." Of course this could be said with equal pertinency of the Dutch and the French.

In his remarkably objective and informative book, *Strangers in India,* Penderel Moon has his fair-minded British colonial observer say:

Princes and landlords support us, but all the youth of India, all the progressive ardent elements in the country, find no inspiration in England. They look for light to Russia. And we, with obstinate folly, try to prevent them. In Russia an experiment is being conducted which is patently of the highest relevance to India. They are attempting there simultaneously a rapid industrialization . . . and a new form of cooperative farming. . . . What they are doing has an obvious bearing on our Indian problems, and ought to be of greatest interest to us.

This statement was made in 1934, but it applies with much greater force to India today—and to China as well. More and more, as the Western democracies fumble and blunder, one and a quarter billion of Asiatics "look for light to Russia." And the longer we fumble and blunder, postponing the substance of freedom and a fixed program for independence for all these Eastern peoples, the stronger the present small Communist parties will grow—in India and Burma, in Indonesia and Indo-China and everywhere else.

But India at least is fortunate in having the powerful All-India Congress party, led by patriots of outstanding ability and inspired throughout its large membership by strongly democratic principles. By keeping Jawaharlal Nehru and hundreds of other Congress leaders in jail throughout most of the war the British have merely increased the tenacity of their movement, and made certain that their drive for complete independence will be pursued with greater intensity—and probably with less compromise. But we in the West must understand clearly that the All-India Congress is not at all "just an Indian political rumpus." On the contrary, Pandit Nehru, Maulana Azad, and all their lieutenants regard India's struggle for independence as merely a part and spearhead of independence for all Asiatic peoples. It was significant that, only a few weeks after Japan's surrender, the working committee of the All-India Congress demanded that India, Burma, Malaya, Indo-China, and the Indonesian islands should be freed from "imperialist domination." Its resolution stated plainly that this was essential to avoid "sowing the seeds of a future war." As for Britain's Asiatic holdings, it said: "No concessions should be given to the new vested interests created by British authorities in favor of foreign capital that curtail the rights of the [Indian] people." A few weeks later Nehru boldly declared it was India's duty to "revolt"; a nation was a dead nation if it was not prepared for a revolution to free itself. This, I believe, was the strongest language that self-disciplined Nehru —so long an obedient follower of Gandhi's passive-resistance policies—had ever used. If Nehru's attitude had stiffened as much as his Bombay speech indicated, it could have very great meaning for future developments in India; and by repercussion, in other countries.

But the development of strong nationalist feeling among important sections of 2,000,000 British-recruited, British-trained Indian troops had also assumed very great significance by the spring of 1946. It developed that "the national idea" had penetrated the Indian Army to such an extent as to wring a public recognition of the fact from Prime Minister Attlee and to create serious concern in the Viceroy's palace in New Delhi. London dispatched a three-man mission of unprecedented powers and scope for concessions to negotiate in India. On March 15th Mr. Attlee informed the House of Commons that Britain's emissaries "are going to India with the intention of using their utmost endeavor to help her attain that freedom as speedily and fully as possible. What form of government is to replace the present regime is for India to decide. . . . India herself must choose what will be her future constitution; what will be her position in the world. . . . If she elects for independence, in our view she has the right to do so. It will be for us to help to make the transition smoother and as easy as possible."

At long last—and nothing shorter—the British Raj, through a Labor government, had recognized and bowed to the irresistible tide of Asia's new times. This was the most promising and revolutionary development that had occurred in the vast colonial East in two centuries. At least this was an utterly new attitude by the world's greatest colonial power. If India won complete self-government or outright independence, the folly-ridden deadlock of British, French and Dutch imperialism in Asia would be blasted wide open. This possibility had become real for the first time. India might well become the example as well as the older brother of the Eastern colonial peoples. Through long over-due

statesmanship a British government had released a great hope.
Yet the obstacles to the final dawn of India's promised new day
would remain extremely difficult to overcome.

This has to be a sharply condensed survey and by no means
a complete or sufficiently balanced picture. I am trying merely
to give some of the essentials to any understanding of what is
now happening east of Suez. But by now, despite the limitations
of space (not to mention your reporter's), it must be abundantly
plain that we must think of Asia as *one*—one kind of past, one
burning sentiment within it, one goal, and one problem. The
Eastern colonial peoples are linked together by the same chains
that have bound them for so many centuries. Today it is not just
one or two sections of chain that are rattling. All of Asia's chains
are rattling together. If all white people do not hear them and
understand what their clamoring means—including seemingly
little-concerned Americans—then we shall all be compelled to
pay for our deafness and stupidity, in due time. Whether we see
it or not, the world's peoples are becoming too united—too conscious of the power in their hands and the justice within their
reach—to be dominated and exploited for many more years by
a white minority.

Perhaps, before it is too late, we—who believe in democracy—
should ask: What can be done to help the Asiatic colonial peoples
toward independence? At San Francisco a very modest beginning was charted. Now that we have some fundamentals of the
problem, let's look at it.

What does the United Nations' proposed system of colonial trusteeships offer?

There are some fine phrases at the start. United Nations members, administering territories "inhabited by peoples not yet
able to stand by themselves," accept the general principle "that
it is a sacred trust of civilization to promote to the utmost the
well-being of the inhabitants of these territories." They agree:
(1) to insure the economic and social advancement of the peoples
concerned; (2) to develop self-government "in forms appropriate
to the varying circumstances of each territory"; (3) to further
international peace and security. UN should establish under its

authority "an international system of trusteeship for administration and supervision of such territories *as may be placed thereunder by subsequent individual agreements. . . ."* (Italics mine.)

Basic objectives of the trusteeship system included: "To promote the political, economic, social and educational advancement of the trust territories and their inhabitants, *and their
progressive development toward self-government or independence,* as may be appropriate to the particular circumstances . . .";
"To encourage respect for human rights and fundamental freedoms for all *without distinction as to* race, language, religion
or sex . . ."; "To insure equal treatment in social, economic
and commercial matters for all members of UN. . . ." (Italics
mine.)

The most important provisions are contained in Section B.
Article 3 reads: "The trusteeship system *should apply only to
such territories* in the following categories *as may be placed
thereunder* by means of trusteeship arrangements:

(a) Territories now held under mandate; (b) Territories which
may be detached from enemy states; (c) Territories *voluntarily*
placed under the system by states responsible for their administration. *"It would be a matter for subsequent agreement as to
which territories would be brought under a trusteeship system,
and upon what terms."*

Article 5 adds: "Until such agreements have been concluded,
*nothing in this charter should be construed in or of itself to alter
in any manner the rights whatsoever of any states or any peoples
or the terms of existing international instruments to which member states may respectively be parties."* (Italics all mine.)

It will be seen from the above portions in italics that the loopholes and escape clauses in this supposedly progressive new
system are much broader than the proverbial barn door. The
word "self-determination" does not appear. The Australian,
New Zealand, Soviet, and Philippine delegations fought at San
Francisco to get much stronger pledges from the colonial powers;
but with very little success. The United States delegation showed
more interest in control of strategic bases than in guarantees of
independence to colonial peoples. General Romulo declared bitterly: "The word independence was not lost at Valley Forge. It

was not lost in Bataan. Why should it be lost here?" Only at the last moment did the champions of the underdogs manage to get the phrase "or independence" inserted in the trusteeship chapter.

But the loopholes, dictated by the big powers' blindness and self-interest, diminished the UN trusteeship proposal to a lamentably half-hearted and inadequate thing. With the whole of Asia on fire for independence, the new family of nations would rush to the scene with a hand-pump and a pocketful of sedatives. The trusteeship charter did not obligate any colonial power to place any territory whatever under trustee administration. Britain could rush to give Burma a new "semi-dominion" status, and France to place Indo-China in a new "French Federal Union"—which is exactly what London and Paris promptly announced plans for doing. The slower-moving Dutch did not have to hurry about Indonesia because there was no compulsion to place the Indies under the trusteeship anyway. A British Information Service hand-out frankly indicated there wouldn't be many territories under British rule that London would consider handing over to the noble-sounding UN system of supervision. "There is abundant evidence," the release reported solemnly, and without mentioning any evidence, "to show that the peoples of Tanganyika, Togoland and Cameroons [Britain's three "B" mandates] would bitterly resent being now arbitrarily handed over to the trusteeship of some other nations, just as the peoples of the British Colonial territories would resent being withdrawn from the Empire and handed over to international rule."

You could read that and wonder what British propagandist had typed it without biting his tongue or roaring with laughter. For all these years India had been repeatedly paralyzed with passive resistance and nonco-operation campaigns—could it be because her people so resented the idea of "being withdrawn" from the British Empire? There were no Burmese resistance forces fighting the Japs to help the British come back; only the hill tribes, but not the Burmese who are in overwhelming majority. When *New York Times* Correspondent Tillman Durdin got into Burma he found an Anti-Fascist League whose chiefs demanded independence for Burma. They had named a National Government, but nothing more was heard of it after the British reoccupied Rangoon. One could also remember how Burma's last governor, Sir Reginald Dorman-Smith, had said in 1943: "Neither our word nor our intentions are trusted in that part of the globe. . . . We have fed such countries as Burma on political formulae until they are sick at the sight and sound of a formula, which has come—as far as my experience shows—to be looked upon as a very British means of avoiding a definite course of action."

But on May 31, 1945, the Churchill government presented Parliament with a bill to give Burma "restoration of the wide measure of self-government which Burma enjoyed before the Japanese invasion, and then [in Secretary Amery's words] to the attainment of that full and complete self-government within the British Commonwealth, commonly described as Dominion status." Whether this was another "formula" would be judged first by the Burmese. But it most certainly was a move to keep rich and underschooled Burma out from under a UN trusteeship. But even Socialist Sir Stafford Cripps assured Parliament that he saw no reason why self-government in Burma should not come within "three or four years at most." He counseled his Burmese friends to have patience. "We do not want to see in Burma, or in any other country, rapid seizing of power by any particular group of people in order to improvise some form of government."

So the trusteeships, after San Francisco's pattern, will apparently be limited to such smaller and remote portions of the earth as do not seriously affect either the strategic power or the pocketbooks of the big colonial powers. If there is not general rebellion throughout Asia—and how can that happen with vast quantities of American lend-lease weapons in the hands of our ruling Allies?—then no very radical or swift changes will be made. In this fashion, wasting these next years of immediate and never-again opportunity, we may all combine to build up and touch off a tremendous Asiatic revolution—which would also mean THE Atomic War, and the white race decimated beyond recognition. Unless teeth of real meaning are put into the United Nations' Trusteeship Charter, this is the logical trend which must result. For if there is anything certain in this world, it is the fact that awakened, nationalistic Asia will not wait with cap in hand for many more years.

What is the fatal weakness of the United Nations trusteeship system as it now stands?

I think we have enough hard facts to note several very serious weaknesses. First, the trusteeship system does not apply—and cannot be made to apply under present provisions—to some 600,000,000 colonial Asiatic peoples who most need its help and protection. Second, it is not truly international in its scope or in its proposed framework as now known. It does not "pool" the colonial experience of the imperial nations and insure that no one government will dominate the administration of any territory. Third, it does not provide regular inspections by an international board of UN colonial experts, nor assure specific UN controls over policies to be enforced in any given region. Fourth, its escape clauses are so broad as to provoke cynicism and resentment among peoples who are promised preparation toward self-government. A sweetened biscuit is not exactly a sedative to long-exploited peoples profoundly stirred by national resentment and revolutionary aspirations.

I think we can best appreciate the dangerous shortcomings and failures of the San Francisco project for trusteeship by contrasting its feeble evasions with what Franklin Roosevelt had in mind. What he hoped would be done represented what enlightened students of colonial conditions believed was both fair and practical. On May 8, 1945, Marquis Childs [4] reported in his syndicated column a conversation he had with President Roosevelt in the spring of 1944. "The President began," wrote Marquis Childs, "by talking about the position of the white man in the Pacific. The white man, he pointed out, had come more and more into disfavor. The quick successes of the Japs had shaken white prestige that was already badly damaged."

"We are going to have to take some positive steps," the President said, "or find ourselves pushed out completely. Some time ago I worked out a form of trusteeship for French Indo-China.

[4] See *New York Post* of that date.

You know, that colony was governed very badly. For every dollar the French put in, they took out ten dollars. Those little people had a culture of their own, but they were badly treated. Now my idea is for a trusteeship to administer Indo-China. I put this up to Chiang Kai-shek and he was strong for it. The idea is to have one Chinese trustee, one French trustee, a British trustee, and perhaps an American trustee."

Mr. Childs says President Roosevelt thought in terms of a fixed period of years—something else which is utterly lacking in the UN charter—in which Indo-China would work toward political and economic independence. The joint trustees' job would be to guide and promote this process. At Teheran Roosevelt said he asked Marshal Stalin what he thought of the plan, and Stalin thought it "excellent." Prime Minister Churchill, interestingly enough, "would have none of it even after the late President reminded him that on this issue there were three votes against one. Churchill was thinking of Burma. He refused to consider such a plan for Burma."

Just before the San Francisco conference began its laborious negotiations President Roosevelt died. What became of his truly international project for trusteeship, in the White House or the State Department, we have never heard. Supposedly, the President's "worked-out" plan for Indo-China, for instance, must have been on paper somewhere, and had surely received the attention and help in formulation of certain advisers. But the United States delegation at San Francisco came forward with no such proposals, nor anything remotely resembling them. The guiding mind and the central purpose had vanished; and America lost one more unique opportunity for humanitarian world leadership. In Marquis Childs's accurate words, Franklin D. Roosevelt "alone possessed the moral force to challenge the rulers on so vital an issue." Yet there is also an ironic side to the way in which the President sought support for his trusteeship plan for Indo-China. The French, of course, were most directly concerned. Their agreement, in some degree, was a first essential. But Roosevelt had somehow tragically permitted himself to be alienated from General de Gaulle and the French Resistance. Thus one of his most statesmanlike projects had become crippled, its chances seriously reduced in advance, by a grave misjudgment of American diplomacy in which Roosevelt himself had played a most important part.

Even so, the idea of a group of international trustees, representing the nations most immediately concerned, as administrators of colonial or native areas has been placed in circulation. San Francisco did admit that "what terms" a territory should be placed under trusteeship must be worked out later. That was far from heroic, and not at all obligatory. Common sense would dictate that the Dutch East Indies or Burma or Malaya would benefit far more from a several-powered joint trusteeship than Indo-China. It is not in human nature to expect the people with the most cold cash and prestige involved to promote, alone and without any prodding, those reforms which are most urgent or most essential to the welfare of subject people. London has sent back to Burma as governor a man who had lost the confidence of the vast majority of British residents, let alone the Burmese, in the period when Burma fell. Does that look like a bright and progressive new deal for Burma? And can we expect the French to act much differently in Indo-China? Or the Dutch?

Admittedly neither the Burmese, Indo-Chinese, nor the Indonesians are capable of complete self-rule in this year of lack of grace. None of the white imperialists ever made a decent, sustained effort to educate these people or prepare them for self-government. As Dr. Soekarno said: "It is the Dutch colonial system we are fighting." The "system"—under any of the dominant imperialists' flags—received precious little tampering with at San Francisco. So the British—with Indian troops—were fighting for the Dutch in the streets of Surabaya, to keep the Indonesians *from what?* No, the Javanese patriots did not expect independence before Christmas. While Surabaya was a battleground, Correspondent A. T. Steele, reporting to the *New York Herald Tribune*, wrote: "Every Indonesian leader I have talked with had underlined his willingness to submit to United Nations trusteeship for a fixed term—but not Dutch trusteeship."

So here were colonial peoples crying for the one thing that the imperialist governments—and the United Nations—had *not* possessed sufficient courage or sufficient vision to give them. By the veto of London, Paris, Amsterdam—and, in effect, of Washington too—joint trusteeships would not be for the 200,000,000 people in the Rangoon-Batavia-Saigon triangle. Real trusteeships would only be for the rag-tag-and-bobtails, which really wouldn't cost the big powers much of anything. *The very peoples whose demands for independence threaten world peace were told to wait.* That might not be very important—except that it happens to threaten the future peace and security of every American, Englishman, and Dutchman, and many others.

The people whom we have asked to wait in colonial Asia are the people who do not have to wait—not for so much as another twenty or thirty years. They do not have to wait very much longer because they know that the most powerful currents in the whole world are with them. They know that India's freedom is inevitable; that the longer it is delayed the more complete her independence will be. They know that China may have to fight a long civil war, but that *China can* fight—and that the Chinese people cannot be exploited, internally or externally, forever. They know that China's industrialization will gradually work to Asia's benefit; that a swiftly industrializing and self-governing India will interest herself in the liberation of 200,000,-000 Malayan people. In short, they know that this atomic world cannot risk a great upheaval in Asia—but that, should the great powers take Doomsday as their choice, it will not be the vast Asiatic peoples who will be most destroyed, or will lose most. As has always been true, the rattle of Asia's chains comes from those who have nothing else of importance to lose.

In April 1943 President Roosevelt said: "We know that the day of the exploitation of the resources and the people of one country for the benefit of any group in another country is definitely over."

But the delegates at San Francisco gave few signs of knowing this. The governments of the colonial empires obviously still do not know it. It is only the *people* who know which day is definitely over. In Asia these people are nearly six times more numerous than the combined populations of the British Commonwealth, France, the Netherlands, and the United States.

Chapter IX

WHICH WAY CHINA AND JAPAN?

I'll be glad when people will live and let live,
instead of some trying to keep others in misery
and slavery. The world can't go on like that.
                                An American Negro woman

As American troops were pouring into the ports of Honshu an Allied correspondent talked with a Japanese fisherman. What did he think about his country's surrender? The fisherman replied: "He who owns nothing has nothing to fear."

This fatalistic Japanese might well have been speaking for a large majority of his people. But a Chinese coolie or peasant, in similar circumstances, would have the same reasons for making an equivalent response. Feudalism is older and more deeply entrenched in China and Japan even than in Spain, or in Hungary until now. In one respect, however, Japan's ruling classes proved unique. They alone grafted a great and highly modern industrial plant upon a feudalistic foundation which they kept completely undisturbed. This same thing *could* happen in China during the next fifty years. It merely depends upon what kind of government China has; upon what persons do the industrializing—and how they do it.

When the Japanese signed our surrender terms in Tokyo bay the United States assumed the role of supreme power in the Pacific. This brings America into more immediate contact with Japan, China and Soviet Russia than ever before. Whatever happens in China and Japan from now on must concern Americans personally, and must also tend either to improve or to complicate our relations with the Soviet Union. We shall establish co-operation in the far Pacific, or we shall drift there toward another great war. China and Japan have suddenly become twin keys to our chances for peace. In the Pacific, American policies can be largely decisive in shaping the future course of the Chinese and Japanese. But is the average American now prepared to judge the soundness of Washington's decisions? Or of our chief Eastern representatives' actions? How much does George Jones know about the basic conditions in these countries? Suppose we join the Joneses and begin by considering—

The common base of feudalism in Japan and China.

After a close look at European feudalism the basic pattern in the Orient is quite familiar, but it is more extreme in the poverty and ignorance which it imposes—and it affects far greater populations. At Potsdam the Big Three pledged themselves to eliminate "all bars to establishment of a free, democratic regime in Japan." That was a revolutionary declaration, because the Japanese cannot hope to achieve democracy unless the Allies promote revolutionary reforms in Japan. And there has never been a country which has enjoyed truly democratic government under a predominantly feudalistic economy.

On November 12, 1945, General Douglas MacArthur got down to rock bottom about our program for Japan. He said: "Japanese farmers and their families are about to be liberated from a condition approximating slavery." If the Allies go all the way through on this pledge—*provided* that we do—one of the chief barriers to democracy in Japan will be removed. To understand why this is so certain facts must be clearly in mind. They can be listed graphically:

5,000,000 pre-war landowners in Japan.

3,500,000 of these owned less than two acres.

Only one-tenth of 1 percent owned more than 100 acres.

Nearly 4,000,000 farmers—probably, with their families, more than one-fifth of Japan's population—were share-croppers.

Only 15.6 percent of Japanese land was under cultivation.[1]

Over 3,500 Japanese landlords held more than 125 acres each.[2]

Emperor Hirohito and the imperial household owned 3,314,242 acres of land, mostly in forests.

The big landlords kept nearly one-third of Japan's share-croppers at near starvation levels, taking 60 or 70 percent of the crop which each tenant farmer raised.

[1] See Professor Hugh Borton: *Japan Since 1931.*
[2] See Andrew Roth: *Dilemma in Japan.*

In the 1920's and 1930's these conditions provoked a continuing agrarian crisis. The small landowners could barely keep their families alive on less than two acres of land. The millions of share-croppers existed in virtual slavery. More than 5,000,000 families (which are very large in Japan) were tight in the coils of this feudalistic system; but when they tried to organize they were beaten down. War gave Japan's rulers their one chance to employ greater repression at home. With the Manchurian and the China invasions, everything could be excused as necessary sacrifice for Japan's future glory.

The mass poverty of the peasants was equaled by the most extreme exploitation of industrial workers in any modern nation. This was what made aggressive war the "only out" for Japan's aristocrats, industrial monopolists, and militarists. The peasants and the workers were notoriously underpaid. So Japan's cheap manufactured goods had to be dumped on foreign markets since few people at home could afford them. Japanese bicycles, watches, and hundreds of other products sold abroad at such low prices that American and European products could not possibly compete. Because the Japanese system did not create a home market (by putting a tolerable amount of cash in the pockets of its own people), Japan had to dump 30 or 40 percent of her products abroad. But to keep that up Japan had to conquer all of Asia, from Korea to the Dutch East Indies. Then she would have a vast market tightly to herself—and enormous raw materials in the conquered lands, at her own prices. War was the only solution. It came—straight out of the feudalistic roots of the Japanese system.

General MacArthur's November 12 directive was a first blow aimed at these roots. It was realistic because about 40 percent of Japan's 80,000,000 people depend upon agriculture to live. The seething rural discontent, as in Hungary and Poland, could be cured in no other way. But it was unfortunate that some Americans in Tokyo—officers or correspondents—presented the announced *intention* for an established fact. An Associated Press dispatch said General MacArthur's headquarters "reported that diplomacy and directives had shattered the nation's war-minded spiritual and economic control systems as completely as Allied bombs destroyed its cities and factories." One wondered why the

American public should be fed such palpable nonsense. Neither the Japanese secret societies, the Japanese Gestapo, the tremendous *Zaibatsu* monopolies, nor Japan's millennial feudal roots could be dissolved merely by waving a commander's orders about "what must be done." In two years, or in five, perhaps we can begin to know how much has been accomplished that some enthusiast in MacArthur's headquarters glibly announced as a fact in November 1945.

But General MacArthur's directing order was none the less a most encouraging step. It proposed to expropriate and redistribute nearly 7,000,000 acres from the large landowners; and another 2,000,000 acres to be reclaimed, possibly including large slices from the imperial forests and such. It served notice that a very important percentage of the Japanese people would be freed economically—and economic freedom is the only ground upon which backward, exploited peoples can move toward education and self-government. It looked as if perhaps the Americans in Japan might be so realistic, on this land question, as to steal what had been some of the Soviets' most effective thunder in eastern Europe. This was only a beginning—on only one of the five or six main Japanese pillars for war-making. But for all that, it promised a straightforward, practical attack upon a key pillar of Nippon's system.

With this in mind—

What about feudalism in China?

Like the Mexican revolution China's revolution, which came into being under Dr. Sun Yat-sen in 1911, is still going on. Dr. Sun's famous Three Principles are still far from realized, but they live on in the hopes and yearnings of the Chinese people. One of these principles demanded the end of feudalism. "Land to those who till it," said the great founder of the republic. After thirty-five years and immeasurable bloodshed and suffering, 80 percent of China's 400,000,000 (who are peasants) still have obtained hardly any land of their own; more than 85 percent are illiterate. Chungking's Kuomintang regime has never got around to a drastic redistribution of land in its regions. Only in Yenan's Red China have the Chinese people received a new stake in their soil. Under the Chungking government local landlords are still local czars, and the abusive traditional warlords still control their own armies and live on the backs of the people in some districts. There is surely no country in the world where the uprooting of feudalism constitutes such a vast and complicated problem as in China.

We must remember that the Chinese are thin not by nature but from persistent lack of sufficient food through many centuries. We need to pause over the brutal fact that the average length of life in China is only twenty-eight years, as it is twenty-six in India. We must consider the terrible implications of the further fact that not more than a tiny fraction of China's "good earth" has ever been owned by the bent, patched figures who till it with such skill and amazing thrift. The Chinese people are incredibly strong for their size and weight—but they are strong in the sense that the survivors must be strong.

Scores of millions of China's peasants spend their short lives as tenant-farmers (share-croppers) in the service of rich or rela-tively wealthy landlords, who hold them in their power until the grave. In China, as all correspondents have learned while work-ing there, it is much easier to get statistics than to maintain faith in their accuracy. Part of "saving face," where officials are con-cerned, is to paint as bright a picture as possible. But when you go into the villages and look at the feudalistic land system you see conditions more eloquent than a million columns of statistics. In the villages—except in so-called Red China today—you see a merciless triumvirate of landlords, tax-collectors, and usurers fattening on the collective misery and hopelessness of the people. This was what caused Dr. Sun Yat-sen to cry out: "Land to those who till it!" And this—if there is ever to be any liberation in China—is where liberation must begin.

The League of Nations once had a health expert, Dr. Stampar, investigating rural conditions in China. In Shensi province he found that small farmers had to pay land taxes and surtaxes amounting to 45 percent of their income—and other taxes totaling 20 percent more. The local militia (usually acting as collectors for some warlord) took some 30 or 40 percent of the municipal budget. When the terrible famine of 1928–30 came, the big land-lords and officials bought out the small landowners at distortedly cheap prices. Then these formerly semi-independent peasants joined the swollen ranks of the share-croppers, or starved. In many districts the rich held large areas of land which they did not bother to cultivate; and in Shensi Dr. Stampar found that the wealthy landowners were usually exempted from taxes.[3]

The impoverished Chinese farmer, owning too little soil to make ends meet, is forced to borrow in advance of his crop— to keep alive. This is how the vicious money-lenders have prospered in China for centuries. It is a typical phenomenon of feudalism. The Chinese gentry and usurers charge the small farmers or share-croppers anywhere from 60 to 100 percent for their loans. They are the village bosses, partners of the big landlords and the local military, and they hold the purse-strings. Peasants who cannot pay are simply dispossessed.

When the Chinese Communists were driven to the north by Kuomintang forces, the Reds began to confiscate the big landlords' properties and turn them over to the peasants. Their policy was to tax the exploiting classes heavily, and win the peasants by carrying out one of Sun Yat-sen's major objectives. The loan robbers were driven out in Communist areas, and taxes on the small farmers were greatly reduced. After the Japanese war began in China there followed some five years in which no American or British correspondents were allowed to visit Communist-governed Yenan. Finally, in 1944, the journalists brought such unrelenting pressure that Chiang Kai-shek's government permitted a few of them to go behind the veil which had blacked out conditions in Red China for so long. During the next few months these correspondents—and the members of a temporary United States military mission—learned many surprising things about the "other China."[4]

What the Communist leaders had done in Yenan and the border region looked very much more like grass-roots democracy to these American observers than anything they had seen over a period of years in Kuomintang China. The Chinese Reds, while holding off and harrying the Japanese, had introduced the only serious land reforms that have yet been attempted anywhere in

[3] See Edgar Snow: *Red Star over China*, pp. 208–209.
[4] For a rounded picture read Gunther Stein: *The Challenge of Red China*, and Harrison Forman: *Report from Red China*.

the country. Gunther Stein, an economist with long experience in the Orient, made a careful study of this frontal attack on feudalism. The Communists, he found, had ceased appropriating land in large amounts. Instead, they had "reformed" many larger landlords; they had the landlords and the peasants working together; the farmers pooled their labor; tenant farmers' rents were reduced to a fixed maximum of 40 percent; the vicious tax collectors and grafters were gone—and Yenan's farm production, despite wartime conditions and acute shortages of many implements, had doubled.[5] Nothing on such a scale as this, nor so basically sound, had occurred anywhere under nearly twenty years of Kuomintang control. Chinese who live in Yenan-administered regions have been estimated variously at between some 65,000,000 and 95,000,000. With the northward spread of Chinese Red armies into Inner Mongolia and parts of Manchuria, after Japan's defeat, it is impossible to make an accurate statement about the new total of population in Red-governed regions. But the fact is plain that Yenan's "New Democracy" has certain very important aspects of tremendous appeal—and novelty—for the great peasant majority in China. The basis of the Communist-controlled regions' strong appeal to a population which is 80 percent peasant, or more, is the progress which they have made toward liquidating feudalism.

But feudalism also still exists in the Philippines.

This fact needs to be emphasized, lest we Americans should harbor the illusion that United States administration of the Philippines has been progressive and beneficial in every respect. It is true that American rule had been sufficiently enlightened so that the only dependent peoples in Asia who fought valiantly against Japanese invaders—*voluntarily* and in large numbers—were the Filipinos. Their resistance guerrillas also played a magnificent part in liberation of the islands. But most of these humble Filipinos were likewise fighting for a better chance to live decently. They have since seen alleged notorious collaborators, like Manuel Roxas, take over high posts in the Philippine government. Since the autumn of 1945 we have had repeated warnings

5 See Gunther Stein: "The Other China," *Foreign Affairs*, October 1945.

that serious trouble might break out in the islands at any time; and one of the immediate causes for this tense situation comes from the land.

The Spaniards transplanted their feudal system to the Philippines, as to most of Latin America. A powerful landed gentry grew up in the islands. The Americans found big landlords holding very large areas of agricultural land, and the landlords took pains to protect their privileges and interests. Thus the same widespread "tenant farmer" system as exists throughout all of Asia remains in the Philippines. The share-cropper may not clear more than 150 or 200 pesos with which to support his family and a carabao and to maintain his house and tools for a year. The former governor of Panay, Tomas Confesor, places the average Filipino farmers' *yearly* income at less than $40. In respect to the Philippines' predominantly peasant population, then, American rule—even with far better educational facilities —did not do very much more to raise the living standards of the average Filipino than British, French, or Dutch rule has done elsewhere. It was not surprising that the Filipino peasant patriots in several provinces took direct action when liberation came. They seized the estates of big landowners, many of whom had collaborated with the Japanese, and started dividing them among the peasants. The popular demand for long-overdue land reforms is bound to provoke more than one crisis in the Philippines in the next few years.

In the twentieth century a medieval system of peasant exploitation is a dangerous luxury for those at the top who seek to perpetuate it. During enemy occupation the Philippine Communists increased their strength some sevenfold. Theirs is the most active party throughout the islands; the political movement with the greatest mass appeal. Thus the feudalistic landlords and those who tolerated their excessive privileges have, in reality, promoted a rising Communist sentiment among Filipinos. Until the common people of the Philippines are given a much broader stake in the land, this Left-wing political ferment seems bound to increase. With a large number of collaborators infesting the Manila government—an affront to the great number of Filipino patriots who resisted so courageously—the outlook in the Philip-

pines is far from pleasant. To the average Filipino what Red
China is doing for its peasants must look like the only kind of
democracy that has much meaning for him.

This raises a question which is of great importance to the American people, as well as to American shapers of foreign policy.

How much democracy is there in China today?

In a previous book [6] I summarized certain outstanding aspects
of the Kuomintang government's nature.

The Kuomintang government over which Chiang Kai-shek
presided well into 1946 remained a one-party government. For
many years it functioned as a strictly totalitarian system, although
promising some degree of multipartied administration after a still
indefinite period of preparatory "tutelage." All government min-
istries and the entire bureaucracy were held as a monopoly of
Kuomintang party members. The most influential leaders in
the Kuomintang, to date, have not been its more liberal elements but the most reactionary politicians—or generals—in the
party. Some of these leaders are described by Chinese moderates
as being pro-Fascist, or Fascist, in their ideology and their methods. Some of the most powerful army commanders under Chiang
Kai-shek belong in this category also.

Although the Kuomintang ruled a considerable portion of
of China for nearly twenty years there is still not a single county,
in its provinces, whose officials have been freely elected. Corruption and graft have been one of Chungking's greatest problems,
in the capital and among large numbers of petty officials, throughout the war. Under the Kuomintang free speech has rarely
existed and the press has been rigidly controlled, with few excep-
tions. Chungking's censorship has been one of the most severe in
any wartime capital. Some correspondents, who have worked in
both capitals, have found Moscow's censorship considerably less
onerous on the average than that in Kuomintang China. Concentration camps—confining professors and students and moderate
liberal critics, as well as Communists—have been maintained for
years. The three separate secret police organizations operated

[6] See Leland Stowe: *They Shall Not Sleep*, Chapter III.

under the Kuomintang are extremely active and inspire much popular fear.

These are facts known to all foreign correspondents in China, and lamented by a great many Chinese who are in no sense Communist—including some impotent progressives in the Kuomintang itself. After General Stilwell's most unfortunate recall in October 1944, facts such as these prompted Brooks Atkinson of the *New York Times* to describe the Chungking government as "a moribund, antidemocratic regime." Atkinson, I am certain, had the agreement of at least 90 percent of foreign correspondents—and of the most experienced men then in our Chungking embassy—when he stated that the United States was now committed to support "an unpopular and distrusted" government, unchanged over a long period, "bureaucratic, inefficient and corrupt."

It was with this regime that Patrick Hurley, then U.S. Ambassador to Chungking, elected to pursue a policy of placation. Whereas the Stilwell-Gauss approach had been realistic—both to get the Kuomintang armies to begin to fight the Japanese aggressively and to promote much-needed reforms in the Chungking government—Mr. Hurley tended to accept promises for deeds. His policy seemed to boil down to the impossible one of trying to outcharm the ever-charming Chinese politicians. It did not achieve the slightest reform of consequence in the regime. It did not promote any democratic gains. Finally, it failed completely to bring Chungking and the Chinese Reds any nearer an agreement. What the United States accomplished during the "Hurley-burly" period was merely to build up greatly Chiang Kai-shek's divisions—for possible use in a civil war against the Yenan Reds—without obtaining any progress or guarantees for the liberalization of China's government.

Conditions in Red China were strikingly different from those prevailing for so many years in Nationalist-Kuomintang China. General Stilwell, with his intimate acquaintance with China, was much better informed about this than Ambassador Hurley could hope to be. U.S. Army officers and corrrespondents all brought back the same kind of reports from Yenan. They said that the Chinese Reds were frankly Marxist in their long-term aims and philosophy, but that they had inaugurated in their regions the only truly democratic practices to be found anywhere in China. They had not tried to impose Communism or collectivism. Instead, they had adopted a compromise known as the "New Democracy." In their regions they had organized the only freely elected self-government the Chinese people had yet known. In each of these units Communists were limited to one third of the elected seats. Thus the kind of coalition government that Chinese democrats and liberals had for years vainly demanded in Kuomintang China was already functioning under energetic Communist promotion in the north. Why had not America's full material and moral pressure been used in Chungking in the critical period of the war to encourage the creation of a similar coalition government, or one even broader? Could Ambassador Hurley explain this convincingly? Or had President Roosevelt, listening to Mr. Hurley, committed as grave an error in regard to China as he had—listening to whom?—in regard to General de Gaulle?

In their regions the Chinese Reds had applied land reforms which vastly increased the number of property holders and which protected private property. They had also attacked many other political and social problems. One of their most notable achievements was a frontal attack on illiteracy—something which the Kuomintang had scarcely touched. In Yenan, Chinese of all ages were learning to read and write. A universal educational program was under way. And the Reds had accomplished something else which the Nationalist regime had had much greater opportunity to do: they had won the support of many landlords and merchants, as well as the peasants, in a clean-up of traditional Chinese bureaucratic and administrative abuses. Foreign observers declared that in Red China graft and corruption among generals and civil authorities either did not exist or was so negligible as to be regarded as eliminated. These great contrasts with Kuomintang China stood up under close examination. Gunther Stein was prompted to write: "For the first time in modern history some of China's great economic problems seem on the way to solution. That is one of the great sources of strength of the communist regime and a portent for the future. To overlook it is to run the risk of an inaccurate analysis of present and future forces in China."

Yet these were the highly important political realities which

Ambassador Hurley's policy of all-out and unqualified support for the Kuomintang regime had overlooked. U.S. armed forces and American Lend-Lease had been used uniquely to strengthen Chungking's discredited government and the Kuomintang's party armies. When Japan surrendered, American planes, troops, and marines were committed to help the Kuomintang do what its armies could not hope to do alone—to recapture control of the heart of China, from Shanghai northward into Manchuria. American involvement in a Chinese civil war was a constant threat for weeks and months, and everything but official in certain areas. It was small wonder that GIs, who had seen plenty during their exposure to Kuomintang China, were filled with disgust and clamoring to come home. A good many American airmen were killed while flying missions to help Chiang's troops stake out additional territory against the Chinese Reds. Their comrades asked bitterly what kind of China they were dying for. It was hard to convince these young Americans that Washington was supporting a democratic opportunity for the Chinese people. Where they had been, the Chinese people had no such thing.

In this emergency the appointment of General George C. Marshall as the President's special ambassador to China was a first great step toward common sense. Further shipment of American materials to Kuomintang China were reported to have been stopped simultaneously. General Marshall was authorized to negotiate peace in China's undeclared civil war, and to mediate for an agreement between Chungking and Yenan as a foundation for establishment of a democratic, multipartied government. Few American ambassadors have ever assumed a more onerous, complex, and seemingly thankless task—nor one of greater significance. But an American of very exceptional ability and stature had patriotically assumed the responsibilities and the risks. General Marshall began by listening attentively to leaders of all factions. In a very short time he had made notable progress.

On January 10, 1946, a truce was declared between the Kuomintang and Chinese Red forces, thereby signaling a first great success for General Marshall's mission. For the first time in eighteen years of bitter Kuomintang-Communist conflict, both sides had been persuaded to attempt to settle their differences peacefully. It was only an armistice, yet one that offered great opportunity. Simultaneously Chiang Kai-shek promised far-reaching governmental reforms and so informed the Political Consultation Conference, representing all parties, which had been called to explore the possibilities for a coalition government.

The reforms which the Generalissimo pledged his government to enact or support covered these chief points: (1) Steps to insure freedom of the press and of assembly; (2) curbing of the much-feared Kuomintang secret police; (3) equality of all "legal" parties before the law; (4) release of all political prisoners except traitors—which would end concentration camps in Kuomintang China; and (5) promotion of local self-government, with popular elections. These were all reforms which the Chinese people had been demanding for years. In the opinion of most foreign observers they could well have been undertaken in 1942 or 1943. That this had not happened was chiefly due to the strength of the anti-democratic and reactionary forces in the Kuomintang—and to the lack of persistent United States pressure in their favor. One was bound to observe that, if Chiang Kai-shek had sufficient power to announce such reforms, as a promise, early in 1946, he had had equal power to do so several years earlier. But late though it was, this was still a hopeful sign.

To accept it as more than a promising development could yet prove to be wishful thinking. Anyone who knows Chinese politics and Kuomintang methods knows that in China attractive government plans often remain in the realm of words. Certainly the Chinese people would believe that the secret police would not arrest them without writ or charges and spirit them away without trial when that no longer happened—but not before. Certainly local self-government will mean nothing unless China's feudalism is attacked everywhere as the Reds have done in Yenan. Every promised reform will be most difficult to carry out, and the Kuomintang reactionaries, after twenty years of power and privilege, will defend their interests with every weapon of oriental deviousness. Thus the pressures on the Generalissimo will be exceedingly great; and in his own book, *China's Destiny,* he did not place much emphasis upon democracy or modern political conceptions.

Whether the Chinese Reds would ever be so rash as to disarm their forces or place them under some of the Kuomintang's most rabidly Rightist generals must remain most dubious. It is still perfectly clear that even the announcement or the formation of a coalition government must leave a great many moderate Chinese democrats, as well as the Reds, highly skeptical—until it has been demonstrated that the Kuomintang's reactionary elements do not still retain all the vital leverages of power. A Kuomintang-dominated "coalition" will remain suspect to an enormous number of Chinese for a long time, simply because of the abuses which have flourished under the Chungking government—and in it—for so many years. But the war-exhausted Chinese people want to believe that Chiang Kai-shek will prove himself a statesman in peace. If the Generalissimo can subjugate his past hatred for the Reds, if he can rise above all parties and factions to unify and to serve the welfare of the entire nation, he will have rendered an inestimable service to his people. This, we may be sure, is the vision that inspired General Marshall, whose contributions toward Chinese unity have already been unique and whose efforts continue to merit the highest praise.

Should China get a "coalition" which is not a coalition and a "democratic" government which dodges all real and fundamental democratic reforms, the showdown of a most costly and destructive civil war would merely have been postponed for a while. Any such extended internal conflict between Kuomintang and Red armies would inevitably undermine Soviet-American relations and menace world peace. This is what is at stake as the Chinese people strive for a measure of genuine democracy and an end to party dictatorship. Many of the best-informed observers in the Orient are also convinced that any Chinese civil war would be long, or very long. Some insist that the Kuomintang, even with its large arsenal of American Lend-Lease weapons, cannot hope to destroy and dominate Red China. The reasons for this conclusion have been amply demonstrated in the course of the war against Japan.

The *New York Herald Tribune,* in one of its consistently outstanding editorials on world affairs, stated:

The Japanese held the principal cities of North China with far better troops than the Kuomintang controls. The communists grew rather than diminished in strength throughout enemy occupation.

The Japanese found it impossible, as the British did in Ireland centuries ago, to wipe out a well-organized opposition of agrarian guerrillas. . . . It is wildly impossible that the American people will
participate indefinitely in a Chinese civil war which goes on for year
after year. . . . It would be far wiser to give up our present program [7]
of all-out support for the Kuomintang and to join with other countries, especially Russia, in bringing pressure to stop the fighting in
China.

The wisdom and soundness of a joint Allied mediation in
China cannot be challenged. We can only hope, for the future
peace in the far Pacific and for our own American security, that
such a course will be not only adopted but pursued tenaciously
until China can be united under a true coalition government.
I think we can best see our own long-term benefits from such a
course, if we ask ourselves—

What does the United States want in China?

Our greatest desires seem simple enough to state. America
wants a peaceful and, if possible, a united China. If we have any
logic and foresight whatever, we also want a democratic China.
After that America hopes to build up a large and growing trade
with China. Such a trade could develop into hundreds of millions of dollars every year, and would do much to boost employment in the U.S.A. But a China torn by civil war, or divided into
two rival and antagonistic parts, would certainly never be a profit-
able market or a dependable one. So we can never have a steadily
enlarging business with one of the world's greatest potential markets unless China is united and remains a peaceful country dedicated to reconstruction and industrialization. This would seem
to dictate an American policy toward China, which works consistently to consolidate world peace. It would also promise very
practical benefits to us.

But the key to all this—so it seems to many others besides myself—lies primarily in the cultivation of a truly *democratic* China.
If the United States should make it possible for the Kuomintang
regime to obtain dictatorial control over all China—supposing

[7] As of November 1945.

that this finally could be imposed—what then? Are we to assume that a triumphant Kuomintang, reactionary and antidemocratic in much of its present leadership, would suddenly become pro-democratic and liberal once it had complete power in its hands? Are we to assume that a party which has failed most seriously to reform itself internally over a period of close to twenty years would suddenly clean house? Would a victorious Kuomintang be likely to industrialize for co-operation with the Western democracies—or to industrialize simply to achieve far greater power?

From any common-sense point of view these questions answer themselves. It seems to me that "which way China?" must in the long run spell war or peace in the Far East. Even more conclusively, it seems to me that a democratic China—at any rate a China faced resolutely *toward democracy*—is the only kind of China that is compatible with the peaceful aspirations and the material interests of both the United States and Britain. If these Western powers do not foster the present tentative upshoots of democracy in China, they stand to lose—well within this generation—400,000,-000 Chinese as a force for democracy in the world. If there is any foreign country in which the American people really *need* a democratic government, it is China.

To think of China in terms of a *buffer* against Soviet Russia is to do one of two things: either to invite a war with Russia in the Orient, or to poison all chances for a peace-promoting world organization. To think of China as a *bridge* between the American and the Soviet systems is to drive the first piles for an intelligent and much more secure future for all of us. In this fashion the lives of our children are as much at stake in China today as anywhere in the world. The Western democracies—in population and ultimate resources—are definitely in a minority in this post-war world. Can you think of any sure way for democracy to survive except by helping build democracy on great and strategic soils which are now ripe for it? That, to me, is the paramount significance of contemporary China for all of us in the West. And this opportunity may never come again. We cannot afford to do less and promise less, democratically speaking, than the Chinese Reds do and promise. Beyond this stands one further and indisputable fact. The great mass of the Chinese people, still having great faith in America, want an increasingly democratic way of life more than anything else. The Chinese masses want schools. They want freedom of speech, a multiparty system, elected public officials, and a far greater degree of broad private ownership of land than they have ever known. If these things are not democratic instruments, then what indeed have we to offer China?

Whatever the United States does to promote and strengthen democracy in China will have an enormous, probably a decisive, effect. But whatever America does, or fails to do, in Japan will prove overwhelmingly decisive. The chief responsibility for reshaping Japan is ours by self-election. That very fact alone ought to be a terribly sobering realization for all Americans. For if Japan again becomes a military menace in this century, or if we do not remove the formidable barriers to democracy in Japan, Americans will be chiefly to blame. Either our military and civilian authorities in charge of Japan's occupation will have proved grossly inefficient; or they will in some serious measure have failed to carry out their announced programs; or Americans will again have become dupes of the Japanese ruling classes. It would be a grave reflection upon the world's greatest power if, with all power in its hands, it should fail to fulfill creditably and effectively the greatest overseas responsibility that Americans have ever assumed. Are we sufficiently shrewd in our understanding of the main aggressive forces in Japan? Will the American tendency to gullibility—and weakness for the "nice people"—make our representatives frequent victims of Japanese dissimulation? Will the American people show the stamina and tenacity to support a twenty- or thirty-year program in Japan? The perils ahead of us are far greater than the American public as yet gives any evidence of comprehending.

Perhaps we should constantly remind ourselves of—

The barriers to the establishment of a "free and democratic regime in Japan."

The most powerful of these obstacles can be named concisely: (1) The emperor system and emperor-worship; (2) the secret Japanese military societies, the militarists, and the viciously thorough secret police; (3) the tremendously rich industrial and financial monopolists known as the *Zaibatsu;* (4) the feudalistic land system and the big landlords; (5) the vast Japanese bureaucracy and the aristocrats; and (6) the Japanese constitution with its "god-emperor" and other antidemocratic provisions.

To eradicate only one or two of these factors, while leaving the others essentially unreformed, would give the Japanese people little chance of ever achieving self-government on any modern, Western pattern. So the Allies' occupational activities, under American leadership, in reality boil down to at least a six-front initiative. On most of these fronts some action has been taken— and the earnestness of our intentions has been proclaimed without bashfulness. But once again long-term performance will be the only thing that will count in the record books, or as a contribution to making peace secure. To accept official pronouncements as results already accomplished or assured would be the most dangerous kind of self-deception. We would do well, here in the U.S.A., to keep steadily in our minds such warnings as these:

General Jonathan M. Wainwright: "I am not for one year's occupation of Japan. I am against five years' occupation. I'm against ten years. *We should occupy the Japanese islands for about twenty years.*"

General Claire L. Chennault: "The Japs are spiritually unde-feated. . . . There will either be a popular revolution . . . or the Mikado will rebuild the old structure and begin new conquests at a future date."

Vice Admiral John S. McCain: "The Japanese war lords are not half-licked yet. They will take a lot more killing in the future. *I don't like the look in their eyes.*"

And after the surrender the Japanese commander of Singapore, Lieutenant General Seishiro Itagaki, told the Sultan of Johore: "We hope the peace will last for twenty years—and *then we will be back here again.*"

If this should happen, the American people can never plead that they were not plainly warned. But has anyone yet devised a system to keep the memories of the citizens in a democracy effectively sharpened?

For the first three months, as American forces were gradually occupying key points throughout the Japanese islands, there was a good deal of unavoidable confusion. Yet General MacArthur

somehow managed to get the Jap armies demobilized with remarkable dispatch; in large measure, perhaps, because Washington had decided to "use" the Emperor's authority. But once
American occupation became secure it did not become at all clear
how much the Americans were "using" the Emperor; or whether
perhaps, behind the scenes, the Emperor might also be ingeni-
ously using *them.* By November, Tokyo correspondents informed
us that Hirohito's prestige was greater than ever with his people.
For the average Japanese it was the Emperor himself who had
brought peace—and look with what respect he was still treated by
the Americans! Even to "foreign devils" Hirohito was evidently
sacred. From Americans with the most intimate knowledge of
Japan we had innumerable warnings that to keep the "god-
emperor" was to court disaster on all of our main objectives in
Japan. I am also one of those who are convinced that Hirohito is
a first barrier to any genuine Japanese democracy. If we permit
the Emperor to remain as the chief symbol and inspiration of the
Japanese, I believe our chances of success in Japan will have been
diminished by at least 50 percent. You cannot re-educate any mis-
guided people by retaining over them the symbol of their in-
grained fanaticism. But aside from this contested point—

Shall we effectively break up Japan's all-powerful industrial monopolies?

Japan's whole modern economy was dominated by interlocking financial and industrial trusts. The Big Four among them are
Mitsui, Mitsubishi, Sumitomo and Yasuda. The *Zaibatsu,* who
owned and operated these colossal monopolies, reaped enormous
profits and expanded their enterprises to fantastic proportions
through four Japanese wars of aggression. Some of the *Zaibatsu*
were the most ardent partners of the nation's militarists and contributed large sums to the latter's secret terrorist organizations.
But all of Japanese big business served Tokyo's war-bent clique
unhesitatingly, and piled up enormous profits out of four succes-
sive wars of conquest. Since 1894 and its preliminary Sino-Japa-
nese conflict, war-making has been Japan's greatest industry—no
fewer than four different wars of foreign aggression launched in
the short period of forty-three years. Japan's industrial monopo-

lists fattened prodigiously on these deliberately calculated conquests. After the First World War, which was of exceptional profit
to Nippon, it was estimated that the five largest trusts controlled
over 60 percent of Japan's industrial, commercial, and financial
wealth. By 1937 the Big Four cartels controlled one third of the
total foreign trade, more than one third of all deposits in private
banks, and 70 percent of the deposits in all trust companies.[8]
Proportionately, they were many times more powerful than a
quartet such as General Motors, General Electric, Standard Oil,
and United States Steel.

Without the support of these gigantic *Zaibatsu* monopolists,
Japan's militarists could not plan to conquer all Asia, but they
could offer fabulous spoils to be exploited by the Big Four—from
Manchuria through China to the Dutch Indies and India. Emperor Hirohito also held tremendous stakes in Japanese expansion, such as: nearly half of the 300,000 shares in the Bank of
Japan, a part control in the Mitsubishis' vast shipping lines, and
more than one fifth of the stock in the Yokohama Specie Bank,
which dominated foreign financing. And the Mitsubishis had
important supporters of theirs inside the imperial palace. When
Japan invaded China in 1937 the great Mitsubishi shipbuilding
company had a declared capital of 120,000,000 yen. In 1945 its
capital was admittedly almost ten times that amount. Decidedly
the big Japanese monopolists were doing very nicely from the
war.

Facts like these make the *Zaibatsu's* attitude after Tokyo's surrender extremely interesting. Suddenly mild-mannered Japanese
business executives, speaking beautiful English perfected at
Oxford or Harvard, were assuring American correspondents that
they had opposed the war all along. The president of Mitsui &
Co., Ltd., Kyoshi Miyazaki, graciously granted a three-hour interview—which he must have hoped would not be time wasted. "We
had no voice. We took our orders," Mr. Miyazaki said. It was
exactly as if the president of the National Association of Manufacturers, or a super-Dupont, should insist that his organization
had never had the slightest influence in Washington—only a lot
more so, given Japan's economic set-up. The Mitsui chief executive, talking to our reporters, was suddenly profoundly concerned

[8] See Andrew Roth: *Dilemma in Japan*, Chapter IV.

about freedom of speech for the Japanese people. Not very subtly he insisted that Japanese business had been muzzled all along; that it had in fact suffered from the hostility of the militarists. But he didn't produce any annual balance sheets to back up that statement. Mr. Miyazaki had served his firm in the United States for eighteen years, and he had a most engaging way in talking with Americans; obviously, a cultured gentleman. He stressed the fact that the House of Mitsui had lost nearly one million tons of shipping in the war. But a *New York Times* correspondent ended by reporting that Mitsui, "protected by investments of millions of Japanese [?—my question mark] and by its remaining assets at home and abroad, seems to be in a position to withstand anything but the collapse of the nation's economy—or revolution." Could Mr. Miyazaki have also raised that delicate point about the danger of revolution in Japan? We were not told, but that's the way the defeated Krupps and their kind talked immediately after Germany's defeat.

Seven others among Japan's leading industrialists tendered a five-course steak dinner to American correspondents in Tokyo's best hotel within a month after surrender. "We didn't dare to speak. We were afraid of death," said Harvard alumnus Ryozo Asano, president of the Japan Steel Tube Company. Solemnly all seven protested they had never harbored the faintest desire for war. Once again there was no mention of those years of massive profits, while millions of Manchurians and Chinese were murdered, starved, driven from their homes, and systematically inoculated with the opium habit. How could a journalistic guest be so impolite as to mention such forgotten incidentals? Besides, their Japanese hosts—so well-mannered and civilized—had other matters on their minds. They were very much alarmed, they explained, by the prospect of widespread unemployment and hunger (though not at all concerned about those countries which had suffered these things for years because of their Japanese conquerors). Mr. Asano was quite frank on this point. "We are alarmed," he said, "because so much unemployment may lead to dangerous thoughts, such as Socialism." By some strange paradox, the "dangerous thoughts" that so suddenly and deeply concerned the Japanese industrialists would be costly only to—the Japanese industrialists! Now wasn't it a pity that the Mitsuis, Mitsubishis, and the rest hadn't thought of that long ago? All they were really propagandizing for was an undiminished grip on war-profits—without any of the inconveniences that might automatically result from having lost a war.

Does this statement seem unfair to the *Zaibatsu*? Any examination of the Big Four monopolies' profits in Manchuria through fourteen years of Japanese exploitation will provide an answer in columns of enlightening statistics. But a single example from Korea is a faithful reproduction of the general pattern. The Japanese-owned industrial octopus in this impoverished land was the "New Korea Company." After liberation, American authorities learned that this gigantic trust had a monopoly of mining, agriculture, industry, finance, transportation, and forestry—and it was merely the Korean *branch* of one of Japan's Big Four. When one company controls virtually all of the above enterprises and resources in a nation one fifth as large as the United States, that is rather Big business.

The New Korea Company's holdings included shipbuilding, port operations, textiles, iron, mica, tungsten, coal, charcoal, ceramics, and food products, and it controlled 64 percent of Korea's dry lands, 80 percent of her rice lands, and 350,000 acres of forests—in short, an exhibition sample of what the Japanese meant when they talked of an "All-Asia Co-Prosperity Sphere." In forty years the Japanese monopolists had completely strangled Korea. They were milking every conceivable profit out of it, into their own pockets. Now would it be terribly surprising if 23,000,000 liberated Koreans should emerge from such an experience with some socialistically "dangerous thoughts"? But there are one or two associated facts of great pertinence for us to remember. What the Japanese financial and industrial monopolies did to Korea and Manchuria was merely a faithful replica of what they had been doing to Japan for several generations. If the Koreans were enslaved, they were no more enslaved than some 85 to 95 percent of the Japanese people. If Korea can never gain true independence without a complete breakup of the monopolies which bound her hand and foot, how can the Japanese possibly be given an opportunity for a "free and democratic regime" unless the *Zaibatsu* trusts are utterly eradicated in Japan?

It is to the great credit of certain key advisers in Washington that American policy adopted this realistic course from the begin, ning. Following Washington's directives, General MacArthur announced that the multi-million-dollar family monopolies would be dissolved. But this is a highly complicated task. It strikes at the roots of Japan's ruling classes. It can be circumvented or camou, flaged in a thousand ways, all of which are perfectly familiar to the entrenched *Zaibatsu*. In Germany it was already being demonstrated that a worthy and fine-sounding "directive" from the top means not a whit more than what its executors, all down the line, do with it. In regard to "denazification," for instance, a great many American and British officers did nothing at all. Thus, in Japan everything depends on the thoroughness and the governing principles of Allied officers who are supposed to break up the nation's big trusts. If that is their only aim, they have the power to do the job. But if they listen to some of Japan's very "nice people" who murmur about the dangers of "revolution"—or if these American officers are more concerned about maintaining Japanese industrial strength as a future "buffer" against Soviet Russia—then, of course, the greatest remaining antidemocratic force in Japan (after the Emperor himself) will survive virtually intact. For the powerful monopolists will need only a little blindness here, and a little secret indulgence there, to retain their power—for future use!

The first reaction of Japan's Big Four was significant. They began to "co-operate"—but according to their own plan. They publicly announced that they were discarding the top layer of officers in some of their huge combines, and divorcing ownership from management. But they did nothing to indicate that control of their enormous financial and industrial enterprises was being altered fundamentally. At this writing, it is not at all clear how much real progress the Allies are making toward dissolving the *Zaibatsu* combines; or whether anything like an effective crippling of their power can be expected. We in America will be prudent if we remain strictly "from Missouri" until Washington's announced intention has been translated into precise, irrefutable facts. Once again, this is a long-term job and perhaps should not be judged too hastily. But it is an all-important job— and for that reason it requires the sustained interest and watchfulness of the American public.

I have outlined only a few of our major tasks in Japan. The object here is not to make a detailed survey, but to emphasize the underlying question which should be of first concern to all of us.

Can we hope to lay the foundations for democracy in Japan?

Surely, we cannot hope to do this—

Unless the average American takes pains to inform himself about the political and economic structure of pre-war Japan;

Unless the American public clearly understands such fundamentals as the nature of Shintoism and the "god-emperor" concept, the feudalistic land system, and the enormous power of the great Japanese financial and industrial trusts;

Unless reporting on American and Allied actions in Japan is frank, fearless, and penetratingly efficient on economic as well as political developments;

Unless the State Department and the Allied command in Japan make regular public reports which can be checked and reported on by independent investigators;

Unless the main objective in Japan is what Potsdam said it was: to eliminate all barriers to a "free and democratic regime."

Unless the United States government, firmly supported by American public opinion, assumes this responsibility on a long-term basis of fifteen or twenty years at a minimum.

All of these things *can* be done—provided that the American people are sufficiently interested to see to it that they are done. If George Jones, the composite American, is too taken up with his personal interests to remain concerned about this tremendously difficult task, then you and I—the George Joneses—may justifiably expect the U.S. Congress and our American representatives in Japan to become indifferent after a few months or one or two years.

We can lay the groundwork for democracy in Japan only if the American people are sufficiently interested to see to it that the job is done—and thoroughly done. In other words, we shall have to possess a great deal of General Wainwright's realism and patriotism, plus a clear conception of our own of what things make a democratic society possible in any country. We cannot get more from the Japanese people than we provide them with the opportunity of achieving for themselves. We cannot expect a united and democratic China unless the American people—and their government—use their influence to promote a coalition regime in China, and unless we understand clearly what forces offer some hope for democratic expression to the Chinese people.

An ignorant and uneducated Japanese and Chinese people can never become a force for peace. But can we with any more reason expect that an American people, ill-informed or largely uneducated about the fundamental governing facts in China and Japan, can promote any real possibility of peace in the Orient? As the greatest power in today's world, we Americans must first look to ourselves to assess any answer to the question: Which way China and Japan? In this final answer the American share of responsibility will weigh very heavily. It could even be decided—with an atomic war as the final reward—by what we Americans do *not do* in the Orient, and through sheer indifference do *not know* about the Orient. For the atomic age has made almost every other people's problems *our problems*. For you and me to seek to escape this hard fact would merely be to seek mass destruction.

NOTE

It seems clear that peace or war within the next thirty years will be decided chiefly by developments in Asia. For this reason I am appending, for any readers who may not have followed recent trends in the Far East very closely, a list of some of the books that have been helpful to me:

OWEN LATTIMORE: *Solution in Asia*

WILLIAM C. JOHNSTONE: *The Future of Japan*

PHILIP JAFFE: *New Frontiers in Asia*

GEORGE HOGG: *I See a New China*

AGNES SMEDLEY: *Battle Hymn of China*

LAWRENCE K. ROSINGER: *China's Crisis*

EDGAR SNOW: *Red Star over China*

MARK J. GAYN: *Journey from the East*

HARRISON FORMAN: *Report from Red China*
GUNTHER STEIN: *The Challenge of Red China*
H. H. CHANG: *Chiang Kai-shek*
ILONA RALF SUES: *Shark's Fins and Millet*
ANDREW ROTH: *Dilemma in Japan*

PART III

The World War of the Isms

Chapter X

WHAT IS FASCISM?

The beginning of wisdom is calling things by their right names.

Chinese proverb

It was left for the Germans to bring about a revolution of a character never seen before; a revolution without ideas; opposed to ideas, to everything better, higher, decent.

Thomas Mann

For anyone who cares about democracy the surrenders of Germany and Japan were in no sense decisive. We defeated the Axis war machines. Perhaps we shall even succeed eventually in making it impossible for German or Japanese armies to attempt world conquest in this century. But we did *not* crush Fascism, and we shall never be able to eradicate it by force of arms alone.

We did not crush Fascism, because the Fascist spirit still flourishes inside the human fabric of most of the world's nations. Fascism can finally be conquered only through an ever-rising spiritual and mental development of mankind. Fascism is the product of diseased minds and corrupted hearts. For this reason bombs and arms alone can never extinguish it. Fascism is inside society; it is inside *ourselves*.

I say this because most of us have not understood and do not yet understand it. I say this, thinking of the fearful contradictions with which the Western democracies waged their war against Fascism. I say it with a personal knowledge of the deep mental confusion which characterized American soldiers, sailors, and airmen as they fought with such bravery and distinction. They fought superbly, yet only a small minority among them could tell you why. Somehow the nation that boasts of the world's highest literacy—and the world's best-equipped and highest-endowed educational system—failed tragically to make its fighting sons comprehend the fundamental reasons for their bitter experiences and their great sacrifices. To the overwhelming majority of Americans in uniform "Fascism" remained, to the end, merely a phrase of identification; a tag hung on Germans, Italians, or Japanese as the case might be.

We have had more than twenty years in which to educate the American people on the fundamental elements of Fascism. Yet somehow we have failed to create any fairly universal understanding of the meaning of Fascism and its basic manifestations. Thus, it is probably true today that not more than one out of fifty American adults—on the average—could name to you off-hand five main characteristics of a typically Fascist movement. A thoughtful citizen, writing to me shortly before Japan's defeat, would unquestionably express himself in identical fashion at this moment: "Sometimes one is inclined to feel terrified at the glaring fact that we are engaged in a gigantic war against Fascism and yet so few people know what Fascism is. Or what it would mean to them, if it should be allowed to rise again in other parts of the world; not to mention the Fascist danger in our own United States."

Certainly it is true that one of America's greatest dangers, both external and *internal,* throughout the next ten or twenty years will be Fascism. The widespread assumption that Fascism was exterminated with the fall of Berlin and Tokyo is in itself an hypnotic drug which will greatly aid Fascist elements in many nations' societies. And the indiscriminate way in which many persons toss about such words as "Fascism," "Socialism," and "Communism" serves chiefly to confuse uninformed or unperceptive or prejudiced people. Perhaps we shall avoid a good deal of confusion if we sort out some precise facts before indulging in a label-pinning contest. This chapter therefore represents a modest but honest effort on my part. I think the best place to begin is by asking the question:

How does Fascism come?

Both in Italy and Germany we have had ample opportunity to learn the processes through which a Fascist movement rises to power. In reality, these processes provide the most important features of Fascism. In their early phases they may indeed not be called "Fascist." In fact, they may be called anything at all. Their partisans may adopt the most patriotic slogans and never admit that they are governed by Fascist aims, ideology, and methods. To expect a postwar Fascist movement, in any country, to parade itself frankly for what it is would be incredibly gullible on your part or mine. Thus we must judge Fascism by what it *does*. We must be alerted against Fascism by *how* it seeks power. To do this we must be keenly aware of what the Blackshirts did in Italy in the early twenties, and what the Brownshirts did in Germany between 1923 and 1933.

With this approach, Fascism becomes less complicated and evasive than any literate citizen might suppose. The Italian and German models show us these things clearly. Fascism comes—

1. By preaching an extreme and chauvinistic nationalism.

2. By exploiting hatreds and mass prejudices against certain minorities in any country, and usually by a brutal fanning of antiracial sentiments.

3. By seeking to destroy free labor organizations and eventually to compress all labor into a tightly controlled governmental strait jacket.

4. By promoting a very large and extremely powerful military machine within the nation.

5. By promoting an imperialistic program of expansion, colonial or otherwise.

6. By posing as champions of internal "order," while training its own hoodlum bands to provoke rioting and bloodshed wherever it can be exploited as "political capital."

7. By assuring big business and property-owners that they will enjoy special protection and privileges, if they help "the movement" to seize power—and by selling them out afterward.

8. By practicing the cheapest and lowest forms of demagoguery, and by posing as "the only defense against Communism."

9. By promising a complete clean-up of press and radio—and planning the suppression of free speech and the suppression of all opposition parties as soon as power has been seized.

All nine of these strategies have been used by the Fascists as powerful levers for the creation of a totalitarian state, whether in

Italy, Germany, or Spain. They can be applied most successfully through a single, highly organized party—but they can be used through the preliminary stages just as effectively through an "underground" interlocking of groups, movements, and parties. In a democracy these methods can never succeed until the soil is ripe, or has been made ripe through deliberate connivance and conspiracy. In a democracy, too, the Fascists cannot hope to win except by winning the wide support of various categories of citizens who are—*unconsciously Fascist*. Both the Blackshirts and the Nazis began as noisy, violent, hate-mongering minorities—but they did not end that way. Their real power and final triumph came from the unconscious Fascists who were won over by their own hatred of certain minorities, by their fear of Communism, by their greed or their ambitions. There is no national society in which these predisposed or pro-Fascist elements are not present in a variety of forms, with susceptibilities which clever and unprincipled men can easily exploit.

But there is another aspect of Fascism which the George Joneses are most likely to overlook. You and I can grasp this most quickly, perhaps, by asking another question:

Where and how is Fascism unique?

This, I think, is what many well-intentioned persons have failed to perceive. It is what Thomas Mann, a great humanist, put his finger upon with precision when he defined German Fascism as "a revolution without ideas—opposed to ideas." In the entire armory of Fascist weapons there is no appeal to reason; no recognition of human values; no acceptance of moral principles or of the spiritual potentialities of man; no ideal which contains the slightest germ of human brotherhood. Fascism has no philosophy but the philosophy of brute force. It is nihilistic and amoral; a code for the enslavement of human beings, without so much as an intelligent program for their general economic betterment—or even so much as a promise that their lost freedom may eventually be recovered by degrees. In this respect the Marxists, whether Socialist or Communist, possess a great advantage over the Fascists. However much a confirmed democrat or confirmed capitalist may repudiate Marxism, it does have a definite basis in logic and a definable program for improved intellectual and economic opportunities for a majority of citizens under its form of state ownership. You and I, for instance, can *argue* the validity or soundness of Marxist principles. We cannot do this with Fascists—because *there is no Fascist philosophy.*

That fact is easily established. For more than twenty years Italian and German Fascists dominated their countries' printing presses and controlled all recordable thought. Their apologists published billions of words and thousands of books. Yet with all this opportunity the Fascists did not produce a single book which gave humanity a single new idea or added an original thought to philosophical and political knowledge. Not only did the Fascists fail to produce a Marx, Engels, or Lenin; from the vast Hitler-Mussolini entourage there did not emerge one writer whose name will ever be mentioned in world philosophy. As for someone who could attempt to challenge the ideas of Thomas Jefferson, John Locke, or Jean-Jacques Rousseau—Fascism did not cast up a single mind capable of conversing coherently with a good intellect, let alone with giants such as these. No intelligent opponent of Communism has ever challenged the keenness and force of Lenin's mind; for Lenin's whole philosophy was built upon tangible and precise ideas. By contrast, the writings of Hitler and Alfred Rosenberg are the rantings of madmen; the belchings of delirious emotionalism.

The Fascists repudiate morality because even the most elementary morality would deny their right to dominate others without any commitments to serve the common good. Fascists enthrone violence and force because it is the only way they can gain and keep power. They have no program for human betterment because, admittedly, they seek privileges and profits for themselves alone. Thus Fascism is antiequality, antirational, and above all antihumanitarian. In short, Fascism is a gangster concept, simple but impure. It is inspired by gangster motives, promoted by gangster methods, and it can retain power only through a nationally imposed gangsterism practiced on an ever-expanding scale—with war against other nations as its ultimate expression.

The wholesale corruption among Fascist leaders in Italy and

Germany has been unparalleled in any other nations in modern times. Inevitably a one-party dictatorship breeds special privileges for high party members. During the Soviet "purge" trials, certain cases of personal graft were publicized. Such abuses became far more widespread in the Kuomintang's monopoly rule in China. But state ownership of all important means of production in Soviet Russia would alone prevent the amassing of great personal fortunes; and there are extremely few ways in which greedy or rapacious public officials could use ill-gotten gains. Such things as better housing, a choice of the best food and clothes, and an automobile for personal use are rewards of important public servants and Communist leaders. But I never heard, or heard of anyone who so much as hinted, that any Soviet citizens were rolling up big personal fortunes during the war. Graft in high places has been the rarest of complaints in Russia, where people have often had plenty to complain of and take a rather Slavic joy in doing so whenever a sound excuse presents itself. So far as I have ever been able to learn, the advantages of Soviet officialdom —real though they are—do not show themselves in the officials' pocketbooks, or in private lives of reckless extravagance. On the average, despite a rigidly one-party system, there seems to exist a definite Soviet morality in regard to public service.

In striking contrast, Europe's Fascists scarcely made any professions of public morality. They sought power and they reveled in all the material manifestations and privileges of unbridled power. When the curtain came down, the personal gangsterism of Mussolini's and Hitler's henchmen became shockingly apparent. The Fascist bigwigs had long lived like grand dukes, in elaborate villas and châteaux and castles. They had summer retreats and hunting lodges, with Marshal Göring the most garish feudal knight of them all. It was notorious that "money talked" among all the important Fascist executives in Italy, and that Hitler alone among the top Nazi hierarchy *apparently* did not seek the extreme in luxuries and ostentation.

But when the curtain came down at last, Fascist leaders in both Italy and Germany were revealed uniformly as men with great personal fortunes. The stolen art which Göring and Ribbentrop had rounded up from all over Europe filled many freight cars and was worth tens of millions of dollars. In due time American officers found the tax records of the chief Nazis. These showed that a long list of Hitler's favorites had benefited by hundreds of thousands of dollars in waived taxes, while Germany's "little man" had half a dozen different kinds of taxes removed from his pay envelope before he ever collected a pfennig. Himmler, when caught, had a princely sum on his person—in dollars, pounds, francs, and other currencies. Mussolini, as he begged for his life like the cowering, abject wretch that he always was at heart, sought to buy his freedom with several hundred thousand lira. Italy and Germany were worse than bankrupt when midnight sounded—and the creatures who had promised these nations unprecedented glory had most of their government's remaining cash assets conveniently in their own pockets. In the flagrant avariciousness of their personal gangsterism the Fascists, as a ruling party, have never been rivaled in modern times.

But this is merely an expression of Fascism's more fundamentally unique distinction. I think it has best been expressed by Herbert L. Matthews.[1]

Fascism [he writes] has taught a whole generation to believe in violence, force and the right of might. . . . Private virtue or morality ceases to exist. You start from the Machiavellian thesis, so heartily approved by Mussolini, that "all men are bad." You deny the validity of the Christian philosophy of natural law. You proclaim the *inequality of men* [italics mine], the value of the "élite," the necessity of considering people qualitatively, not quantitatively. Where you find these ideas you find fascism. You may find them in an American industrialist or union leader. You may find them in hundreds of thousands of German war prisoners. But wherever they are, there you have fascism; and there you have the true enemy of liberalism and democracy and of communism, which has very different aims and ideas under a similar governmental structure.

First in Italy, then in Ethiopia and Spain, and later in Italy again, Mr. Matthews has had an exceptional opportunity to observe what is truly unique about a "way of life" which still finds champions almost everywhere.

In our own investigation the next step is highly practical.

1 See *New York Times,* Sunday magazine section, May 27, 1945.

From what does Fascism grow?

The record of Italy and Germany shows that Fascism gets its big chance from a great depression and accompanying mass unemployment. When people are without work, with little food, and with little hope, they are in no mood to listen to reason. On the contrary, they are embittered and open to violence. They are ready to hate and quick to hate. They demand radical changes. They are looking for someone to blame for their miserable plight, and the greater the demagogue the surer he is to gain their attention. This is why we shall not know how strong Fascist tendencies are in the United States until another great depression paralyzes our economic life—something that is more than likely to happen within ten years of the war's end. Whenever we may again have twelve million or more unemployed in America, a shrewdly misnamed American Fascism is virtually certain to become a sinister force in our national politics. You may check off the nine points of Fascist methods, as listed above, and decide for yourself whether or not the essential ingredients now exist in our American society.

I was not in Europe when Italian Fascism seized power. But I was in Europe, from 1926 onward, when German Fascism maneuvered its way into supreme control of the Reich. From Paris, or inside Germany for that matter, the Nazis never loomed as a serious threat until after the Wall Street crash late in 1929. Europe's great depression was provoked and accentuated by our own. That's a serious thought for Americans today, because—if the United States has another such economic paralysis in the next decade or two—the repercussions from our collapse will inevitably precipitate political upheavals in many parts of the world. For four years after our 1929 crash one European country after another slid into economic disaster. Even the mighty British pound went crashing into enforced devaluation. At the end of this period, in the dawn of 1933, Hitler came into power in Germany. Thus the Wall Street crash did more than pulverize our banking system, destroy American fortunes, and make millions of our people jobless. It went a long way toward making certain that the United States would fight the costliest war, in lives and cash, in all history.

For without the American depression Germany's unemployment could have been curbed. Without Germany's unemployment Hitler's Fascists could never have come to power. Without Italy's serious unemployment in the early twenties Mussolini would have sunk back into oblivion. But because the people lacked work and sufficient food, because street disorders and violence spread increasing disorder through Italian cities, the Blackshirts found many listeners for their wildly emotional and nationalistic appeals. In a few years the same circumstances arose in Germany, with the same results. Like the Fascists before them, the Nazis waged a ruthless civil war against Socialists and Communists. The Brownshirts organized their own "shock battalions" from the most brutal and lawless among German youth. Any political meeting was an excuse for bloodshed or murder. And—note this particularly—the police, as in Italy, usually favored those thugs who smashed skulls while shouting: "Down with the Bolshevists!" But when municipal authorities in any country abdicate control of law enforcement, they open wide the door for a violent seizure of governmental control, either by the Right or by the Left. When Fascists are confident that the police or the army sympathize most with them, then riots and disorder are worth promoting. Immediately it is the reactionaries who have most to win. Only the bulk of the people and the law-abiding middle class have everything to lose. Yet in times of such internal dissension these people rarely organize to act. They rarely demand a strict neutrality on the part of all police. They lean toward one extreme or the other; the street-fighting and civilian warfare grows; and suddenly a small minority marches on Rome—or an election is won with clubs and blackmail and bribery—and Fascism is in power.

Here again the unconscious Fascists prove to be the most effective enemies of parliamentary government. It is they who have been duped by preachments of arrogant, better-than-anybody nationalism. Or won to the Fascist cause by promises that "labor will be put in its place." Or impressed by a program for creation of an "unbeatable" military machine. Or enlisted by fear of Communism or by the poison of a rabid antiracialism. Without mass unemployment and harshly restricted living conditions, many of these citizens would never have been swept into support of the

Fascists. But the Fascist demagogues offer them all sorts of things to fight *against*. In their emotional outpouring of fighting against something, these harassed and resentful citizens forget, quite humanly, to inquire what—if anything—they are fighting *for*. The others, those who lead them, know perfectly well what they are after. In Italy and Germany, and in Spain, we have seen what they have done with their power.

You may remark that Fascism must have provided some important benefits, or it would not have won an important following through its early years. This is certainly a point to be considered. We may ask—

Are there any important benefits under Fascism?

Italian and German Fascism both made their first domestic gain by providing jobs for almost everyone, except those who dared oppose the regime. They banished unemployment—but by spending billions in the war industries, *not* by producing consumer goods. The Fascist dictatorships expended fortunes to impress their subjects—and extremely little to improve their individual existence. Splendid public buildings—yes. Railroad trains that ran on schedule—yes. Great new highways and *autobahns* (designed primarily for wartime use)—yes. Greater profits for certain industries—yes. In Italy the Fascists also made some important permanent improvements, such as aqueducts and irrigation projects in Sicily and the draining of the Pontine marshes. With a party-controlled press and radio, such improvements could be presented to the public in fantastically exaggerated terms. Fascism specialized in presenting a glittering façade. But the economic "good times" which it promised remained far more artificial than real.

While Fascism gave the Italian and German people employment, it also proceeded consistently to reduce their pay envelopes by an increasing variety of special taxes and party contributions. The apparent economic improvement became more superficial with each passing year. After being lifted slightly, the standard of living relapsed. Here and there certain gains were registered. The Italian Fascists organized children's colonies, and inaugurated social insurance, maternity leaves, and hospitalization.

These were creditable innovations. The workers lost their free unions, but in some respects they obtained more security than they had had. But the same workers received the privilege of paying much higher taxes and eating less food—as part of the cost of the glory of conquering Ethiopia and investing millions of dollars in the defeat of the Spanish Republic. The "benefits" of Fascism were decidedly ephemeral compared with the moral and material sacrifices the people were compelled to make.

But we must recognize, as Sonia Tamara points out, that both Italian and German Fascism had a very strong appeal to the youth —what might be called an antimaterialistic appeal. It was a kind of mysticism, presented as a national idealism. Time showed that it was based on lies and cynical opportunism, but it caught the imagination of young men and women, boys and girls, who sincerely loved their country. Both Hitler and Mussolini laid great emphasis on organizing the youth. They and their followers understood that a strongly idealistic molasses was needed. So the impressionable young were told that Fascism was above materialism; Fascism was an elevated, mystical expression of Italianism, or of Germanism. Rituals, oaths, parades, and other shrewd trappings were used to enhance this lofty conception—and millions of the youth passionately believed the lies they were told. Were they lies, entirely? Well, look at the loot which the Fascist champions of "antimaterialism" ended up with. They had used a diabolical idealistic window-dressing to make cannon fodder out of the cream of their countries' youth.

In the same fashion the Nazis, particularly, went about hoodwinking the great mass of workers. They created the great Strength-through-Joy organization (*Kraft durch Freude*), which provided free tours for laborers and their families all over Germany—and even into Scandinavia and Switzerland. These vacation trips for scores of thousands of workers were unquestionably beneficial as to health. They were very popular, and they had their good points. But as a demagogic device to lull the grumblings of the hard-driven laborers, and to further indoctrinate them with Fascist ideas, they were a remarkably successful investment. "Bread and Circuses" was the applied slogan of the Fascists, and Strength-through-Joy was an effective branch of the circus—so long as the Fascist regimes were on the up-grade. As the war came nearer, the "benefits" of Fascism were in notable decline. In 1939 neither Rome nor Berlin could produce evidence to show that Fascism had improved the general standard of living of their peoples. War blasted the entire false façade to bits.

Fascism won in Spain in the spring of 1939. After that Spain managed to remain neutral throughout the Second World War. It's true that Franco's Falangist regime inherited the destruction which its own rebellion had inflicted: damages and ruins which were very serious for a country as poor as Spain. Even so, Fascist Spain had virtually unrestricted trade with Italy and Germany through the greater part of five years. Her steel, copper, olive oil, and other products were essentials which could command high wartime prices. In addition Spanish ships were free to ply the seas, and the Madrid government benefited by some rather extraordinary concessions from the Allies. Thus, after nearly six years of absolute rule, what had Spanish Fascism done for Spain by the beginning of 1946?

In Fascist Spain the nobility, the landlords, the party members, and the rich in general still live lives of great luxury—while millions of the Spanish masses exist in semistarvation. The life of the average Russian under severe wartime rations was unquestionably much better than the lot of the Spanish peasants and workers. Numerous correspondents have reported the shocking facts about present-day Spain. De luxe restaurants in Madrid, San Sebastian, and other cities abound with a wide choice of delicacies. But Fascism does not provide one adequate meal a week for a majority of the Spanish people. This is not surprising, perhaps, since General Franco agreed in 1942 to pay Italy $50,000,000 worth of commodities over a 25-year period—as part payment for Mussolini's armed aid in Spain during the civil war: that direct Fascist intervention which Franco's propagandists denied for so long. And Hitler's bill was also being collected "in kind." But if Fascism offered anything to the common people, Falangist Spain still required years in which to begin demonstrating it.

In Madrid today a chambermaid still is paid about thirty cents a day. A Spanish workman earns $1 a day, or sometimes $1.40, and up to $2 if he is a skilled laborer. But a dozen eggs—even more than a year ago—cost exactly $1.40, or as much as a workman receives for a day's labor. A chicken, if available, costs approximately $1.00 a pound; thus a small chicken would consume at least three days' income of a workman. A cotton shirt in Franco's Spain costs the equivalent of five days' work for a common laborer. General living costs in Spain have increased roughly between 250 and 400 percent. In some categories wages have scarcely increased at all; in others no more than 70 percent. In 1944 a Spanish marquis sharply reproved a foreign friend for paying his servant $12 a month, saying that the figure had always been $7 a month, and to pay a servant more than that was "unthinkable." This is the mentality of feudalistic and Fascist Spain.

Pedro Gomez, a Spanish seaman who jumped ship in the United States in the spring of 1945, reported: "The workers are starving. They do not earn enough money to buy the food they need. I have seen young girls, of twelve or thirteen, trying to pick up men to get enough money to buy food. . . . Oh, yes—there is work, but only the Falangists get work. The Falangist trade unions alone give work. Anyone suspected of republican or Leftist sentiments cannot get work. The Falangists have taken over all the trade unions." This means there are no free unions; strikes are outlawed; there is no collective bargaining. Fascism selects the workers, and pays them what it pleases. The Syndicate fixes the wages and prices—and its members are all Falangists. Meanwhile government employees (who work for the system) are paid approximately ten times as much per day as the average worker.

These are merely a few samples of the basic economic facts about the "benefits" which Fascism—allegedly saving Spaniards from "the menace of Bolshevism"—has given the Spanish people. It is difficult to see how they could remain alive and in a more hungry, repressed, and hopeless state under any other system, whatever its name or credo.[2]

But we need not confine ourselves to Europe. We have ample opportunity to see how Fascism takes hold here in our own hemisphere, where the future of American democracy is definitely menaced by the rise of any Fascist movement.

[2] For an authoritative and objective record of Spain under Fascism, see Thomas J. Hamilton: *Appeasement's Child: The Franco Regime in Spain.*

Is there anything Fascist in the Argentine dictatorship promoted by Colonel Perón?

Since Argentina's military clique ended all pretense of popular government, we have had ample evidence that this was not just another typically Latin American "army grab." Throughout the recent war liberal and democratic newspapers were repeatedly suppressed, while openly Nazi-propaganda dailies were favored by the government. Fascist spies and Nazi-controlled enterprises functioned with impunity in Argentina. Franco's agents were equally favored. Secretary of State Cordell Hull's strong condemnation of antidemocratic activities tolerated (and aided) by the Buenos Aires government was based upon a long accumulation of ugly facts. We have also had such illuminating and detailed reports as *The Battle for Buenos Aires* by Sax Bradford and *Argentine Diary* by Ray Josephs, more recently the State Department's *Blue Book on Argentina*. The Argentine militarists' regime has been more than pro-Fascist. Under the shrewd manipulations of Colonel Juan Perón it has revealed unmistakable Fascist aspects.

In the end events forced Colonel Perón to drop part of his carefully manipulated mask. In October 1945 he was suddenly ousted from power, actually with the aid of a general. But in eight days Perón wriggled out of confinement and staged a sensational come-back. How did he manage this slick trick? Chiefly, thanks to three time-tried Fascist devices: by the help of his own "Gestapo," the federal police whom he had built up and indoctrinated with the aid of German Nazis; by disorderly street demonstrations in which Perón's well-subsidized minority labor group intimidated the populace; and by the complete connivance of the Buenos Aires police force, which Perón had personally increased from 10,000 to more than 30,000. *New York Times* Correspondent Arnaldo Cortesi, who has had a long acquaintance with Fascist tactics in Italy, reported:[3] "It was the police, in both Buenos Aires and the provinces, who determined the course of events by severely crushing all demonstrations against Colonel Perón and by favoring those in his support."

[3] *New York Times*, October 19, 1945.

On that critical day Perón's rowdy young hoodlums filtered into Buenos Aires from the suburbs and terrorized violently while the police watched without interference. The same thing happened in Italy in 1922; in Germany from 1928 to 1933. Of course, there was shooting; even machine guns were used. The Perónista Fascists, assaulting the offices of the democratic newspaper *Critica,* were unmolested for more than an hour. Then Perón's allies, the police, took sixty members of *Critica's* staff off to prison! In every sense this was organized Fascist terrorism. It was worked by a mob minority. Perón's so-called "laborites" were one third as numerous as the throng of Argentine citizens who had demonstrated against him and for democracy only a few days previous.

American reporters confirmed the fact that none of Argentina's legitimate labor unions participated in the uprising to put Perón back in power. The mob consisted solely of those "unions" which Colonel Perón had created or controlled. To buy up young nationalist hotheads, Perón had used a portion of a huge slush fund that he had accumulated in the previous two years. The Colonel, thoughtfully and significantly, had reserved for himself the ministry of labor in the first generals' cabinet. He reportedly possessed secret funds running into scores of millions of dollars. Much of this powerful financial support is believed to have come from sympathetic Argentine industrialists, including a good many wealthy German Nazis. After all, the Austrian armaments king, Fritz Mandl, had been doing extremely well in Argentina for several years; and he was only one among many pro-Germans. In Germany, Fritz Thyssen and other great industrialists had contributed their millions to supporting the Nazis. In Italy the Pirellis and many more had done the same for Mussolini. Fascism in Argentina is merely running true to form.

Soon after his remarkably successful *coup d'état* Colonel Perón made a revealing announcement. He would quit his fine residence in the aristocratic section of Buenos Aires and live thereafter in one of the city's lowliest workers' districts. The Colonel was out to get "elected" president by "buying up" or winning over the largest possible following among the poor—with the help of his powerful allies in the police. Since he also had most of the upper army officers in his pocket, Perón's chances were bright. But his tactics, once again, were typically Fascist: a combination of demagoguery, hard cash, and jingoistic nationalism—linked to the police and the army. As one reporter wrote privately from Buenos Aires: "The show is taken right out of the pages of *Mein Kampf*."

Shortly afterward came the next clear signal. Perón's followers began to indulge in violent anti-Semitism. Young Perónista hoodlums invaded the Jewish quarter of Argentina's capital, smashing Jewish-owned shops and beating up citizens of Jewish faith. Some yelled: "Neither Jews nor traitors will ever govern!" Again the Perón-controlled police failed to intervene, or to protect those who were attacked. They stood passively by while Jews were knocked to the ground and savagely kicked. This is probably the most shameful and dangerous outbreak of anti-Semitism that has ever occurred in the Western Hemisphere. Unmistakably it means that Fascism is now fighting to conquer South America. Less than two weeks after these events a most lamentable thing happened. The publication of one of the Argentine provincial bishoprics urged Catholics not to vote for candidates of the Democratic Union, formed to oppose Colonel Perón. The article stated that it was "a directive—not merely advice." [4]

There are other countries in Latin America where Fascist upshoots are alarmingly evident. Brazil, which is of extremely great strategic importance to the security of American democracy, is by no means immune. It will bear close watching for a long time. Bolivia, in the grip of an oppressive regime, is strongly influenced by developments in Argentina. And in Paraguay the army's chief of staff—a Colonel Bernardo Aranda—has published a sort of *Mein Kampf* of his own. Aranda's book has had virtually no publicity in the United States, but Paraguayan businessmen are deeply perturbed by his Fascistic pronouncements. Colonel Aranda demands that pacifism and hatred of war should be eliminated from Paraguayan education: that in peace "the only measures that count are those that will be useful in war." People, he declares, should be taught to be less individualistic. Aranda is another champion of Fascism in America. Paraguay, it happens, is

4 See Associated Press dispatch from Buenos Aires, *New York Times*, December 4, 1945.

just next door to Argentina. Thus a Fascist bloc of three or four
South American nations could emerge at almost any time—and
it would have the energetic support of Spain, so long as there is
anything less than a freely elected republic in Spain. For us to
assume, then, that Fascism was destroyed in Berlin would be to expose all of the Americas to a most powerful threat to our future
peace; most powerful because all the elements of *greatest potential power* are behind the Fascist-imitators in Latin American
countries.

When Argentina's late February (1946) election results were
finally announced the gravity of the new Fascist menace to Latin
America could no longer be ignored. Colonel Perón not only
had won the Presidency but his supporters captured two-thirds
of the seats in the Chamber of Deputies and all but two of the
thirty places in the Senate. Yet the democratic opposition had
polled only slightly less than half of the total votes cast. Could
one dare to assume that the millions of dollars which Perónistas
had used to "subsidize" Argentine laborers, a portion of the press
and most of the nation's police had not in reality decided the
elections? Or was it likely that the Argentine Army had remained
strictly neutral throughout? In any case only the most naive in
other lands would be deceived by Colonel Perón's initial efforts
to present a "moderate" face to the United States and other
democracies. In the Western Hemisphere a most dangerous and
cunning Fascism, led by a ruthless and ambitious man, is en-
trenching itself in Argentina. It will conspire to create an His-
panic-American Axis, and it will use every weapon and every
wile. Time will show, short of a miracle of early overthrowal,
that Perón's Fascism will find increasing sympathy and support
among North Americans. For us, then, there is greater need than
ever that we understand clearly what Fascism is, what it does
and whom it uses.

I do not think that any adequate discussion of Fascism can neglect this last point. We must take careful note of one thing.

Where does Fascism get its chief support?

Here, too, the record is indisputably plain. It required more
even than acute unemployment to put Mussolini and Hitler in

power. It required plenty of hard cash, such as Colonel Perón had at his disposal. The cash has always flowed into Fascist hands from the Pirellis and Thyssens—from conservative industrialists, aristocrats, and landowners who were most frightened by the Left parties or most plagued by the growing strength of labor unions. This, I believe, is one of the chief reasons why the Communists have never won a revolution in a predominantly industrial country. That fact seems to me of great significance. In industrialized nations like Italy and Germany the counter-revolutionists—however brutal and repugnant in their actions—have always won important financial aid from citizens of wealth who would rather lose political freedom than risk socialistic reforms.

I have never heard of any millionaires or huge corporations that secretly supplied Communist or Leftist movements with large amounts of money. The wealthy and the big business interests in any country would be pretty crazy if they did. But when a "Red menace" exists or is consistently promoted in any society, a very considerable amount of big money always gravitates to the organizers of Fascism. The Hitlers and Mussolinis are sure of ready cash if they ballyhoo Communist "threats" consistently. This is one reason why I cannot conceive that an American Communist movement can ever gain power—even by force—in the United States—unless we invite the supreme chaos which an atomic war would precipitate. The army, the police, *and* an enormous amount of American capital will always be marshaled against any extreme Left movement in the United States. Unless wealth has far greater perception in America than in most other countries, it would throw its weight behind an American Fascism —sincerely believing it the lesser of two evils, but really because the Fascists pose as protectors of big business, wealth, and property. To their ultimate sorrow, Fritz Thyssen and the others learned what Fascism does to capitalists in due time. Had they spent the same huge funds defending a free parliamentary system, they might well have saved most of their fortunes, as well as their honor.

But the Fascists have always made beautiful promises, and played their chief benefactors for suckers once they had them in their power. The Italian and German industrialists had their labor troubles solved, it's true. But in short order they were left without a glimmer of free enterprise. Their taxes were boosted tremendously. Their foreign markets were killed by Fascist policies—in any case, were under rigid state control. At every turn businessmen had to take orders from officious and arrogant Fascist bureaucrats, and expend large sums in endless bribes. They had been "saved from Bolshevism"—and look what they got! In the end most of their factories were also bombed-out ruins.

The *Encyclopædia Britannica* has a deserved reputation for historical accuracy. This is what it says about the way in which Fascism duped Italy's big businessmen:

From its start the fascist movement received substantial aid from Italian businessmen and landowners. . . . In the end too many condoned and even supported the fascist campaign of violence against the free trade unions and cooperatives, *in order to maintain their position of* economic privilege at the cost of political self-government. [Italics mine.]

But after the Fascists were firmly in power—

Italian businessmen learned that they, like the rest of the Italian population, were subject to the lawlessness and personal insecurity implicit in a totalitarian regime of arbitrary authority. . . . Personal insecurity permeated all social and individual relations, so private enterprise was exposed to serious dangers which constantly threatened its very existence.

For the German record we have such authoritative books as Douglas Miller's *You Can't Do Business With Hitler,* Wallace R. Deuel's *People under Hitler,* Edgar Ansel Mowrer's *Germany Turns the Clock Back,* and William Shirer's *Berlin Diary.* These and other documented reports will still bear rereading, for neither Fascism nor its most seductive tactics are dead.

In *The Fruits of Fascism* Herbert L. Matthews has also provided a mass of evidence of the kind that short-memoried democrats can so easily overlook today. "The way in which the authorities fought them [the Socialists] and favored the Fascists," Mr. Matthews says, "was typical of this period and symptomatic of a state of affairs which played an important part in fascism's success. The powerful element, the vested interests, the conservative classes, were all giving the fascists at least a tacit blessing." And in 1922 an Italian journalist, still free, reported of the Fascists: "The idea was to *create or to maintain chaos,* and then say, 'Only we can restore order. The country needs a strong government.' "

If we want democracy in the United States, or in our neighboring republics, we shall forget these things only at our extreme peril.

In summation let us see Fascism for what it is: supernationalist, breeder of violence, exploiter of fear, and disseminator of anti-Semitism and all other antiracial hatreds—opportunistic and aggressively demagogic. Fascism denies equality of treatment for citizens in any country. It is an implacable enemy of the rights of man. It appeals to mob emotions and brutal instincts. It knows no morality and has no spiritual motivation. Fascism is a merger of hatreds and fears, of ignorance and greeds, of chauvinism and an unquenchable thirst for power. All these primitive and anti-Christian instincts are latent in every human society. For this reason there can be no truce in humanity's struggle against Fascism. We cannot conquer the Fascist demon until we have conquered ourselves.

This is why Hitler could rightly hope for his final revenge *inside* American society. If Fascism should one day destroy our democracy, what greater triumph could Hitler have? The victors, ravaged by the political syphilis of their defeated enemies, would merely fulfill one of Hitler's prophecies. It is the nature of a democracy to be forever exposed to Fascist foxes that nibble at its vines. A free society presents precisely the opportunity for those abuses which may ultimately bring it down. In the United States today, anti-Semitism is greater than it was in Germany in 1928. Other racial and religious animosities run dangerously high. Millions of our soldiers have returned home in an extremely nationalistic mood. Labor and capital are engaged in bitter quarrels. Here, too, there exists a widespread fear of Communism—and scarcely any popular conception of how Fascism exploits that fear to its own destructive ends. Yes, we should do well to look in more than one direction if we hope to bring American democracy safely through the unpredictable crises of the next ten or twenty years. For it is on middle ground—not in either extreme—that democracy's safety and greater development can alone be found.

Chapter XI

THE WHAT AND WHY OF COMMUNISM

> *There are at the present time two great nations in the world . . . the Russians and the Americans. . . . Their starting point is different and their courses are not the same. Yet each of them seems marked out by the will of heaven to sway the destinies of half the globe.*
>
> *We both have much to do before we can afford to damn rather than help each other.*
>
> T. V. Smith

It's strange how many books about Soviet Russia you may read without once encountering in their pages any clear-cut definition of Communism. Ever since 1918 we have been up to our necks in a competition of Isms. Now we shall be up to our teeth in the Isms-argument for the rest of our days. Perhaps we shall find life a little less confusing if we try to be pretty specific about what we mean by what we are talking about. The Isms'll confound us—if we don't watch out.

I intend to write this chapter with my shirt buttoned—as well as on—with my head screwed on as tightly as possible, and without any rise in my blood-pressure. If I can be of any small help in evaluating some of the fundamentals of a very muddied and controversial subject, I suspect an approach of sober analysis will be my only salvation. But at the outset I shall lean rather heavily on Dr. Hans Kohn, professor of history at Smith College. Dr. Kohn must have a delightful sense of humor. In the *Encyclopedia Britannica* he launches his discussion of our topic with these words: "Communism, a term often loosely used—."

I stopped right there. Isn't that wonderful? . . . "Often loosely used!" How true, how true. For haven't most of us bandied about the word Communism pretty loosely at one time or another? I'm sorry to admit that I have. I am still shamefaced about one case in particular. Under the pressure of writing a book during a very short leave between war zones (*No Other Road to Freedom,* 1941), I described the Hitler regime as "Brown Bolshevism." It was a facile phrase, but it was both misleading and inaccurate. As I look back, it was an inexcusably confusing expression to use, but it now serves as a reminder that a weakness for alliteration is a dangerous luxury when one is dealing with such serious subjects as Isms. And here was the good professor inadvertently pointing his finger straight at me—and quite a good many others, sadly enough.

"Communism," in Dr. Kohn's definition, is "a term often loosely used to denote different systems of social organization aiming at common property of the means of production—or at equal distribution of wealth and income, or both." My *Macmillan's Modern Dictionary* defines it as a "system of society in which property is held in common." But Dr. Kohn makes a further helpful observation: that in recent times the word *Communism* has been narrowed down to denote that interpretation of Marxian doctrine proposed by Lenin when he came to power in Russia. Dr. Kohn then makes clear a very important distinction, which so many critics ignore when they most loosely describe almost anything left of center, politically, as "socialistic" or "communistic." Here is the distinction: "While socialism puts its faith in an *evolutionary* development and in *democratic* means of attaining the liberation of all men from economic servitude [italics mine], communism regarded revolution and an ensuing dictatorship of the proletariat as a necessary period of transition to the future free and equalitarian society. . . ."

Thus, at the outset, we must understand that Socialism represents a democratic, parliamentarian program to achieve state ownership of the means of production; that Communism, by its original theory, advocates revolutionary and dictatorial methods to reach finally a similar end. In the years since Russia's great October Revolution it has become a general practice to regard Communism and the Soviet system as one and the same thing. That's where most of us, at one time or another, first begin to become confused about Soviet Russia. For there is no such thing as pure ideological Communism in the U.S.S.R. today; and there are even a good many authorities who are convinced there never will be.

With this statement you may interject a question:

Why does Soviet Russia not have Communism at present?

The answer is that Lenin, almost as soon as the Revolution was consolidated, was forced to compromise in the face of enormous difficulties. His compromise came in 1921 in the shape of the New Economic Policy, soon famous under the name of NEP. In a Russia ravaged by war, revolution, and civil war, economic disintegration and paralysis was too formidable. The Marxist theory, despite its glittering goal of "equal distribution of wealth or income," simply could not be imposed under such conditions. Lenin saw that the Bolsheviks must make frank concessions to personal incentive: to that central governing motive which all capitalists regard as the essential spur to economic progress, and usually describe as "the profit motive." With NEP, Communism in Russia lost much of its inner essence. It became a future goal; a system to be evolved, and achieved when—or if—it could be afforded. As Walter Duranty has said,[1] the New Economic Policy "marked not only the abandonment of Militant Communism but a distinct regression, as Lenin admitted, to non-socialist methods."

From 1921, through the various five-year plans and to the present time, Soviet Russia has remained in no sense purely communistic. As in capitalist countries wages and salaries are paid on sliding scales, according to the efficiency of work performed and the responsibility of the individual post. Thus in wartime Russia an unskilled laborer might earn approximately 700 rubles per month, a first-class workman perhaps more than 1,000 rubles per month, and a young engineer or executive perhaps 2,600 rubles per month. An outstanding Soviet ballerina or journalist might enjoy an income of more than 12,000 rubles each month.[2] In Soviet factories the differences in income be-

---

[1] *U.S.S.R.: The Story of Soviet Russia,* Chapter V.

[2] The official exchange rate of the ruble has been kept pegged at 5 rubles to $1. This, however, is so artificial that it has no meaning whatever. When I was in war-

tween the manager, the various executives and specialists, and the common laborer are inevitably very considerable. The strict Marxist theory has no relation to this whatever. In its most central economic aspect there is, as yet, no Communism in so-called "Communist Russia." Private ownership of homes and small garden plots exists in the U.S.S.R. as in the U.S.A. As yet, it is merely not so widespread nor on so high a level of modernization.

What remains in the Soviet system is state ownership of all important means of production, accompanied by a widespread collective farm system. These innovations could be made as easily by the British Socialists as by the Soviet "Communists." In fact, the British Labor Party is now inaugurating a good many of these reforms—by free debate and a free vote in Parliament. Simultaneously the British are retaining a great deal of free enterprise. But in much more socialistic Russia free enterprise has been reduced to an absolute minimum. For this reason the Soviet Union was, during the Second World War, probably the only nation whose citizens could not and did not reap any private war profits. That, I think, is a phenomenon worthy of some reflection. For one, I should feel much happier if all profits and wages in the United States had been rigidly frozen from the day that our country entered the war. It also seems to me self-evident that modern nations cannot continue to indulge in more war, and retain the utterly unfair and lopsided privilege of war profits for those who do not fight or die. If that sounds communistic, make the most of it. To me—when I look around me in America today and think of some 300,000 Americans who died in uniform —it is elementary morality.

It is true, then, to say that the Soviet Union—if by no means Communist—is sufficiently Socialist so that Soviet labor did not receive vastly swollen wages during the war and that there were no private corporations or stockholders to reap unprecedented surpluses and profits after taxes. This is one way of making plain

---

time Russia in 1942 some foreigners, on the basis of prices and living costs, estimated that the exchange ought to be at least 60 rubles to $1, and some insisted that a rate of 80 rubles to $1 would be fairer. I do not know of any reliable and fair assessment of living costs by which a Russian workman's monthly wage can be transposed into American dollars. One can only say that a first-class Soviet worker, earning 1,000 rubles per month, had to spend all but a minute portion of his income for food, rent, and other bare necessities—at least until the war's end.

what Russia *has* got without getting Communism. It is extremely important, even if generally overlooked in Western democracies. But, of course, it is only one feature of a very large canvas. To get a fairer perspective there are many things about the Soviet system which must be borne in mind. Let us first list those limitations or abuses of which most democrats are most clearly conscious.

What are the outstanding antidemocratic elements in the present socialistic Soviet system?

Because these characteristics are most obvious to us Westerners, they are most easily identified. The bitter critics of the Soviet system base their unqualified rejection of it upon such factors as these. Soviet "Communism" is a totalitarian state, governed by a rigid and all-powerful one-party dictatorship. It tolerates no freedom of speech and of the press as we know them in western countries. It is a "police state" in which the secret police (NKVD) dominates and controls the entire population. Arrest without writ and detention without trial severely limit the civic liberties of its citizens.

(While the Bolshevik Revolution was being consolidated, after a most bitter civil war, the Soviet state obviously had to protect its still exposed internal situation through rigid supervision both by the army and by the secret police. Eventually the OGPU was replaced by the NKVD—a change of letters rather than of method and organization. The Soviet secret police are still ever-present, and in many respects all-powerful, throughout the U.S.S.R. The continued scope and importance of their role has had two unfortunate results. Critics of everything Soviet Russian point to the secret police as a ruthless and flagrantly oppressive organization, and they can often cite personal tragedies and abuses of elemental private rights to support their charges. In addition, many emerge from the U.S.S.R. testifying that public fear of the NKVD is very widespread there. The reports about displaced Russian citizens, in Poland or Germany, who made desperate efforts to avoid being returned to the Soviet Union have not decreased foreign criticism of its secret-police system.

It is undoubtedly true that a relaxation of police controls, and the expansion of civilian liberties of action and expression, would be warmly welcomed by most Soviet citizens. It would also remove one of the most important sources of criticism and friction between the U.S.S.R. and its wartime allies.)

The Soviet system necessitates a great and powerful bureaucracy in all departments of its governmental administration. Besides eliminating free enterprises it places many serious limitations on personal initiative. All these pronounced restrictions upon individual freedom and self-expression are real and highly important. Very few inhabitants of Western democracies would prefer to live in a society dominated by these restrictions.

In addition, the emphatic or passionate critics of the Soviet system denounce it for its early revolutionary excesses; its original antireligious policies; its liquidation of the *kulaks;* its ruthless purges of the higher ranks of the party; the vast loss of life that resulted from the famines and the imposition of farm collectivization. In Soviet Russia these were all features of a sharp break with the past. Many of them were also characteristics of the first and violent phase of successful revolution and revolutionary reform. The cost, in human lives and in suffering, has been enormous; almost inestimable. So, in its time, was the cost of the French Revolution to the French people—beginning especially with the more privileged classes. In any just appraisal this cost cannot be overlooked. But any attempt at just appraisal should also take note, I believe, of what history has demonstrated repeatedly. In any revolution large numbers of innocent people inevitably pay a fearful price for fearful wrongs inflicted upon previous generations. No great or important revolution has ever avoided the imposition of this cumulative, overdue price which society exacts in order that its members may make a fresh start.

I say this because we humans, in every land, often pursue a blind course which finally makes us the chief victims of our own neglected opportunities, or our own lack of perception. Count Carlo Sforza's warning words bear repeating: "It is strange how frequently in history revolutions and disorders are promoted by people who believe themselves to be conservative." The aristocrats around the Bourbon kings of France did this very thing. In our day I saw the most favored of the subjects of Alfonso XIII do precisely this in Spain. In the Czar's Russia the ruling classes, more than any others, "bought" the Bolshevik Revolution and made its extremism unavoidable. I insert these reminders because so few Americans seem to look at Soviet Russia with any regard for those Old Russian factors which, in reality, *made* the Bolshevik Revolution. It is as if we started studying our American Revolution with the shots fired at Lexington, and completely disregarded the cumulative pressure of British misrule which—in the end—actually pressed the triggers of the Massachusetts rebels.

After more than a century and a half we have begun to be somewhat objective about our own Revolution, even to a healthy debunking of some of the objectionable fairy tales which had been built up on our side against the British. But to be equally objective about any great revolution which, in *our* day, shakes the ground beneath our feet—this is a most difficult thing for human beings to achieve. Any revolution breeds partisanship. We, who live in one of history's greatest revolutionary epochs, can always see today's crimes or abuses far more easily than tomorrow's long-term gains. Thus, we are naturally much more sensitive to the Russian Revolution's excesses than to whatever constructive results it may already have brought in its tragic train.

The "ten days which shook the world" have made an indelible impression upon most of mankind. We remember the immediate consequences of that stupendous October upheaval almost as survivors remember an earthquake. Certain impressions are profoundly fixed. This is why most of us, perhaps, tend to regard what has since happened in the Soviet Union as "fixed" in fundamental ways and tendencies. Yet a revolution—as Mexico and China both so well illustrate when we review their past eventful thirty-odd years—descends from its fierce, blood-streaming crest, and gradually flows away and onward in a broadening flood of *evolutionary* processes. This, too, has been happening in Russia. The end of antireligious propaganda, the new official recognition of the Russian Orthodox Church, the sharp reversal from free-love tendencies to a strong emphasis upon the sanctity of the family, the remarkable rise of nationalism in the U.S.S.R.

in the past few years—all these are phenomena of the pronounced evolution in Soviet policies and thought. To this observer they dictate one imperative necessity. We cannot accurately judge the New Soviet Union of today by what it was in 1923, in 1931, or even in 1940. To do this—in all accuracy—would be like judging the United States today in terms of the American scene of 1885 or 1900.

This fact, however, is actually an advantage to you and me—provided we are inclined to take advantage of it. For the coming-of-age of the Soviet experiment, as shown clearly in these recent war years, at last gives us an opportunity to reach an estimate based upon an enlarged perspective. While remembering the revolutionary costs in Russia we *should* be much better situated to take stock of the gains.

What are some of the great gains of the Soviet Revolution?

I should be strongly tempted to place the mass education of nearly 200,000,000 people, as discussed broadly in Chapter IV, as foremost of them all. Obviously the distinctly improved standards of living throughout most sections of the Soviet republics also mark a very important advance. The tremendous progress in industrialization, with its coincident creation of trained or skilled labor running into many millions, is another great historic gain. Most Americans today, I think, would admit that the following statement of fact (culled from Foreign Commissar Molotov's 28th anniversary speech) represents an accomplishment of considerable magnitude. "We have no more unemployment, and shall not have any," Molotov said. "In our country there is work for all." This, too, comes as part of the cost of freedoms which are rightly prized in our American democracy; but a job for every healthy citizen is not despised in any part of our postwar world.

Under the Soviets, libraries and certain community services have been greatly increased. New standards of sanitation and vastly improved housing facilities characterize thousands of collective farms, and are available to a great many industrial workers. Maternity leaves and special aids for all women workers are provided by law. Communal kindergartens for the children of factory-employed mothers exist in great and increasing numbers. All health services are free to all the people. Many thousands of clinics have been established in every corner of the U.S.S.R., and the prevention of illness is a state responsibility pursued on a constantly expanding scale. At the *New York Herald Tribune's* annual forum in October 1945, Dr. Henry E. Sigerist of Johns Hopkins commented on the medical centers which Henry J. Kaiser had installed in his shipyards during the war. Dr. Sigerist, who has spent three summers in Russia, said the health services "that are practiced on a small scale in the Kaiser shipyards are of the same type as those that the Soviet Union has been practicing on a nation-wide scale for over twenty-five years." In 1941, Dr. Sigerist reported, the U.S.S.R. possessed 13,461 urban medical centers, 13,512 rural medical centers, and about 35,000 smaller rural medical stations.

One of the things that impressed me most in wartime Russia was the tremendous role that women played, not only in military organizations but in every phase of industrial, professional, agricultural, and civic life. I do not believe there was another Allied country (and I speak from personal observation in these lands between 1939 and 1945) where women contributed so decisively to their nation's war effort. The more I observed the Soviet scene the more I became aware that Russian-Soviet women have stepped forward into a much enlarged influence and importance. Curiously enough, Russian women have also acquired certain striking similarities to their American sisters. They, too, are self-confident, energetic, unabashed—and rather prone to have their own way and to demand their full quota of masculine attention.

Of course, history indicates that the Russian female was never exactly a suppressed creature within the limits of her own social status. Old Russia even had a remarkable quota of empresses, and her literature abounds with strong feminine characters. I gather, and some shrewd observers of Russian society of other centuries bear me out, that the Russian woman on the average has never been any shrinking violet. Under the late Czars she had already won a good many privileges—at any rate in the educated minority of the upper classes. But the Revolution opened wide the doorway of opportunity for the humblest daughters of peasants and workers everywhere. Accordingly, you find the Soviet generation of women literally doing almost everything. They have swarmed into the professions, and constitute more than 50 percent of all Soviet physicians today. They are railroad engineers, or first mates or even captains of cargo boats on the Volga. They are agricultural specialists, geologists, chemists, or what have you. Many millions of them are industrial workers or collective farmers. What you sense today in Russia is that her women consider themselves as aggressively important a force in the national destiny as the men. Far more Soviet women are educated and skilled specialists than is the case in any of the Balkan countries; and in larger percentage and with freer scope than is true even in France or Belgium.

Under the Czars 80 percent of Russian women were peasants or servants. By 1937 in Soviet Russia 88 percent of such women were employed in offices and industries, in intellectual professions and state trade enterprises. Less than 2 percent were household servants, while 45 percent of university students and some 15 percent of engineers and technicians were women.[3] What to me is most striking about this tremendous change is the fact that in Fascist countries women have never been raised to any such new level of activity as this. Under Italian Fascism the gains of women were very moderate, if not nonexistent; in no sense widespread. Under Hitler's Nazism a "man's state" was frankly decreed. Women were breeding animals for Fascism and virtual servants, and were supposed to glory in it. The *Küche, Kinder, und Kirche* (kitchen, children, and church) of the Kaiser's day was restored as a slogan—with scant stress on the church. As Wallace R. Deuel has recorded in detail,[4] women's role was definitely oriental. They were barred from the Reichstag and their access to public office was made almost impossible. At a meeting of the Supreme Soviet I was attracted by the variety of feminine costumes. There were scores of women delegates—possibly several hundred—of many different nationalities. If they did not debate in the fashion of our feminine Congressmen, nevertheless *they were there*.

Somehow it seems to me that what Fascism does to women

[3] See William Henry Chamberlain: *The Russian Enigma*, p. 105.
[4] *People under Hitler*, Chapter VIII.

has received very much less attention in Western democracies than it deserves and requires. It is a universal attribute of Fascism that it relegates women to a cramped and rigidly inferior position in society. It not only repudiates any liberation of women in a twentieth-century sense; it takes pride in dominating women and confining them to a narrow and often stultifying, or even debasing, role. The "Communist" Soviet system has not made this great error. It has enlisted women as equals, and has given them unprecedented opportunities and exceptional responsibilities. The Russian woman today, in one short generation, seems to take these great advantages for granted; but she would never tolerate being nothing but a home-body again. If she saw women in Italy or Spain she would be amazed at their docility.

These paragraphs represent no more than a rough balance sheet in which, on the credit side, are listed some of the essential gains which stand opposite the frightful costs of the Russian Revolution. Once again, these impressive social advances have been purchased through the deaths and suffering of millions of people. They are held today at a continuing cost in many freedoms which are indispensable to us. But despite the large and sometimes oppressive debit column, the fact remains that the Soviet nation today has won tremendous progress from where it started in 1917—and has become the second most powerful nation on earth. In this federation racial equality and cultural equality are by no means the least of its humanitarian achievements. And when we have even listed these great essential gains we must be struck by the fact that Fascism could not, at the peak of its power, in either Italy or Germany, begin to point to attainments of an equal validity and stature. Mussolini and Hitler certainly possessed equal power. Could it be that their ideological scorn of all humanitarian values had something to do with the bankruptcy of their results?

But surely, you will rightly interpellate, there is little or no democracy as we understand it in the Soviet Union. There you find the same sort of one-party dictatorship, a similarly dominant secret police system, the same rigid control of press, radio, and speech as existed in the Fascist states. The Soviet government and system is probably more totalitarian than any others in the world today. And you would put the further question:

Is there, after all, any important difference between Fascism and Soviet "Communism"?

Upon careful examination, I am convinced we shall remark more than one important distinction. I have mentioned several already: the far more widespread—and freely available—educational opportunities in the Soviet Union; a more definite and more permanent lifting of the living standards of the great mass of the people than Fascism ever achieved in Italy or Germany; the pronounced emancipation, rather than the subjugation, of women. But the chief difference between Fascism and the Soviet system (or the Communist idea) goes much deeper than this, and is not merely structural or a matter of practical application.

However much we may dislike the conception of a "dictatorship of the proletariat," or any kind of totalitarianism, the fact remains that Marxism of any variety rests upon an unquestionably humanitarian ideal. "From each according to his ability, to each according to his needs" may be utterly impossible of attainment in any human society. Nevertheless, this idea is motivated by a recognition of the intrinsic brotherhood of man; by a desire to develop the generosity of human beings; by the profession of a goal of a greater justice in human society. Beside these fundamental conceptions, the Fascists' glorification of a "master race," their preachments of violence for its own sake and of bitter racial hatreds, sink to the lowest levels of primitive barbarism. However painful and slow the task has been, the Soviet Marxists have kept their eyes on the welfare and ultimate progress of the common man. It does not seem to me that this can be dismissed as nothing but materialism. If that were true, then the United States—with its incessant striving toward an ever-higher standard of living, and its unveiled pride in its unique progress—must be regarded as the most materialistic nation on earth. Fortunately there is also a spiritual quality in the American way of life. Despite the Russian Revolution's costly excesses and its elimination of many personal freedoms, it is still true that there is a spiritual factor which inspires Soviet partisans toward their goal. By contrast with Fascism, there is an ideal—and an idea.

Without this inner meaning and broader human view it seems to me indubitable that the Soviet Union could never have retained the loyal support of its people under the impact of a German invasion which swept to the edge of their capital, and nearly 1,000 miles deep into their territory. Without the basically humanitarian conception behind the October Revolution it would never have stirred the hearts, and fired the imaginations, of scores of millions of humble people—from Korea to India, from Poland to Peru and Tierra del Fuego.

It is worth remarking and remembering that the Italian and Nazi counterrevolutions *never spelled hope* to the common people in foreign lands. The Fascist ideology never enlisted imitators who championed human rights. On the contrary, the Fascists won the support of the Quislings and Joseph Darnands; of lickspittles and despicable persons who sold their countries for their own ease and profit. Mussolini's and Hitler's revolutions never shook the world through the impact of an idea, but only by the eventual and passing power of their guns and their implements of conquest.

I am aware that some Americans, perhaps many, would deny the existence of any idealism whatever behind Soviet Marxism. But is not this emotionalism rather than analysis? Why, indeed, has the idea of Communism spread and grown until Indonesian natives in remote islands ask themselves if this may not offer hope to them? It seems to me self-evident that the chief reason why Communism so greatly worries many of us, who are democrats or capitalists, is precisely that we recognize subconsciously that this is the challenge of an idea linked to an ideal. If it had not had within it a concept of human betterment it would never have inflamed imaginations in every corner of the world. This is not to say that Soviet Russia has yet adequately fulfilled the humanitarian promise in its ideology. It is not to assume for a moment that greater steps toward society's improvement and progress could not also be achieved, if we Westerners were to make democracy more enlightened and more economically democratic. It is merely to assert that the ideals of Jefferson, and of the notable British and French democratic thinkers, at last have a great and serious competitor in the realm of human aspirations.

Professor T. V. Smith will be challenged by very few of his colleagues in philosophy and history for saying: "To begin with, Russia and we share a great revolutionary tradition. The Russian Revolution, like the French and the American, belongs to those that spring from love of mankind, as contrasted with Fascist and Nazi revolutions which proceed from hate. These Revolutions of the uplifted vision share the great ideals of liberty, equality and fraternity." Then Professor Smith makes a penetrating observation: "We Americans have specialized, as it were, on liberty; whereas the Russians have emphasized fraternity. Each has perhaps overdone its part; certainly has underdone the other's part." This, in concise form, is a great truth.

Those who have informed themselves thoroughly on Lenin, his career and speeches, recognize the sincerity of the idealism which inspired him. William Henry Chamberlain expresses it in this way: [5]

No shadow of scepticism ever clouded his white-hot conviction that in fighting for the overthrow of capitalism he was fighting for the higher good of humanity. Impersonal faith that he was marching with the progressive forces of history replaced, for Lenin, that strong sense of divine mission that helped to sustain a Cromwell and a Luther.

In the Soviet Union today there are nearly 6,000,000 members of the Communist Party—more than 2,000,000 of these admitted during the war.[6] But there are also some 12,000,000 to 14,000,000 *Komsomols,* or junior Communists; and another 14,000,000 or more "Young Pioneers" between the ages of eight and fifteen. From these two large younger groups come the future members of the Soviet Communist Party. In their ranks, as foreign correspondents have learned from personal contacts, the predominant characteristics are an extraordinary faith in the Marxist ideal and great patriotism. A very large proportion of Soviet Communists have the same conviction as Lenin had: that their state is struggling "for the higher good of humanity." It was almost impossible to find an Italian or German Fascist who ever had this idea, or made any pretense to having it.

[5] *Op. cit.,* p. 81.
[6] See *New York Herald Tribune,* Moscow dispatch by Joseph Barnes, November 14, 1945.

But what about Joseph Stalin? Is he merely a cynical opportunist who loves enormous power? That, of course, will be debated by some for decades. Yet this is not at all the predominant impression that Stalin has made on most foreigners who have talked with him. Once, when Walter Duranty showed him a copy of a dispatch he planned to file to New York, an interesting thing happened. Duranty had referred to Stalin as the "inheritor of Lenin's mantle." Stalin scratched out that phrase and wrote in its place: "Lenin's most faithful disciple and the prolonger of his work." [7] You may or may not believe that Stalin meant what he wrote. I believe that he meant every word of it, even though powerful circumstances have sometimes forced him farther from the Communist ideal. But whether the Soviet Union will ever be able to evolve back to a more purely Communist reality is open, at least, to serious question for the next twenty or thirty years. Circumstances can also be most powerful dictators.

We should also remark and remember one more thing about Soviet Russia. Unlike the Fascist regimes, it has an officially fixed goal of increased civic and political liberation for its peoples. This is another fundamental difference from Fascism, which never pretended that any except its own "élite" should ever enjoy full privileges. Communism, as Dr. Hans Kohn underlines, "regards dictatorship as a transitional institution, and full democracy as the goal," while Fascism believes in "the unalterable and beneficial *inequality* of men and races." The Soviets still have very far to go if they are to achieve a reasonably complete democracy. But they also still have a great deal of educational lifting to do. When the Soviet Union has at least two highly literate generations, what will happen? Will there be as little democratic freedom, in the Western sense, as today?

It so happens that Lenin foresaw this situation with amazing clarity years ago, and that he faced it frankly in an interview with an American correspondent.

[7] *Op. cit.,* p. 171.

What effect did Lenin think the education of the Soviet masses would have upon the Soviet dictatorship?

This question is highly important and its answer is most revealing. It is regrettable that Lenin's answer has not been widely known. I am indebted to Miss Bessie Beatty for this information, and I report it here with her kind permission.

During and after the Bolshevik Revolution, Bessie Beatty was a correspondent for the Associated Press in Russia. In 1920 or 1921 she had a lengthy conversation with Lenin. Suddenly the leader of the October Revolution asked her:

"What do they think of us in America?"

"They say that yours is a dictatorship and it's as bad as the Czar's," replied Miss Beatty courageously.

Lenin did not wince. He paused reflectively for a brief moment. Then Lenin said:

"That's true—with one exception. The Czars had a deliberate policy of noneducation, on the theory that you could control the people more easily if you kept them in ignorance. We Bolsheviks have a *deliberate policy of education. And no educated people will long tolerate a dictatorship. Therefore, we have in our dictatorship the seeds of its own destruction.*" (Italics mine.)

Seeing clearly that mass education would create eventually "the seeds of destruction" of the Soviet proletarian dictatorship, Lenin—without hesitation or compromise—made the progressive liquidation of mass illiteracy and the steady broadening of higher education a key plank in the Soviet Communist program. That is not the mark of a man without humanitarian ideals. It is certainly not the mark of a dictator who is at heart afraid of the people. Definitely, it is the mark of a great leader with rare insight and a long view piercing forward at least half a century. It is *not* an accident that those Western nations which possess the highest levels of education in the world—whether the Scandinavian countries, Holland, Belgium, France, Britain, or the United States—have survived two gigantic world conflicts with their democratic institutions intact. The average level of education made all these peoples cling to their democratic liberties.

In the Soviet Union education marches on, avidly and energetically. The evolution in Russian "Communism" proceeds with it. It may be that what Lenin told Bessie Beatty will materialize in the Soviet Union before the end of this century. That the Soviet peoples will eventually change their one-party dictatorship to new and greater freedoms cannot, it seems to me, be doubted. The seeds of that final evolution are indeed there—planted by Lenin himself.

Chapter XII

WHAT TO DO ABOUT COMMUNISTS?

What I don't like," says George Jones, "is the way those Communists are cropping up all over the world. If the Russians prefer their system, and want to kid themselves that it's democratic, that's all right with me. But these Communist parties all over Europe and in China and South America—yes, and right here in the United States—what do they want to spread all around like that for, if they don't mean revolution? It's pretty plain they take their orders from Moscow. Well, I don't like the way they operate. Let the Russians keep their Russian ideas to home. Anyhow this Communist business sounds un-American to me. All those fellows do is stir up a lot of trouble."

You can sympathize with George's impatience because the Communists have become pretty much of a universal political and social headache. The Communists use the privileges of a capitalist democracy to keep reminding us of all the things which they insist are wrong or unworkable in that system. They are the naughty boys who are always making annoying or embarrassing remarks. George Jones says that, as far as he's concerned, they're a perpetual nuisance; and why we have to put up with their outlandish notions is more than he can see. All of which reminds me of an old French saying: The more things change, the more they are the same.

In the late 1700's the American colonists and the French people got taken with a consuming idea—about equality and the rights of man. In the furnace of revolution they gave this idea the indestructible quality of steel. In those days neither the American democrats nor the French republicans made any organized efforts to spread their idea in other countries. But the moving pen had written. The words had been spoken. The idea leapt from mind to mind, and there were no frontier guards who could conceivably intercept it. Today we tend to forget what devastating and revolutionary consequences the *idea,* spawned in the American and French revolutions, had in countries far removed from the place of its germination. Through much of the nineteenth century Europe's monarchs and ruling classes were as terrified of this "unspeakable democratic-republican idea" as a great many of us in our times are fearful of the Communist idea. Kings and dukes and feudal landlords in many European countries united, politically or spiritually, to defend themselves against that foreign "ism" which had sprung from Philadelphia and Paris. Here was an upstart and vulgar challenger to their traditional privileges and their own "inalienable rights." Great coalitions were formed between emperors and czars. Wars were fought. The French republic was overthrown, only to return again—and then a third time. In less than one hundred years parliamentary democracy was more strongly entrenched in western Europe than ever before; and inside even the Austro-Hungarian, Russian, and Prussian empires party systems and parliamentary procedures had struck new roots directly traceable to the "subversive" influence of the French and American revolutions.

Then, in the latter nineteenth century, Karl Marx wrote a book and published a manifesto which proclaimed another momentous idea. Marx insisted that capitalism was as vulnerable and mortal as the system of feudal monarchies had ever been. He held that the class struggle is inevitable in the capitalist system. He contended that a society's class structure, politically and socially, tended to lag seriously behind economic changes; and in the end, he maintained, this serious and accentuating lack of balance would be readjusted by revolution. Inevitably the Marxian theories, with their new emphasis upon the *economic* rights of man, won an increasing hearing among the workers and the most exploited classes of Europe. The idea, once more, was out of Pandora's box. It spread almost as swiftly as Franco-American democratic ideas had spread some seventy-five years earlier. Thirty-four years after Marx's death the Bolshevik Revolution brought the first great opportunity for his theories to be tried out on a vast scale. The Marxist idea became the greatest and most challenging new force of the twentieth century.

So, as we wrestle with the problems of peace after humanity's greatest war, we find a new Europe in which Socialism and Communism have not only become fully mature as great politico-economic forces. We find a new Europe in which Socialism and Communism are, in varying degrees, two of the most powerful forces; and a new world in which the converts to one or the other must be expected to grow steadily. These similar philosophies, with their different conceptions of the means toward a common end, constitute a tremendous challenge to accustomed ways of thinking in capitalist or democratic countries. They deny that *laissez-faire*, go-as-it-will capitalism can avoid catastrophic, periodic depressions which must eventually—their adherents believe —prove fatal to the system. The Marxists are not only unafraid of change; they demand serious fundamental changes. They insist that *economic* democracy must be achieved before any society can become truly democratic; they stubbornly maintain that their solution is the only one that will meet the requirements of our supermechanized age. When you cross verbal swords with them you find they are usually expert logicians. Paraphrasing the remark a Yankee teamster once made to my father: "They may or may not be very smart—but they *know history*."

Thus, if we are going to face the hard facts of twentieth-century existence, we must begin by recognizing that—

There will always be Socialists and Communists.

Terrible though this thought may be to the kings of industry in Western nations, and especially to the very large number of American conservatives, we shall always have Socialists and Communists with us for the rest of our own and our children's days. We may call them "Reds" or "radicals" or "Bolsheviks," but we shall never find any combination of words or gestures that will spirit the Marxists out of existence. It won't help to blame the Russians because—even if there had been no Russian Revolution—the theories of Marx and Engels would still have millions of followers today. Dr. Einstein also once had an idea. When ideas are important they become immortal from birth.

So this may be an appropriate time for you and me and the George Joneses to bear in mind what inadequate success we had when we concentrated on destroying the Fascist conception by force of arms alone. We could shoot and bomb everything—*except* the Fascist mentality. We could kill Germans, Italians, and Japs galore, but we could not kill Fascism. Now, after victory, we can combat the strong Fascist tendencies in our society only with more perceptive education, with a much greater development of our spiritual values, with an enlarged sense of justice and human brotherhood—in short, with *more democracy*. Against even the sub-idea of Fascism, armies, navies, and air forces can never win a permanent victory.

The other night I heard a speaker remark that some Americans "are against war—except with Soviet Russia." Of course, you and I know people like that. But supposing our leaders were to become so reckless as to decide that we must fight Russia "in order to stamp out Communism." That would mean nothing less than *the* Atomic War. Even if we could win, most of our cities and one third or more of America's population would be destroyed. Let us pause to consider the ghastly conditions and the social disintegration which would then exist in the United States and in every important country of Europe and Asia. Would the dazed, half-starved, embittered survivors in all these lands—in the aftermath of an atomic Doomsday—be much less disposed to accept Communism than they were before? I wonder. That, at any rate, has clearly not been the consequence of this war among European peoples. It would seem to me far more likely—if not inevitable—that a few hundred or thousand atomic bombs would produce a world dictatorship; and most probably some form of communistic world dictatorship. Capitalism and democracy would be the first victims of such a war. Why? Because Western survivors would hold capitalism and democracy as chiefly responsible for having failed to prevent such a holocaust. The survivors could see no future safety except in an international society—and the strongest *international* political and economic idea in today's world is the Marxist idea. Atomic bombs might devastate half the globe, but they could never destroy that idea.

We may as well face the fact, then, that both Communism and Socialism are international ideas; and that this is one of their deepest sources of strength. Religious creeds are also international and that, as Catholicism demonstrates, is the great source of their strength. It is no accident, either, that Communists usually have the crusading spirit of religious zealots. However abhorrent the notion may be to some of us, to most Communists their philosophy is based upon the ideal of a larger measure of the brotherhood of man. We may justly say that certain most elemental freedoms do not exist in Soviet Russia today. We may remain skeptical that Communism can ever be attained or create a truly classless society. But however well-founded such objections may prove, in this century and longer there will always be Communists because theirs is an international idea which champions a broad community of aims and desires among human beings.

But the great majority of us Western democrats believe that democracy could, and should, offer much more in freedom, justice, brotherhood, and international co-operation than Communism as yet seems to offer. In this I agree that democracy *should*—IF we made an intelligent and co-ordinated attempt to win the world's masses to democratic processes; IF our governments would bend their greatest efforts to encourage and build democracy abroad; IF you and I were as willing to serve our democratic ideals and ideas as devotedly and unrelentingly as the Communists serve theirs. As you look about you in the democracies you do not see much evidence that any of these things is very likely to happen. Thus it is easy for many of us to become frightened and embittered toward others who seem willing to give more and do more, on the average, than we are willing to give or do, on the average, for the way of life which we profess to cherish. In this mood of fear or anger we make sharp charges against the Communists; some of them true and others clouded by emotionalism. One of these popular accusations is that—

The Communists organize in every country.

Please bear in mind that I am not conducting a defense for the accused. I am looking for some practical answers to the question: What can we do about the Communists? Since we are always going to have them with us, in small numbers or in larger, I think this is a practical question to which some rational answers—or at least suggestions—must exist. I don't think we need to play make-believe either.

We may even pause to list certain Soviet policies which have aroused most criticism in the Western democracies in recent years. I suspect the indictment would certainly include the following items: That the Soviets have deliberately imposed Communist-dominated, minority governments in countries like Rumania, Bulgaria, and probably Poland; that parties, which were moderate and in no sense Fascist, have been declared illegal or rendered impotent in these countries; that in several cases the electoral rules have been "Communist-weighted" in advance and that truly free, uninfluenced elections have not been held; that freedom of the press and free reporting are still prohibited, or curbed in various degrees, in most eastern European nations inside the Soviet orbit; that the revolt in northern Iran in the autumn of 1945 must have been maneuvered or encouraged, for political reasons, by the Red Army's forces of occupation; that Soviet talk about "democracy" seems an expedient or a subterfuge to most Westerners; that, whether or not the Comintern has been officially dissolved, the Communist organizations in other lands obviously continue to follow a "Moscow line" on most essentials. These are among the most prevalent complaints which citizens in the democracies make against Communist policies and tactics. They are factual complaints. They are important because they illustrate clearly what the *New York Herald Tribune* has called "the ideological chasm" between Western peoples and the Soviet peoples.

These criticisms exist because Moscow permitted her understandably acute anxiety for security against future attack from eastern Europe to dictate extremely realistic but repressive measures of initial control in most of the countries from which the Red armies drove the Germans. The evidence seems to be increasing that these policies—in Rumania, Bulgaria, Hungary, and Poland—have proved a boomerang in more ways than one. The Soviets have aroused much distrust in the West which could have been avoided. The prestige of the U.S.S.R. has suffered through certain undisciplined actions of Red Army soldiers. Anti-Soviet sentiment reportedly has grown very considerably among the populations of all or most Russian-liberated lands. To anyone who knows the Balkans, for instance, it is difficult to see what Moscow has gained by alienating Maniu's strong Peasant

Party in Rumania, or the important Agrarian Party in Bulgaria. In the Slavic countries, especially, the Soviets might well have won the sympathies and support of an impressive majority if they had followed much more liberal policies, based upon the assurance of completely free elections. The gains for Russia in world opinion would have been very great. Because this unique opportunity was lost, a harvest of distrust has been reaped instead. To balance the picture we must also remark that Britain and the United States, through blundering or indefensible policies and actions of their own in the past few years, have also brought the motives and prestige of the democracies into serious disrepute in many places. North Africa, Italy, Germany, Greece, Indo-China, and the Dutch East Indies immediately bring lamentable illustrations to mind.

But for present purposes we may concentrate on Western concern over the fact that Communist parties exist in most of the world's countries; and that their actions and propaganda upset some of us no end. A great many Frenchmen are certainly unhappy over the fact that the largest single party in the French Assembly is the Communist Party. The Communists have emerged from the war very much or considerably stronger in almost every European country, except Britain and Denmark. They have small but vital parties in India and Asia's colonial lands. They are a powerful force in a large part of China. They exist in Korea and Japan and throughout Latin America. There is also a very small but energetic Communist Party in the United States.

The first observation to make about the above is that, in most countries, there also exist democratic parties of every hue; from conservative and moderate, to progressive or Socialist. In most nations today democratic parties are as free to organize as the Communists, though they are often less aggressive and less expert at the art. What Western democrats really object to is that their own domestic Communists take so many of their cues from Moscow, either by suggestion or by instinct. This is admittedly a difficult thing to combat. But is this really the ground on which to do most of the combating? American missionaries also organize and carry their idea all over the earth. The Vatican, in its field, offers guidance and support to its followers in every land. We, as believers in democracy, are free to do the same. An idea, whether religious or political, cannot be isolated. If we have any valid replies to the Communist idea (which surely we have, if we will use them intelligently) the place first to meet the Communist challenge is on our home ground. This is why I am repeatedly surprised by a certain type of violent anti-Communism in America. It seems to me so amazingly self-defeatist, or so blindly emotional—or both. Since we are bound to have a certain number of Communists always with us, I would prefer to ask—

Why should Americans fear Communism?

Do we fear Communists in the United States because they are so numerous and so financially powerful? In 1940's presidential elections the Communist candidate received 46,251 votes out of a total popular vote of 49,815,000. Even making the most liberal allowances, I do not believe any experienced political observer would estimate present-day Communist Party membership in the United States at more than a few hundred thousand, at most. The Communist Party has not elected a single senator or congressman in Washington, nor a single Governor; and very few of any of these who could be described as "Communistic" or even "Socialistic." Virtually the whole corporational and private wealth of America is arrayed against the Communists. Even their strength in our labor unions is minor—and spotty—compared with their showing in European unions. In addition there is no other country in the world where so large a proportion of citizens, including those persons and organizations with tremendous influence, are actively or even aggressively arrayed against everything Communistic.

Finally, the American Communists have performed so many backward flips and *volte-face* spins in the past twenty years that they have seriously discredited any standing they might have won as an American party. Perhaps the most general criticism of American Communists has been that they followed the Moscow party line so furiously and completely that they are repeatedly tripping themselves up in its coils. Their overnight switch in June 1941—once Russia was invaded—from fierce opposition to "the imperialist war" to crusading support of "the democratic war against Fascism" will rise to haunt America's Left-wing crusaders for many years. Their tactics may eventually have helped us unite to prosecute the war. But they were not tactics to win them any widespread mass support in the United States.

In view of these and other demonstrable facts I frankly do not understand the scope and violence of American fears of Communism. It oftentimes appears to be purely pathological; rather like Don Marquis's old maid who rolled a ball under her bed every night to make certain that a man wasn't there. Freud would probably say that many American conservatives have a fixation; or perhaps even an inferiority complex. Is it, in part, because many of them have been obsessed for so many years by a *glandular* antagonism to the New Deal? I can remember newspapers that were shrilling "dictatorship" as far back as 1936—and one that carried a front-page box during that election campaign which warned all readers: "Only—so many more days to save the American way of life." Yet the U.S.A. is still functioning under freely elected representatives; and cries of "Wolf! Wolf!" have been uttered indiscriminately for so long that a majority of American voters do not seem to place any credence in them. As for most European visitors, I have found them uniformly bewildered. To them the New Deal was about as "socialistic" as a glass of grape juice is intoxicating. Europeans mostly could not, and still cannot, understand why so many Americans are deathly afraid of anything that could be remotely described as "socialistic." They have learned that we Americans today are politically the most conservative people on earth—and perhaps, rather frequently, the most confused.

Nevertheless there is scarcely anything that will get many votes and so quickly in the United States as a shrewd, demagogic exploitation of the fear of Communism. This fact has prompted me to ask *why* many Americans should fear Communism so greatly. *If* the American system really is the best in the world, what are we afraid of? *If* our capitalist democracy has achieved the greatest production of goods and wealth and has established a consistently higher standard of living than any other nation has ever experienced, *what* are we afraid of? Does any free people ever deliberately join in destroying what has given it unique opportunities

and unrivaled well-being and prosperity? I have never heard of
a nation, in circumstances even relatively comparable to our own
most privileged circumstances, which threw away what it already
had—merely for the excitement of trying something new. And
how, given our instinctively and emphatically conservative army
and police forces, could any small Communist minority hope to
seize control in the U.S.A., either by direct or by indirect action?

It seems to me that we must reach one of several conclusions
about those Americans who are incurably haunted by the "Communist menace." Obviously, they have astonishingly little faith
in the solidity of American democratic institutions. Obviously,
for all their marked conservatism, they must have pronounced
lack of confidence in the stability of the American system. Apparently they believe that our average citizen has obtained so little
from the American way of life that he might be lured away from
it by Marxist soothsayers with dangerous ease, and by tens of millions. Or could it be that many of those who have for so long
reaped the biggest profits from American capitalism are secretly
afflicted by a twinge of conscience? Sometimes, in all honesty,
some of them manage to sound that way. In any case I do not
see how some people, well-intentioned or fanatical, can act so
frightened-out-of-their-wits by Communism (as it limps along in
America)—unless they are completely defeatist about American
capitalism and the future of democracy in the United States. If
the American system is anywhere near as weak and exposed as
they—by outspoken intimations—make it appear to be, then this
house of ours must indeed be built upon sands. I never met anyone in Soviet Russia—and never heard of any American col-
league's meeting anyone there—who had so little confidence as
that in the stability and future prospects of the Soviet system. On
the contrary, it is undeniably true that the vast majority of some
200,000,000 Soviet citizens are convinced that a great and increasingly fruitful future is assured to their country—barring only
another war.

I suspect that Americans who fear Communism greatly and in
bugaboo fashion are reacting to glandular secretions or pocket-
book-protection reflexes, instead of doing much thinking. Certainly, I am not a defeatist about the American system; not unless

we, as a people, are incapable of learning the most obvious lessons of our times; not unless we are so blinded by our various self-interests that we refuse to consider intelligent compromises which conservatives in the other Western democracies have made or are now making; not unless we are so foolhardly as to suppose that it is not absolutely imperative that we seek *middle ground* in our industrial and other controversies; not unless a majority of Americans are so stupid as to believe that we alone can remain unchanged and unchanging, in our economic and political life, in a world of *dynamic change*. I am a Jeffersonian democrat (with a small d), who believes democracy can grow with the times; that modern technological developments compel our democracy to make commensurate readjustments and to find a minimum of controls which are still compatible with a free, parliamentary system.

I am also an American of Jeffersonian allegiance who believes that Communism and Communists are phenomena which are actually good for our heads—and perhaps even for our souls. They jolt our complacency and jar our self-assurance and our conceit. They are forever reminding us that we cannot stand still. Sometimes they are like the *banderillas* which, in a bullfight, are plunged into the shoulders of the bull. They draw blood and they enrage. The bull answers this by wheeling about and wildly charging the matador's red cape. It would be a tragic commentary on the intelligence of the American people if we were to prove capable of no more effective retort than that.

For it seems to me that the only valid answer to Communism— the only thing of dignity and lasting pertinence that we can do about the Communists—is to make democracy *better* and to make it *more democratic*. Instead of playing the Communists, we should play ball. We should play ball by insisting that industrial management and labor make concessions for the national welfare. We should play ball by taking intelligent precautions to prevent another great depression. We should think less of immediate profits—and much more of making available sufficient customers to consume the enormous flow of goods that we can produce. We should face the fact that capitalism, as we have known it, is going to go under or blow up—unless it goes a lot better than it has gone for the past two generations or more. Those are rather simple things to recognize—unless you are preoccupied charging a Red cape, or a Fascist cape, or something else down a side alley.

It is an historical fact, beyond contesting, that Communism is brought about *by internal conditions*, as Sir Samuel Hoare (for whom I have no other use) has said. "If you fear it," Sir Samuel added: "You should *so set your house in order* [italics mine] that your social and political conditions will silence any demand for its introduction." If you can talk or wriggle your way around that statement, you will find no saving grace when you have done it. In a world where there will always be Communists, and probably more and more of them, the first full-time job in any democracy *should* be to get to work and "put your house in order." Not with policemen, but with jobs and production and a fairer distribution of the benefits of democracy. The world is being swept by terrifically high winds. We shall set our democratic and capitalistic house in order—or it is *going to come down*. But the only people who can destroy the House of the British Commonwealth, or the House of the United States, or other similar houses, are the people who *live* in those houses.

Must the dwellers in the House of Soviet Russia inevitably operate to try and tear down these other national structures? William Henry Chamberlain remains a severe critic of Soviet life and policy. Nevertheless he expresses this opinion: [1] "A communist party that is taking on more and more the functions and psychology of a combination Rotary Club and National Association of Manufacturers, under Soviet conditions, is not likely to be a torchbearer of international revolution." In a very provocative examination Professor Pitirim A. Sorokin [2] cites facts and figures to demonstrate that the chief difference between the American and the Soviet systems "relates almost exclusively to the means and instruments of large-scale production"; and that this difference is much less actually than we generally assume. Professor Sorokin states:

When we examine more closely the forms of ownership in Soviet Russia and in the United States we observe that they have tended to

[1] *U.S.S.R.: The Russian Enigma*, p. 116.
[2] *Russia and the United States* (New York: E. P. Dutton & Co., 1944), Chapter IX, pp. 200, 204.

converge more and more, and that they now differ much less than the formal statement of the recognition of private property here and its abolition in Russia implies. Full-fledged private property—in the sense of the right of the owner to possess, use, manage and dispose of it—is greatly curtailed in both countries. . . . The bulk of the means of production are managed by those who do not own them; and their theoretical owners do not manage them.

Perhaps—while we protest and sometimes indulge in bitter mutual recriminations, and while the various peoples denounce the systems of others while extolling their own—perhaps while these things happen the tides of our times roll strongly and heedlessly onward toward their predestined goal. Perhaps we could learn much from each other, if we earnestly desired to learn. But time grows fearfully short; and it is much easier to condemn than to seek to understand. Even in this fast-shrinking world with its manifold and so marvelous means of communication, it is our mutual ignorance of each other which makes any sane and peaceful solution appear so far removed, if not so hopeless. If the Soviet peoples know little about the peoples of the West, we cannot— for all our advantages—claim as yet to know a great deal more about them.

How much do we know about Soviet Russia?

Let's be frank about our own handicaps and our own dilemma. We are trying to build peace with the help of a powerful new neighbor, with the second greatest power in the world. But despite our exceptional educational opportunities most of us Westerners, and especially the Americans, are woefully ignorant about the Soviet Union. Our average citizen has scarcely skimmed Russian history; has never learned the basic facts about Marxist and Communist theory in school (after all, it would be "subversive" and dangerous for teen-age pupils to be exposed to much information on such subjects!). Our average voter knows little about the Russian people. His knowledge of the record of Soviet developments since 1917 is featured chiefly by those lurid revolutionary developments which he does not like. The structure of the Soviet government is pretty much of a mystery to him. About

Russia he is lamentably short on facts—and quite long on opinions. This is probably about as true of average Englishmen as of Americans. Yet our peoples are now compelled to co-operate with the Soviets—and to succeed at it somehow—or resign themselves to a lost peace and eventually another war. If the Russians annoy us with their brusque diplomatic methods; if we find their psychology rather consistently baffling, can we rightly expect our own actions to be much more comprehensible to them?

It is true, I think, that Americans are showing an increased interest in Soviet Russia today. But it is equally true that we have a long way to go before our general knowledge is lifted to a respectable level. In its September 1945 issue *Fortune* published an exceptionally detailed survey of American opinions on Russia. This was a combination of the *Fortune* Survey and its management poll, thus being a much broader inquiry than most. It indicated some striking aspects of general American opinion, such as the following:

When asked to express their own ideas about Russia's good points and bad points, 43 percent of Americans queried could think of no particular good points; as many as 33 percent could cite no particular bad points. On specific questions about Soviet policies, the "don't know" replies were remarkably numerous; as much as 48.3 percent had no opinion on the way Moscow handles our news correspondents, and 57.3 percent had no opinion on the way she handles justice and the legal rights of her own people. It was indicated that some 70 percent of Americans think that the U.S.A. provides its people with a better sense of economic security—a conclusion which is certainly highly debatable, if you are at all informed about Soviet employment security, public health, and similar benefits. *Fortune* reported: "When people are asked not for their opinions but for matters of fact about Russian policies or practices, the 'don't knows' sometimes run higher still." Asked whether Russia sympathized with Czechoslovakia or Germany at the time of Munich, 25.8 percent of the answers incorrectly placed Soviet support with Germany—and nearly 60 percent did not know. Asked whether Russia supported Ethiopia or Italy when the League was trying to prevent Mussolini's war, 13.6 percent had Moscow backing the Fascists—and another 73 percent did not know.

On factual matters of this sort the American public's ignorance appeared to be shockingly great. Roughly 66 percent of those questioned were either "poorly informed" or "uninformed," and divided about evenly. The survey made one revelation which seems undoubtedly accurate. "Those who rate as well informed about Russia, those who have been to college, those who are in the upper economic level in the United States—all these express far more favorable opinions than do the 'uninformed,' the less well educated and the poor." The paradox was reported that Russia's best United States friend is the businessman, and that she has fewest friends among the American "proletariat." If America's lower classes are most prejudiced against the Soviet Union, we may wonder how Communism can ever be expected to get a big following among them. Equally interesting is the evidence that American businessmen and others who are best informed about Russia are most tolerant and most inclined to seek means of mutual co-operation. It seems indisputable that we can improve our relations with Russia only through a much greater popular knowledge of the Soviets and their system.

Even then the Western peoples would not find understanding an easy thing. For we have been learning in recent months that Soviet citizens and Western citizens are also separated by a very wide gap in regard to certain of their key definitions. They use the same word—and mean very different things. Perhaps the most difficult example of this is our common confusion when we and the Russians talk about democracy. Our conception and theirs are such poles apart that we are compelled to ask—

What do the Soviets mean by "democracy"?
What is the Russian Communists' idea
of the term?

To a Scandinavian, French, British, or American democrat it is almost incomprehensible to explain such statements as these. According to *Pravda* the Soviet Union is the "foremost and most consistent democracy in the world." Another authoritative Moscow daily, *Izvestia,* defines a true democracy as a system "in which the peoples' aspirations are the concern of the state, and state laws are put into effect by the inspired effort of the people." There is nothing here about government through the freely elected representatives of the people, with opposition parties playing an important role in legislative debate. Yet Soviet leaders seem absolutely sincere in their conviction that their system has produced a more developed form of "democracy." They simply do not regard free elections with secret ballots as one of the essential tests of functioning democracy. One Russian writer explains this by saying: "In the Soviet Union there is nothing to warrant the existence of several parties, since classes with radically different interests no longer exist in our country." Because capitalists, landlords, and such do not exist and all citizens have the status of workers, the Soviet spokesmen see no reason for nonexistent classes to be given a theoretical voice in government.

To call a one-party system a "democracy" on these terms is by no means valid to Western minds. But the Soviet logician insists that the democracy of a regime must be determined by "whom does it serve?" Therefore, it is his view that "Soviet democracy" serves all the people—not merely a majority who may win an election. We in the West are the more confused because in the Soviet Union "its freedoms, like its suppressions—its liberties, like its tyrannies—are almost the direct opposite of our own." [3] Something of this was in Mr. Molotov's mind when he mentioned the anti-Semitic and racial-equality clauses in the Soviet Constitution. Although some of its bravest provisions have still not been realized, we need to remember that the Soviet Constitution guarantees many economic privileges: the right to a job, to health services, to education, and to old-age security. Such rights as these are regarded in Russia as fundamental democratic rights. As for the still unfulfilled constitutional guarantees, such as free speech and certain personal freedoms, the Soviets take the view that these are state-recognized objectives—a commitment and a goal. Certainly they can also point to the fact that Fascist regimes never made any such commitments to their peoples—and never put into force any such broad and important economic guarantees.

It was significant that Foreign Commissar Molotov placed such emphasis, in his 28th anniversary speech, on the "true democracy" of the Soviet Union. "Unlike parliamentary democracy," he as-

[3] *New York Herald Tribune,* editorial, November 23, 1945.

serted, "the democracy of the Soviets is a true democracy of the people." Then he spoke of trade unions and other working-class organizations, of the Soviets' vast cultural programs for its numerous racial groups, of collective farms and the classless society as demonstrable proof of "Soviet democracy." At another point he said: "Only in our state, in which there is no room for exploitation of man by man, in which there are no exploiting classes—." This obviously is regarded as an essential part of democracy by Soviet definition.

Unquestionably a Soviet leader has all these things in mind when he speaks of "democracy." But we Westerners naturally think of a very different set of symbols which have become fixed in our minds by a very different basic philosophy, and throughout many generations. Thus we can scarcely fail to feel that there must be an intentional hypocrisy—at any rate, serious contradictions—when the Russians insist that "democracy" has been established in Poland or Rumania. By our book the regimes in these lands are far from being democratic. So it becomes a most difficult thing to reach common ground on many issues when we negotiate with Soviet representatives. We forget the frequent self-contradiction of democracy in our own American or British foreign policies, whereas we can easily become morally indignant about the contradictions that are palpably apparent to us in Soviet policies.

In this fashion the Big Five Council of Foreign Ministers rode to a tragic and costly failure in London in September 1945. The Anglo-Americans, neglecting the central issues of Germany and Japan, concentrated on elections and more democracy in the Russian zones of eastern Europe. But when the Soviets showed an equally keen interest in certain matters within the Anglo-American Mediterranean zone, our representatives cleary felt this was none of their business. Walter Lippmann put their own self-contradictions in a nutshell when he said: "They were more interested in arguing about democracy behind the lines of the Red Army than in reinforcing democracy within their own lines." He might have added: Look at Greece!

The upshot of our conflicting conceptions of democracy is that both Westerners and the Soviets will be compelled to make a persistent effort to understand each other's point of view. Neither party can expect the other to abandon his variety of democratic loyalties. Each party might begin to understand that the other's democratic emphases are merely in different places; and that neither in the Western countries nor in the Soviet Union has democracy become well rounded or complete. We can see quite easily where some of our democratic freedoms would mark a great forward advance for the Soviet peoples. They believe quite as sincerely that in our systems any true economic democracy is lacking. And the Communists' conception of "economic democracy" possesses a tremendous attraction for the exploited masses in Asia, and wherever else the great majority of a nation's inhabitants live forever close to the hunger line or on it.

The emergence of the Communists' idea of democracy as a powerful world force leaves no choice to the governments and peoples in the capitalist democracies. The competition is very real, and realistic. We must build better democracies, and make them more democratic economically as well as politically. This is the true and inescapable challenge of Communism in our time. For there is no Western democracy, surviving this war, whose house has been put in order; whose functioning, as yet, offers much if any safe hope for the future. But are our minds clear about our goals and what they will require of us? Do we practice at all effectively what we preach most assiduously? Do we know where we are heading, and what we want?

That's another chapter.

Chapter XIII

WHAT DO WE MEAN, DEMOCRACY?

A democracy is a state where the freemen and the poor, being the majority, are invested with the power of the state . . . that the poor shall be in no greater subjection than the rich; nor that the supreme power shall be lodged with either of these, but that both shall share it.
Aristotle

We gained democracy. There is now doubt whether it is fit to survive. . . .
It is the issue of human rights against property rights: an issue that will continue supreme in this country long after Judge Douglas and I are gone.
From *Abe Lincoln in Illinois*

Democracy is a word we have used so much that we often seem to have become very hazy about its meaning. Very frequently, too, we speak of democracy as if it were a fixed quantity like a chunk of steel, rather than a *process*—a process of living which is under constant pressures and subject to a wide variety of fluctuations. If there are laws that govern democracy, they are not a strait jacket bearing the date "1776" or some other date for Frenchmen or Englishmen. They are general laws which leave a wealth of room for self-expression, experimentation, and fluctuation; in short, for growth. But democracy, along with Fascism and Communism, is deeply involved in this present world war of the isms. To defend it with any intelligence or success we need to understand precisely what we are championing.

"Democracy is a form of government based upon self-rule of the people," says Dr. Hans Kohn.[1] "And in modern times upon freely elected representative institutions and an executive responsible to the people; and in a way of life based upon the funda-

[1] Encyclopædia Britannica.

mental assumption of the equality of all individuals and their equal right to life, liberty and the pursuit of happiness." That is a clearer and far more concise definition than most of us could possibly offer, even after some reflection. But these are the distinctions which we accept, or *think* we accept, as distinguishing our political philosophy from others. We would also agree with Clement Attlee that "democracy is not just majority rule, but majority rule with respect for the rights of others." Of course we do not always practice that respect. Like some other aspects of democracy it is idealized far more than achieved.

When you investigate democracy two facts are striking. You cannot define it without one phrase becoming predominant—"the people." You cannot elaborate upon it without emphasis upon "equality." Abraham Lincoln compressed those elements with a unique genius when he gave humanity "government of the people, by the people, for the people." So long as this kind of government does not perish from the earth, this triple emphasis upon the people's role must dominate the convictions—and the practices—of those who profess allegiance to democracy.

Because the Greeks gave us the word, and its first flowering into practical expression, perhaps we need to remind ourselves of the clarity of their ideal. That ideal has never gone out of date in the aspirations of mankind. Aristotle's "that the poor shall be in no greater subjection than the rich," that the supreme power shall be shared by both, may seem a remote Utopian goal. Yet this is the spiritual genesis of the long, slow march of many centuries toward a more just and freer society. In different epochs and in different national laboratories, men have shaped and improvised their variations of democratic institutions. The variety of their methods marks the inner strength of the democratic ideal. It gives us a justified hope for further progress. But for this very reason one question is more pertinent today than ever:

What is our general conception of democracy?

I think you and I must get straight about this because the American, British, French, and Scandinavian concepts are by no means identical in every respect. In Scandinavian countries and in Britain the symbol of monarchy has been retained while parliamentary democracy registered consistent and remarkable gains. Monarchy became the protector of representative government and democratic freedoms. In Sweden, Norway, and Great Britain today outright Socialist majorities govern. Yet there are no countries where democratic practices are more deeply entrenched or more staunchly defended. In fact, the Scandinavians, the British, the Australians, and the New Zealanders have shown—by elected majorities—that they regard increased measures of Socialism as a natural expression of *increased* democracy, rather than its enemy. The rise and growth of industrialism provoked, in these lands, a broadening conception of democracy to include important socialistic reforms. Though it has not yet happened in the United States, this is definitely the most striking trend in modern democratic states.

In the European democracies several differences from the American model (in practice) could be mentioned. For one thing the prime minister or chief executive is usually much more directly responsible to the electorate, and even to parliament. Unlike our president, the victorious party chief in Britain, France, and elsewhere has to defend his government's policies repeatedly before the people's representatives. He may not be content with an occasional message to Congress or an occasional radio address to the nation. He is more personally accountable for key projects of legislation, and often for foreign affairs. In most of Europe's democracies the government and the party in power do not enjoy the assurance of a fixed term of years in office; they can be ousted by an unfavorable vote on almost any outstanding issue. In these respects Europe's parliamentary systems often have a much greater direct *responsibility* than unfortunately is true either of the U.S. Congress or of America's chief executive. A European cabinet minister is also required to defend the administration of his department on the floor of parliament; a democratic provision which would serve to improve the caliber of American cabinet members very greatly.

There is another distinction that Americans in general tend to ignore. In the western European democracies which I have mentioned, and also in Holland and Belgium, labor unions are more politically active than they have been in the United States until very recently. The trade unions in these countries for the most part are older organizations. Accordingly they are more mature and, in general, have produced an increasingly responsible leadership. In western Europe, labor's role in the national life and its place in political expression were firmly established many years before this began to happen in the United States. This means that labor and unionism are more integrated into the democratic fabric of Europe's governments "of and by the people" than in our own. It also means that a safer balance between labor and capital-management has been created in several of these lands; notably Britain and Scandinavia.

In addition, I have frequently been impressed by the fact that the western European democracies usually place a greater emphasis upon fraternity, and certainly upon racial equality, than is true in the United States. In France and Scandinavia color prejudices are virtually unknown. While Britishers who administer their colonies usually win enemies by a reckless drawing of color lines, the British people at home are remarkably tolerant—as many American Negro soldiers learned to their great relief. Anti-Semitism has never flourished among the Scandinavians, the Belgians, or the British; and it was utterly foreign to France until diabolic and powerful Nazi propaganda succeeded in poisoning a minority of French minds in the years of France's greatest humiliation and suffering. But all antiracial discriminations are utterly foreign to the French spirit and French traditions. The free acceptance of peoples of all races and religions within her gates has been one of the great glories of France for generations, and will be again. Although there are definite class lines in all of western Europe's democracies, there nevertheless exists a racial equality which puts our American scene to shame.

Perhaps this is the place to point out—

Certain contradictions between American democracy in theory and in practice.

There is scarcely a literate American who has not memorized: "We hold these truths to be self-evident; that all men are created equal, that they are endowed by their Creator with certain unalienable Rights . . ." This is part of the noblest inheritance of the American people. Yet this, too, is the measure of one of the greatest failures of American democracy. Most Americans, I suppose, rarely let their minds dwell upon this glaring discrepancy in our national life. But there is probably no blot upon our record of which the world at large is more acutely conscious; and more so today than ever before. For a vast number of millions of people beyond our shores American democracy will remain only a part-democracy until we have given a far greater measure of equality to all our citizens.

Some of the most penetrating books about the Negro question in the United States have been written by foreign visitors. Although our Negroes have made considerable progress since 1864, the intelligent European is vividly aware of the cruel limitations under which this large percentage of Americans is still compelled to live. A surprising number of foreigners know that one out of ten Americans is a Negro, and that most of these 13,000,000 citizens do not begin to enjoy the fundamental rights guaranteed by our Constitution. A majority of Soviet Russia's 200,000,000 people certainly are keenly aware of this serious gap in America's democratic armor. But this is equally true of the more educated classes throughout Europe, and a great many of Europe's underprivileged as well. Thus, when some eminent American speaks sincerely in defense of the democratic rights of smaller peoples, I have often encountered abroad the immediate retort: "Yes, but what about those lynchings in America? How many rights do your Negroes have?" On this question we are continually on trial before the jury of world public opinion. The force of many highly moral presidential pronouncements is repeatedly weakened by what the world knows about the antidemocratic abscesses in our own American system.

When we are critical of British treatment of "natives" in India or elsewhere, or when we have bitterly denounced the bloody suppression of riots in British or French colonies, the resentment of Britons or Frenchmen is easy to understand. We, from our glass house, are throwing stones. To many outsiders we appear to be Pharisees or hypocrites. It may appear grossly unfair to us for the British to use some 2,000,000 Indian troops to defeat German and Japanese Fascism, yet fail to give the Indian people so much as a fixed date for their independence. To our neighbors it seems equally self-contradictory of the United States to put hundreds of thousands of Negroes into our armed services without offering these colored citizens a far greater degree of political rights and economic independence. Aside from this dangerous fundamental injustice, every race riot that breaks out in an American city serves notice to the world that inequality is still one of the gravest discrepancies in our democracy.

In seven southern states the poll tax still robs 10,000,000 Americans, Negroes and whites, of their right to vote. Yet it falls to the lot of Secretary of State Byrnes, coming from one of these states, to champion the right to vote of all Rumanians, Bulgarians, or Poles before the Soviets' foreign commissar. Whether or not Mr. Molotov made any acid inquiries about voting privileges in South Carolina is of slight consequence beside one further fact. Any foreign spokesman, in such a circumstance, would have been completely justified in doing so. Jennings Perry, chairman of the Committee to Abolish the Poll Tax, was a credit to America and his native South when he said: "It is indecent of the U.S.A. to attempt to enforce our concept of free elections on Yugoslavia or Bulgaria when we don't have the free vote at home." [2] This is how we ourselves have undermined, and continue to undermine, the moral force of America to promote democracy in other lands where democracy would be of inestimable benefit to *us* quite as much as to the people who live there.

But this undermining of democracy is much more serious and far more menacing in its disintegrating effects upon our own American society. Because the Negro was asked to sacrifice as much for our country as any fully privileged citizen, the war has naturally aroused in him new dissatisfactions, new discontents, and a new determination that the "Four Freedoms" should begin at home. On the other hand, all of America's young men in the services return with sharp demands of their own; and millions of these have become calloused or habituated to bloodshed and the use of brute force. Serious interracial clashes therefore seriously threaten many parts of the United States in these immediate post-war years. The tinder for race riots is dangerously great in the overcrowded Negro sections of New York, Detroit, Chicago, and other cities. In recent months an unheard-of phenomenon occurred almost simultaneously in the New York and Chicago areas.

2 In Washington, October 30, 1945.

Racial "strikes" were declared in schools where white and colored pupils had shared their lessons without any trouble in the past. It is significant that these unprecedented disruptions were reported to have been precipitated, not by students but by adult hatemongers. This is precisely the way that Fascists operate. It is precisely the way in which to promote increasing waves of disorder, to be exploited eventually for demagogic and antidemocratic political purposes.

If it cannot be denied that there are very dangerous anti-Negro elements at work in America today, it is equally true that anti-Semitism has grown menacingly in our country in recent years. Certain speeches inside Congress by creatures like Bilbo and Rankin have been a disgrace to our nation. Gerald L. K. Smith, the "Christian Fronters," and many others preach a racial hatred that is as vicious as anything ever mouthed by Hitler's Jew-baiters. Within the past two years Jewish students have been beaten up by organized gangs of adolescents in the suburbs of Boston. "Kill the Jews" was chalked up on walls or houses, and other slogans as inhuman and terrible as any ever painted in German cities under the Nazis. In Chappaqua, a peaceful little town in northern Westchester County (supposedly the center of the élite among New York City's commuters), similar offensive epithets marred a newspaper window not long ago. One such incident has occurred in my boyhood home town of Seymour, Connecticut, where I never heard of such a thing as anti-Semitism when I went to school there. This sort of disease exists and is spreading in many parts of the United States; and if we do not defeat it, it will one day be used to destroy such American democracy as we now have.

While speaking as a radio commentator during the past two years I felt it my duty to take particular note of patriotic services by our Jewish and Negro citizens in uniform; and also to point out the dangers to our American way of life if we fail—you and I and each one of us—to combat *all* racial discrimination *wherever* we encounter it. Whenever you tolerate racial hatred you help it to spread. Those who listen and say nothing are allies of Fascism. So I tried, now and then, to help radio listeners to understand how this mounting tide of anti-Negro and anti-Semitic sentiment (and propaganda) imperils the immediate future peace of our American society and the existence of our most important American institutions. I received many letters of encouragement. But I also received a good many letters, almost always anonymous, which were so scurrilous and poisonous as to frighten one about our future. Here is a portion of a typical letter of this sort:

The Jews ordered British and Americans to bomb German civilians. The barbarians of this war are none other than the Jews. The Jews have caused the slaughtering of many millions of Christians. . . . The Jews have always been barbarians. All I can say is, the Jews got what was coming to them. Too bad God didn't strike them down— wipe them out completely. Today we American Christians are slaves. We already owe the Jews 300 billion dollars. . . . No, I have no ill feeling toward the Germans for wiping out the rats of humanity. And I'll say that if they enslave us like they did the German people, what the Germans did will seem like a picnic compared to what the brazen parasites and cheats will get here. There is no such animal as a conscientious, honest Jew.

If this is patently the product of a diseased mind, let us remember that this antihuman, anti-Christian germ found fruitful soil among scores of millions of Europeans in our day. Especially let us face the fact that many millions of Americans are showing themselves receptive to this kind of poison; that another serious depression would increase its spread many times over. The writer of that letter might well have been Julius Streicher, or Robert Ley, another of Hitler's most vitriolic anti-Semites. After years of this kind of hatemongering Robert Ley, too despicable to face the Nuremberg trials, committed suicide. But he left a strange and amazing political testament. Facing death Ley wrote:

I am torturing myself to find the reason for the downfall, and this is the result of my contemplations. We have forsaken God, and therefore we were forsaken by God. . . . In anti-Semitism we violated a basic commandment of His creation. . . . We Nazis must have the courage to rid ourselves of anti-Semitism. We have to declare to the youth that it was a mistake. . . . We have to meet the Jews with open hearts. . . . A complete reconciliation has to be found.

What an extraordinary end to a life devoted to the most vicious racial hatred! But the light came only after the German republic had been destroyed, and all Europe ravaged, and millions of Jews tortured and killed.

If we tolerate the accentuation of intergroup hatreds in the United States, can we expect that a final justice will fail one day to exact a terrible retribution from our entire society? It seems to me inescapable that Americans, like all people and nations, must reap what they sow—or what they *permit* to be sown. Anti-racialism in our midst is a moral decay threatening the very life of American democracy. The warning voices among us are noble and eloquent, yet still far too few. The finest and best in American traditions is at stake. Associate Justice Frank Murphy of the Supreme Court was defending democracy in the truest sense when he said: [3]

We still have to mount guard against those in our midst who have been nurtured on the myths of the superior and inferior races, and who practice discrimination against fellow-Americans because of the color of their skin or some other arbitrary racial sign. There are still among us, calling themselves Christian, those who follow the Nazi line of anti-Semitism and fail to see that in attacking the Jews they undermine the basic tenets of Christianity. We must remove the economic insecurity and social frictions which tempt the weak to seek scapegoats on whom to blame their troubles, or on whom to pour their blind hatred, born of frustration and defeat.

When we re-examine our American democracy we see that it does not rest alone upon the lofty pronouncements of the founding fathers; nor merely upon immortal phrases of Jefferson, Lincoln, Wilson, and others; nor can it be judged solely by the fact that we have freedom of speech and of religion, and are governed by freely elected representatives—who often act and sound too dishearteningly like the Composite American himself. We have also placed the claim frankly before the world that the unrivaled American standard of living is one of the greatest accomplishments of our democratic system. Most of us are convinced this is a fact, so we have never been bashful about making it vocal to others. American democracy, we insist, has given our people such freedom of opportunity as has been provided in no other land.

[3] In Hollywood, July 4, 1945.

The key to this remarkable scope of opportunity we frequently express in the phrase: free enterprise. Because this is so generally taken for granted, perhaps we should examine it more closely.

How much free enterprise exists in America today?

No, I do not hope to be able to provide—least of all in this space —any complete and documented findings. I merely suggest that we do a little preliminary exploring. Of course, there is not a very wide range of free enterprise for the majority of 13,000,000 American Negroes or for many Jewish Americans—who often cannot live where they would prefer to live, nor work where they would like to work, and many of whom are barred from medical and other professions or seriously restricted in practicing them if they succeed in attending the limited schools available to them. Free enterprise is never very free for races who are discriminated against.

But we conveniently do not think of this large fraction of our citizenry when we speak of free enterprise. In New Deal years the term has been accepted as being synonymous with business, and has been championed chiefly by big business. Frenchmen and Scandinavians have enjoyed more free enterprise because their democracies have protected and encouraged small and medium-sized businesses far more than our system has done in the past fifty years. The proportionate number of their citizens who have a personal, active stake in capitalism—men who own and operate their own enterprises—is considerably larger than in the United States. In fact, it can easily be demonstrated that many of our most vocal and ardent champions of "free enterprise" in recent years have been representatives of large firms which are highly monopolistic in their practices. Do we mean by democracy a system where small, independent businesses are constantly and increasingly "squeezed out" by large monopolies? If free enterprise is not freely available to the small capitalist, with initiative and an idea, how much "free enterprise" in reality remains?

The record of the lawsuits filed by the Anti-Trust Division of the Department of Justice over the past decade is an enlightening but shocking record. Dozens of the largest corporations in the

United States have been named in these prosecutions; among them such powerful firms as the General Electric Company, Westinghouse Electric Corporation, and the Aluminum Company of America. International Telephone & Telegraph, Ford, General Motors, and many others have been linked with great German cartels. The O'Mahoney bill to require full publication of the terms of all international cartel arrangements was prompted by widespread abuses which frequently hindered or restricted American wartime production. Americans who profess to believe in democracy have paid far too little attention to the monopolistic activities of most of our largest corporations. We cannot have anything remotely approximating "free enterprise" if these strangling, price-fixing arrangements are allowed to continue and spread.

The case of the Aluminum Corporation of America illustrates a widespread trend among the giants of American industry and production. In September 1945 a Department of Justice report revealed that ALCOA, as it is called, still held a tight monopoly on the nation's war-essential aluminum production. In submitting an eighty-page, closely documented report to Congress, Attorney General Tom Clark stated that the Reynolds Metals Company is the only operating competitor of ALCOA in the United States. He said that this firm is dependent on ALCOA for some of the principal raw material, alumina, because ALCOA has 96 percent of the nation's alumina capacity under its control. The Attorney General warned that "prompt action is imperative" and "competition must be firmly and unmistakably established." Despite the industry's sevenfold expansion since 1939, ALCOA still maintained a stranglehold. The report narrated how ALCOA had lowered prices to destroy competition before the war; had raised prices when it held a monopoly; that it had operated on a policy of high profits and low production at the expense of the consumer.

The continuing threat of American trusts to American democracy is factually and uncontradictably recorded by David Lasser in his revealing book *Private Monopoly: The Enemy at Home.* Out of a wealth of his unchallenged facts I will summarize a few here briefly. In the past forty years, or less, the right to manufacture in the United States has come increasingly under the control of some 200 leading industrial corporations. These giant corporations have gradually controlled whole industries through "umbrella patents," or have blocked the entry of competitors into their fields by "preventive patents." In 1909 the 200 nonfinancial corporations had one third of the total American corporation assets; in 1930 nearly one half. By 1933 their share had risen to about 60 percent. Mr. Lasser reports that by 1929 they had 43 cents out of every dollar of corporation income in the United States; while small businesses, constituting 75 percent of the number of our corporations, had their share of the total corporate dollar reduced from seven to only four cents. "By 1937 the network had so tightened that only 50 companies (out of the 146,000 engaged in manufacturing) had nearly 16 percent of all employees. The $17,000,000,000 of goods these fifty companies produced was nearly one-fourth of the entire national production." In 1929 we had a three-billion-dollar corporation; but in 1941 American Telephone & Telegraph had assets of nearly six billion dollars.

The Congressional Monopoly Committee of 1938 found that the du Pont, Mellon, and Rockefeller families alone controlled directly fifteen of the 200 largest corporations; that thirteen other family groups controlled a score of other industrial giants. The TNEC report stated that in 80 of the 200 largest corporations "one family or a small number of families exercises either absolute control or working control. . . . About 60 of these corporations . . . are controlled by one or more other corporations. Thus a small group of dominant security holders is *not* in evidence in *only* 30 percent of the largest 200 corporations." This could be said in much clearer terms; a small group of dominant security holders *is* evidenced in about 70 percent of the 200 giant corporations.

Professor Pitirim A. Sorokin states that "in 1930 the 200 largest corporations controlled approximately *38 percent of the business wealth, and 22 percent of the total wealth of the country.*" He remarks that in these 200 corporations none of the presidents or directors owned even 1 percent of its shares in 1930. He adds: "Then full-fledged private property in the classic sense of the term, especially in the field of large-scale production, *was given the first fatal blow by the corporations,* which have been rapidly expanding." [4] (Italics mine.)

It was not surprising that President Roosevelt frankly said to Congress: "Among us today a concentration of economic power without equal in history is growing . . . which is struggling so hard to master our democratic government. . . . Private enterprise is ceasing to be free enterprise and is becoming a cluster of private collectivisms." Indeed, it is through the enormous expansion of these "private collectivisms" that many alert economists see the United States moving closer and closer to Soviet collectivism. That is a neat paradox worthy of some thought.

It seems to me that any American who really believes in free enterprise and wants our democracy to survive must inform himself on the structure, actions, and consequences of our giant monopolistic corporations—and consider what can be done to limit their further encroachments. In 1929, David Lasser reminds us, only *1 percent* of America's population, with incomes of $20,000 a year or more, had as much total income as the lowest *60 percent* of the population. Surely this is as great a discrepancy in material benefits as existed in most of Europe's recently feudal countries. Surely Thomas Jefferson's conception of democracy envisaged nothing so discriminatory and lopsided as this. To put an end to such discrepancies the European nations are turning more and more to Socialism. Mr. Lasser, interestingly enough, does not think this the wisest or most practical course for the United States. Instead, he suggests a definite program to "democratize" our giant corporations, especially through placing representatives of workers, consumers, and government—amounting to perhaps 30 percent—on their boards of directors. When corporations have won such monopolies of wealth and power it would certainly seem imperative—and democratic—that all the important elements of society should have a direct voice in their decisions and procedures.

In any case it is clear that "free enterprise" is a far more serious challenge to American democracy than most of us have recognized. As Marquis Childs has said: "Many who today talk so glibly about 'free enterprise' are the very ones who advocate government privileges and favors for themselves. They cry out in

[4] Sorokin: *Russia and the United States,* p. 201.

pain and rage at strict enforcement of the anti-trust laws, although —if they were consistent—they would support this means of opening up free competition." Let me add emphatically that I believe in free enterprise when it is and means free competition; and in my conception this, too, is an essential of Jeffersonian democracy under twentieth-century conditions. When I write and speak of American democracy, the right of our citizens to indulge in free economic competition is included in that phrase.

And we should also take careful note of the fact that this kind of democracy has become increasingly more of a guiding principle and accepted fact throughout our neighboring democracies; in Scandinavia, France, and the British Commonwealth. In highly industrialized countries there can exist no true democracy in our times unless it includes an important and increasing amount of economic democracy. Our American conservatives will fight this tooth and nail. They will buck the swelling tides of the whole world—and eventually they will lose. Perhaps they will lose only after we have Fascism and another war. But if those things happen, then in the end they will surely lose. But so will *all of us.* Yet there will always be survivors—and *survivors who have been hurt most learn most.* In our century some of us, fortunate or unfortunate, will live and learn.

There is another aspect of our sister democracies which commands consideration. They have accepted completely into their own functioning of democracy something that is still rejected by many Americans in positions of exceptional power. We can see this clearly by asking—

Is collective bargaining an essential of democracy?

It has so been accepted in every modern democratic state, with the United States the last of all to fall in line through national legislation. The Wagner Labor Relations Act, by guaranteeing the rights of workers to organize and bargain collectively, merely brought us to a stage of development already reached in several leading countries abroad. That we still have a great deal to do to perfect and humanize labor-management relations is plainly shown by our postwar strikes, and the manner in which certain big monopolists have refused arbitration flatly or as long as possible. In some quarters it is indicated that large corporations still hope to force the repeal of the Wagner Act, or to render it innocuous.

In the middle of the twentieth century collective bargaining has become an established and inseparable part of democratic processes. However we may lament the extremism of certain labor leaders and certain big industrialists, we must recognize that collective bargaining cannot be tossed out of the window without precipitating an economic and industrial civil war. Both labor and management must devolp increasing social responsibility. It can come only through many costly struggles and many errors, but it must come—if our democracy is to survive.

But despite this obvious and unavoidable fact, we find—as recently as August 1945—such evidence of antediluvian influences in our midst as the following. John W. Scoville, chief economist for the Chrysler Corporation, then stated: "If you believe in economic freedom and competition, then you will be opposed to collective bargaining." He added significantly: "*As industrial turmoil increases* [italics mine], more and more people will see the evils generated by collective bargaining, and we should look forward to the time when all federal labor laws will be repealed." That, at least, has the merit of frankness. Does Mr. Scoville mean that some of those who most strongly oppose government planning are in favor of planning for "industrial turmoil"? If this were conceivably true, then the internal peace and prosperity of the American people would be menaced by elements a million times more powerful than the on-again, off-again American Communists.

As chief economist for Chrysler Corporation Mr. Scoville undoubtedly makes, and earns, a fairly handsome living. This evidently makes it quite reasonable for him to say: "Fair wages are wages that are just high enough to attract the required number of employees of the desired quality." In other words, fair wages have nothing to do with the size and amount of the profits that the workers' products bring in. If there is anything democratic—or remotely just—in that idea, then I am General Eisenhower. Writing in *Barron's,* Economist Scoville puts forward another idea which would fit perfectly into the seventeenth century, or into present-day Fascist Spain. "The right to a job," he asserts, "is one of the most absurd of the current fallacies"; it could be established only by "replacing freedom with communism." So the Truman administration is introducing Communism when it seeks to assure the right to a job for every returned veteran. Apparently the well-paid Mr. Scoville considers the "right to starve," for such as become superfluous in any given labor market, as one of the inalienable rights in the American way of life. Could any union leader—even the wily and unspeakable John L. Lewis—be more irresponsible?

I prefer to turn to the words of an outstanding American public servant and humanitarian. It is strangely true that only a *human* being can speak like a human being. While championing the Full Employment Bill, Senator Robert F. Wagner said: *"There will be no such thing in the postwar world as the possibility of continuing freedom plus continuing mass unemployment."* Whatever certain dinosauric advisers of a few giant corporations may say, this is a fact which we shall all of us disregard at our extreme peril. In the past thirty years the world's peoples have increasingly shown, and especially in industrial countries capable of producing plenty, that they will not tolerate great unemployment. In our mighty machine age the right to a job has become a primary right of people who want work. If the "pursuit of happiness" does not clearly include this right, then it means nothing at all. For men can be truly content only when they have work to do.

It is also true that the average citizen is much better informed about the facts of our economic system than he was thirty years ago. People have available such facts as these from the Security and Exchange Commission's quarterly report. On June 30, 1944, the total current assets of American corporations was $99,300,-000,000—virtually 100 billions—as compared with only $54,600,-000,000 in 1939. "As of March 31, 1944," SEC records, "American corporations had net working capital which was almost $11,000,-000,000 in excess of their working capital at the end of 1941 —the time of the highest peace-time production of goods in our history. . . . The continued increase in working capital and in liquid funds of corporations since the end of 1943 re-emphasizes the ability of American industry as a whole to reconvert, and also undertake considerable expansion without recourse to outside sources of funds."

American labor's demands for postwar wage increases are not at all surprising to anyone familiar (as relatively few white-collar folk seem to be) with the extraordinary size of industrial war profits. Official U.S. Treasury figures, released in September 1945, curiously were treated as front-page news by very few newspapers. These figures showed that American corporations, in the years 1936–39, averaged $3,323,000,000 in profits—after taxes. In the war period from 1941–45 *total corporation profits—after taxes—averaged 250 percent of the prewar levels.* After Pearl Harbor they averaged $9,000,000,000 of profits per year—after taxes. In 1944 profits, after taxes, of American corporations were $10,000,000,000.

Thus the war profits of American industries have been much greater, after taxes, than in any peacetime year in our history, including the great boom years of 1928–29. If these facts had not been buried deep in the financial pages of most newspapers, the George Joneses of our nation would be less surprised at labor's insistent demands for higher wages. But when American corporations have accumulated such an unprecedented reserve cushion of assets and profits it would seem rather logical that our large working class should also insist very stubbornly upon "the right to a job." It would also seem necessary that our government "of, by, and for the people" should seek to distribute some of these enormous wartime profits with an effort toward equality and fairness.

Look objectively at America's internal labor-management strife and I believe you can discern that strict self-interest is not its only motivation. If selfishness often seems to predominate on both sides, there is also evidence of a growing conception among rank-and-file Americans that our democracy must provide a more even distribution of economic benefits than it has in the past. Without embracing Socialism, Americans are increasingly concerned over a fairer distribution and division of the national income. In reality, this is the emergence of the idea of economic democracy. Its general motivation is much the same as in Britain, France, and other western European countries. The American gives this motivation far less precise ideological expression. But he is in no mood to go back to the 12,000,000 unemployed of 1930–31. He is rightly convinced that America's colossal industrial plant must be used to produce a greater prosperity *for all*.

I believe we shall see that the majority of American voters regard this kind of common betterment and common opportunity as being strictly within their unconscious definition of democracy. They have sensed the fact that "continuing mass unemployment" is incompatible with "continuing freedom." For any American political party willfully to oppose this fact would be to invite nationwide disorder or eventual revolution. Majority rule means that the issue of full employment must be faced, and somehow solved, by our democracy. For this reason we must understand clearly that *political freedoms alone are no longer enough in the world's greatest industrial state*. The Frankenstein-monster machines that we have created now compel us to define and work out an economic democracy—or yield to totalitarianism.

When we turn to the rest of the world another embarrassing question arises.

Do we Americans believe in democracy for other peoples?

Of course, we say that we do. But if this is true, then one would suppose that American foreign policy ought to support democracy abroad with a fair degree of consistency. Agreed, this is not always possible. But both Washington and London, in their wartime record, have revealed an incredible incapacity to support democratic forces in foreign lands. For years we gave important material support to Fascist Spain. For years we tolerated the pro-Fascist activities which brought a totalitarian dictatorship into power in Argentina. Under the excuse of military expediency Anglo-American policies succeeded in disillusioning or alienating most of the popular movements in Europe. Very late in the day, and well after Germany's defeat, our governments finally began to show an interest in democracy in eastern Europe—the one place where they had the *least* direct influence.

If the Anglo-American powers had possessed any enlightened self-interest, let alone a sincere desire to promote democracy in

Europe, they would have given early and wholehearted support to the patriotic French Resistance. They would have become genuine allies with the Italian guerrillas and patriots in northern Italy. They would have co-operated sincerely with the largest and most ardent Greek Resistance group, the EAM. They would not have been afraid of popular movements, or of Socialists or Communists. The only democratic policy that could make any political sense was for the United States and Britain to welcome and promote the widest *popular* coalition movements in any European country, to assure them of free elections at the earliest possible moment, and to practice democracy inside these liberated nations in such a fashion that it would have a greater mass appeal than Communism could possibly have.

But the Anglo-American approach placed its chief emphasis on "order" rather than on democratic institutions. The Anglo-American attitude was one of suspicion of the people. The Anglo-American tactic was to push the people back, and tell them that they would be told what was good for them in due time. These people had suffered long and were naturally impatient. They had also been betrayed and they were naturally sensitive in their self-respect and their pride. Many of them had been sold down the river by prewar republican governments, so they had their own sharpened ideas about how to make certain that democracy should be more than an impotent façade.

To such people, in such a state of mind and in such urgent need, the Anglo-American armies brought officers chiefly concerned with military controls and military problems. On their part there was little or no recognition of popular rights or popular desires—and to very many of these officers a Socialist was a "rabid Red." Yet the most important democratic friends that the United States and Britain needed on the European continent were precisely the Socialists. Our policy was to ignore them as long as possible. "Government by the people" was what Americans and Britishers made speeches about, but had amazingly little interest in so long as a war was being fought on European soil.

But the European masses had a curious democratic idea: that there *is* such a thing as the right to revolution, and that the right to change is the eternal right of all peoples who have been victimized by flagrant misrule. We prattled of "order" and we liberated our section of Europe without any clear political program whatever. In the east the Russians had a political program. In the west the Allies had none—and the results were exactly as might have been expected. In the west, very clearly, most American representatives did not know what they meant by democracy. Whatever they meant, it obviously did not include any convincing degree of *trust in the people.* But what is democracy, if it does not connote trust in the majority of the people? We had not trusted the majority of Frenchmen or of Italians or of Greeks. Ours were liberating "democratic" armies which did not know how to promote democracy, and were not even seriously interested in trying to do so. If the Soviets had shown as little comprehension or intelligence, they would not stand where they stand today.

To a conquered Germany we brought no more political awareness than to other lands. Our Military Government officers tolerated Nazis in important civic posts until it became a scandal. Instead of worrying about denazifying the German municipal and regional administrations, American officers usually concentrated on restoring the sewage systems and judged Germans by whether they "got things done." As a political or even a cleansing influence in Germany the U.S. Army soon proved a disastrous failure. The majority of its personnel showed not the slightest conception of what we mean—or should mean—by democracy. General George S. Patton expressed a prevalent attitude when he said: "In general far too much fuss has been made regarding denazification of Germany. This Nazi thing is just like a Democratic and Republican election fight." It would be difficult to find a statement by an American of importance which reveals a more abysmal ignorance of what the war was about. Yet with attitudes approximately as superficial and unrealistic as this, uniformed Americans were supposed to awaken in Europeans a personal interest in democratic principles and a democratic way of life. Without any concise conception of what they were bringing, they were relied upon to sell it.

Without reviewing many of the heartbreaking details, we must ask ourselves where do we go from here? The fundamental definition of democracy as majority rule has not changed, but most of the *majorities* in the world's nations *have* changed. Their conception of what makes democracy has become far more specific and demanding. Their desire for freedom has become just as economic as it is political. Their grasp of what they want has gone far beyond prewar concepts. Their idea of the peoples' strength has deepened with the demonstrated endurance of the people. These awakened, hungering, impatient peoples of Europe and Asia cannot tolerate yesterday or the status quo, but they have no fear of change. If we champions of democracy are afraid of change, then our kind of democracy obviously is not for them.

So the question remains whether we can betray the majority of the people in any of these lands without betraying ourselves. Unless we know what we mean by democracy we *shall* betray both them *and* ourselves. For democracy cannot be static. Democracy must grow and serve the people in the conditions of their times. And in fact, for so long as democracy has in it life and hope it must inevitably continue to grow and to serve the people. *But democracy can grow only in so far as its citizens grow* in their comprehension and vision and awareness.

A few days before he died Henry George made a speech in New York. He was introduced, so Professor Woodbridge tells us, as a friend of the working man. In a hall crowded to capacity Henry George began to speak.

"I am not for the rich man," he said.

There was thunderous applause.

"I am not for the poor man."

With that came a sudden, astonished silence.

"I am for *man!*" he announced.

A hush—and then a tumult of cheers.

We say we believe in democracy.

Are we for Man?

Chapter XIV

MR. CHURCHILL BRINGS "DEMOCRACY" TO GREECE

*They joined battle, and the Phocaeans won, yet it was
but a Cadmean victory, and the victors suffered as much
as the conquered.*

Herodotus

It's the tailor's fault, and they beat the cook.

Greek proverb

That flight from Athens to Italy was the worst I had sweated
out anywhere, around the war and around the world, in five and
one half years. By the grace of Providence our plane did not hit
the shrouded island peaks beyond the Gulf of Patras or quite clip
the Mediterranean whitecaps which we skimmed. So on January
20, 1945, I was able to make the following broadcast to the ABC
network from Rome:

I've just come back from Athens. Athens is the saddest city in
Europe. For some it's a city of rejoicing and revenge. For others, a
dark well of fear and despair. Day and night the manhunts continue
in Athens. The police are still cramming the jails with those suspected
of belonging to ELAS, or of having Left-wing sympathies. Some of
these same policemen fired the first shots on December 3. That's the
testimony of every foreign correspondent who was on the spot.

That police volley touched off thirty-three days of civil war and
bloodshed. It brought armed intervention by British troops—using
American-made tanks and half-tracks—and supplied by American
trucks—often fed by American food. In Athens in bitter street fighting,
somewhere between two thousand and five thousand persons were
killed or wounded. Hundreds of buildings were destroyed, with property losses estimated at two hundred and fifty million dollars. Today
barbed-wire barriers still encircle sections in the heart of the capital.
Those who were riotously welcomed as liberators in October have
fought their way into complete control. Scores of their tanks are

parked close to government buildings. Some Athenians are convinced they've been saved from a Red uprising. A great many others are beaten down and broken-hearted.

All this is part of an Athens I never dreamed of when I was with the Greeks as they threw back the Italians four years ago. All this is a great and heartrending Greek tragedy. But it's also a British-American tragedy. Neither the British nor the Americans are without their share of responsibility. With the Greeks, of the Left and the Right, we have also made serious mistakes. But tonight I shall speak only as a reporter.

I knew the Greeks in their days of imperishable grandeur. I longed to return to Athens—to see once more the noble columns of the Parthenon, standing like an eternal sentinel above the brown-tiled roofs which lie at its feet. I returned. These are some of the things I found.

Across from the Acropolis rises the lofty summit of Lykabettos. On the lower slopes of Lykabettos is the Kolonaki district—the Park Avenue of Athens. Wealthy and well-to-do Greeks have their apartments there. Ordinary Greeks call the upper-class people who live there "the Kolonaki."

I talked first with these upper-class Athenians. They are almost hysterical in their fear of ELAS and the Communists. One of them said: "What we've had here wasn't Communism. It was just gangsterism and anarchy." On every side well-to-do Greeks talked of mob violence. Others told me that criminals had jumped jail and joined the ELAS during the fighting—that they had looted and sometimes murdered—that ELAS leaders could not control them.

But in the Kolonaki district—where people are obsessed by a Red phobia—not a single burned building exists. The Kolonaki were inside the British lines—a fortunate thing for some of them.

But I noticed one other thing. In Athens the well-to-do Kolonaki all look prosperous. They obviously had plenty to eat all through the German occupation. About twenty thousand Athenians live in this district . . . whereas the population of greater Athens totals one and one quarter millions. The vast majority of these are terribly poor people—people who are worse off than the poorest slum-dwellers in America.

So I talked to these "forgotten men" of Athens. "Did many of the well-off Kolonaki resist the Germans?" I asked. The worker laughed out loud—a bitter laugh. "When the Germans are here the Kolonaki are with the Germans," he said. "When the English are here they are with the English. But why are the English shooting the ELAS, just like the Germans shot the ELAS?"

I didn't try to answer that. I kept questioning Greeks—from the highest to the lowest. I talked with Archbishop Damaskinos, the new Regent, with General Plastiras, the new premier, with the British and American ambassadors, with Greek officials and editors who are old friends. From all sides—including American and British officers who were with the ELAS guerrillas long before liberation—you get one overwhelming verdict. The ELAS resisted and fought the Germans more, and more consistently, than any other group in Greece. Now these same guerrillas are referred to in British communiqués as "the enemy."

This is part of the great Greek tragedy. I speak as a reporter—a seeker for facts. Let me repeat. The overwhelming evidence inside Greece is that the ELAS–EAM coalition resisted the Germans more than any other Greek organization. Whether they were more recently misled by Communists or other extremists—or to what degree they're responsible for the civil war—is another question.

But you must go to the workers' districts of Athens to learn what the majority of Athenians think and say. I went to one of these districts, where the ELAS stubbornly fought off the British-Indian troops for over two weeks. We went beyond the street barricades, far up the hill. In the center of a long square zigzag trenches are now a common grave. Thirty-six pitiful crosses made out of boxwood were stuck in the fresh earth. But the neighbors said over one hundred and fifty persons are buried here—only the names of thirty-six are known. I checked the names on every cross. Eighteen out of these thirty-six dead were old men, women, and small children.

At the foot of the trench a large sign had been put up. This is what it said: "Here lie Greek traitors who collaborated with Germans, Bulgarians, and Italians for the destruction of Greece."

So these workers' women and children had collaborated with the Nazis? I asked an old woman. "We didn't write the sign," she said. "It was written by the new soldiers of the National Guard. Of course, what it says isn't true. We know that."

All around us the heads of hungry people nodded in agreement. But how did these women and children die? One woman answered: "About forty people were killed here by bullets from the British planes. One day we were waiting in line to get food. Seven planes came diving and shooting. They came back three times. Seven were killed and forty wounded that day."

A Greek gendarme—a supporter of the new government—came up. He said many people had been slaughtered by the ELAS on top of the hill. When he went away the same woman said: "They were officers and cadets of the Greek royalists. They were executed by the ELAS, but they were not civilians. I could tell you more, but we can't speak freely now."

Again and again, when I spoke to Greek workers, they said the same thing. The Plastiras government is making wholesale arrests of everyone suspected of ELAS or Left-wing sympathies. Unless you see them quite alone, the workers in Athens do not dare to tell what they know or what they think. This is true of hundreds of thousands of people in Athens.

I went to Kaisariani, where ten thousand people live in hovels and shacks. The people of Kaisariani fought forty-nine pitched battles with the Germans and the Quisling Greek police. In one day 204 of their sons and husbands were executed. In Kaisariani there's scarcely a family that does not have one or more who died resisting the Nazis. In well-to-do Kolonaki I never met one Greek family who said they had lost one of their members fighting Nazis in the resistance movements. Some must have done so, but I never met any.

Here, in Kaisariani, we were surrounded by ragged, half-starved women and children, their eyes dark and drawn with tragedy. The British and the royalist Greek Mountain Brigade had to fight for every foot of Kaisariani. Its ugly homes are blasted by shells or bombs; many of them are burned to the ground; many more are riddled with bullets. Almost no men are left here—none except old men.

One old woman burst into tears, crying: "Why did they burn our homes?" Another tall, emaciated woman sobbed: "The English planes killed my daughter, while she was sewing." Another said: "We expected the English to come to free us . . . instead, they fought against us."

Everywhere I found ruin and heartbreak and unanswerable questions. Everywhere hunger branded hopeless faces. But in all Kaisariani I did not see a single Allied soup-kitchen. . . . I opened a tin of Army peanuts. Children went mad, clawing at my hands for a few peanuts.

Mothers lifted their babies, fighting to get near me. In one half-demolished shack a woman sobbed:

"I'm a widow. I have just lost my last son, who supported me. My first was killed in Albania. My second is in a hospital. There's nobody to care for me. . . . What shall I do?" Outside I asked: "Why did the British fight the ELAS?" A sailor said: "There are many reasons—which we don't speak about." When I gave away what little food I had, people stooped and kissed my hand. Later I talked with a working woman—a woman with fine face and intelligent eyes. "We can do nothing but hope," she said. "All we can do is hope."

When I finished this broadcast an American officer in the control room said: "How in hell did you get *that* by the censors?"

"But I didn't express any personal opinions," I replied. "I merely reported what I saw, and what I heard from all sides." That, of course, was the chief reason that my script had got by untouched. It was the first complete and free report on Greece that any radio correspondent had succeeded in making from the Allied Mediterranean zones since the so-called "civil war" began more than six weeks previously. Perhaps an American, rather than a British, censor happened to handle my script that afternoon. Perhaps it was luck. But, in any case, you couldn't cram into a twelve-minute broadcast more than a tiny fraction of the truth about Greece. The American public did not have the background facts on which to base a judgment; nor did the British people. The entire Greek situation had been clouded and distorted for nearly a year by a severe and unscrupulous British censorship in Cairo. To explain the tragedy in Greece one had to expose facts long suppressed. The public also needed—

A political dictionary of the factions and
personalities involved in Greece.

EAM—The largest Greek Resistance Movement, dominated by Communist leaders but including a wide range of Socialist and moderate republican groups.

ELAS—The armed guerrilla forces of EAM, numbering some 60,000 or more fighting patriots.

EDES—Another guerrilla force, commanded by General Zervas and active only in the Epirus. It co-operated with the Germans through most of the occupation, was finally paid by the British, and continued to fight ELAS. Top strength: between 5,000 and 10,000.

The Mountain Brigade—Organized by the British in Egypt in the spring of 1944 and deliberately packed with Greek royalists.

X-ites—A small fanatical group in Athens. Like EDES, royalist and antirepublican.

The Security Battalions—A Greek Quisling militia, formed under the Germans and their Puppet-Premier John Rhallis. Equipped with German uniforms and weapons. Greek traitors who hunted down patriot guerrillas and delivered them to torture and death at the hands of the Nazis' Gestapo.

Papandreou government—The British-picked "puppet" government in Athens when hostilities broke out.

Sir Reginald (Rex) Leeper—British ambassador in Greece, who advised and actually controlled the Athens government.

Lieutenant General Sir Ronald Scobie—Commander of British-Indian troops in Greece.

With these chief characters identified, it is possible to trace the causes and course of the Greek tragedy. It is highly important to do this because the Anglo-American democracies were supposedly restoring free self-government to the bravest and most long-suffering little nation among the Allies. When the small Greek Army hurled back the Italians and thrilled the world in 1940–41—in those days when I saw that the British uniform was the object of touching adoration in every Greek village—who could have dreamed that British "liberators" would one day return to fight the unquestioned majority of the Greek people? Who would have believed that British soldiers and planes would kill several thousands of Greeks, very many of them civilians, in their own capital? The fair-minded, decent British people would never have countenanced such shameful warfare. But the facts about Greece—and especially the Churchill government's policies toward Greece—had long been concealed from the British people. They did not know what was now happening. They could not find out more than a small part of it until long afterward. Are

these statements biased? Let us look for the facts—and begin at
the beginning.

What was the Greek "Mountain Brigade," and who sponsored it?

In April 1944—while Germans still occupied Greece—a
"mutiny" broke out in the Greek Army and naval forces in
Egypt. These were Greeks who had fled their country to fight on
beside the Allies. The EAM Resistance leaders had smuggled
delegates out of Greece and sent them to Cairo. These Resistance
delegates came to ask that they—like the French Resistance delegates to the French National Committee in North Africa—should
be represented in the British-dominated Greek government-in-
exile. The Greek patriots who were resisting and dying at home
felt they should have some representation in their government.
In Cairo the EAM delegates were received with harsh words—
and locked up; finally they were shipped ignominiously home to
Greece. BUT the British and American correspondents in Cairo
were severely muzzled by censorship. They could not report any
of this, nor explain what followed, until long afterward.

What followed was officially described by British officials as
a Greek "mutiny." As a protest against the highhanded ousting of
EAM delegates, thousands of Greek soldiers and sailors refused
to obey orders. They felt that the greatest Resistance Movement
in Greece had every right to be represented in the exile government. Fighting broke out. Many were killed. Thousands of
patriotic Greeks were jailed—and Allied correspondents were not
permitted to tell the world how and why this incredible thing
had happened. Eighteen months later, in the late autumn of 1945,
some 1,500 anti-Fascist Greeks, victims of this "mutiny," were still
imprisoned in *British* concentration camps in remote Eritrea.
They had been guilty of demanding a Greek government of
national unity. (At least until July 1945, it was charged that they
had never been granted the right to see a representative of the
International Red Cross.)

It was immediately after this ruthless suppression of Greek
soldiers and sailors in Egypt—when British guns first shot down
Greeks—that the Churchill government proceeded to organize

the Greek Mountain Brigade. All Greeks in Egypt were carefully "screened." Greek *republicans* of all nuances from moderate-conservative to Leftists, officers or men, were barred from the new brigade. It was built up as a strictly royalist and antirepublican fighting force. Was it a coincidence that the Churchill government was a frank champion of King George of Greece? A Greek officer, a lifelong republican whom I knew well in Albania in 1940, told me in Athens: "In Cairo I saw the whole thing. They jailed or banned all republican officers from the Mountain Brigade." Allied correspondents saw this, tòo; but they were not allowed to inform the British and American people. If the Greeks had "mutinied" in Egypt, then the Mountain Brigade was a Churchill-approved (or invented) *royalist* plot.

So the British whipped the monarchist MB into fighting trim. The Mountain Brigade fought in Italy for about one month, long enough to help capture Rimini. Then, soon after Athens was liberated in mid-October 1944, the British brought in the Mountain Brigade. The Athenians cheered these men wildly because they were the only Greeks who had fought the Germans as a regular army unit. But the EAM–ELAS leaders knew that the Mountain Brigade was ardently royalist. And when General Scobie demanded that ELAS, the patriots' half-armed forces, should give up their arms, these Greeks naturally said: "Disarm the royalist Mountain Brigade, too—or no, thank you."

It was this dispute over disarming the *British-created* royalist brigade which precipitated the government crisis, which in turn produced the "civil war." In Athens I checked over this, step by step, with Greeks and correspondents—and Allied officers— who were on the spot at the time. Premier Papandreou finally agreed that both ELAS and the Mountain Brigade would be disarmed. Then Papandreou retracted. He gave an EAM member, then in the government, a letter from General Scobie. The letter said that Prime Minister Churchill *would not permit* the royalist Brigade to be disbanded, along with ELAS. The American ambassador in Athens confirmed to me that this rejection came either from London or from General Scobic. This decision provoked the resignation of the EAM ministers. That brought on a huge EAM street demonstration on Sunday, December 3. The police fired into the unarmed, peaceful paraders. The "civil war" began.

I asked a strongly anti-Communist Greek doctor why Churchill forbade disbanding the Brigade.

"Well, who created the Mountain Brigade?" asked the doctor.

A Brigade officer made this frank remark to a friend: "We were brought here for one purpose—to suppress the Left. Our men have been promised jobs in the new police force which is going to be formed."

While I was in Athens, Mountain Brigade men were being incorporated wholesale into the new Greek Army, called the National Guard; or into the police. So were the pro-monarchist EDES followers who had co-operated with the Germans through most of the occupation. But to get the picture straight—

How did the Greek civil war start?
Was there a "Red plot"?

In Parliament Prime Minister Churchill gave this explanation: "From the depredations and ravages of ELAS there developed . . . a well-organized plot by which ELAS should march down to Athens and seize it by armed force and establish a reign of terror."

In his January 18th (1945) speech Mr. Churchill quoted a report from the British ambassador to Greece. Ambassador Leeper charged that a small, well-armed Communist Party had been practicing a "reign of terror" all over Greece, and added: "Nobody can estimate the number of people killed or arrested *before the revolt in Athens actually began*." (Italics mine.) This statement implied that Left-wing guerrillas had been pillaging and killing in Athens, and throughout most of Greece, for weeks before the police began shooting on December 3.

In Athens I investigated with great care what had happened between the capital's liberation on October 12–14 and December 3. For those first two October days ELAS forces held Athens alone, until the British arrived. Naturally, they were wildly elated—and, of course, they went after Quislings and traitors. Some were killed; and in the furore of those first two days of liberation some innocent citizens possibly became victims of passions long pent up. But as soon as the British came, General Scobie requested ELAS to withdraw their forces from Athens—

and ELAS withdrew. That, indeed, was a strange procedure for "well-organized plotters" who, in Churchill's version, later planned to march on Athens and "establish a reign of terror." On October 14 ELAS vastly outnumbered the British and held Athens in their power. Why, then, did they obediently withdraw?

In Athens I met many old colleagues. We had worked together in many parts of Europe. These British and American correspondents I knew by long observation. They were journalists of great integrity and reliability. I asked them, as I asked Greek friends of the Italian war period, if looting and killing occurred on any important scale before December 3. Since British troops arrived, they told me, there had been nothing remotely resembling a "reign of terror" in Athens. The terror had started only with the civil war—and then it was *war*, with ruthless fighting on both sides. Frank Gervasi of *Collier's* and M. W. Fodor of the *Chicago Sun* had journeyed from Athens all the way north to Salonika and back without encountering any "massacres" or hint of ELAS "depredations." In Salonika the British commander, Major General Hollworthy, told them there had not been a single reprisal execution by ELAS since that city was liberated on November 7. Although I sought evidence on every side, Ambassador Leeper's statement about vast killings "*before* the revolt in Athens actually began" simply could not be substantiated. Along with other correspondents I had to conclude either that Sir Reginald had been a victim of highly emotional rumors, or that he had become involved somehow in a deliberate falsification.

Once the civil war started, many upper-class Athenians talked wildly about acts of "Communist terror." Certain ELAS extremists had run amok, they said, and committed all sorts of crimes. But when you tried to get specific dates, you could almost never place serious disorder before December 3. And American officers and officials, on the whole, confirmed this important distinction. Mike Fodor, as foreign correspondent, had known Greece for more than twenty years. No one who has ever met Fodor can question his honesty. He summed up the pre-civil war situation to me in these words: "In twenty-five years I've seen almost every revolution in Europe. This, right here, was the

quietest, calmest, and most civilized revolution I've ever seen—
until the shooting began by the police and the British inter-
vened."

But how did the shooting in Athens begin?

During the week before December 1, the Papandreou government was stalemated on how to get ELAS and the Mountain
Brigade disarmed and disbanded. When the British command, or
government, insisted that their hand-picked Brigade of royalists
must have special treatment over the Resistance patriots (who
had opposed the Germans at far greater cost), the six EAM
ministers quit the government. Yet when Winston Churchill
told the world about the Greek civil war he made no pretense of
reporting all the facts. He never so much as mentioned his government's stand in support of the royalist Mountain Brigade—nor
so much as mentioned the existence of the Brigade.

On December 2, EAM leaders asked for governmental permission to stage a protest demonstration—and gave their word that
it would be unarmed. Papandreou granted permission for the
parade on December 3, next morning. Out of 1,250,000 Greeks
in the greater Athens area, probably 80 percent or more were
EAM supporters; mostly workers and the poor. That afternoon
they got word that the demonstration was permitted. Most of
them had never possessed telephones or radios. They went to bed
early, so as to get up at four or five o'clock and start marching to
Constitution Square in the heart of Athens. But Papandreou had
a long parley with General Scobie that night, and shortly before
midnight the premier cancelled permission for the parade—when
the people could not possibly be notified. Papandreou also decided to declare martial law. From British sources I was told that
General Scobie told Papandreou it was time to "get tough" with
EAM.

On Sunday morning tens of thousands of Athenian workers
and their wives and children marched toward and into Constitution Square. The police had machine guns on the roofs—something no correspondent had seen before then. The EAM supporters carried placards. Some of the slogans read: "Why,
America, have you abandoned us?" . . . "America, we are tired

and we don't want civil war." . . . "Bring the traitors to trial."
. . . "We want a real national unity government." The square
was jammed with people, but correspondents close beside the
police lines said there was no disorder. Then, suddenly, some of
the police began firing into the tight-packed throng. In a short
time twenty-five were dead, including a boy aged six. Scores more
reddened the pavements from their wounds. Now it was not
merely martial law, but civil war.

Later on I had a long conversation with British Ambassador
Leeper. He talked so readily that I had little opportunity to ask
questions. At the end of some forty minutes I was keenly aware
of the fact that the British ambassador had scarcely looked me
straight in the eye twice throughout his prolonged monologue.
This is a fact which I am compelled to report. There was a further
fact. In years of rather frequent encounters with ambassadors
of many nations, I had never left a consultation with such an
unpleasant impression as I took away this time. I regret to have
to say this, but I believe it is too important to be glossed over.
This happened, oddly enough, without my so much as asking an
embarrassing question. Perhaps this was because the official
Churchill-Leeper version of the tragedy in Greece had won only
one ardent supporter among some twenty British and American
correspondents who were making their own investigation of facts
in Athens. The Churchill-Leeper version badly needed support
in the world press, yet about 90 percent of Anglo-American correspondents on the spot rejected large sections of it *in toto*. As a
more recent arrival, I was probably thought to merit an extensive
official review of the situation. In the course of this review Ambassador Leeper said: "The police did not shoot first. Grenades
were thrown first by the ELAS. The Communists put their wom-
en and children in the front row, as they always do, to hide their
armed men. They had their guns behind and were shooting."

This statement was so completely contrary to everything I had
previously heard that I maintained a poker face to hide my
amazement—and did not question it. But I went back and talked
again to about a dozen correspondents who—unlike the British
ambassador—had been eyewitnesses. Again I asked if there had
been any shooting by the EAM demonstrators.

"None whatever. Only the police shot."

That was the unanimous verdict. "We never saw any EAM people with weapons in their hands," they said. "If any of the EAM were shooting, how was it that not a policeman was wounded?" The British correspondents were particularly incensed over their ambassador's statement. One of them said: "There were never any women and children out in front to hide men with weapons. That's a lot of ——."

I am absolutely convinced that he was right.

In fact, the absurdity of Ambassador Leeper's accusation was demonstrated by the news photographs which Dimitri Kessel of *Life* risked his own life in taking that morning of death and disgrace. These pictures show Greek workers—men, women, and children—being mowed down by police fire, without a weapon in their hands. Was it merely as a precaution that Papandreou was persuaded, the night before, to declare martial law? By the record of what happened, the Athens police should have been placed under martial law.

The massacre by the police prompted the EAM–ELAS supporters to attack police stations all over the city. British troops were ordered to uphold the forces of "law and order." And within twenty-four hours the British and their Greek royalist bands were in serious danger from ELAS forces, which outnumbered them greatly and were backed by the overwhelming mass of the Athenian population. That was when 100 U.S. Army transport planes were called upon to intervene in the civil war. American pilots flew in British and Indian troops as reinforcements. All of Athens, that lovely and shining metropolis beneath the brow of the incomparable Acropolis, became a battlefield. For *thirty-three* days the common people fought against Lend-Lease tanks and RAF dive bombers. They were bombed and machine-gunned in their pitiful shacks and hovels in Ghizi and Kaisariani. They were "terrorists" and "Communists," the "liberators" said. The strongest of EAM and ELAS leaders were Communists, and so were a small minority of their extremely large following. But who were the terrorists? Who had started the terror? Let history answer—let time bring its own retribution.

But in these first days, even with all the organized military units on their side and even with the best and heaviest weapons, the British and the Greek royalists were pushed backward and backward. So it happened, just two days after the fighting started, that General Scobie accepted other allies—the Quislings and Lavals of Greece. By Scobie's order, or by his permission, the traitor "Security Battalions" were released, rearmed, and thrown against the ELAS forces.

What did the Security Battalions do in Greece?

They were formed under the Germans as Greek Quisling militiamen. In the battle-scarred Kaisariani section of Athens women and old men told me how these traitors had rounded up their sons, husbands, and brothers for the Gestapo to execute. Thousands of the bravest Greek patriots—chiefly workers and peasants—were sent to their deaths by these hired servants of the Germans. When liberation came, the Security Battalions rushed to surrender to the British, knowing the fierce hatred which the Greek people held for them. The British obligingly put them in barracks, sometimes even allowing them street liberty. While the people cried out that these traitors should be punished, nothing was done. An Allied officer got some of them drunk, and they then said they had been promised that nothing would happen to Security Battalion men.

Just as the French patriots cried: "Death to the Vichyites!" so the Greek patriots clamored that the SBs (a wonderfully apt designation) should be executed. But the British and their puppet-premier Papandreou were pleading that people should be reasonable. Then the EAM—ELAS leaders made a remarkable concession. To avoid general bloodshed they agreed that only the chiefs of the Security Battalions should be tried. Despite all the deaths these traitors had inflicted among their own comrades and loved ones, EAM and ELAS agreed that the SB rank and file should be relieved of any penalties. That, too, was a strange kind of mercy for "terrorist plotters" to show. Yet these same EAM—ELAS people were charged by Winston Churchill with plotting "wholesale massacre." It is a matter of record that between October 14 and December 3 they spared the miserable lives of thousands of SB traitors.

On December 5 or 6 the EAM—ELAS Resistance forces were rewarded for their generosity. General Scobie needed reinforcements badly. Some 5,000 Security Battalion men, or more, were armed and thrown into battle against ELAS in the streets of Athens. Until then the British probably had no more than 6,000 Mountain Brigade Greeks as allies; and a thousand or so more Greek royalists—the X-ites—were holding the Temple of Theseus area. Without the assistance of the *German-uniformed* Greek Quisling battalions, ELAS patriots might well have *liberated* Athens from the British. Later on a British officer was so amazingly frank as to tell a correspondents' press conference that the Security Battalions "fought very well." When the civil war ended, the British-controlled Athens government put thousands of these SB traitors into the new National Guard—where they are still doing very nicely today.

I reached Athens before the truce had been declared. I learned how the Security Battalion men were being enlisted in the new army, along with all royalists, while republicans of all shades were being barred. So when I had an interview with the new British-selected premier, General Plastiras, I brought up this subject. General Plastiras seemed neither surprised nor embarrassed.

"Of course there are Security Battalion members in the new army," he said. "Why not? They fought well beside the British."

When I pursued my questioning, a high government official, sitting beside the general, explained: "The Security Battalions were formed to prevent Communist excesses and lootings. They fought the ELAS." He admitted that "some of them" had fought for the Germans. But he insisted their chief role was protection of property and protection from EAM guerrillas. General Plastiras added: "I wasn't in Greece then, but I don't believe the majority of the Security Battalions were pro-Nazi or collaborators." This, most emphatically, was *not* what the majority of Greeks believed. It happens that *they were* in Greece all the time.

What Greeks loyally and persistently resisted the Germans?

Prime Minister Churchill told Parliament that "the ELAS armed bands, at any rate for the last two years, *played very little part against the Germans."* (Italics mine.) This statement is diametrically opposed by the overwhelming majority of testimony gathered by correspondents and Allied officers in Greece *before* the civil war. Both the British and the Americans had many liaison officers working with the Greek Resistance inside Greece for many months before "liberation." I have talked with some of these officers. Other correspondents talked with more of them. These on-the-spot intelligence officers had all publicly *contradicted* Mr. Churchill's effort to belittle EAM and ELAS, weeks before his statement was made to an uninformed world public.

A British brigadier (equivalent to a brigadier general in the U.S. Army) had worked with the Greek Resistance forces for approximately two years. He said: "The only real resisters and fighters against the Germans were the ELAS."

At an Athens press conference, about October 18, a British brigadier—Brigadier Barker-Benfield, who personally directed all British liaison with Greek guerrilla forces over a long period —told assembled British and American correspondents: "We should never have been able to set foot on Greece had it not been for the magnificent efforts of the Resistance Movements of EAM and ELAS." Within forty-eight hours this British brigadier was *withdrawn* from Greece. Correspondents insisted he had been "banished" upon the demand of Ambassador Leeper, who considered him too pro-EAM. Several other British officers, who had served with the Greek Resistance, were dispatched out of the country before December 3, and there were ugly rumors as to why they had been removed from Athens.

Many months before Athens was "liberated," an Allied intelligence officer reported from inside Greece: "One of the chief dead things in Greece today is the monarchy. We crossed parts of Greece which were strongholds of royalism in the past. Now people appear ashamed if you ask whether they would vote for the return of the King. Every day I talk with scores of villagers. As much as is humanly possible, I try to gather the truth about things and issues as they are. What amazed all of us is the amount of control that the EAM exercises in every part of Greece. The greater part of the country is ruled and controlled by EAM.

EAM has established self-government in most of the country, and these changes are very popular with the people. Every village has its own organization."

The Allied officer continued in his report: "At present all the forces of reaction—special interests, old politicians, Fascists, German collaborators, and some of the wealthy—have united with the single purpose of beating EAM. All these people have either stayed inactive too long (and thus let the initiative of national leadership pass to the radicals who lead the EAM), or they were active selling the country to the Germans. . . . *The initiative passed to those who were willing to fight and risk their lives. . . .* The old politicians grabbed the anti-Communist harp and started playing the German tune. They led many officers into collaboration. They thought they were being clever."

More than one Allied officer who had worked in the Greek underground frankly stated that the only Greek organizations which never collaborated with the Germans were EAM and ELAS. I sought out a Greek editor, who was considerably concerned about the Communists. He was an old friend in whose judgment and fairness I had great confidence. He said: "ELAS fought the Germans at times, and sometimes they fought the Greek middle class. But they really *did* fight the Germans." He admitted he could not say that much for most of the Greek upper class. In the workers' districts, where the vast proportion of Athens' population lives, we found nothing but hatred of the Germans and Greek collaborators, and a universal loyalty to EAM. They were amazed and indignant when I asked if any of their neighbors had helped the Germans. "Nobody," the workers' women replied in a chorus. Watching these people's faces, you knew they were speaking the absolute truth. In Athens' Park Avenue district I heard much talk from the Kolonaki about the "Communists," almost none against the Germans, and no talk about relatives who had died fighting in the Resistance. From all I could observe or learn, talking with all categories of Greeks, there was extremely little *active* resistance to the Nazis among upper-class Greeks. They were also the only uniformly healthy-looking, well-fed Greeks that I met.

Why did Mr. Churchill make such a slighting remark about the part played by ELAS in resisting the Germans? *Six months earlier,* in August 1944—as CBS Correspondent Eric Sevareid reported [1] —Churchill ordered the BBC Overseas Service to *eliminate "any credit of any kind"* to the ELAS or EAM. Was this a deliberate plan to distort the Resistance role of ELAS before European public opinion? Or was it an accident that Cairo correspondents, well before "liberation," were instructed to limit any estimates of ELAS strength to no more than 30,000? Actually, its strength was conceded to be at least 60,000 guerrillas. Why did the British censorship in Cairo insist that ELAS strength should be played down and minimized? And again why were those British intelligence officers, who knew better and could speak with authority about EAM and ELAS, ordered out of Greece before the fireworks began? These are fair and pertinent questions which the Churchill government never faced, never acknowledged, and, in fact, dodged by never admitting their existence. Since the Churchill-Leeper school were equally hazy on another key question, let's face it.

How Red and Communistic were EAM and ELAS?

As was true in the Spanish Civil War, a relatively small minority of Greek Communists became the most active leaders in the Greek Resistance. EAM was a coalition of moderate republicans, agrarians, Socialists, and Communists; but the Communists developed more strong personalities and greater capacity for organization than any of the other parties or groups. In ELAS, the fighting branch, four career army generals were in command, some of them reputedly Communists. But even the British, in the midst of the civil war, admitted that the Russians never gave any help to EAM or ELAS. The Soviets, by common testimony, never lifted a finger; and the Greek Communist movement developed under the Germans as a strictly national expression. Actually, these Communists had been jailed for long terms under the prewar pro-Fascist Metaxas dictatorship. A keen Greek observer assured me that Metaxas "made" and educated their Communist leaders—because they studied Marxism while in jail.

Although Communists provided the greatest leadership in EAM, the mass following of that coalition was in no sense Com-

[1] See his "Censors in the Saddle," the *Nation*, April 14, 1945.

munist. What, in fact, was EAM's political program? It was chiefly a program for much-needed social welfare in Greece: more schools, better child care, the development of co-operatives as in Scandinavia, clinics, and the expansion of public health. Like all the European Resistance Movements, EAM also demanded equal rights for women. Neutrals who lived in Greece during the German occupation describe the EAM reform program as democratic, surprisingly moderate, and surprisingly un-Communistic. EAM likewise favored the inauguration of a permanent civil service with adequate pay—something which Greece has needed for many years. Throughout most of Greece anywhere from 70 to 90 percent of the people are said to have supported this program. And throughout most of Greece before "liberation," as I know for a fact, from 65 to 85 percent of all Greeks were pro-republican and antiroyalist. For the Churchill government to attempt to impose a monarchy upon these people was the height of folly, as well as of injustice.

Anyone who is informed about Greeks and the economy of Greece must be very naïve to imagine that these people would ever go Communist—unless pushed into it by Allied stupidities. The Greek is a fierce individualist by nature, and also an extremely shrewd businessman, with a curious mixture of the poet in his make-up. Greece has relatively little big industry and virtually no big landlords. The people are small peasant landowners or shepherds, small shopkeepers or workers. They have a passionate love of freedom and are so sharply individualistic that they have a hard time governing themselves—and any dictatorial group has an infinitely worse time. Communists had no foothold whatever in Greece until General Metaxas and his dictatorship tripled or quadrupled their very small ranks. The Greek Communists had little success in selling their ideology. They merely gained respect by their unflinching opposition, first to Metaxas, then to the Germans and Quislings. When the Churchill-Leeper school went out to smash the whole of EAM as a "Communist menace" they completely underestimated the temper and character of the Greeks, and alienated forever the mass of the Greek people.

As to where the sympathies of the great majority of the Greek masses stood, the blood and rubble of Athens gave their own answer. If EAM and ELAS were not the only patriotic coalitions which commanded a very large mass following in Greece, how did ELAS manage to fight off British troops, tanks, and planes for thirty-three terrible days in Athens? Even with the help of thousands of Greek royalists and traitors, British arms had to conquer Athens street by street. A large majority of the people supported ELAS to the end, not because they were "Reds" or "Communistic," but because ELAS had fought the Germans for Greek freedom—and, in their minds, was still fighting for Greek freedom.

The Greek people lost the "civil war," but they have not changed. On the fourth anniversary of EAM, in September 1945, more than 100,000 people filled the huge Athens stadium and overflowed in a great mass in surrounding streets and on the hills. All the suppressions of the past nine months failed to deter them. The British-supported Greek royalists had never been able to muster a demonstration like this. These were the "outs" defying their minority rulers. Edmund Wilson, of the *New Yorker*, sent this report that same month:

"It had become very plain to me since I had been in Greece that the movement which the British had disarmed, and which the United States had allowed them to disarm, was neither a chess play directed from Moscow nor a foray of bandits from the hills—but a *genuine popular movement* which had recruited almost all that was generous, courageous and enlightened in Greece; the most spirited among the young, the most clear-sighted among the mature. This movement has been broken; the prisons are crammed with tens of thousands of political prisoners, and the government police have been practicing just such methods of torture and terror as the Gestapo formerly used. . . . While the British, after calling out their tanks against EAM and expressing indignant horror over outrages perpetrated by the Left, have done little or nothing to curb the Right."

This is the nature of the Churchill government's Pyrrhic victory in Greece. It is the "damned spot" which must remain on the record of a great and brilliant war leader to whom people in all Allied lands—*except Greece*—are uniquely indebted. For the tragedy in Greece is equally a great British tragedy. This is true beyond slightest question because—

The civil war in Greece could have been avoided.

I had always said I would rather be in Athens on its day of liberation than in Berlin when it surrendered. I had lived with the Greek soldiers and the Greek people in those unforgettable months of grandeur and self-abnegation as they expelled Mussolini's vaunted Blackshirt invaders. I knew with what incredible enthusiasm and warmheartedness they would receive their liberating allies. That was what happened on October 14, 1944. All of Athens went delirious with joy at the sight of General Scobie's small columns. Everywhere the Greek people showered the British with adoration and affection. The Greeks gave them their hearts as few, save the Greeks, can give their hearts.

"The Greeks welcomed the British as if they were gods," a friend said to me. "These people in Athens are overwhelmingly for EAM and ELAS, but they showered British Tommies with flowers and kisses. They gave them everything they had to give. The British had the ardent support of the whole Greek people— and they threw it away. All London had to do was take in EAM, along with everyone else; treat them fairly, and build a real government of national union. The British had the firmest and most loyal allies they ever had, right here—and they threw them away."

I went around Athens for days asking Greeks, British, and Americans: "Could it have been avoided?" There was far more agreement on this than on anything else—something close to unanimous agreement. Yes, the civil war *could* have been avoided. My Greek editor friend spoke sadly of British blunders. A Greek officer, republican but strongly anti-Communist and one who had seen how the Greek "mutiny" was handled in Egypt, said: "The British have committed every blunder and stupidity. If they try to bring the King back, I'll go with anybody—even the Communists. This did not need to happen. Don't talk to me about Leeper. I know what he has done." That was the verdict of an anti-ELAS Greek.

I talked with the workers, and I remember particularly the

expression and words of one very intelligent working-class woman· "If the British had let us alone, these things would have been settled in forty-eight hours." The majority of British correspondents—whose fearless efforts to try to tell the truth from Athens I shall always remember with professional pride—these honest and best-informed Britishers admitted sadly that the civil war could have been avoided. An American with an exceptional background in Greece said: "This whole thing has been a colossal British blunder. The British ambassador overrode the advice and warnings of his own army's intelligence service—and got rid of them. He badly underestimated the great mass following of EAM and ELAS. His attitude was that ELAS represented only about 10 percent of the population, and it didn't matter. But whether Leeper convinced Churchill, or Churchill convinced Leeper, their policy naturally led to civil war."

And one Britisher, shamed by what he had seen and what he had learned, replied slowly with an expression I shall not forget: "It would have been easy enough to find a peaceful solution." He paused, and I understood why. Then he looked me straight in the eyes, at an obvious cost. "You can't escape the conviction," he said, "that the main idea was to smash the Left *at any cost.*"

Strangely enough British Ambassador Leeper (who at this writing still remains in Greece, representing a British *Labor* government) said as much to me with the utmost frankness. These were the concluding remarks of my interview with Sir Reginald Leeper: "I think we have smashed here any chance of a dictatorship of the Left. It will have a big effect in Italy; in France, Belgium, and Holland as well." In the mind of Ambassador Leeper any Left coalition government would be a "dictatorship." But EAM had never proposed or championed any kind of dictatorship. Seemingly, that fact was irrelevant.

But the death toll in the "civil war" is by no means irrelevant. Months later it appeared that first estimates, such as mine, were far too low. Ernest O. Hauser reported in December 1945 that the Greeks had suffered 76,000 casualties—the British, 1,810.[2] Others stated that approximately 11,000 persons were killed, and

2 "Europe's Most Frightened Country," the *Saturday Evening Post*, December 29, 1945.

that 6,500 of these were *civilians*. The overwhelming majority of the victims were Greeks, and the majority among them were thousands of civilians.

The fundamental issue of the British-Greek war has been blacked out by charges and countercharges of atrocities, coming especially from Greek royalists, the "Kolonaki," and Churchill government apologists. But certainly more than 90 percent of the atrocities came only after the street fighting started. In the British Parliament Sir Richard Acland [3] blasted this propaganda fog with unanswerable logic.

"In any civil war," Sir Richard declared, "the question is never settled by asking . . . 'Who has committed the most atrocities?' . . . or 'Who committed any atrocities?' The question is: 'Which party pushed the whole situation over the dividing line which separates the possibility of discussion and compromise from the impossibility of discussion and compromise?' " In other words: Who was primarily responsible for the beginning of the shooting? As Professor L. S. Stavrianos of Smith College has remarked: "It is significant that this question has been evaded both in the British White Paper and in the parliamentary speeches of Churchill and Eden." But any search for facts is certainly justified in asking—

What are the Churchill government's responsibilities in the Greek "civil war"?

These, I believe, are irrefutable:

1. British formation of the royalist and reactionary Greek Mountain Brigade under veil of rigid censorship, and London's early adoption of an antirepublican policy for Greece.

2. British failure to get the Greek Resistance Movement represented in the Greek government-in-exile in Cairo.

3. British refusal to disarm the royalist Mountain Brigade, thereby precipitating the crisis in Athens.

4. Pressure by General Scobie to have Premier Papandreou cancel permission for the EAM demonstration on December 3; and British approval of Papandreou's declaration of martial law.

5. Winston Churchill's refusal to accept the Greek moderate,

[3] Speech of January 19, 1945.

Themistocles Sophoulis, in place of Papandreou on December 4 or 5.

These are five specific responsibilities of the Churchill government, and their total effect was to prevent or make impossible any government of national unity after Athens' liberation—and to make civil war inevitable.

I think it is highly significant that Prime Minister Churchill, in his long and acrimonious public speeches on the fighting in Athens, never once mentioned—let alone discussed—any of the first four of the above five points. Upon rereading Mr. Churchill's speeches before Parliament on the subject of Greece I was shocked by their omissions and distortions. I am compelled to say that few dictators in our time have made speeches more essentially misleading and fundamentally dishonest. Future historians will study these speeches to observe how a truly great statesman can reveal feet of clay.

I speak here as a reporter. Lest there should be any misconception I owe you this statement. All the factual developments reported by me in this chapter were included in a series of eleven articles which I wrote for the New York Post Syndicate, upon returning from Greece in February 1945. They were examined and passed for military security by British officers in Washington prior to publication. Thus their contents were known to British authorities well in advance. As I write now, nearly a year later, I can say that not one line of my eleven-article report on the Greek civil war has even been challenged by any British authority. If my report had contained any serious misstatements, I think it most probable that some British agency would have challenged them. But how could the Churchill government question facts which Mr. Churchill himself was most careful never to mention when he appeared before Parliament?

At this point I want to make it clear that I do not place the betrayal of Greece in this record with any pleasure whatever. I do so strictly out of necessity; in the interest of clarifying what our actions and our choices are in this postwar world. I have been careful to place an unfortunate and major share of responsibility for the Greek civil war upon the Churchill government—not upon the British people. If the British people had been given the facts —if they had not been gravely deceived by the "Iron Curtain" of the Churchill government—Mr. Churchill would rightly have faced the greatest storm of his career in Parliament, and possibly not have survived it. To any readers who are by conviction anti-British I would say: I am not writing this for you. Any American who can forget the tremendous debt we owe the British people—and Winston Churchill, first of all—for their magnificent service when they fought alone; any such American is guilty of an ingratitude and a lack of fairness which, to me, are unpardonable. I am not and I shall not be anti-British. But I am a reporter.

But before any American begins to wax self-righteous over these unhappy pages, I think we must ask ourselves—

What did the American government do to prevent the Greek tragedy?

The answer is—precisely nothing.

The government of the world's greatest power sat by and lifted no finger to prevent or stop the civil war in Greece. We treated the Greek people's desires for self-government as though they were of no conceivable interest to us. We had supplied the tanks and trucks and planes and food—but Washington treated Greece as strictly a "British zone." We were Allies in Italy and the Mediterranean, but we did not send in any American troops beside the British. Our representatives in Athens watched the crisis come threateningly to a head, but they kept on the sidelines. Once the fighting started, Washington never once offered to mediate. There are more citizens of Greek blood in the United States than anywhere else in the world. These Americans of Greek descent have been among the bravest fighters in our armed services. In the most remote villages of Greece you always meet a Greek who once lived in the United States. I found among the Greek people a deeper and more universal affection for America and Americans than I have encountered in any other country around the world. Greek faith in America surpasses words. The friendship of the Greek people for Americans is one of the most spontaneous and unselfish things to be found in any nation. The EAM marched with placards saying: "America, why have you abandoned us?" The Greek people meant every word of that—and that, precisely, is what we did.

If my British colleagues were filled with shame at the actions of their government in Greece, the American correspondents were equally ashamed of the indifference and inaction of their own government. I have never lived days of greater spiritual agony and heartache. I shall never forget the sadness in the voice of George Weller of the *Chicago Daily News,* and the helplessness and bitterness of many others. These men, Americans and British, had seen plenty of war in all its cruelty and suffering and idiocy. Here, in Athens, we saw a betrayal infinitely more ugly than war—with the United States turning its back. You could wear a thick armor of journalistic cynicism, but you could not laugh that off. The Greek people wanted freedom and democracy; and the government of that nation in which they believed more than any other on earth—the government in Washington—betrayed them by its shocking inaction and indifference. Ours was the prestige. Ours was the power. We alone had the complete confidence of the Greek people. But Washington had no policy for Greece—except to do nothing.

Now, early in 1946, the Allies have teams of observers in Greece (British, French, and American) supposedly to insure that the announced Greek elections will be free. But—

What chance is there of free elections in Greece under present conditions?

Royalist and reactionary Greek bands have been waging a so-called "white terror" throughout the country ever since ELAS was conquered. One year after the civil war began a widely-known British journalist, Philip Jordan, reported: "Almost every day reports of beatings, of murder and rape are printed in the Athens press and cannot be denied." Jordan said the Greek Minister of the Interior's promise of law and order "will not prevail so long as men and women are being murdered by *his own* henchmen and supporters."

Saturday Evening Post Correspondent Ernest O. Hauser reported [4]

4 Issue of December 29, 1945.

Today, as a result of their victory, the Right-wing forces are making hay while the sun shines. Conditions reminiscent of early Nazi Germany leave Greece with less freedom than any other liberated country outside the Russian sphere. Armed vigilantes maintain "order" in the villages, and a private army of stormtroopers, called Organization X, terrorizes the city folk. . . . Neither the Greek Army nor the police seriously object to Right-wing excesses.

This last is not surprising. Both the new Greek Army and the police were recruited and packed—under British encouragement—with monarchists, reactionaries, and Security Battalion traitors. Yet these are the very forces of "law and order" which will police and control the "free" elections. They are all selected enemies of all groups, however moderate, who were formerly in EAM—and most of them fought the EAM and ELAS with the British. After more than fifteen months of "white terror" in the Greek towns and villages, and with the monarchist-SB Quislings watching them with guns, are the Greek people likely to vote as they want to vote? Many of them know they would be murdered a few weeks later for doing so.

Of course, the elections will be "orderly" when they are held. Of course, a few hundred Allied poll watchers will assure the world that the elections were "free" and "uninfluenced." But the French, British, and American electoral supervisors will not investigate the political affiliations, and past records, of the army officers, gendarmerie, and police in charge at the polling places. Nor will any of the Allied observers revisit the same towns and villages several months later, to inquire what has happened in the meantime. If the Allies wanted free elections in Greece, they would have to send the present Greek Army and police forces to Egypt for a vacation—and perhaps send the 70,000 or more British troops, which still patrol Greece, along with them.

Under present conditions elections in Greece cannot fail to be anything but a farce and a mockery of self-determination. The monarchists and reactionaries—all of those who never fought the Germans or who collaborated with them—are almost certain to win. Winston Churchill, who could not win the last elections in Britain, has every chance of "carrying" Greece. Yet even if the amazingly courageous Greeks should be so rash as to defeat

Churchill's "ticket" by a narrow margin, the full voice of the Greek people would still not have been accurately registered.[5]

(The preceding paragraphs were written three months before March 31, 1946, when the Greek elections—boycotted by the Left parties—were held. The official results, as now known, merely demonstrated that the Greeks were no more "free" to vote their honest preferences behind the Churchill-Leeper-Greek monarchists' "velvet" curtain than Rumanians or Poles may have been behind the Soviets' so-called iron curtain. Although the Populists—otherwise royalists—emerged with more votes from those who did vote, the number of abstentions totalled approximately 50 percent. If the registration lists were not padded with the names of scores of thousands of dead citizens—as the Left and some neutral observers had charged for many weeks—this fact proved that EAM supporters would surely have emerged as the strongest party in Greece, had they dared go to the polls. The only other possible interpretation was equally derogatory to the British-sponsored monarchists and collaborating Greek Quislings. Athens' puppet government had proclaimed a total registration of 2,200,000—nearly 500,000 more supposed voters than had voted in 1936—in a country of a population of less than 7,000,000, in which more than 1,000,000 persons died during the war—and in which women are not allowed to vote. Even British Ambassador Sir Reginald Leeper would find it difficult to explain this highly suspect matter of simple arithmetic and make it spell or smell like "free elections." As Correspondent Hauser prophesied, the Greek elections were most thoroughly "prepared". What they have really prepared is another and more bitter story.)

5 This, incidentally, is what Ernest O. Hauser has to say about "preparations" for the Greek elections. The monarchists "hope that many Greeks will vote for the king—whose popularity is almost nil—simply because they consider him a bulwark against communism. Anyway, as long as thousands of EAM followers have to stay away from their homes and from the polling booth, as long as the Right-wing policy controls the pre-election registration, a Left-wing victory appears unlikely. I have talked with numerous Greeks who frankly told me they did not dare to show up for registration, for fear of being thrown into jail when they presented themselves. Known royalists, on the other hand, are reliably reported by competent British and American observers here to have obtained more than one polling card, enabling them to cast several votes." This, I believe, is sufficient indication of how "free" elections in Greece can possibly be, and how thoroughly they are being "prepared."

It seems now that the true opinion of the Greek people can only express itself, some day or other, in another civil war.

I left Athens still hearing the voices of the Greek people, and the voice of George Weller. We had all lost: the Greeks, the British, the Americans. We, the Western democracies, had sold our birthright. Some day we should all have to pay the price—and the Greeks, who had lost one out of every eight of their fellow countrymen in this war, again would pay most heavily.

Our plane was pushed close to earth by thick clouds. It skimmed precariously above the treetops along the southern shore of the Gulf of Patras. A heavy gale whipped and tossed it. The ceiling closed down and down as we reached the ugly sea, with the island mountains fogged out somewhere in front of us. When I could get my mind off these ugly realities, and between the lurches, I was obsessed by the heartbreak of Athens. One woman's words in particular kept coming back to me. She was a fine-browed working woman, with an unquenchable sadness in her splendid dark eyes.

"But do they think that nothing has changed in the world?" she asked me. "And why do you Americans let them destroy the Greek patriots?"

"Yes," I had said. "They think nothing has changed in the world."

She stood there, straight and unconquered and somehow unconquerable; a slender woman with work-calloused hands and slender fingers. I saw her grappling with her thoughts—not to make them clear, but to make the truth behind them clear.

"But why," she asked again, "are the British shooting the ELAS just as the *Germans* did? . . . Why are they afraid of the people?"

Why are we afraid of the people?

There were many things I wanted to tell her about that. But it was too long a story. It would take this book to try to give a partly adequate answer.

Chapter XV

IS SOCIALISM THE NEW MIDDLE GROUND?

*We are confronted with a problem that is old in Europe.
How do we reach a compromise between control and
liberty? That is the problem that confronts our age.*

Edward R. Murrow

*A social system that cannot be changed cannot be
maintained.*

Holbrook Jackson

*What private property any of us enjoys represents the
acquiescence of society in our private control of it . . .
and, like every privilege, it carries with it certain obligations. . . . Those who neglect the obligations, I am
convinced, speed the day when this privilege will be
curtailed or perhaps denied.*

Marshall Field III

It was just before Christmas 1944. In a Paris restaurant my
friend, the French journalist Geraud Jouvre, was discussing De
Gaulle and the Communists. But he turned suddenly to the bloodshed in Athens.

"In Greece the British are losing all their influence in the
Balkans," said Geraud with much seriousness. "That's a bad thing
for France. We should have worked together there. Churchill
is a great fighter, but a very bad politician. He is working to
communize Greece. It is a terrible blunder—and we shall all have
to pay for it, even you in America."

I recalled this comment when, early in the following June,
I scanned the morning newspaper. Winston Churchill had
warned the British electorate that the result of a Labor victory
would be a Socialist totalitarian state whose authority would be
a Gestapolike political police. "Socialism," Mr. Churchill said,

"is in its essence an attack not only upon British enterprise, but upon the right of an ordinary man or woman to breathe freely without having a harsh, clumsy and tyrannical hand clashed across his or her mouth." From any European politician, that was an amazingly alarmist and inaccurate statement. Would the British people swallow anything as exaggerated and emotional as that? I doubted it very much. And when the answer came, it came in the form of a crushing repudiation. The British people knew perfectly well that nowhere, inside or outside Europe, had Socialism ever been "Gestapolike" or "tyrannical" or antidemocratic in its methods.

But the extreme and distorted language used so incomprehensibly by one of this century's great leaders has been resorted to, in the heat of electoral campaigns, by conservatives in many lands. We in America have heard the same kind of picture painted in the same lurid terms rather often since 1932; yet the prophecies of dictatorship vanished into thin air, and our representative government plods or stumbles along much as usual. In the case of a statesman of Mr. Churchill's stature it merely came as a shock that he should suddenly sound like William Randolph Hearst or Colonel Robert R. McCormick. Is it not usually true that when a conservative goes glandular in a big way he sounds so overwrought and illogical that he loses much of his effectiveness? This, at any rate, was Winston Churchill's reward from the level-headed British voters.

This, in turn, brings us to what I believe is one of the outstanding characteristics of our times.

These are days when life is really pretty tough for an ultraconservative.

There are few nations in our world where an *extreme* conservative can be very happy or has much, in the long run, to look forward to. Almost everywhere, including the United States, human rights are being demanded with increasing insistence. Almost everywhere, including conservative America, property rights are being challenged with greater force. The more I have watched these tendencies grow and expand, the more grateful I have become that I was not born loaded down at birth with the world's goods, nor with any ambition to try to accumulate a large amount of them. Without such encumbrances it is much easier to observe and study what is happening in human society. A modest share of bourgeois blessings need not be a hindrance, unless you permit them to be. It should and can be an advantage to be, relatively speaking, a spectator with some intellectual or scientific interest in what may happen next—and why.

But the well-heeled conservative, in our revolutionary times, in most cases is as inevitably an ardent partisan from the outset as are the very poor and the exploited. The one fights for what he has; the other for what he has not. The spectator is obliged to note that it is those who have most who more frequently betray impatience or indulge a mood of violence. Long ago Machiavelli explained this by saying shrewdly: "Men complain more of losing a fortune than of losing a brother or a father. *For we forget our grief over a death, but never over a loss of property.*" If Machiavelli had been mistakenly cynical, how much happier the intervening centuries would have been.

Thus any close examination of contemporary society underscores the plight of those conservatives who are usually described as reactionaries. Whatever happens, they have nothing much to gain. The trend of the times runs strongly against them. They have nowhere to go that promises them any lasting relief. If they embrace and underwrite Fascism in an effort to save their fortunes and their privileges, the end-consequence of that policy of desperation—as has now been clearly demonstrated—will be that they lose most of both; a Fascist-inspired war would take care of whatever remnants might have survived. A completely disinterested and indifferent observer today might remark: Pity the poor reactionary. He was born in conflict with the times, and out of joint with his time. The twentieth century has made him its prisoner. His only escape is to bend like a willow in a high wind. But how can he bend? If he *could* bend with the wind, he would *not* be a reactionary. He would be an intelligent conservative, conscious of the practical value of compromise. But, on his side of the fence, what is so rare as an intelligent conservative?

These observations are not facetious in spirit or intent. I am merely looking at our present world and thinking out loud. The evidence is everywhere about us that the lot of today's ultraconservative is in no sense a happy one; and this, I have repeatedly noticed, is to be seen in most of their faces. They themselves have seen the handwriting on the wall. But like the incorrigible Winston Churchill, with his feet and much of his mind firmly cemented in the imperialistic era of Kipling, they cannot free themselves from the heritage of their past, or from their environment and the mounting demands of their preoccupations. The peoples of the modern world have a place to go, and the ultraconservatives haven't. Sometimes it must seem as if their choice lies between a military atomic bomb and another which is political and economic. To envy the lot of our present-day captains of finance, industry, and vested wealth might almost justify a psychiatric examination for initial signs of lunacy.

But a reporter from Neptune, being utterly uninvolved, would probably stay his tears and stifle his sighs. He would note that most ultraconservatives are in no mood for sympathy; and he would rightly conclude that humans of this particular type will never learn, except the hard way. Having noted these pertinent facts, we can again turn our attention to this Europe which is as surely the cradle of our Western nations' *future* as it has been the cradle of our past. In this Europe Today grapples with Tomorrow, and no holds are barred. We can see there how the ground has shifted, and why much of the shift will be permanent. The Second World War has made—

Socialism the new middle ground in Europe's
politics and economy.

This is the factual result of Labor's smashing victory in Great Britain and of the French elections where the Socialists emerged precisely in the center between two other main parties of almost identical strength. But the Socialists have held or gained in much the same way in most European countries. The prevailing weight was left of the old center in Hungary. In reality, it is the same in Greece, however much army- and police-dominated elections might seem to camouflage the fact. In Italy, too, the fundamental popular trend is left of center. In Austria alone, at this writing, have the Communists shown no strength at all and the Catholic Right won a considerable success. Yet the Austrian Socialists proved about as strong as ever. In Belgium and Holland the Socialists remain important, and certain of their socialistic proposals—as in most other countries—have the support of more moderate or conservative parties. In Norway and Sweden the Socialists are dominant.

What is perhaps most striking in these postwar developments is *the fact that Socialism has become the middle ground precisely in those western European countries where democracy is most deeply embedded.* In these lands peoples with the firmest traditions of representative government have accepted Socialist parties as a central bastion of democracy's defense. Since this could not possibly be true in the United States today, it reveals the gap between the American system and the more experimental and progressively inclined European democracies. For a majority of these peoples what is Socialist may or may not please them mightily—but it is obviously *democratic.* For a large proportion of Americans what is Socialist is obviously radical, or "communistic." But a Frenchman who wants to keep as many of his property rights and as much of free enterprise as possible is compelled to regard the powerful French Socialist party as his last line of defense. A last line, because state ownership of key industries and the like would come only gradually. Middle ground, because the great Socialist Party can decide an issue if it throws its full weight either to the Catholic Popular Republicans or to the Communists.

These are all evidences of how times have changed in Europe. But it would be misleading to assume that the more conservative elements in European countries have resigned themselves to the change. Like convinced conservatives anywhere, they will not bow to the inevitable without using every weapon in their hands. So we must consider the question—

Can Europe's Rightists recoup their losses?

It is clear that the conservatives in Britain, France, and elsewhere are dedicated to a stubborn, uphill fight. Near the close of 1945, and at seventy-one, the unrepentant Winston Churchill set out heroically to salvage or save the Tory cause. Though he sounded to many like a political King Canute, bidding the postwar breakers of popular will to stand still, the old bulldog of Britain barked and gnashed like a Victorian mastiff. He declared war on "the gloomy vultures of nationalization" and those "hagridden by socialist doctrinaires." Knowing full well the financial and economic nightmares inherited by the Attlee government, Mr. Churchill declared: "We are being harassed, harried, tied down and stifled for vaguely thought-out and physically unattainable plans for a socialist future." The old Churchillian invective flashed brilliantly and bitterly. If British conservatives' capitalistic privileges could be saved by magnificent rhetoric, Winston Churchill would save them yet. But admittedly he faced a task as seemingly hopeless as the Battle of Britain had appeared five autumns earlier. In the Battle of Britain, however, Churchill did have the people on his side.

In Italy the uneasy coalition government headed by the Resistance patriot, Ferruccio Parri, had fallen. The unliberal Italian Liberal Party, aided by the Catholic Christian Democrats —both conservative in their following—broke the six-party unity which appeared to offer Italy's one hope for some sort of political stability. This was the Rightists' first blow against the Left. It succeeded because the Anglo-Americans had bolstered the despised and pro-Fascist Italian royalty; because they did little or nothing to strengthen the Parri government in its helpless economic plight. It succeeded, some charged, because the British and Americans were afraid that popular disorders might grow out of the people's hunger and want. But the conservatives were also greatly aided because Italy's most politically developed provinces, those in the Po valley and the north, were still under Allied military administration. As everywhere, the Allies had retarded or smothered political self-expression. By supporting the king who made Mussolini and his antidemocratic son, Prince Umberto, they betrayed the Italian people's hopes for a republic. But the issue was far from decided yet.

So the prospects for a conservative come-back were nowhere bright in Europe, though one great intangible made outright prophecy of their final chances a risky matter. What would one or two more winters of undernourishment, unheated homes, and increased suffering do to the masses of the people? Would they blame the predominantly Left coalitions and give new heed to promises from Rightist groups? Or would they swell the ranks of the Communists at their next electoral opportunity? If there were no certain answers to these questions—perhaps not even in convincing form before the spring or summer of 1947—it remained a fact that social disorders anywhere would galvanize the conservatives against the menace of "Bolshevism." It also remained a fact that any threat of Fascism, once Allied military forces had withdrawn, would very likely precipitate civil war in most European countries. Extremists of Left or Right could be the only ones to gain. That, once again, meant that Socialism was—and would remain—the only *orderly* and safe middle ground throughout much of the Old World; not completely Socialist governments, but coalitions in which moderate and conservative groups co-operated on a compromise basis with the Socialists.

Without a working coalition of all or most democratic parties with the democratic Socialists, the Communists stand to gain most in Europe in the long run. Any prolongation of mass misery, as the war showed, adds to the appeal of the Communist doctrine. The Soviets may not worry too much about feeble or retarded reconstruction in much of Europe, since they may estimate that Communism's long-term prospects in these countries will be definitely improved as a result. For these reasons conservatives in Italy, France, Austria, and elsewhere will be extremely short-sighted if they refuse to make compromises with their Socialist nationals. In the new Europe half a loaf can be much more nutritive than none at all. A degree of Socialization, adopted with the checks and controls of free parliamentary procedures, may well prove to be the only middle ground that many European nations can find. In this difficult situation a certain amount of Socialism may be the only kind of democracy that the majority of voters will support or accept. This is perhaps the most important political fact which we have seen crystallizing throughout the continent ever since the war's end.

To a veteran observer like William L. Shirer, the change in late autumn of 1945 appeared impressive. Writing from Germany, he said: "The old struggle between Right and Left appears finished. There is no more Right. The new struggle appears to be between socialists and communists. It is going on in each country. But it may also split Europe in two. . . . The major problem of our time in Europe may well be relations between these two forms of socialism."

Alongside this overall pattern we should take note that Soviet Russia's influence registered a recession in eastern and central Europe, dating from the late summer of 1945. The continued presence of Red Army forces, living off the land, had much to do with this. The fact that many Soviet soldiers got out of hand in their first free months in more bountiful lands accentuated it. Probably the severe control exercised by the green-capped Soviet security police added to the restlessness in Poland and the Danubian countries. National pride naturally reasserted itself in these proud peoples. For these and other reasons Soviet prestige was reported to have declined, even in the Slavic nations. In some places local industries were pretty well stripped and machinery was shipped to Russia—which did not enhance the conception of "Big Brother Ivan."

Although the Red Army had been longest in Austria the Communists there made little progress. In Hungary the distribution of lands made the peasants more attached, momentarily anyway, to private ownership. In eastern Europe there was as yet no indication that the masses had rallied strongly to Communism. But there were indications that the Soviets had decided it would be more practical not to push their dominant influence too hard. According to one theory, Moscow could not lose much by letting central and eastern Europe stew in its bitter juices. In the next twenty years or so she might expect most of Europe to go Communist anyway; the more blindly the conservatives fought in their national arenas, the more hopeless economic and political conditions would become. It was not surprising, perhaps, that some Soviet citizens should predict confidently that Communism was bound to win in Europe eventually; and that may become true.

But the drop in Soviet prestige and Soviet magnetism in central and eastern Europe unquestionably gave the Western democracies important, if temporary, opportunities. The evidence is still strong that the peoples in most of these countries would prefer democratic governments under parliamentary systems. In no sense does this mean that any of them would welcome strictly conservative regimes. But it means that an enlightened and progressive democracy could win a great deal of popular support in central and Balkanic Europe *if* the Western democracies were unitedly to encourage it in every possible way—and especially by their own example.

Our initial record in postwar Europe, however, has shown the British and Americans more often destroying their own propaganda and their own prestige than building these. In Italy and Germany the Anglo-Americans were usually afraid of Socialists. In Greece the British fought all the Greek political groups left of center, branding even mild Socialists or milder republicans as "Reds." As practiced in military occupation and in diplomacy, the "democracy" of the Allies offered no mass appeal whatever to Europeans. Frequently it smacked of anything but democracy. *How, then, can we hope to promote democracy without winning the people?* That is what Washington and London have never, in Europe or Asia, attempted to answer with clear and consistent policies. To an observer it would seem quite explicable why neither the Soviets nor the European Communists need to be in a hurry. Time works for those who see clearly and know what they want.

Once Great Britain had given the Labor Party an overwhelming mandate of power, the London government became the natural leader of western Europe's middle-ground orientation. The tough scales of the Tory-Churchillian foreign policy could be dislodged only gradually, and they stuck fast in some imperial regions. But domestically the British Socialists' reform program closely resembled those reforms being urged in continental countries. The blueprint was Labor's booklet entitled "Let Us Face the Future." It proposed public ownership of fuel and power industries, especially of all coal mines; nationalization of all railroad, air, and canal transport services; public ownership of the entire British iron and steel industry; and extensive state control of exports. In its first weeks Labor nationalized the Bank of England. All of Britain's airlines and also her empire cable and wireless communications (a powerful and far-flung system) were marked for public ownership. How much of this bold program can be carried out in four or five years remains to be seen, but this is what the British people voted for; and many of these measures will be adopted.

In France action was delayed by the fact that a new Constitution, the structure of the New Fourth Republic, must be drafted. The delegates were assigned to complete this task before the summer of 1946. Then national elections to the new Chamber of Deputies, or National Assembly, would be required. But the October 1945 elections gave a tremendous majority to three parties, all of which favored the Resistance Movement's broad program for state ownership of mines, heavy industries, public utilities, insurance, and the like. André Geraud, who is known internationally as Pertinax, has been a friend of mine for some fifteen years. He has always been a Rightist in French politics, writing chiefly for Right-wing journals; but he has also proved himself to be an intelligent conservative. In prewar France Pertinax was seldom in agreement with the Socialists. Yet he was prompted to write, shortly before the French elections:

The Socialist program has become an accomplished fact. It has already been woven into the national structure. Exchange control and a regimented economic regime have come to stay. Therefore the Socialists are no longer dangerous innovators. *Moreover, they operate as a barrier against the Communist revolution on one side and against the Vichy reaction on the other.* . . . The Socialists, nowadays, are a *center* party. [Italics mine.]

This, by virtually unanimous testimony of the most experienced European observers, is the measure of Europe's political transformation. But we, who are Americans, are not at all prepared to face and understand this sudden emergence of Socialism —of partial public ownership through freely elective, democratic processes—as the new middle ground in the Western political world. We have been sidestepping the question of our age: How, as Edward R. Murrow says, do we reach a compromise between control and liberty? In the United States a strong chorus of voices has been telling us that compromise is unnecessary; that any national planning or any degree of state control means the end of free enterprise. The honest concern of many of these Americans cannot be doubted. Aside from a minority of strident reactionaries, most of us want to know—

Is any important degree of state ownership destructive of democratic processes and democratic government?

This is more than a fair question; it is a "must" question. That many Americans should be sincerely fearful of greatly increased state control is, I think, understandable. That most of us should desire to keep as much as possible of our capitalist structure intact is equally understandable. That we should take every precaution against the creation of a totalitarian government is certainly justifiable, so long as we make certain that what we fight to retain is truly democratic. But this great central problem of our machine age can never be solved by loose talk or emotional heebie-jeebies. Let us try to inspect the unescapable facts with all the objectivity we can muster. When we do this, certain outstanding features of our times are much easier to see.

We can see that the capitalist nations have not been functioning with smooth motors for more than half a century. We see that the booms and depressions become increasingly more violent. We see that each new high in mass unemployment precipitates a more violent social and political crisis; that popular demands for sweeping and fundamental reforms become much more insistent. What the American people voted for in 1932, for instance, was not merely *change*. They voted for *more control* and a more even distribution of the national income. More than 12,000,000 unemployed were saying: We demand that this shall not happen again. If we should have perhaps 20,000,000 jobless in our next depression, what would our people demand? They would certainly demand very drastic action to put and keep America's colossal industrial production under control and in some tolerable balance.

In the fields of invention, technology, and industry we Americans have been the revolutionaries of this century. We have completely revolutionized how man works, what man can produce, and what man *can* enjoy. It seems to me we have been equally revolutionary in our *methods,* because revolutionaries always pay little or secondary attention to what is destroyed; they ignore the abuses and social upsets. In our fierce rush toward superindustrialization we have until now paid comparatively little attention to the human dislocations and the millions of jobless which our progress periodically created. But we have not yet by any means demonstrated that we know *how* to control our incredible machines; and we have tended to treat their repetitious social and political ravages as largely secondary. Now Americans have played a foremost role in ushering in the age of the atomic bomb and atomic energy. This, truly, is one of the greatest technical revolutions in all history. We, despite all our conservative yearnings, have in fact become the promoters of an unpredictable revolution. As atom-smashers we are the superrevolutionaries—and yet a great many Americans would like to believe that the emancipated atom somehow will fail to have stupendous social and political repercussions upon human society. As atomic revolutionists we would like to be antirevolutionary! It would take more than an economic Einstein to figure out how this can be done.

Can we get any perspective on a problem vaster than mankind has ever faced before? Surely that will require a tremendous effort on the part of all of us, and the clearest thinking of the best minds of our times. But we must also try to do our own thinking as clearly as we can. This is why it seems to me that, beside the supreme problem of the atomic revolution, the problem of seeing Socialism for what it is must surely be within the reach of most of us. We need not assume that because the steel industries, gas and electricity, coal mines, or insurance are passing under government ownership and control in western Europe, therefore any socialistic reform in the United States would be equally sweeping. We need not assume that necessarily any great amount of government ownership need become imperative in America; certainly not in any predictable future—*if* we put our own economic house in much better order than it has been in this century. Unless we are sadly short on intelligence, foresight, and national self-discipline, we need not assume that any serious amount of state Socialism is inevitable in the United States—*unless we are!*

But should we not be equally extremist and blind if we did not now inform ourselves much more accurately as to exactly what

Socialism is? Should we not be extremist and self-deceptive if we, the American people as a whole, do not study more closely what the socialistic democracies have tried and have made work in the past forty years? Unless we make a widespread effort now to achieve this kind of fundamental fact and fundamental understanding, I believe we shall be shouting in the dark—shrilling empty catch-phrases and slipping from one quagmire into another—for the next twenty years or longer.

So let us look at the well-governed, well-living and democratic Scandinavian countries.

Is Socialism a menace to capitalism in Scandinavia?

Throughout most of this century Socialist parties have been increasingly powerful in Norway, Sweden, Denmark, and Finland. Since 1914 co-operatives and state ownership in certain industrial fields have progressed steadily in most of Scandinavia. These countries have also had their periods of prosperity and of depression, but the depressions there have been relatively less severe than in the less socialized neighboring nations. The standard of living of Scandinavians, since state ownership became more pronounced, has continued to rise. In fact, these northern countries have been models of relative prosperity and high living standards. Their peoples have had more protection—more in health clinics, public nurseries, social security, and old-age pensions—than almost any other peoples anywhere. Yet nowhere have citizens been more free, and nowhere has democratic government functioned with greater vigor.

Since Sweden is the largest and perhaps most typical, take Sweden. At this moment in our history it seems to me that Marquis Childs's remarkably informative book, *Sweden, the Middle Way,* should be discussed in all our communities and studied in every American high school. It would not be a menace to American free enterprise. It would inform us on some of the most important trends in the world today. It would remind us that some state and community ownership can be successfully integrated with private ownership. It might even show some of us how free enterprise *can* be saved from its own most costly abuses. Many of the innovations that have been made in Sweden were also introduced, years ago, in Denmark, Norway, and Finland. But the Swedish picture will serve as the general pattern of all.

Consumers' co-operatives are one outstanding feature of Sweden's economy. By 1935 these co-operatives, operated on a non-profit basis, conducted one third of all retail trade and over 10 percent of the wholesale trade. A large proportion of the Swedish population went into business for itself—to get as good or better goods at lower prices. The Swedes were aided in this by a powerful and highly responsible trade-union movement. Big monopolies in private enterprise were limited or prevented by the remarkable success of the co-operatives.

What did the Swedish co-operatives do? Marquis Childs tells how they tamed that country's flour-milling monopoly and averaged to sell flour at from 12 to 25 cents a sack below the trust's price. Because the Swedish rubber trust was reaping 60-percent annual profits, the co-operatives took to manufacturing galoshes. Within a year they reduced the price of galoshes, a winter necessity in Sweden, by $1.25 a pair. That brought the price of galoshes down to reasonable figures for all Swedes. The co-operatives went into dairying, they operated department stores, they formed co-operative insurance companies. They formed a Scandinavian Co-operative Wholesale, and broke an international monopoly that was charging inexcusable rates for electric lamps. A co-operative leader told a monopoly executive: "You want prices up, we want them down. You want to benefit stockholders, we want to benefit consumers." The majority of Swedes were the consumers. There did not seem to be anything undemocratic about that. Monopolies bred the great Swedish co-operative movement by persistently charging more than the traffic should bear. In this fact there is food for thought for all American monopolists.

In the same fashion the unions and co-operatives went into low-cost housing in Sweden. Their dwellings, both in small houses and in apartments, are notably modern and moderate in rental prices. Well before this war Mr. Childs reports that Swedish co-operative houses contained some 25,000 flats; and in Stockholm alone co-operatives housed 65,000 people. "About $90,000,000 has been spent on low-cost housing, by the state and its political subdivisions and through co-operatives such as H.S.B. This is nearly $15 for every man, woman and child in the country." In the United States today this would represent more than $2,100,000,000 for low-cost housing in city and suburban regions.

In the field of outright state ownership the Swedish government owns and operates many of the railroads, the airlines, and the telephone and telegraph system, which is one of the best operated in the world. The state owns power companies and contributes some 40 percent of all power produced. Not only do these state-owned power companies compete with private companies, but the two often co-operate and link up together. The Swedish state owns or administers several million acres of forests, and operates its own lumber mills on the same basis as private companies. The state holds the rights to the country's largest iron-ore deposits, but usually permits private companies to mine under its control. The Swedish radio (which inserts no advertising) is under a combination of public and private operation. The same is true of the state tobacco and liquor monopolies, whose profits are reserved as government revenues. It is interesting that the tobacco monopoly was started to provide funds for the launching of Sweden's old-age pension system.

For this summary of Sweden's established socialized institutions I am indebted to Marquis Childs. From such a condensed list as this we may begin to perceive how changed the American economy would be if we had approximately as much socialistic enterprise as exists in Sweden. But the striking fact is that—while this has been going on there for about fifty years—Sweden today still has a predominant degree of private enterprise, and this enterprise is as energetic, free, and prosperous as any to be found in the world. Let us note that it also seems to be considerably more stable than our own. Certainly, when I first visited Sweden in 1939 and 1940, the Swedish capitalists were busy and prosperous, and they gave no evidence of being haunted by fears of Socialism. Most Swedes did fear Communism. But Socialism was no bugaboo to them. They had long ago accepted the fact that state ownership, in certain fields, could provide a healthy and constructive competition to private enterprise. The Swedish capitalists gave every appearance of being far less harassed and worried than most American big businessmen. They were living on *middle ground* and making very decent profits at that.

Perhaps this was also because the Swedes are very level-headed and practical people. They now have a completely Socialist government, but this government does not have to rush into large-scale nationalization because the division of labor between public and private enterprise has been established gradually, through intelligent compromise and intelligent experimentation. Thus, in late 1945, Sweden's Socialist premier told C. L. Sulzberger of the *New York Times:* "We are now discussing—but so far only in theory—the possibilities of extending the nationalization of industry . . . of nationalizing the shoe industry, stone quarries, insurance companies, and a new tenement project. Our principle is not expropriation. We redeem properties taken over at a fair rate, more or less as the London government is doing with the Bank of England—but with cash payments instead of bonds. . . . We wish to nationalize industries only where the state can run a business more efficiently and justly. Where private enterprise can do a better job we wish it to keep going. Efficiency is our standard."

That sounds like common sense. But what many Americans still seem to ignore is the fact that the Swedes have proved that state ownership can be, and *is,* more efficient than private industry in certain fields. Accordingly, Scandinavia stands as an inspiration and a measuring rod for those socialistic reforms which are now being pushed forward throughout western Europe. Monopolies and swollen profits and price-fixing, these and similar abuses of power, created the popular demand in Britain, France, and elsewhere for a much greater degree of state ownership. The same factors, of course, could produce a similar demand in the United States. I think we must conclude that whether or not we eventually have very much state ownership in America will depend upon the wisdom and foresight of the directors and executives of our 200 greatest corporations—upon them more than upon any other factors.

But the experience to date of all other Western capitalist democracies has been to seek an increasing mixture of private and public enterprise. The Second World War has given this long-apparent exploratory development a tremendous impetus. If we examine with cold objectivity, we see that Socialism—in the European democracies and throughout most of the British Commonwealth—has indeed come to represent and constitute middle ground. Perhaps America can get along with only a dash, comparatively speaking, of state ownership. But if the experience of all these other nations is any criterion, America cannot hope to do that after tail-spinning once or twice more into a great depression—or into one more war.

In an address to the Association of National Advertisers in New York on November 20, 1945, Walter Lippmann warned that the United States is now the only large industrial nation committed to the perpetuation of free enterprise. Anyone "is deluding himself dangerously," Mr. Lippmann said, if he imagines that business leaders can survive without considering an enlightened public policy as much as scientific research, production, and finance.

"We have unwise friends in business," Walter Lippmann added. "They are to be found in politics, on public platforms, on the radio and in the press. . . . They prey upon the most innocent and gullible of the businessmen. They paint a wholly false picture of the world. They make it out that the American business community is beset on all sides by enemies; that it is attacked by the government, the labor unions, college professors, Russia, Britain. I think it is time the business community dismissed these people who impair their dignity. Let the captains of industry be captains, and go forward unafraid in the days to come."

If the American champions of free enterprise really desire and hope to maintain a system of free and private enterprise, I can conceive of no other way in which it can be done. We can keep democracy only by being more democratic in our acts and functions. We can keep free enterprise only by making enterprise more free and more truly competitive. We shall make our own American middle ground—with foresight and with compromise and with a broader sense of social responsibility for all. Or many of us, from the extreme right and the extreme left, will combine to make our chances of reaching any middle ground impossible.

By its partial record to date, what we have to fear is not Socialism or some degree of Socialism. Paraphrasing that memorable phrase of Franklin D. Roosevelt, and speaking in the economic and political sense, we Americans have nothing to fear but— ourselves.

PART IV

The Road to World Citizenship

Chapter XVI

ARE WE EDUCATED FOR PEACE?

The dogmas of the quiet past are inadequate to the stormy present. The occasion is piled high with difficulties and we must rise with the occasion. As our case is new, so we must think anew and act anew. We must disenthrall ourselves.

Abraham Lincoln

Today we are faced with the pre-eminent fact that if civilization is to survive we must cultivate the science of human relationships—the ability of all peoples, of all kinds, to live together in the same world, at peace.

Franklin D. Roosevelt: From a speech written, but not delivered, before he died.

Your chaps haven't hesitated to tell us what's wrong with us."

My Scottish friend Captain "Mungo" Park wasn't being bitter. His smile was half-amused, half-sardonic. Four years earlier, at the war's outset, he had been a deputy provost-marshal of London. Since then few British officers had had a closer view of the American "occupation" of England. Those four years of blitzes, buzz bombs, and the rest had left their mark. As with everyone in London in November 1944, I could see and sense his fatigue. He was more serious now, and especially about this.

"Your American boys have such natural technical ability," Captain Park said earnestly. *"But they have no appreciation of the outside world.* It seems they haven't been educated to make any real effort to understand other people. Sometimes I get frightened when I see how true this is of most Americans. It's really a shame. *You have such wonderful human material—but so much of it is wasted.* . . . How are we going to be able to work together after the war?"

One of the by-products of being a war correspondent was precisely this. Wherever you went people told you what they thought of the Americans. These Europeans or Orientals were looking at our mass-exported citizens with fresh eyes—from the outside. What they saw and remarked was often quite different from what folks back in the U.S.A. had ever imagined. What the more thoughtful American war correspondents themselves observed was frequently chastening, or shaming to their sense of national pride. But because we did not wish to undermine the morale of the home front we seldom wrote about such incidents. As a consequence, the American people got an extremely distorted and overglamorized picture of the conduct of our officers and men overseas. To have put the picture in some true proportion we should have had to report, week after week, such every-day occurrences as these:

The information clerk at the American Express center for GIs in Paris was not only an unpaid volunteer and very good-looking. Besides being very well dressed, she was a young Frenchwoman of obvious education and refinement. An American soldier noticed the handsome diamond ring, in modernistic setting, which she wore. He pulled out a package of Camels. "I'll give you a pack of cigarettes for it," he offered—in dead seriousness. The ring was certainly worth a thousand dollars, or much more. "Oh, they often do things like that," said the young Frenchwoman. She laughed. But I wondered what she secretly thought of the upbringing of Americans.

Across the hall a dozen mesdemoiselles worked at feverish pace, eight or nine hours a day, wrapping and mailing home-bound packages for thousands of our GIs. They, too, were volunteers. They were cheerful, well-bred young women, many of them from the most aristocratic Parisian families. It was not an uncommon thing for one of them to be asked: "Say, where can I find a girl to sleep with?" Sometimes GIs made the question more strictly personal than that. I marveled at the tolerance and good temper with which they tossed off such unsavory recompense for their generous assistance to our fighting men.

At the bar attached to the Olympia dance hall, a rather disconsolate *demi-mondaine* was sitting on an adjacent stool, so I bought her a drink. It was an easy way to find out what she might have to

say. "I've been much deceived about the Americans," she remarked with typical French frankness. "Their manners are very
bad. In general they have no education." Yes, I knew what she
meant; and there was no denial or excuse that I could offer. Just
the same it seemed strange and sad—such a reproof as this, coming
from a prostitute. Now she was pointing to the floor. "I have seen
two American officers so drunk—right there—that they couldn't
get up," she said. "In all the years they were in France I've never
seen a German officer drunk in public—not once. German officers
would never act like that."

On my way out I made a jesting remark to the hat-check girls.
It was always the same when a uniformed American spoke their
language. The French beamed and their words fizzed; the unexpected pleasure of being able to express themselves freely to an
overseas ally. With her third remark one of the hat-check girls
asked: "But why do the Americans treat *all* women like prosti-
tutes?" That same question was asked me too many times, in
Belgium and Italy as well as in France. I was never able to offer
any explanation that made much sense—even to me. Would you
say that the average American male could not tell the difference
between a lady and a harlot? Was it just incredibly bad manners?
Or did too many young Americans simply not know how to
behave in foreign lands? Wherever United States servicemen have
been stationed in considerable numbers, the residents of those
countries are still wondering—or have reached an uncomplimen-
tary conclusion of their own.

Incidents such as these have been repeated so many thousands
of times over that, it seems to me, citizens of the United States
might do well to ask themselves—

Are Americans exportable?

Having recently exported more than 8,000,000 young Americans, we now have an exceptionally broad basis of judgment. We
are also pretty thoroughly aware of what our servicemen chalked
up in their credit column overseas. They were magnetically
youthful and energetic. They were gay, self-confident, and full of
initiative. Their humor was contagious. They were fond of children. At their best they made friends quickly and were warm-

hearted. Everywhere people welcomed the Americans with open arms. Almost everywhere a great many people cooled toward them after a while. The Yanks won popularity much more quickly than the British, Canadians, Australians, or French. Usually they lost it more quickly, too. Their cockiness, their unconventionality, and their boldness toward women were a novelty at first. Later on this same frontierlike crudeness often came to be resented.

In a score of lands today any sufficiently exposed foreigner will give you his candid portrait of the average American—meaning, of course, our recent tourists-in-uniform. He will mention the attractive qualities that we all know. But he will add something like this: "Most Americans are very undisciplined. They drink too much, and they are destructive or nasty when they get drunk. They are extraordinarily self-satisfied, and that often makes them arrogant. They have little or no respect for other peoples' ways of living or other nations' culture. When they meet strangers, in their own cities or homes, most Americans start telling them that they don't know how to do things. They are intolerant about almost everybody's habits except their own. I do not know what to say about the manners of Americans—for many of them manners do not seem to exist. It's amazing how rude and insulting so many of your fine-appearing young men can be toward women. I hope you'll forgive me, but truly, the Americans are a very strange mixture. We liked them in many ways—but we also found them very difficult. Many of them did things that will never be forgiven."

As a reporter I know this is an abbreviated but accurate summary of impressions left behind by United States officers, airmen, soldiers, or sailors in Europe and Asia. While demonstrating their superb qualities as fighting men, their efficiency and high-spiritedness, our servicemen overseas were equally profligate and indifferent in displaying the faults of their virtues. On the average they did not act in any sense aware that they, and they alone, were painting a picture of America and American civilization in the minds of millions of foreign peoples. As exportable human beings, a dishearteningly large proportion of them were failures. But are any nation's soldiers or citizens really exportable? "We thought we were different," a friend remarks. "Now we have shown we are just the same as other people."

To a certain extent this is true, but it is not entirely accurate—because there are differences of degree. Peoples of every country are nationalistically self-satisfied. Neither the Englishman nor the Frenchman is a perfect example of a mixer when abroad. The German, too, is arrogant. The Russian is quite as boastful as the American—which is saying a good deal. In short, none of the world's peoples seems to have been adequately educated to serve as ambassadors of goodwill in foreign lands with uniformly marked success. But the Europeans have had much more contact with foreigners and foreign cultures than Americans have had. The Asiatics, perhaps in part because they have a much older civilization, are far more tactful; and they have also maintained a high tradition of good manners. It may be that George Jones, the average American, is definitely less exportable than citizens of most other countries for reasons such as these. It may be that Americans, being a much younger race, are more scornful of other peoples' customs and traditions. It may be there are certain other important reasons—as I believe.

The fact remains that the recent war showed Americans to be considerably *less* exportable than most of our allies. As a war correspondent I served with the armies of seven different nations and traveled in forty-four countries. Honesty compels me to report that, wherever I have been, the deportment of Finns, Norwegians, British, Greeks, Russians, Indians, French, and Chinese (in uniform)—and also Canadians and Australians—has been very considerably better, on the whole, than the average conduct of the uniformed forces of my own country. Perhaps the Russians were as bad when they got out of hand in eastern Europe after V-E Day; I was not there then, and I speak here only from personal observation. But the places around the world where I have seen the largest percentage of indiscipline, violence, excessive drinking, insulting of respectable women, and callous indifference to the opinion or the customs of foreign peoples have been where these regrettable incidents came from uniformed Americans. These are facts that are humiliating, but a reporter cannot gloss them over. They raise the question: To what degree are the American people yet prepared for world leadership? They raise the question sharply as to whether, collectively, we are capable of holding or winning the friendship of most of the world's peoples.

Americans at home have perhaps taken little time to consider questions like these. We were further handicapped because we could not begin to get a rounded, bad-with-the-good picture of our servicemen overseas until hostilities ceased. Since then the seamy side of the canvas has been shown increasingly in dispatches from Europe and Asia. If we have read them with any care, we have had too many occasions on which to feel shocked or ashamed. Perhaps you have sometimes asked yourself—

Are Americans really like this?

At Le Havre, France, there was Grandmother Feret, sixty-three years of age.[1] Her left index finger was broken and her left eye blackened. That was the retort of two drunken GIs when she refused to serve them more liquor. In agonizingly hurt tones Madame Feret told *Life's* correspondent how it happened and their café was smashed up. "We expected friends," she said. "Instead there came incomprehension, arrogance, and incredibly bad manners—the swagger of conquerors."

Up to this present writing not a small fraction of the violence or crimes of American troops in Le Havre and many other French cities has been published. I remember being told how the residents of Rheims did not dare to appear on the streets of their own city after dark—least of all, women. I remember being told of GIs in Paris who tried to hit French girls over the head with their steel helmets when their proposals were refused. I remember that executions for rape or murder were seldom published by our United States commands abroad. In Shanghai, early in January 1946, a band of American bluejackets tore the British flag off an automobile and hurled it in the driver's face. Another group of gobs seized sailors from an Indian ship, tore off their uniforms, and accused them of masquerading as "niggers." It was a common practice in Shanghai to see our sailors hurling torpedo firecrackers into groups of Chinese civilians—for the sport of seeing them run.[2]

From Tientsin, *New York Post* Correspondent Robert P. Mar-

[1] See *Life*, December 10, 1945.
[2] See *New York Post*, January 4, 1946.

tin reported [3] that when Americans stagger out of night clubs the Chinese scatter like leaves in an autumn wind.

They have seen too much brutality when Americans cannot make themselves understood. . . . Every night in Tientsin, Peiping and Tsingtao the shattered bodies of Chinese killed by American trucks and jeeps are dragged away. . . . Almost any hour of the day, smashed rickshas and bicycles—which may mean bankruptcy to each owner. Some incidents are almost unbearably ugly. . . . This is not a blanket indictment. An M.P. lieutenant estimated that not more than 10 percent of the Marines were involved in crimes.

Not more than 10 percent!

If that percentage seems shockingly high for criminality in any American unit overseas, it does not include the wholesale blackmarket profiteering which uniformed Americans have indulged in everywhere. Returning from the European theater, officers, nurses, and noncoms whom I know for their reliability could not conceal their dismay or revulsion. "It's every man for himself," one reported. "GIs or captains or colonels, it's all the same. Almost everybody is in the black market, piling up all the money they can get. Some brag that they've sent home $20,000, and some twice as much. Why, I know GIs and officers who actually bought hotels in Austria or Germany—with Army cigarettes and stuff. They showed me the deeds to prove it." An officer nurse said: "Our own soldiers rifle the belongings of our returning troops in Le Havre. One of our girls had spent about a thousand dollars over a two-year period on Irish and Belgian linens and lace for her own trousseau. They stole every bit of it. We even had soldier's suitcases rifled under the beds in the hospital while the wounded men were asleep—by other Americans, mind you." It was not surprising that a veteran correspondent like Paul Scott Mowrer should write: "I consider myself hard to shock. Yet I was nauseated, as the war neared its end, by the way a large part of our Army turned into peddlers, selling government property at exorbitant prices in the European black markets."

You listen and read, and wonder whether this picture could possibly be exaggerated. But if you have served in the war zones

[3] January 9, 1946.

of the world, alas, you know that nothing on this scale—in both violence and illegality—has occurred in the British, Greek, Norwegian, or any other army you have been with. If there was as much profiteering and graft in China, the Chinese soldiers at any rate were the least offenders—and on their part violence against civilians was relatively rare. After having been with the British in Norway, Greece, Burma, and Egypt I never saw a single incident of lawlessness and destructive violence of the type I have mentioned in the paragraphs above. As I recall this fact now, it seems to me a great tribute to the social responsibility and self-discipline of the British Tommy.

But for our own men in uniform any valid explanation must take some searching of souls on our part. Is it that the American people are suffering from a reckless and indiscriminate leveling-down of all social and moral values? Is it that *more* of us have learned much *less* respect for law and property and the culture of others? Is it, by any chance, the evidence of a widespread American crisis in character?

We know that what has been summarized here does not apply to anything like all of Americans who served abroad, and that much of it applies only in part; that some portions of these observations do not apply to most of them. Only a long and painstaking investigation by sociologists could possibly give us percentages of some accuracy. But the precise percentages do not matter. What matters is the fact that the *pattern of conduct* of our millions of overseas Americans, in whatever war theater, has been strikingly identical. What matters, when all aspects involved are considered, is that no other nation's uniformed fighting men have written this overall record to any such degree. Omitting the violence and crime, and considering only the phenomena of attitude, manners, psychology, and social behavior, it is significant that American servicemen, by and large, have acted in foreign lands and toward foreign peoples almost precisely as I saw our average tourists act during nine years that I worked in Europe. This is not surprising. In this war most of our overseas soldiers and sailors were really civilians, by conditioning and long experience. If they proved quite questionably exportable, they were still extremely representative of Composite American George Jones.

Thus, what foreign peoples have become rather acutely conscious of, while most folks living in the United States have been scarcely conscious of it at all, is a pretty general American indifference to or scorn of the way of life of other nations. So far as some 8,000,000 overseas servicemen were concerned, it appeared to indicate—

A widespread American inadequacy in
human relations.

Being from a land of plenty, our visitors-in-uniform were naturally shocked by the terrible mass poverty in the Orient and the Near East. But they rarely thought to look for the causes—to grasp that these hundreds of millions had been the prisoners of feudalism or imperialism for centuries. In our American schools they had *not* been taught to pry beneath the surface. Having no real comprehension either of feudal slavery or of colonial exploitation, the average GI exclaimed impatiently: "What's the matter with these dopes? Why didn't they fight for their rights long ago?" And having grown up surrounded by machines and fancy gadgets, our innocents abroad usually measured the intelligence and the national stature of other peoples by their plumbing facilities. Material progress and efficiency seemed to be the chief gods of the products of our (self-admitted) "best educational system in the world." In such fashions as these our world-exploring youth rang up an embarrassing score at alienating people who were originally their admiring friends. They were so sincerely convinced that "everything American is best" that they felt compelled to tell other people what—in their firm opinion—was wrong with them.

This is not exactly the most effective manner in which "to win friends and influence people." If a majority of our overseas Americans had been looking for something good or something to learn from Europeans or Asiatics, it would have taken much of the sting out of their self-assertive attitude. But who had ever bothered to train American youth to respect British justice and British quality products? To admire French creative arts, including clothes and food? To detect the highly different qualities and accomplishments of Italians, Belgians, Czechs, Greeks—or Russians? Where —in our educational system or our armed forces—had any systematic effort ever been made to explain to young Americans the differences in mentality, background, and customs of these older peoples whom they now encountered for the first time? Many of these peoples were exhausted by two world wars fought on their own soil. Without a thought as to what this fact meant, it was common for GIs to declare loudly: "They can give this place back to the Indians!" In their highly superficial view, the one thing wrong with these people was their "shiftlessness." Defeat and national enslavement for years, the terrible bleeding and sapping of energy of the other war, lack of food, political betrayal—such obvious contributing causes as these were not at all obvious to unanalytical, unthinking Yanks in uniform. Was it a curious lack of imagination? Was it youthful blindness alone? Or was it, fundamentally—miseducation?

The parents of Mlle Rouselle de La Pereire, whom I quoted in Chapter VI, entertained many United States officers and men at their ancient château in Normandy. "Among the Americans we met," she told me, "the only really cultured ones were Jewish. They were always the Americans who were interested in music and art, in my father's library of old books, and in the wood carvings and period furniture in our home. I never had any great liking for Jews, but among the Americans they were the most interested in other peoples' culture." Of course, that particular French family's experience did not establish any hard-and-fast rules about culture among Americans. Nevertheless, in our anti-Semitic age, Mlle Rouselle de La Pereire's testimony was worthy of some meditation. Residents of the Old World were not finding any great number of representatives of the New World who had much interest in Old World civilization.

When our armies took over in Germany, American GIs were soon saying what a majority of American tourists repeatedly said between the wars. "The Germans are more like Americans." "The Germans are efficient." Our soldiers chorused approvingly that "the Germans are cleaner and better dressed." (Having robbed all European countries of their clothes, and the French alone of 90 percent of their textiles, there were sound reasons why the German people were so well dressed. It was amazing how seldom that simple fact occurred to the Americans. Why did over 90 percent of Berlin women wear attractive stockings? And why were fully 90 percent of Parisian women going bare-legged? Most GIs did not possess sufficient perception to figure even that out for themselves.) Saul Haas, a Seattle radio executive, returned from Berlin in a pessimistic mood.

"American soldiers are beginning to admire the Germans, both as a people and ideologically, more than any other people in Europe," he reported. "Our boys are impressed by appearances— that's what counts with them. They don't think what's behind it."

When he saw a Russian captain in a patched uniform an American officer exclaimed: "What untidy people!" Once again— appearances. The chances were that this Russian had seen five, ten, or twenty times as much front-line combat as the man who judged him by a patch on his coat. An enormous lot depended on getting along with the Russians, and General Eisenhower made a tremendous success of it, at the top level, simply by being friendly and going out of his way to give generous credit to an army which had fought much longer than ours. As one correspondent noted, the Russians wanted to be noticed and wanted to be praised. In this, of course, they were 100 percent like most Americans. The correspondent went on to report that the Russians "are damned well hurt and mortified by the lack of attention they are getting." Just a slight amount of fair play and human psychology would have gone very far, in those days, to promote friendliness where friendliness can contribute most toward an enduring peace. Just a reasonable spirit of giving credit to the other fellow. Our American troops were not up to it. They had never made any real effort to give credit to any of our Allies—yet they had always expected a large and glowing amount of credit for themselves.

An Australian correspondent, Thomas E. Healy of the *New York Post,* was in a position to be far more neutrally objective than most. From Vienna he wrote: "Americans are die-hard conservatives in all matters affecting their way of life. They can see little good in any other. That's why they never really take to their allies. . . . I have not heard a single GI utter a word of praise or friendliness for his Russian comrades."

It is unquestionably true that we Americans, on the whole, can see little good in any other nation's way of life—and also that we expend alarmingly little effort trying to discover any. Yet we are undoubtedly the greatest cocktail of races and nationalities in the world. Why do we act as though a cocktail were superior to the ingredients that go into it? In truth, it is the immigrant sons and daughters of dozens of older nations who have combined to keep the United States prosperous and powerful. For three centuries Mother Europe, in particular, has regularly given us new blood; and the new blood was swiftly transformed into new energies, new dynamism, and new dreams. In reality there is no nation that owes so much to so many different peoples of the world as our own U.S.A.

Somehow, therefore, it seems curiously illogical and tragic that Americans of this generation should show such slight capacity for understanding their cousins, aunts, and uncles in other lands. Because we have made scarcely any real progress toward mutual respect and understanding, while fighting side by side as allies under the greatest of stresses, it augurs ill for future peace in the world. The particular facet of evidence which we have considered here—as pertinent to Americans—applies, of course, in varying degrees to peoples of all nations. All have been suckled and fed with heavy doses of nationalism. Unconsciously, we have all been educated for war. But somehow, it would seem that, with our extraordinary intermixture of many national and racial strains, the Americans have had a much greater opportunity than most other peoples to acquire something more of breadth and tolerance, a somewhat more adequate basis for world citizenship. In this we have made no more progress than many peoples with far less opportunities; and in some respects the wartime evidence indicates that we have achieved considerably less than some other peoples. I believe one of the chief reasons for this is—

The persistent miseducation of American youth.

In the classroom of the Second World War, the United States serviceman, collectively speaking, unquestionably flunked the course in Manners and Social Behavior. With a little reflection we can see that this was bound to happen. In how many American homes do we find any consistent emphasis upon courtesy, respect for others, and self-discipline? Go to the average movie or listen to a fair sampling of radio entertainment programs, and you will note the dead-level sort of things that are being presented to

American youth as models for their conduct. Our most popular newspaper comic strips are devoured daily by from 30,000,000 to 40,000,000 readers—among them the vast majority of young Americans. Most of the language and much of the manners which they absorb from these are either of the street ragamuffin or the gangster type. The most omnipresent and impressionable instruments of mass appeal in the United States are predominantly geared to *a process of general vulgarization.* But the wise-cracking and tough-boy pranks, which in our society pass as being funny or just high-spirited, still rightly rate in older civilizations simply as bad taste. In much of the United States it may be regarded as no more than a friendly joke for a young blade to slap a girl on the buttocks and yell: "Hi-ya, Toots!" In Britain, France, China, and most other countries it is regarded as crude boorishness, or worse.

When you consider such simple things as these, you touch an aspect of American miseducation which is highly nonexportable. It might be of relatively slight consequence, were it not for the fact that millions of air-minded, footloose Americans are going to be traveling all over the world in the next decade or two. Of course, they will behave in general—as they have grown up behaving. Yet these same Americans will all be observed and judged as representatives of the world's most powerful nation—as samples of the people who are expected to supply world leadership for peace and understanding. We are compelled to wonder whether our new legion of tourists and business travelers will be much more successful as emissaries of goodwill than were our wartime soldiers and sailors. After all, we can scarcely hope to lead the world until we have demonstrated a considerable capacity to lead and discipline ourselves.

But world citizenship for a world at peace is much more than a question of individual manners, important though these may be in many subtle and enduring ways. We must look sharply at our entire American system of education. For generations and from the first grade through high school (at the very least) we have been educating our children for war; and this we are still doing in a blissful sort of blindness. Admittedly, the school systems of most other countries have done precisely the same thing. But the vital question is whether any nation can now afford to

turn out minds that are "easy meat" for cannon-fodder—or atom-
fodder. Under the United Nations a totally new emphasis on
mutual understanding and co-operation could—and should—be
injected into a large proportion of the world's school-rooms. If
we Americans, however, really wish to avoid the disaster of an
atomic war, we would do well to take the initiative within our
own borders. The place to begin building peace is at home.

When I say that we are unconsciously educating for war, I mean
things we can put our fingers on. Nationalism that promotes a
feeling of "better than thou" and "everything American is best"
is education for war. Any nationalism that is arrogantly self-
assertive and scornful of other peoples' way of life is a mental conditioning to "put other nations in their place." We have had so
many just reasons to be proud of the United States, and we are by
nature such a patriotic people, that we have not realized the
extremes to which we have been carried. This pronounced American nationalism once whipped us over night into a war with hap-
less Spain. It applauded wildly the "big stick" effusions of Teddy
Roosevelt. It encouraged a great many Americans to regard our
own brief participation in the First World War as the only heroism or exploits worth mentioning. Today it prompts many of us
to give scant credit to any of those allies without whom we would
have been lost.

It is possible to admire and love a wife or a husband while
recognizing clearly that person's faults and limitations. In reality,
this is virtually always the case. But how often—if ever—have you
heard of a classroom where America was presented in a human
cross-section of qualities and shortcomings? It seems to me we
shall begin to build a better and mature United States only when
Americanism is taught in our schools with a frank enumeration
of our national handicaps: in character, in temperament, and in
habits. Certainly, we cannot hope to begin to build a world capable of maintaining peace until the entire American educational
system inaugurates a conscious program to produce young men
and women who are trained to be better Americans—and therefore capable of being citizens of an atomic world. The cult of
"anything American is best" or "my country right or wrong"
works out in practical result to a mass mentality highly susceptible
to nationalistic war. For hundreds of years, such nationalism has

produced nothing but wars. Our new world cannot exist very much longer with this kind of education. To educate for peace we must clean much of the slate, begin anew, and *begin at home.* American taxpayers paid more than \$2,000,000,000 for the atomic bomb. Suppose we were now to spend another \$2,000,000,000 for a new and modernized national system of education? In one generation this might well give us far more protection from mass destruction than 100,000 atomic bombs can ever provide. First of all, it is unseeing minds and shriveled hearts which produce war. For if there is to be any peace, it is people—and only people—who can achieve it.

But the world's peoples are still chained to rampant and brutal bloodshed as an illusory solution for their ills and desires. The world's peoples, abroad quite as much as in our own land, are not yet being educated either to conquer war—*or even to survive.* As the most powerful nation on earth, we can scarcely hope to produce men and women able to exercise world leadership in these menaced times without making a great and specific effort to produce them. Since leadership is ours, so the responsibility and the necessity are ours. As with automobile mechanics or physicians, we shall get what we teach and what we train. Let us look, then, at another aspect of the urgent opportunity which confronts American education.

American understanding of foreign peoples is an imperative requirement for winning the peace.

This much is self-evident because of the unique power position of the United States, and because misunderstandings and festering animosities between nations inevitably breed wars. Since no other nation has so much power as America, no other nation's people could possibly contribute more toward removing war-irritants and hate poisonings between peoples. But are we now prepared, or are we now being educated, to fill this role of such great possibilities? Are we producing any notable quota of minds of mediation, comprehension, and tolerance?

The small-town public schools which I attended in Connecticut were reputedly somewhat above the average. But I do not remember that any teacher ever told us how much the United States owes to the countries of Europe. I was never taught that Italian immigrants had brought to America a love of music, and that the Germans and the Jews had done the same. I was never taught that the Scandinavians had brought with them a pronounced industriousness. No teacher ever impressed on my mind what we owe to British processes of democratic government, to French logic and French art, to the Greek concept of democracy, or to the staunch independence of our Polish, Baltic, Russian, and other immigrants. I was not taught that the strength and variety of American society were indebted in any degree either to our constant inflow of European immigrants or to European civilization. So I graduated from high school, as most youthful Americans had always done and are still doing today, serene in the conviction that virtually everything splendid and praiseworthy in the United States was strictly a product of American environment and American soil. I had been perfectly educated to be a sincere, enthusiastic, and unquestioning nationalist. I was supremely confident that nothing could quite compare with "God's country," while anything foreign inevitably must be rather inferior or very much so. In patriotism my mark was never less than 100. In understanding of other nations and the qualities of their peoples, it never could have been much over 5 percent. It is safe to say that this discrepancy and disproportion are very little less in most American schools today.

It is not surprising, then, that our American servicemen overseas predominantly betrayed a feeling of superiority toward foreign peoples; that they "could see little good in any other way of life"; that they were seldom interested in the customs and manifestations of other civilizations and too often were scornful where respect and consideration were due. Few of our GIs had been educated for any of these things, and only a relative few had been schooled in tolerance. Yet these things, too, constitute indispensable foundation stones upon which any world peace must be built.

Here we are simply exploring a problem based upon a set of facts. The alarming degree of racial intolerance in the United States today must be included as one of these facts, because intolerance is unavoidably a question of miseducation—in the home and in the schools. There is probably no country in the world where racial prejudices are so deep and so dangerous as in the present-day United States. Our Jewish, Negro, and Mexican-American citizens and our citizens of Japanese descent are all the butt and the victims of discriminations which daily violate the pledges of the United States Constitution. Naturalized Americans who came here from Germany have assured me there is as much anti-Semitism in our country today as there was among Germans only three or four years before Hitler. If these racial animosities continue to be exploited and spread by our Bilbos, Gerald L. K. Smiths, and many others, our American society will be torn by dissension and serious civil strife before very many years. The seeds and the threat of what happened to Germany and France are already present in our midst. No country can be divided against itself more seriously than through the dissemination of racial hatreds. Having watched democracy being destroyed in other lands by these precise tactics, I know that we in the United States cannot afford to be complacent. And unless we are truly *united* States, we shall inevitably throw our vast weight toward another world war rather than toward a world at peace.

Some of our most thoughtful young veterans like Bill Mauldin are awake to this danger. They are fighting, courageously and patriotically, for a tolerant America in which no lines are drawn because of color or creed. But what are our public schools and colleges doing about this? And how many citizens in your community or mine so much as voice a reproof when an acquaintance preaches anti-Semitism or other racial prejudices?

Not long ago I spoke at a teachers' convention in New Haven, Connecticut. The subject was the subject of this chapter: education for peace in an atomic world. So I asked how many of these teachers regularly emphasized the dangers of racial prejudices and the need of tolerance in the course of their classroom instruction. Something less than 50 percent of the teachers were doing so. Yet Frank Sinatra, during that same fortnight, could take time out to address a Harlem high school assembly—a school where someone had promoted a hitherto unknown "racial strike." "If you have to call someone a name, don't put a racial prefix in front of it," he told a packed auditorium of hero-worshippers. "That's the most dangerous thing you can do in the U.S.A. . . . No kid was born and starts saying: 'I hate Jews or colored people.' Somebody taught him that!" But what long-term result can you and I expect unless our homes, and our schools in particular, are teaching the opposite? It required a young radio crooner, as a practitioner of democracy, to contribute infinitely more toward an enlightened, peaceful American society than nearly half of the teachers in the New Haven district could admit to teaching in their classes, week after week.

In Springfield, Massachusetts, every schoolroom is an organized workshop for democracy, international understanding, and tolerance. For more than five years the so-called "Springfield Plan" has been training young Americans in that city for intelligent leadership in the kind of a world we live in. It began through the vision of Dr. John Granrud, Superintendent of the Springfield schools. A committee of all categories of citizens, including Protestants, Catholics, and Jews, drew up the list of objectives. Here is the first objective:

"It is imperative that pupils understand all the constituent groups of our population, the historical backgrounds of these groups, *and their contributions to American life.*" (If all of our 8,000,000 fighting men overseas had grown up in that sort of school system, imagine how different the newspaper reports from Europe and Asia would have been over the past year or more. Imagine how much more goodwill might have been won and spread!)

The second objective reads: "Youngsters [previously] were given to understand that we in this country had already achieved a perfect society. Experience soon disillusioned them. . . . Teachers must emphasize the fact that we have not yet achieved the perfect democracy which is our goal. Weaknesses in our democratic processes should be pointed out, and ways of eliminating them should be discussed realistically." [4]

If this is anything at all, it is educational statesmanship. It is education for a better America—and education for peace, not for war. Yet the Springfield Plan has not spread, in these five years, throughout the United States; nor even to Boston, nor to many other important cities in Massachusetts. The hard fact is not only that the American people today are seriously unprepared for world leadership; it is equally true that we remain bogged down

[4] See C. I. Chatto and A. L. Halligan: *The Story of the Springfield Plan,* New York, Barnes & Noble, Inc., 1945.

in the same miseducation of our narrow and self-centered past, *that we still do not have a nationwide educational system capable of training our youth to help shape a world in which they can hope to escape atomic doom.*

On the basis of the facts which are all around us, it is difficult indeed to be an optimist about a world in which we Americans exert the decisive balance of power. Most of us do not read much more than the headlines about what is happening in this revolutionary world. Only the most biased and sensational of our daily press are read by the millions. If self-education and the informative, discriminating reading of newspapers and periodicals would go far toward giving American citizens a sound basis of judgment —some equipment for salvation—what are our chances? The pulp magazines: the "true stories," the "love stories," the "western," the "detective," the "movie star" publications—all so expertly designed for the paralyzing of thought—are read by tens of millions of our adults. And our most powerful instruments to reach the overwhelming majority of citizens, the motion picture and the radio, are used only intermittently to awaken the George Joneses to the neglected opportunities and obligations which push us toward war and away from peace. The atomic time-fuse means that human beings, of all nations, have never before needed so urgently to inform themselves—and *to think.* Instead of this, for the most part, the movies and the radio are drugging us with entertainment.

What with all these factors—and the atomic bomb thrust suddenly on top of them—a correspondent who looked forward anxiously for the end of bombings and bloodshed finds that the armed truce under which we now live is far more frightening than war. I am not scared of the Russians, the British, or anyone else. I am scared of ourselves. For of all our complicated world problems and all the recurring political crises among the great powers, *the most frightening thing in today's world is and remains the terrible unpreparedness of the American people either to co-operate constructively for peace or to assume their necessary role in world leadership.*

It is perhaps understandable and pardonable that we Americans have been miseducated in the past for the pressing task of helping our world civilization to survive. It is another matter, and in slight degree excusable, if we continue to miseducate ourselves. In every land in reality, but especially in our superbly equipped United States—

We need a revolution in education,
and in our civic consciousness and our thinking.

"The dogmas of the quiet past are inadequate to the stormy present"; utterly so in the face of our immediate atomic deadline.

If we examine what we are not using or are misusing, as well as what we are not teaching, I think we can quickly understand why such a huge part of America's truly wonderful human material is being wasted. At once we come to the largest, most comprehensive press existing in any country; to the world's most highly developed and widely distributed motion-picture and radio industries. A few sample observations are sufficient.

The scientists' testimony before the McMahon Senate Committee were of life-and-death importance to every resident of every industrialized United States city—i.e., to some 60,000,000 Americans, at least. Yet not a single United States newspaper published the full text of the scientists' most vital testimony; not so much as three columns per day containing what Americans *must know,* if we hope to survive. Nearly a year after Hiroshima scarcely a handful—if any—among some 1,500 United States daily newspapers were carrying a daily column or more devoted to atomic information, international and domestic. As an instrument of mass education regarding humanity's most gigantic peril, the "world's greatest press" functioned at something like 10-percent efficiency. On our radio stations there was a good deal of atomic talk at first—but only a small part of it by qualified experts; and none of it presented in a co-ordinated and consistent educational program, week in and week out, in accordance with an announced radio station policy. It was amazing that not one nationwide radio network, during those first formative eight or ten months, set aside a regular half-hour period once a week to educate the public on the ABCs of the atomic menace and what we might do about it. The men who control and decide the policies of our greatest mass dispensers of information were obviously still chained to the habits and dogmas of a past not only dead, but buried.

Is our supposedly "world's best-informed" public opinion really well informed at all? Could it be rated much above a twelve- or thirteen-year-old level? Hadley Cantril, director of the Office of Public Opinion Research at Princeton, reported: "People are thinking in terms of their own everyday lives—lives that just aren't concerned with the big, important issues that make headlines." Even months before Hiroshima—with papers full of data and maps about the Pacific war—Mr. Cantril's organization uncovered the following facts: Some 27,000,000 (or nearly one out of three among 90,000,000 adults in the U.S.A.) did not know that the Japanese occupied the Philippines; and 50,000,000 did not know the Japs held Wake Island. Of all adult Americans who were asked whether the United States had ever been a member of the League of Nations, 30 percent replied in the affirmative—and another 26 percent did not know. Only 32 percent could say how a treaty is approved in this country. Facts like these are difficult to square with the proud boast of "the best educational system in the world." They also raise an important question. If between 30 and 50 percent of American adults do not, and will not, read their daily press sufficiently to pass a fair current events test for twelve-year-olds, how are they going to get the knowledge on which to vote or act intelligently upon the supreme problems of war-or-survival which now beset us all? Is not an informational and educational revolution both overdue and an imperative necessity in the United States?

In the tremendously influential field of motion pictures, un-excelled and unprecedented opportunities to create an informed citizenry are still being wasted to an alarming degree. The percentage of good educational and informational films produced by Hollywood has improved, but it remains highly inadequate—still seriously disproportioned to the drug of entertainment. We have trained an entire generation to acute receptivity to the eye-and-ear appeal of the movies, with television soon to be added. Yet, after some thirty years, the educational motion picture is still virtually unknown in the classrooms of our schools and colleges. A nation that prides itself on its technical progressiveness and modernity has not begun to use one of the most effective educational instruments ever developed. When all of America's schools devote perhaps 20 percent of their classroom instruction to highly skilled documentary and expository movies, our educational system will have moved into the twentieth century—but not before. What could better explain, for instance, either the workings of the United Nations Organization or the essential meaning of the atomic crisis? We are wasting fantastically our human material, adult as well as youthful, because we are not using more than a fraction of our tremendous motion-picture and radio instruments to inform the people—to help them to basic knowledge—to help them to think. Our imaginations are paralyzed by a fearful time-lag. Our great technical proficiency is almost matched by the adolescence of our minds. But somehow, within a few short years, we must act our age. Somehow we must learn how to factually indoctrinate tens of millions of Americans who simply will not read those things which are vital to the continued existence of all of us.

But it will take a sweeping revolution in American education and in the goals which we set ourselves before we can—

Grade up and speed up our average citizens' thinking, instead of leveling it down and throttling it down.

We have a large number of organizations—from all those prominent ones that are civic, professional, religious, and fraternal to others like "Americans United for World Government" [5] and the "National Committee on Atomic Information" [6]—which could devote their efforts to this task. For if we understand rightly that our present civilization and our present world possess only one last lease on continued existence, we have no other choice save to unite our efforts for the only supremely important objective which remains for our generation: our common safety against atomic war. It will take both a mental and spiritual revolution before more than some 5 or 10 percent of Americans can be expected to face this fact.

[5] 1860 Broadway, New York City.
[6] 1621 K Street N.W., Washington, D. C.

Accepting the Freedom House award [7] General Eisenhower, a great general who has also proved himself an outstanding citizen of the world, emphasized significantly the vital role of education as a means toward achieving peace. "From the primary grade to the master's degree," he declared, "educators must seek objectivity, honesty, and a broadly human approach to subjects affecting all peoples of the earth. In the pulpit, the press, the radio and every type of public organization *we should differentiate clearly between patriotism and jingoism. We should teach that knowledge leads to co-operation; ignorance to disaster!*" (Italics mine.)

Earlier, speaking at West Point, General Eisenhower said: "Keep your mind open in your relation with other human beings. That way lies co-operation between nations, or co-operation between allies. . . . Learn to understand man and his problems. . . . The major thought I bring you today is to cultivate *mutual understanding* of anyone you think you have to get along with. *In my mind that is the whole civilized world.*"

The scientists, who are most accurately aware of the menace of doom which must overshadow us for the next five, ten, or twenty years, have been speaking to us urgently in the same language. If you read their full testimony before the Senate's McMahon Committee, you get an enlightening new perspective on our immediate future and the obligations imposed by the atomic crisis. Dr. Irving Langmuir, Nobel prize winner and associate director of General Electric's Research Laboratory, boiled things down to the essence of your responsibility and mine—the multitude of separate personal responsibilities which, collectively, will decide the fate of this civilization and of scores or hundreds of millions of men, women, and children.

"Of course," said Dr. Langmuir, "the whole problem—all of these details that we are discussing—really emphasize that we have got to learn to live with our neighbors in this world. We have to. It is a question of relations between human beings. That is the problem that has got to be solved. . . . *It is either our own existence, or learn to get along with other nations.*"

It is a question of relations between human beings—between peoples and between nations. Yet these are precisely the matters

[7] In October 1945.

for which neither Americans nor any other nation's people have ever been half-educated. Nor have we yet any plan or program, or any proposal co-ordinated on a nationwide scale, to begin to educate ourselves for survival.

At the close of this particular hearing of the U.S. Senate's Special Committee on Atomic Energy the following dialogue occurred.

Senator Johnson: "I have one further observation to make, and that is that you scientists have got a long way ahead of human conduct; and *until human conduct catches up with you, we are in a precarious condition*—unless you scientists slow up a little and let us catch up."

Dr. Langmuir: "Scientists are not going to slow up. They are going faster."

Senator Johnson: "Then, we will have to speed up."

Dr. Langmuir: *"You will have to speed up."*

Chapter XVII

ATOMIC DEFENSE AND THE MILITARY MIND

We have made technological warfare so dreadful that we cannot survive if we practice it.
Dr. Harold C. Urey, Nobel prize winner

Let's begin with three excerpts from the hearings of the Senate Committee on Atomic Energy.

Excerpt I. Time: November 28, 1945.

CHAIRMAN BRIEN McMAHON: Assuming that forty of these [bombs] were planted around forty of our centers of population and were detonated in some mechanical way. Of what value would 10,000 of these bombs be to us, distributed around the country ready to launch at an aggressor?

GENERAL GROVES: I would say the value would be that although we had suffered a loss through the damage of forty such bombs—

THE CHAIRMAN: Which might mean 40,000,000 people?

GENERAL GROVES: Which might mean 40,000,000 people—but the rest of the people would still win the war.

Excerpt II. Time: The next day.

DR. HAROLD C. UREY: In such a case we would have to have very large stores of material before the war started in order to be able to continue it. . . . A further assumption: that our atomic bomb launching sites were not destroyed. We would destroy the other fellow's cities next. I think after that that the war would languish. I think we would all be so busy taking care of our own homeless and wounded people, probably without leadership (for our leaders would probably go with the first Pearl Harbor attack), that we wouldn't pay very much attention to the war for quite a long time; and neither would our enemy. . . . We would hunt the open spaces and try to get enough to eat to take care of ourselves; and it would be pretty much of a stalemate from that time on.

Excerpt III. Time: The following day.

DR. IRVING LANGMUIR: As was mentioned yesterday . . .
40,000,000 people might be wiped out in the United States by an
attack of that kind, and it would not help us much to destroy
40,000,000 people in the nation of attack.

THE CHAIRMAN: Do you believe, Doctor, that any nation which
suffered that kind of catastrophe *could* proceed with a war?

DR. LANGMUIR: No. I think it would be crippled for perhaps
hundreds of years, and with [the loss of] far less than 40,000,000
people. . . . The whole of the Government would be wiped out;
all our railroad terminals would be wiped out; and we would have
to go back to living, as in the case of colonies, on the farm to survive as best we could. . . . It would be complete annihilation
of the existence of the country as such.

How many statements of greater personal significance to the
entire American people have been made in your lifetime and
mine? But perhaps the most extraordinary thing about them is
this: They were not published in large type or on the front pages
of more than a small fraction of our newspapers. The precise
verbatim quotations were not published by more than a few of
the nation's dailies. In most of our press these all-important facts
and opinions about the probable scope of "the next war" (as
some of our editorial writers already describe it) were buried well
down in much-condensed and seriously inadequate reports. Hence
it is highly probable that no more than 2 or 3 percent of our adult
citizens ever read these atomic facts or pondered their terrible
meaning. Despite our vaunted mechanisms for spreading information, the American public was still ill informed, indifferent,
or inexcusably muddled about the inevitable nature of another
war, even one year after Hiroshima. A definite majority of
people are still living in the same sort of utterly unreal, make-
believe world. It requires a serious effort by most of us to become
prudently acquainted with a reality which our imaginations, at
their extreme awareness, can scarcely begin to comprehend. Very
few of us have consistently sought to assemble the essential facts
and to put them into a pattern. This is why it's not repetitious to
attempt to do this. For our own safety we must remind ourselves
and ask ourselves—

What would one more war be like?

Yes, it is difficult indeed for mere cold words in print to convey what could not fail to approximate the end of the world. If we could all sit down with a group of the scientists who made the bomb, for one evening; if we could listen to them talk and ask questions, we should get a far more accurate, electrifying, and alarming picture of what now confronts all mankind, both as a clear possibility and as a direct menace as yet undiminished. I have been so fortunate as to have had this kind of experience with some of the key atomic scientists from the Manhattan District and at Oak Ridge. Here are a few of their quietly emphatic statements:

"In this last war we had 'block-busters.' Now we have *city-busters.*"

"One bomb equals one destroyed city. Perhaps it will take as much as three bombs to wipe out New York City."

"You can smuggle atomic bombs into any city."

"If Sweden devoted 10 percent of her production effort to this project, she could have atomic bomb plants in five years."

"The bombs make small nations as powerful as the largest nations. A few thousand bombs are enough to knock out any country of any size."

One of these scientists stated: "We regard any attempt to describe an atomic defense as a complete hoax." He then cited a recent news announcement, released from U.S. Navy sources and describing a radar-type device called "huff-duff." As a defense against atomic rockets or bombs, the scientists dismissed "huff-duff" as nothing more than dangerous "wishful thinking."

Dr. Langmuir describes the Hiroshima "baby" atomic bomb as "a million times more dangerous than anything we have had before." But he says we can confidently assume that new discoveries will be made within ten or fifteen years. Conclusion? . . . "It is almost certain that we will have atomic bombs *a thousand times as powerful* as those that now exist—by means that are now undiscovered." (Dr. E. V. Condon has since assured us that these bombs are already under way; can soon be produced.)

The Hiroshima type of pioneer bomb obliterates four square

miles of a city. It is equivalent to 20,000 tons of TNT, or to the
total bomb load carried by a thousand of our B-29s. But Britain's
foremost atomic authority, Dr. L. M. Oliphant, warns us that "improved bombs" equivalent to 1,000,000 or even 2,000,000 tons of
TNT are "just around the corner." This means . . . that close
to 1,000,000 civilians could be annihilated by a single bomb on
each of America's leading cities. In short, Hiroshima's devastation and death-toll could be multipliable at least by 100 within
a very few years. Dr. Oliphant reports [1] that there is a definite
possibility of producing an atomic poison gas that would kill
everything within a thousand miles. Terrifically powerful radioactive materials are by-products of nuclear fission. Dr. Oliphant
states: "They could be extracted by an unscrupulous country and
sprayed or otherwise distributed over enemy territory in sufficient concentration to prohibit the survival of any living
thing. . . . There is no known method of decontamination."
Thus it may soon be possible, through atomic poison gas, for
every living creature—in this and other countries—to be annihilated in thousand-mile strips. To live two hundred miles from
New York, Chicago, or any other great industrial center would
then be utterly futile as protection. Dr. Oliphant's final conclusion is this: "The only complete solution is offered by a mutual
determination of the peace-loving nations of the world to *give up
completely the use of war.*"

The testimony of the scientists has been factual and terrifyingly
explicit. They are the greatest, the only real, authorities on the
subject. They alone truly know the thing they were commissioned
to make. But there are other minds—by contrast, still in the
thirteenth century—which attempt to assure the public that, in
reality, nothing much has been changed. The *New York Daily
News* [2] declared, while discussing "our next war" as something
to be taken for granted: "We should pick the sea and the air
for our battlefield" and pick it "a long way from us." That reduced everything to a wonderful simplicity—on paper. But the
scientists for months had been telling us that the atomic bomb,
by its very superhuman power and purpose, has already "picked"
all the future battlefields in all the countries of the world. *In an*

1 See the *London Star,* November 15, 1945.
2 October 30, 1945.

*atomic war the only important battlefields are—and must be—
the great centers of industry and of population.* If the United
States should use the bomb again, cities and masses of civilians
would be chosen exclusively as the "battlefields." From the moment that other nations possess a supply of the bombs, American
cities and American civilians become the first assured "battlefields"—the top-priority targets—in event of war. To speculate
in a tone of pseudo-erudition about choosing a battlefield "a long
way from us" is to reveal and spread colossal ignorance about the
manner in which atomic weapons have revolutionized the whole
nature of war.

Our military leaders have been frank in telling us about these
fantastic and frightening changes, and others which will soon
become facts. General Arnold's final report [3] described pilotless
aircraft, jet-propelled bombers, rockets of fabulous range and
precision, speeds varying from 700 to 3,000 miles per hour, un-
manned missiles striking targets "many thousands of miles" away,
"space ships" which are "all but practicable today," and atomic
bombs "destructive beyond the wildest nightmares of the imagination." This was to say that just one more war must certainly
equal or exceed anything ever envisaged in the wildest nightmares of Jules Verne, or by the creators of Buck Rogers. Anyone
who is able to read General Arnold's summary of future weapons,
now on the verge of being perfected, must be able to add the two
plus two at the end of his paragraphs of plain fact. . . . One more
war would send earth's radically diminished survivors far back
into the Dark Ages.

As General Arnold has said, these incredible instruments of
mass destruction are forerunners of a "push-button warfare."
They have made the form and functioning of armies and navies
as men have used them for the past century, or for centuries,
antiquated to degrees still not accurately measurable. On this
point our generals and admirals are much less talkative publicly.
But Hiroshima prompted Hanson W. Baldwin, authoritative
military editor of the *New York Times,* to write: [4]

If it be one of the objects of armies and navies and air forces to keep
war from one's own soil and to carry it to the enemy's, *all of these*

3 November 11, 1945.
4 August 8, 1945.

armed forces, as we now know them, become obsolete. Mass conscript armies, great navies, piloted planes have perhaps become a part of history.

But what are our generals and admirals—and we ourselves—going to do about all this? In hard fact, what and how much can be done? This is where the military mind speaks one language and the scientific and atomic experts speak another. We civilians —who must remember that *we* are the future battlefield if one more war does come—have urgent reason, then, to consider another question.

What kind of solution do our military minds offer in this grave crisis precipitated by atomic weapons?

One evening, in a comfortable private dining-room in New York, a small group of us heard the opinions and the viewpoint of one of our foremost generals. He agreed entirely with General Arnold's remark that we must have the most modern weapons of all kinds—"so that we can beat any potential opponent to the draw." The gist of his argument ran something like this: "We're ahead of the whole world now, and we've got to keep ahead. We've got such powerful weapons and armed forces, here in the United States, that nobody will dare attack us now. But we've got to be able and ready to lick any other nation, or any combination of nations—*at the drop of a hat*. This is the only way to get peace."

The General was a distinguished and excellent soldier and a sincere patriot. But he seemed much more gifted as a technician than as a psychologist. The more enthusiastically he developed his thesis, the more dismayed some of us became. At certain passages we could have closed our eyes and imagined we were listening to one of Hitler's Prussian-reared field marshals. The omissions and the limits on the General's thinking were frightening. In his long discussion he did not once so much as mention the possibility—let alone the necessity—of a world authority to control the atomic bomb and other weapons of mass murder. It almost seemed as if he had ruled out any such alternative as impracticable. Quite frankly he assumed that the United States would be able to "keep ahead" in a nonstop race in atomic armaments. His only prescription was this: We should spend more and more on weapons of greater and ever-greater destruction—and keep our fingers eternally on the push-buttons. What that boiled down to was equally frank and plain, if you analyzed it at all: *American "safety" through our domination of the world through ever-expanding destructive power and ever-deepening worldwide fear.* Yet the General seemed to have no conception whatever that this was what he was really prescribing. The inescapable conclusion from his whole argument escaped him completely. That is one of the things people mean by "the military mind."

Like a large proportion of career officers, this able professional soldier was utterly engrossed in the immediate mechanics of keeping the United States military machine out in front. Like so many of his associates, he could not look beyond the technical problems. Did he really think peace could be maintained for any length of time through *global fear?* Rather, he did *not think*—not that far. Not about where wars come from: suspicions and dread, the alarmed reactions of other governments and peoples. Like professional soldiers everywhere, the General had never been educated in how to remove the psychological causes of war, or in how to prevent wars. He had been educated almost uniquely in how to fight wars and win wars. He thought solely of *national* defense and preached it because that had been his lifelong occupation and preoccupation. Supposing that these new atomic weapons mean that strictly *national* defense will no longer provide any real safety? The General had no answer. In his book such a contingency had never been admitted as remotely possible. Desperately clutching the tail of a 3,000-mile-per-hour atomic rocket, he was still clinging to the ancient four-cylindered theory of national defense. Global and *internationed* defense simply was not in his book. The military mind—before Year One, Atomic Age—was never trained for or compelled to consider either the possibility or the need of world security.

The military mind revealed itself with astonishing nakedness when Major General Leslie R. Groves calmly admitted that 40,000,000 Americans might be killed in an atomic attack, and then added: "But the rest of the people would still win the war." The next day he explained that he was convinced we "would wage war for quite a while on that basis if we still had the will to win . . . that we could still go on fighting." Yet the General himself had testified earlier that the Hiroshima bomb—the baby of all atomic bombs—"is an unendurable bomb to anyone." How could he conceive that forty American cities could be annihilated, by bombs probably hundreds of times more terrible, without the survivors throughout our entire nation being thrown into the most frenzied mass panic this earth has ever known? Can anyone imagine that under the impact of such terror any nation's people would not rush madly and hysterically toward plains, forests, and mountains?

Yes, the truly unadulterated military mind can imagine that this would not happen. It can say "we would go on fighting," while also claiming loudly that two baby atomic bombs knocked all the fight out of Japan's rulers and the Japanese people— that they really ended the war with Japan. Obviously, one or the other of these conclusions must be false. You can't have it both ways. It seems to take a traditional military mind to stretch elementary logic and fundamental human psychology that far.

Terror of supernatural forces and supreme horror is a far stronger instinct than patriotism. In turn, patriotism is much weaker in a holocaust than is the instinct for survival. We came to respect the remarkable patriotism of the Japanese, and did not pretend that Americans could hope to do more than equal it. One atomic bomb completely finished off the fighting patriotism of Hiroshima's survivors. But we have already had one most impressive demonstration of how Americans may be expected to react against a terror weapon of mass dimensions. The Orson Welles broadcast of "The Invasion from Mars" created an amazing amount of panic—without so much as Baltimore or Boston going up in flames, or ten persons being killed. In case of a nationwide atomic attack, out of the blue, I should not dare expect anything less than what Dr. Urey and Dr. Langmuir very briefly forecast. Such reactions and consequences would, we may be sure, be just as inevitable among any other nation's people. Human nervous systems have definite limitations. Human minds are human—whatever a military mind, prompted by a soldier's dogged determination, may conceive them to be.

It is true, of course, that not all our generals or admirals belong in the category of what is universally known as the military mind. It seems to me that some of our outstanding commanders —such exceptional men as Generals Marshall, Eisenhower, and Omar Bradley, and probably a good many others of whom I cannot speak from personal observation—stand very much above that classification. Nevertheless, the character of the routine military mind seems to have largely dominated the U.S. Army's atomic policies and proposals during the first year after Hiroshima. And it is a *channeled* mind, too rigid and grooved to do much exploring for possible alternatives to a strictly national program for defense against an atomic war. Thus far our military spokesmen have offered us more and bigger weapons of destruction, more and greater world fear, and not much else. Nor have they, up to this writing at any rate, given us anything like a rounded or adequate picture of what a *national* defense in this atomic age would necessitate.

After all, the first practical question that confronts every American citizen is this:

Would a strictly national Atomic Defense be workable?

On this vital matter, oddly enough, we have been given much more factual information by the scientists than by our Army or Navy. Perhaps this is partly due to the fact that the atomic experts have explored the whole field. In addition, the scientist cannot have a channeled mind: his whole life is an endless exploration. As Dr. Szilard says, science is the art of the impossible. And to overcome the supposedly impossible one must search in all directions; think unconventionally; examine every conceivable combination and alternative. As practical men, confronted with their unparalleled destructive weapon, the scientists asked themselves how this weapon would transform any country's national defense. "It is the people of the United States who face destruction and death," said Dr. Urey. "They should have the privilege of making their own decision."

If we are to attempt to stand alone, guarded only by a radically new system of *national* defense against atomic weapons, we shall need to understand clearly what that system must be and what it implies. Many months after Hiroshima, our military commands had not given us more than piecemeal descriptions; and their omissions were serious. The most authoritative summary I have seen was given by Dr. Henry DeWolf Smyth, author of the U.S. Army's initial report on atomic energy.[5] After stressing the high premium which atomic weapons put on surprise attack, Dr. Smyth said:

Defense against such an attack therefore becomes *the problem of maintaining in peacetime for twenty-four hours of every day, year in and year out,* a system of radar networks covering this entire country, together with constantly alert antiaircraft and fighter-plane defense. The cost of such a system of defense, both in terms of taxes and of implications for our attitude as a nation, makes it an expensive program in every sense of the word. *Even if it were attempted, I doubt that it could possibly be completely effective.*

First of all, then, we should have to live under a permanent, round-the-clock alert of our army, naval, and air forces wherever they were stationed. That would require, I suppose, three full eight-hour shifts for most of our army and air forces and for part of our naval forces. How many millions of men—all specialists—this would necessitate, we have not been told. As this is written, at any rate, our military commands have not taken us into their confidence at all. The American public has not been given any clear conception whatever of what a purely national defense against atomic surprise would mean. But there are other related matters of which the public has not dreamed. Dr. Smyth shocked a few hundred minds into swift clicking and utterly new speculations when he pointed out, to his New York audience, that the United States—if we try to go it alone—must also set up a fantastically thorough and equally round-the-clock *national* inspection system. Why? Because the fissionable material of an atomic bomb can be carried in a suitcase. Bombs and atomic mines could easily be smuggled piecemeal into our country. A nation that once had the world's most efficient bootleggers would now be menaced by a world of potential "bombleggers."

Against such secretly planted atomic bombs [said Dr. Smyth] the only conceivably defense would be an elaborate peacetime system of

[5] Speaking at the Nation's forum on Atomic Problems in New York, December 1945.

coast and frontier guards; and continuous X-ray inspection of every item of freight or baggage coming into this country. I do not believe such a permanent defense system could be maintained with anything near complete effectiveness.

Thus, if we accept the strictly national alternative championed by certain of our military minds, we shall have to organize the greatest army of supercustoms inspectors and superdetectives the world has ever seen. Every ship, plane, train, truck, or private automobile entering the United States from any direction would have to be searched with unfailing efficiency, day and night; every ship's hold, every cargo, every trunk, every suitcase. The bombs could be smuggled through in parts, and assembled afterward. None of our important cities could ever be safe unless this X-ray "lifeline" around all our borders, coastlines, and airports functioned with 100-percent effectiveness. Every 100 yards of our Atlantic, Caribbean, and Pacific coastlines—our Canadian and Mexican borders—would have to be constantly patrolled, day and night. How many hundreds of thousands of inspector-detectives, working in three eight-hour shifts, this would also require we have not been told. Given the size of the United States, they would probably have to total much more than 1,000,000.

But could we hope that either the "permanent alert" for our radar, antiaircraft, and similar defense forces or this round-the-clock, round-the-borders inspection system would begin to give us real protection? I do not see how our armed services could possibly provide an "ever-ready-to-push-the-button" defense unless every officer and man in an American uniform became an absolute teetotaler. Just a few hang-overs, almost anywhere, could make a "push-over" of the entire U.S.A.—any time. Certainly many millions of American males would be compelled suddenly to achieve an abstemiousness such as most American males have never practiced—and have shown no capacity or intention of tolerating. As for making a national inspection system bribe-proof against ten or fifty crisp $1,000 bills, you and I may be forgiven for wondering just where and how we are going to recruit hundreds of thousands of positively incorruptible men —even for a job that might spell life or death for most of us.

Here, at the outset, are two concrete and pretty terrific problems which are centered right at the heart of any proposed *strictly national* atomic defense system. There are undoubtedly a good many others. But the point is that our military minds have not informed us in any detail about either of these two key problems. They have been talking, chiefly, as if our job were simply "keeping in front" with bigger and more powerful weapons. But when three bombs may shortly be able to destroy virtually all of New York City *before* we can act—or perhaps destroy twenty of our great industrial centers *before* our forces can strike back—of what practical use would an assortment of somewhat more powerful bombs be? Dr. Smyth and other atomic authorities have raised key questions which cannot be dodged. If the two related systems of "permanent alert" and round-the-clock X-ray inspection cannot be made to function close to perfection, then the United States simply would *not have any national defense* that was truly a defense at all.

At this juncture we must agree that General Eisenhower has been promoted into one of the least enviable jobs in the world. But neither his headaches nor our own have as yet been more than hinted at. Right here another highly pertinent question pops up which might possibly be of personal interest to you and to every American.

What degree of protection can a national defense system give to some 60,000,000 people in our larger U.S. cities?

This is another tremendous problem about which our military minds have been curiously reticent or completely silent. But the cannon-fodder—more accurately, the bomb-fodder—of an atomic war are overwhelmingly the civilians. For every man in our armed services who was killed we might logically expect forty, fifty, or sixty civilians to be consumed in the furnaced doom of our major cities. It would seem, therefore, that any national defense would be a mockery which does not take positive and elaborate steps to reduce to a minimum the chances of civilian mass destruction. In any event we, civilians, stand to lose most or lose all. In any atomic, supersonic war, *the civilians become the chief expendables*. The survival expectancy of all our city-dwellers would be far lower than that of our recent paratroopers or of our fighting men who went onto the Normandy beaches and Okinawa in the first waves.

Since millions of civilians would be the principal bomb-fodder, perhaps we are entitled to know whether our government will provide us with any appreciable life insurance in advance.

I do not mean to sound impertinent. It happens that I have been bombed somewhat and intermittently by the air forces of five different nations—the U.S. 9th Air Force having been the last to do this. So I've contracted a kind of personal interest and a rather keen appreciation of what bombs can do. And in the course of this strictly involuntary "indoctrination" it has occurred to me that an important part of any modern nation's military precautions *ought* to be thoroughly adequate protective measures for civilians. I cannot be impressed by any so-called defense, especially if it is operated on a solo national basis, which largely writes off one fourth or one third of the nation's population. Of course, Washington and our military command would never contemplate such a thing as that. But the city-dwellers of the United States might reasonably ask, at this moment: "What *do* you plan? If another war would be a button-pushing war, precisely what do *you* propose to do to protect *us* from the future button-pushers?"

What the government and the U.S. Army may finally recommend will depend, of course, on whether or not the presently budding atomic-arms race is nipped during the next few years. If all atomic weapons are not outlawed and abolished by international agreement within a brief margin of years—perhaps within ten years, but perhaps within only five, or even three—then history's maddest competition will be under full steam in many places. The competition would be to determine which nation could equip itself to burn up the largest number of millions of human beings in the shortest time—and stand ever-ready to do it first. No wonder Bob Casey remarked, at our latest reunion in Chicago: "Well, Lee, you and I have seen *the next-to-the-last war*. There won't be much war corresponding in the next one. It'll be over in too few minutes."

In this particular view, our "Two World Wars" Mr. Casey finds himself in quite close agreement with some 1,500 members of the Federation of Atomic Scientists. The atomic experts would greatly admire, I'm sure, the near-indestructibility of the dean of all American war correspondents. But they wouldn't cite any attractive survival percentage even for Robert J. Casey in the event of another war—even though nobody's airplanes and nobody's navy have ever managed to prevent "Two World Wars" Casey from coming to the surface under his own steam. Consider then, the relative chances of ordinary civilians, if the nations keep playing with atomic fire.

The scientists are considering the terribly reduced chances of civilians from every angle. If the nations elect to rely only upon *national* atomic defense, they insist that the United States will be forced to carry out the greatest mass transfer of population ever undertaken by any government. Before the war 30,000,000 people lived in cities of over 250,000, but the number in metropolitan areas totaled 63,000,000—nearly half of the nation's inhabitants. "Preparedness," warns Dr. Szilard, "means also the relocation, in time of peace, of 30 to 60 million people, together with the industries which they serve and which serve them." [6] It is this atomic authority's conviction that without this extreme action "there can be no policy of 'preparedness' which makes any sense at all." Meanwhile, the longer the atomic-arms race develops uncurbed, the more conscious of "being inside the target" our city-dwellers will inevitably become.

"Tensions will increase slowly at first; then beyond anything we have seen or experienced," states Dr. Urey. "In a few years we will begin moving our families far from big cities and industrial plants, if we can afford to do so. Finally, every ripple on the international scene will make us wonder whether the atomic bombs may not arrive before morning." [7]

Thus we should have either to transfer tens of millions of our city civilians by governmental order over an eight- or ten-year period, or risk paralyzing and disorderly mass evacuations at some moment of serious international crisis. The scientists say that all our great cities *must* be depopulated by schedule over a fixed limit of years. But is such gigantic dispersal politically or psychologically possible? Would thirty or fifty million Americans—rugged individualists that they are about their personal lives—obey such orders? Or could they be persuaded to move even if Congress dared to give the government the authority of a national emergency law? We have already had a minor but extremely

6 Statement to the Senate McMahon Committee, December 10, 1945.
7 Statement to the Senate McMahon Committee, November 29, 1945.

vociferous demonstration of the probable American reaction. It was estimated that fewer than 5,000 residents of the Westchester-Greenwich area might be obliged to move in order to provide a site for UN; perhaps not more than 3,000 persons. Nevertheless, a good proportion of the Westchester-Greenwich citizenry uttered protesting cries that echoed around the world. Imagine what collective roars we should hear were 4,000,000 New Yorkers ordered out into the country—or 1,000,000 Chicagoans, including Colonel Robert R. McCormick. The more you examine the amazing complications of a national atomic defense, the more seriously you wonder how we could ever make it work.

But there is a further matter which could never be classified merely as an item. We cannot possibly have a realistic approach to our own American atomic problem until we have asked ourselves and our military planners—

Can we afford to support an atomic-age national defense program? How much would it cost us per year?

Admittedly, it's extremely difficult for the heads of our War, Navy, and State Departments to make more than very general estimates at a time when long-established methods and concepts of war have been turned topsy-turvy. Nevertheless, not even the broadest general estimates have yet been given us regarding the important and unavoidable innovations which we have been discussing here. Under the heading of General Atomic Defense Costs even a partial list of enormously expensive new items makes doleful contemplation for American taxpayers. Among these atomic-age blessings would be a worldwide atomic secret service; special 24-hour atomic alert systems in the Army, Navy, and Air Forces; a round-the-clock nation-girding X-ray inspection system; a greatly expanded Coast Guard; a gigantic dispersal program both for United States city-dwellers and for our industries; and underground installation of virtually all major defense industries.

What would all these elaborate innovations and precautions cost the American people per year? One single item would be quite an "item." Two experts of the Cowles Commission at the University of Chicago, figuring on a ten-year program affecting

60,000,000 people, have estimated *that relocation of our city populations alone would require a yearly expenditure of no less than $20,000,000,000.* The other categories of a national plan for atomic defense, as mentioned above, would certainly cost many more *billions* of dollars annually. In addition we cannot afford to forget our new and mounting expense load to provide hospitalization and other benefits for some 12,000,000 new veterans. For these the United States government anticipates yearly expenditures of between $2,500,000,000 and more than $4,000,-000,000 throughout the next generation. Thus, before we take the plunge for national "preparedness" on an atomic scale, American taxpayers would be wise to demand a carefully documented itemization of what the whole colossal bill is likely to be.

Throughout the war the British people had to pay income taxes of 50 percent on every pound of their income, above annual earnings of less than $500. They are still paying taxes at a crushing rate—without any special atomic protection whatever. Could we Americans maintain a national system of atomic defense without paying average taxes of approximately 50 cents on every dollar of income? Or possibly more than that? It seems unlikely, to say the least. Certainly the taxes on incomes of the middle and upper brackets, on corporations' earnings, and on luxuries would probably have to be boosted to punishing rates. Our wartime taxes of 1941–45 might well appear generously light by comparison. It is not exaggeration to ask whether it would be less than social and economic folly for the American people to shoulder the massive costs of a national atomic defense.

But what is particularly striking is the fact that American public opinion has remained for so long blissfully unaware of the staggering size of the bill which strictly national preparedness would assuredly present to all of us. We have not heard many governmental leaders or congressmen presenting columns of precise estimates about the probable costs. I have not yet noticed, in fact, any inclusive or global "new defense" estimates from governmental or private agencies. Would any rounded program which our War and Navy Departments would regard as "reasonably sufficient" necessitate defense expenditures of some $40,000,000,000 per year? Or something less than that? Or considerably more? Yet the answers to such questions as these are essential to the individual future-planning of all of us.

The truth is that hard facts of this kind may largely determine whether the United States enjoys any real prosperity or any genuine improvement in its standard of living over the next ten or twenty years. A national atomic defense must come unless a worldwide race in atomic armaments is prevented. But in such a world it would also be impossible for international trade to be expanded on the scale now necessary for large employment and general prosperity in the United States. Taking all these factors into consideration, the "we must keep out in front" arms slogan of the military minds loses all of its simplicity. That kind of pseudo-solution could not fail to be one of the costliest financial and economic gambles that any nation ever accepted—if we should accept it.

One further matter is of infinitely greater importance than any that we have previously considered.

Is a strictly national atomic defense possible without dictatorship or virtual dictatorship in the United States?

First of all, it is unquestionable that a nationwide, round-the-clock readiness for a "push-button" war would necessitate giving the military much more rigid controls over many phases of civilian life than the United States has ever known or tolerated, even in wartime. We should have to have greatly increased zones "prohibited to civilians." Americans' freedom to travel, especially outside our country, would have to be much restricted and closely supervised. Every United States beach and shoreline would have to be constantly patrolled. The size of the FBI would have to be increased by tenfold or by twenty. Every house, apartment, cellar, and warehouse in every corner of the United States would be subject to entry and search by federal police, the Army, or the FBI at any hour of the day and night—in strictly dictatorial, Gestapo-fashion. Federal or military controls over the nation's scientists might well become intolerable. All civilians would have to carry special identity cards at all times. These are merely a few items which come immediately to mind—not forgetting the mass transfer of many millions of our city-dwellers that would have to be faced sooner or later. When you conjure up this hypothetical but possible national scene, you remark striking similarities to the Germany that existed under Adolf the Despicable. The evolution would have to be in that one direction. We should be compelled to have such regimentation as Americans have never known and never tolerated.

This fact raises another extremely pertinent problem. Speaking at the *Nation's* atomic forum, Thomas K. Finletter observed: "A case may well arise where it will be politically impossible for any United States government to enact the kind of law which the experts will say is necessary for the national defense." (This certainly does not appear far-fetched when I read in my morning newspaper—apropos of a new bill for a special volunteer occupation force for the U.S. Army—that Congressman Carl Vinson says: "The American people would not continue to permit their sons to be drafted for occupation duties.") Mr. Finletter added: "The people may prefer having the country open to devastating attack *rather than accept the drastic regulation of their lives* which may be necessary in the light of the then-existing weapons in the possession of other countries."

In a November issue of the foreign letter of the Whaley-Eaton Service from Washington [8] we were presented with some startling revelations on "the nature of a nationalistic atomic defense" which War Department planners had come up against in seeking a necessary alternative to international control of the bomb. The planners not only found—if we relied on a national defense —that we must keep much of our armed forces "in a state of permanent wartime alert." We must also organize "an extensive secret service to give immediate warning of any other power's hostile intentions." And provisions finally must be made, it was reported, "for the President's pushing the button . . . the moment the warning is given."

What would this mean? The news letter expressed it concisely:

The difficulty is that planners had not completed their plans before they saw that the program was *impractical in a democratic society.* It would obviously be unconstitutional for a President to press the button for destruction of an ostensibly friendly power without secur-

[8] See extracts quoted by Raymond Swing on November 9, 1945.

ing a prior declaration of war from Congress—the mere mention of which would cause the potential enemy to press his own button first. *It is this which led higher echelons of the General Staff to consider the feasibility of constitutional change.*

This means, of course, that we cannot be adequately prepared against an atomic war—nationally and by ourselves—without giving every future American President dictatorial powers to put our nation into war at a moment's notice. This would strip Congress of one of its most important powers. It would equally strip representative, democratic government in the United States of much of its reality. A handful of military-naval leaders and the Chief Executive—all of whom, at some period, might be either ambitious, demagogic, or merely jittery—could hold the power of life or death over 40,000,000 or more United States civilians. Under such a national defense system, how long could American democracy be expected to survive?

The War Department's planners are understood to have shied away from such a dangerous alternative as this, and we must hope that all our military policy-makers will remain firmly against it. At any rate the Whaley-Eaton letter, reporting their reaction as in the autumn of 1945, stated: "While it is admitted that international control is at best a dubious experiment, it is argued *that it will be better to gamble on a system which has some chance of working, than to adopt one known to be unworkable.*" (Italics mine.)

Thus, in the phrase of Dr. Vannevar Bush, "the entire pattern in which we are accustomed to think of war is scrapped." And the scrapping of that pattern inevitably scraps the whole conception of classical national defense. The "unendurable" bomb is truly unendurable in the possession of various nations' armed forces. It is logically impossible—and livably impossible—for intelligent humans to do anything else than accept the measured verdict of all of America's atomic scientists; a verdict which Dr. Smyth expresses in these terms: "There is still one other alternative for defense against the atomic bomb. It is to build with our fellow-nations a world in which there is no need to resort to war."

As Norman Cousins says, we must transform ourselves "from national man to world man."

Chapter XVIII

THE DEADLINE FOR OUR SURVIVAL

Naturally, I am not really worried about the future—except perhaps the next fifteen years!

Dr. Leo Szilard, atomic expert

The men who *know* are frightened men. That's why they're frightened. Because they *know*. One of the most eminent of these hundreds of nuclear physicists is Nobel prize winner Dr. Harold C. Urey. He is a modest man who has never sought the spotlight. In his field, nevertheless, he is one of the intellectual giants of this century. He has a scientist's extreme respect for accuracy. This is what he says:

"As a scientist, I tell you there must never be another war." [1]

I don't think we can digest that statement in one gulp. I think it should be read and reread. I believe it should really be printed like this:

"As a *scientist,* I tell you *THERE MUST NEVER BE ANOTHER WAR!*"

This is what Hiroshima demonstrated. Not that the atomic bomb knocked Japan out of the war, but that atomic weapons will knock out mankind—unless mankind rallies and knocks out war. The dawn of the atomic age has left us no other tolerable, livable, or endurable alternative. To "control" these fearful new weapons, leaving them in some nation's or group of nations' hands, will not give us any real or lasting safety. They must be abolished. But if this is done, and later the world's powers permit themselves the luxury of one more war—what then? Obviously, the rival nations will start furiously from scratch once more. Whichever side can build the first plants and produce the first bombs might win the war—and become dictators of the world.

[1] Dr. Harold C. Urey: "I'm a Frightened Man," *Collier's,* January 5, 1946.

One way or another any future international war must lead to this final madness: the destruction of most of modern civilization accompanied by the mass murder of scores of millions—perhaps hundreds of millions—of human beings. On these facts some 1,500 atomic specialists are more nearly unanimous than such a group of exceptionally endowed men of learning probably has ever been in several centuries.

Thus we have been given the essential facts. There is no more chance of the scientists' being proven wrong about the political and social meaning of the atomic bomb than there was that time would make heretics out of Copernicus and Galileo. It is no more likely than it was likely, in 1492, that Columbus would sail off a flat earth into space. But the world's peoples today are probably no better prepared for the political imperatives of the atomic revolution than Europeans were prepared in the early sixteenth century to accept the Copernican theory. This is why the temptation is so strong among us to cling to the anachronistic, war-breeding concept of defense built on strictly nationalistic lines.

It should be clear by now that we must look beyond national defense when all of the great centers of population and wealth in the world lie at the mercy of atomic weapons. A tremendous world peril dictates nothing less than a world solution. In turn, any worldwide solution must inevitably require pronounced effort, repeated negotiations—and these will require considerable time, probably a good many years, even if eventually successful. So the question is not merely: Where are we going? The question also is—

What is the margin in which we must find safety from the menace of Atomic Doom? What is the probable time-limit within which atomic weapons must be outlawed?

Even the scientists admit they have to guess about this. But it's of interest that most of them estimate our atomic deadline to be something like five to seven years. Dr. Urey, speaking carefully, says: "I think that we should not think of a longer time than about five years." Dr. Langmuir of General Electric has given precisely the same opinion. "The security which we now possess through the possession of atomic bombs will be short-lived," he warned. "During this period of five or ten years it is of vital importance that steady progress be made to develop means for the effective world control of atomic energy." [2]

Unless the scientists are very much mistaken—and the facts support them too eloquently—the deadline of safety cannot be counted upon, then, to extend much beyond the year 1951. The time-limit for the rescue of our present world, and of ourselves, may not be postponable much beyond that date. This is not to say that an atomic war would be probable in five years, or necessarily even in ten. It is to insist that what governments and voters do—or fail to do—by 1951 or by 1953 is virtually certain to have fixed the world's course either for peace and safety, or for the war to end all wars through its indescribable devastation.

Historians and political observers today are quite generally agreed that the Second World War was largely determined and assured by the blind errors of numerous nations' governments immediately after the First World War—between 1919 and 1924. The false peace which led to September 1939 was shaped in those highly formative years. The governments and peoples of our doubly revolutionary world are now grappling with fate in an even more decisive five-year period. What we decide and do before 1951 may well chain our hands and paralyze our wills in 1955 or 1965. A united world society, capable of repudiating war and abolishing all atomic weapons, can be hammered out only while the metal of mankind's receptivity is at white heat. We dare not hope that this white-heat metal of awakened mass conscience and mass revulsion against war will remain internationally malleable for as much as ten years, or even seven. It is by no means certain that it will not cool off within five years.

But why do they place the atomic deadline so close as 1951? you ask. That's where the terribly ironic rub comes for us who are Americans. The scientists did not make the deadline. The deadline was made when our generals decided to use the bomb destructively; when our government did nothing for nearly four months to prevent the launching of a race in atomic armaments. Dr. Urey expressed this in the plainest language when he said: "Atomic bombs must *not* be made by any country, and they must

[2] Testimony before the Senate McMahon Committee, November 30, 1945.

not be stored any place in the world, if we are to have any feeling of security in this or any other country on this all-too-small planet. We are making bombs and storing them, and are thus a threat to other countries *and are guilty of beginning the atomic armament race*. If continued, it will lead to dire disaster. . . . I wish very much that the statement of the President, Mr. Attlee, and Mr. King had been made in August instead of now. I believe our international situations are being poisoned day after day because we are accumulating a supply of bombs." [3]

It bears repeating that the first stage of a race in atomic armaments is now under way; that the fear and insecurity created by our stock-piling of the bombs had to be translated by the Russians into an atomic defense program of their own; and that Stalin was in reality announcing that Moscow had taken up Washington's incredible challenge when he declared that Soviet scientists "will not only catch up with, but surpass, those abroad." This is how our military minds blundered and pushed us into a squirrel-cage revolving wheel of their own making. This is why our senators, when they diplomatically ask the scientists about how long it will be before "some other country" may have the bomb, are really worrying about what the Russians may be able to do. In speaking with such vagueness the senators were being true to a gentleman's code. But when you and I study this problem we cannot hope to get something like an accurate picture without being realistically frank as well as well-mannered. What all the anxiety and concern centers upon is this question.

Can the United States keep ahead of Soviet Russia permanently in a long-term atomic arms race?

Of course, no one asked the star witnesses at the U.S. Senate Atomic Committee's hearings this question with quite this baldness. But General Groves was asked if we could "keep several steps ahead" of any foreign countries "for a long period of time." His answer was truly remarkable.

"I believe we can keep ahead of any other nation in the world for all time to come," said the General, "provided that the rules are the same for the two nations."

[3] Testifying before the McMahon Committee.

The joker in this statement is as big as a house. It is impossible for any Western democracy to operate under "the same rules" as any totalitarian, one-party system whether that system be in the Soviet Union, in Spain, Argentina, or elsewhere. It is precisely in this regard that the testimony of Dr. Irving Langmuir commands widespread attention.

Dr. Langmuir stated flatly that, whereas the United States held the chief short-term advantages in a competition in atomic weapons, Soviet Russia might have very important long-term advantages over us. He outlined four possible stages of such a race. The fourth stage, he said, might give one nation (possibly not the United States) such overwhelming superiority "that in one surprise attack an enemy nation can be so completely incapacitated that no retaliation can occur." Coming from a foremost scientist-industrialist authority, that is an arrestingly sober statement. But Dr. Langmuir continued in his precise scientific manner.

"There are many reasons," he said, "for thinking that Russia might reach Stage Four before we do. For example, Russia—as in her preparations for her war against Germany—may be willing to forgo any increase in living standards and devote *10 percent or more* of her producing power in a five- or ten-year plan for the development of atomic energy and bombs.[4] We, on the other hand, may conceivably dissipate our energies in increasing our standard of living, in building a strong but obsolete navy, and in shortening our hours of labor."

That last sentence brings up some embarrassing but very pertinent points. How many Americans would be content with a re-

---

[4] In his commentary over the ABC network on October 12, 1945, Raymond Swing made these interesting observations: "Before the war the expenditure on pure and applied science in this country (by all agencies, governmental, industrial, and by public foundations) came to between two and three cents on every $100 of national income. It rose during the war. The government alone spent at the rate of 44 cents for every $100 of national income on pure and applied science in 1944. . . . But the Russians are going for science in a much more basic and sweeping way than we are. They might decide to spend 10 cents on every *dollar* of income, or even twenty cents on the dollar. . . . If they spend 10 cents on the *dollar* and we spend 6 cents on hundred dollars, the Russians would be spending at a rate more than 16 times greater than ours. . . . The bit of engineering know-how which is our margin of safety today might dwindle to less than nothing, if the Russians should decide to marshal their resources and effort in a big way."

duced standard of living over a ten- or twenty-year period for the sake of "keeping out front" in atomic weapons? How many labor unions would accept a 48-hour or perhaps a 52-hour week? How many United States corporations would cheerfully accept either a 25 to 50 percent slash in their profits, or an equal increase in their taxes? How many average American citizens would tolerate going without new motor cars, radios, refrigerators, and other luxuries or near-necessities so that a large percentage of American production would enable us "to keep ahead of any other nation in the world for all time to come"? The answer is, of course, that none of these things can be expected under our free enterprise system or our habits of living. In Soviet Russia none of these serious limitations applies. The Russians have no unemployment, no strikes, no big industries working for private profits—and they are accepting important sacrifices in limited consumer goods under their new five-year plan, as they accepted them under three previous five-year plans. In addition, the U.S.S.R. possesses many scientists of exceptional ability. Dr. Langmuir and other Americans were much impressed by Russian scientists during their visit to Moscow shortly before Hiroshima.

These considerations prompted Dr. Langmuir to make two statements that cannot be brushed off lightly. "If an atomic armament race develops," he said, "I believe the Russians will produce their first atomic bombs in about three years." (As from November 1945.) Later, in answer to Senator Tydings's query as to what countries might be ahead in ten or fifteen years, he stated: *"In ten years, to my mind, it is very uncertain whether the United States or Russia will lead."*

As one who was in the U.S.S.R. throughout the most critical six months of the German invasion, and as one who was greatly surprised by both the organizational and the technical ability displayed by the Russians, I believe Dr. Langmuir's general thesis is absolutely correct. Those who seriously underestimated the military prowess of the Red Army in 1941–42 may misjudge the Soviets' scientific prowess and capacity for industrial organization just as greatly in the course of the next two decades. I expect they probably will. For Americans to assume that the United States can "keep ahead" indefinitely in any atomic arms race would be one of the most dangerous illusions imaginable.

Not because the Russians want to fight us, any more than most Americans are itching to fight the Russians, but because this state of mind—the utterly false idea that the United States could remain in front with superior weapons and forces for ten years or a lifetime—can only serve to undermine *our* efforts to meet the atomic deadline. We are not competing with any other nation for a prize for brute force. We *are* competing against death and Atomic Doom. There is no safety in making superior destructive force our goal. *There is safety only in understanding that the single valid goal for all nations and peoples is now the same thing—survival.*

The natural tendency of Americans is to be abundantly conscious of their assets and abilities, and to disregard limitations or weaknesses which must also be taken into account. Any assessment of a nation's power or its possibilities becomes a distortion —a false guide—unless it is most carefully balanced. The scientists have been trying to give us this kind of perspective. They see what our average citizen seldom stops to think about. Take, for example, a relatively simple truth. Dr. John A. Simpson, Jr., of the University of Chicago, states: "In any atomic armament race the United States, in the long run, will find itself in a very unfavorable position due to its highly concentrated population and industry." That should be self-evident, but it still isn't to the rank-and-file of our George Joneses.

To grasp the real significance of Dr. Simpson's statement we must examine our map. Where, indeed, are the most vulnerable targets in the United States? Most of our industries are concentrated in two dangerously compact belts. The first extends roughly 800 miles between Boston and Philadelphia, in the east, and Chicago. The second runs approximately 1,000 miles from Seattle down to Los Angeles, but it is grouped tightly around only four Pacific coast cities. From Britain to Berlin you find an equally concentrated industrial area—but nowhere else on earth. The Soviet Union, for instance, has already dispersed widely its key industries over a vast region 5,000 miles wide; and its population is far more scattered than ours. Speaking in atomic terms, there is a very considerable amount of geographical immunity and civilian security for the Soviet peoples in these facts. Speaking in the same terms about ourselves, if a strip some

800 miles long and 200 miles wide should be completely obliterated from Chicago to New York, the United States would be virtually knocked out from that time on. It is perilously easy for public opinion to overlook a fact of this importance.

In order to discover a means of survival we must first have an accurate and realistic understanding of the nature of the house in which we live. We must focus our minds on the essential problem. We must see our disadvantages as clearly as we realize our widely heralded advantages. This is what I have been trying to do here. Having examined the requirements for a national atomic defense, its risks and its frightful costs both in fear and in taxes, there remains the alternative of a world control of atomic weapons. Can these weapons be abolished? And can any potential aggressors be prevented from secretly manufacturing and building up a supply of such weapons afterward? Concisely, this means—

Can an international inspection system be made to work with sufficient efficiency?

This is rather like asking whether anyone can fly to the moon and come back to tell the tale. Actually, no one can be certain whether it will or won't work until it has been tried. Some of our generals and admirals are highly skeptical. One thing about their attitude strikes me as odd. The same militarists who insist that an international inspection system cannot be made sufficiently "airtight" have not told us that—without this—we should be forced to have a national, round-the-clock inspection system which would positively *have* to be airtight, if Americans were to enjoy any real protection at all. Yet this second fact brings the debate about inspection systems down to two questions which really make some sense.

Would *you* feel safer if the United States were to attempt to keep free of smuggled bombs only through her own national inspection system, with other nations making and stocking bombs and rockets galore?

Or would *you* feel that your chances were better if all bombs and bomb plants and similar weapons had been destroyed; if fifty-odd nations had joined in a common control of all sources of uranium and plutonium; if their joint inspection system was worldwide; and if a United Nations Police Force, backed by all these nations, stood ready to move against any nation that was shown to be violating its pledges?

If we were incapable of preventing another war, it seems to me the United States would feel far safer in being assured of having the vast majority of the world's nations as allies from the outset. In that event we should have the overwhelming power of the world on our side immediately. Proportionately we should be infinitely stronger than our thirteen original colonies, when united, were in comparison with the colony of Maryland. And if some fifty-odd nations—or even forty—will go into this kind of united front against atomic weapons and national wars, what other country would quite dare to remain outside and attempt to go it alone?

But would every nation open its factories and research laboratories to inspectors from the outside? And would American automobile manufacturers, for instance, tolerate having foreign inspectors in a position to observe what their new and improved models would be like? When it comes down, in a few years, to international inspection or the likely destruction of all the plants of Ford, General Motors, and Chrysler, it may be that our great automotive corporations would prefer to be fairly certain of being in existence and making a few profits. Whatever we do, we are not going to have any dead-sure thing to choose. But the scientists are convinced that an international inspection can be devised that will be workable. If no bomb plants or rocket plants are left intact and inspection starts from scratch, they insist that an adequate control can be developed.

For one thing—and it's very important—any aggression-scheming government would have to work a long time to build an atomic-bomb plant in some hidden locality. It would have to maintain that secrecy over some two or three years before it could get into production and acquire several hundred bombs. And to make these two steps possible a great many of that country's nuclear physicists would have to disappear suddenly and completely. Our scientists maintain that it should not be difficult for roving nuclear experts and inspectors to keep tabs on the key atomic specialists in every country. This should not be difficult because no other country has more than a few scores of them at most—and the complicated task of building an Oak Ridge plant cannot be done without a great many of these top scientists on the job. Our scientists also say that the production of the pitchblende mines, which yield uranium, can be controlled. They do not predict that any inspection system will be perfect. But they are virtually unanimous in the conviction that some type of world control, *with the abolition of atomic weapons*, constitutes humanity's only—and last—hope for escape from a world catastrophe.

However you or I, or the generals or the industrialists or other people, may first react to this complicated problem, the fact of the atomic deadline remains unalterable. This is the most urgent and perhaps the most difficult question that governments and individuals have ever faced in all history. No generation has ever before had to decide how to save the world from being devastated by a weapon that can annihilate all of earth's richest cities and possibly 500,000,000 human beings in the course of a few days. And the time-limit which destiny has given us for working out the safe beginnings for some kind of solution resolves itself into a matter of only some five years—or perhaps seven years at the most. If the people of America and the other leading countries of the world are intelligent enough to see, to think, and to act, it should be possible to meet the atomic deadline. But to do this we must see—we must think—and we must then act in the direction of man's common safety.

The greatest collective crisis of the past twenty or thirty centuries will probably come at some juncture within the next ten or twenty years; perhaps a little later than that, but perhaps considerably sooner. The only possible chance that we may escape it will be if we meet the atomic deadline by scotching the race in atomic armaments and initiating a program to outlaw war as well as all atomic weapons of destruction. As of today it does not seem as though our chances of success were any better than fifty-fifty; and some of our scientists would put them considerably lower than that. This, again, is why we must become aware of our peril. Five years will be much too fast and fleeting. Humanity has been given a suspended sentence, but its days of grace are fearfully short.

General Eisenhower has said that the atomic bomb might "blackmail the world into peace." Fortunately, this possibility also exists. But it does little good to blackmail people unless they understand that they are being blackmailed. That is where survival is by no means the immediate and imperative task of statesmen and generals only. Survival and how to make an atomic war impossible—these are the personal tasks of you and me, of all those men and women in the democracies whose votes determine the kind of men whose decisions in turn must decide *whether we act for Life, or whether we act for an Atomic Doomsday.*

Nigel Tangye, a Wing Commander in the RAF, poses the question of our century as it merits being phrased: [5]

"Is it too much to hope that there can be one law and one controlling authority in a world, any part of which can be laid waste by the pressure of a single finger?"

Once again there is a passage which should not remain buried in the verbatim report of the hearings of the U.S. Senate's Committee on Atomic Energy.

SENATOR BYRD: Human nature doesn't change.

DR. LANGMUIR: I don't know what human nature is; and in the second place, I don't know that it won't change.

SENATOR BYRD: It hasn't changed for the better in my lifetime. I think human nature in the last war was at the lowest level ever known.

DR. LANGMUIR: Let's hope for something better.

SENATOR BYRD: We cannot base our future on hopes alone.

DR. LANGMUIR: *The alternative of not doing something is absolute destruction.* The risk in whatever you do is better than total destruction. Don't think there is a risk in undertaking these things. It is the only possible salvation. This is the thing we have to make clear. *The worst thing that could possibly happen is to do nothing.* So, therefore, let us do something—and let us make it good.

[5] In his article, "Flying Bombs and Rockets, This Time and Next," *Foreign Affairs,* October 1945.

Chapter XIX

WORLD GOVERNMENT, OR WORLD ANARCHY

> *There is no need to talk of the difficulties in the way of world government. There is need only to ask whether we can afford to do without it. . . .*
>
> *Once the nature and the imminency of the peril are understood by the peoples of the world, their differences will not be a bar but an incentive to common government.*
>
> Norman Cousins in *Modern Man Is Obsolete*

Dr. Leo Szilard has remarked that it will take only man's lack of imagination to make a Jules Verne type of atomic-war nightmare come true. A continued and fatal time-lag in our individual and collective comprehension would be sufficient to push our world into the calamity of the ages. Thus *our greatest peril is not the bomb itself but the persistent hang-over of our preatomic thinking*. There can be no solution or escape unless we expand our imaginations and our minds in some such measure as the emancipated atom has expanded man's powers of self-destruction.

We can summarize this in simple terms. Atomic war means that every nation involved must suffer stupendous and incalculable mass destruction. Therefore no nation can hereafter afford to indulge in war. Therefore nationalistic wars can no longer be tolerated by an endangered world society; war itself must be permanently curbed and abolished. But how can the right of nations to wage individual wars be curbed without the creation of a common and supreme law above all nations? This means, in turn, that nothing less than a new world sovereignty can hope to restrain nations from actions which would destroy most of our civilization, probably for many generations or for centuries.

As logic these facts would appear impregnable. But the hangover of our preatomic habits and ideas still palsies the cerebral processes of most of us. This was why Senator Tom Connally could expostulate that he was not going to run after "some butterfly" of world government. The trouble was that our veteran Senator from Texas did not explain where he did plan to run, nor make it clear in precisely what direction he might possibly choose to walk. For, unless our men of government determine America's course with greatest wisdom and prudence, in a few more years Washington will surely become one of the most unhealthy places on the globe in which to live. The "butterfly" which Senator Connally dismissed so hastily might offer infinitely greater protection than billions of dollars' worth of atomic weapons.

Perhaps Senator Taylor had a far shrewder sense of self-preservation. He declared he'd rather be outvoted in a world government than have an atomic bomb dropped on him. That might be a much more comfortable risk for you and me as well. This much is unalterable. The only thing on this planet which is indestructible enough to oppose and tame the atomic bomb is an idea: the idea of some form of limited world government.

"Isn't it visionary?" a Congressman asked Dr. H. J. Curtis, leader of the Oak Ridge atomic project.

The scientist replied: "I will simply state that the possibility of developing atomic energy was also labeled visionary a scant six years ago. Today it is a reality. We can see no reason why a similar miracle cannot be achieved in international relations."

That is the answer of a highly skilled and rational mind. It is also the voice of hope. It is the reaffirmation that man can still be the master of his fate and the captain of his soul. The scientists, those allegedly antispiritual and cold-blooded technicians, have been first to champion this unique hope for mankind. But they have been joined by a notable chorus of public and private citizens in Britain and France and around the globe as well as in the United States. The idea of a world sovereignty is an all-encompassing idea. Like the brotherhood of man, as expounded by Christ some nineteen centuries ago, it surpasses all national boundaries. Although the road is painfully long we do not renounce man's brotherhood as visionary. We can look back to the social conditions and the dumb silence of most of the world's masses only one or two centuries ago and see what considerable progress has been made. We can also survey the brief record of this phenomenal twentieth century and see with clarity how the conception of world co-operation has grown at a truly extraordinary pace. Almost unconsciously we have come to talk and think—and act—in world terms. Now we are still gravely unprepared, and a majority among us seems to be almost totally unprepared, for the immediate necessity of world citizenship. But I still would ask one question: What previous generation has been one half so well-prepared as we?

Almost unconsciously we have accepted a large measure of world co-operation—in the control of white slavery and traffic in narcotics, in the regulation of shipping and aviation, in educational and scientific exchanges, in international political conferences and agreements covering a vast range of human activity. In the United States alone the change in public thinking has been so great that it is startling. After repudiating the League of Nations in 1919–20, the overwhelming sentiment of Americans was to join a world organization after this war, and to exercise an active United States leadership in an admittedly revived and enlarged League of Nations. We have changed its name, but the idea is identical. Today it marches on, and we march with it. There is nothing "butterfly" about the fact that from a United Nations Organization to a World Government (naturally limited by common sense as well as necessity) is only another few steps.

What are the steps toward a world government?

They are the steps that are imperative to make another global war impossible. The atomic bomb and its associated weapons of mass destruction have simply made it unavoidable that these steps should be taken within a very few years. We are like a gang-ster who has been given five years of probation in which to reform himself—or face the imposition of a death sentence within a definite time-limit. If he is at all intelligent the gangster now knows that neither the judge, the jury, nor the outraged public can be wheedled or bought off any longer. But this antisocial offender has been given a chart by which he can yet work out his redemption. The charter of San Francisco is the beginning of such a salvation chart for us; but the supreme magistrate of human destinies, the bomb, has also warned us that it alone is not nearly good enough. We have not built a House of Safety; we have only laid a portion of its indispensable foundations.

Since Hiroshima we have been driven hard by the gale of circumstance. At London in September 1945 we tried to ride into the teeth of that gale by temporarily abandoning Big Three agreement. At Moscow in December we snatched back the main oars of the Big Three with obvious relief. In those intervening dark months Americans, British, and Russians alike learned there could be no conceivable atomic solution, no possibility of a hopeful debut for the United Nations Organization, no facing up to the tangled issues of our messed-up world, without the central amalgam of these three powerful governments' working together or striving to work together despite all obstacles. So the Moscow agreements marked a sudden relaxation from a perilous period of strain and stress. Although they did not solve many things, they cleared the decks and pointed the ship back on its main course. The barometer of hope rose again, and the weather began to clear. The gales tempered and the seas calmed down, however, not because harbor was anywhere in sight, but simply because we had all recommitted ourselves to a program of collective co-operation.

In doing this the necessary steps toward an eventual world sovereignty became much clearer. The Moscow chart was only half a chart, it's true. The boundaries of western Germany and the status of the Ruhr had not been fixed. The future of Iran and that of Turkey were still clouded. The clash of British-Russian interests in the eastern Mediterranean remained as acute as ever. Joint Allied supervision of Japan must still be worked out. Soviet-American co-operation in Korea and in regard to China was still merely a pledge. Yet all these and other problems remain subsidiary to one predominant central fact. At Moscow the Soviet Union had recommitted herself to leading participation in UN with Britain and the United States, and had accepted a United Nations commission to determine the future role and control of atomic energy. Without the Russians' acceptance of this course, the world would have been split in two. UN would have been fatally crippled at its birth. We should have had no common course and no mutual mechanism. We should also have had no common hope. But with these three things we could see at last what we had to do and something of the order in which we must begin to do it. The main steps in this chart for a new world co-operation might be summarized roughly in this fashion:

1. The United Nations must be put effectively to work, in all its councils and subdivisions, in the first year of its existence.

2. The peace treaties, and the status and administration of Germany and Japan, must be handled with dispatch.

3. The whole range of atomic problems must be assaulted by UN's Atomic Commission with the least possible delay.

4. A world control of atomic weapons must be devised and negotiated. These weapons must be abolished.

5. UN's San Francisco charter must be modernized and strengthened so that it may begin to measure up to the vastly increased stresses of an age of atomic energy. In this process the veto right of the great powers in the Security Council must be eliminated—sooner rather than later.

6. Finally, a new world sovereignty must emerge in the form of a new world law. Although this would be strictly limited, it would constitute the beginning of a world government, dedicated to the prevention and abolition of the supreme crime of atomic war—of war itself.

When we examine these steps and check them with the daily headlines we shall see that, for all the recurring slumps and crises —such as that over Iran—the gale of circumstance drives us all irresistibly toward increased international co-operation; toward the ultimate harbor of a world federation. We *have* to co-operate because failure to do so means chaos, anarchy, and war—in whichever order you may care to place them. We are compelled to pin our hopes upon the growth and development of the United Nations because—in all our shrinking world—there is no other agency of slightest safety in which to place them. We are forced to struggle, often reluctantly and often in the face of serious disillusionment, along the path toward a world sovereignty, because national sovereignty is far too narrow and deceitful an instrument with which to confront the Goliath of the Atomic Age. Instinctively, and almost against their will, the peoples of the earth are whipped and driven in the direction of their only conceivable safety. This is one of the incomparable dramas of the ages. We are swept up in it, millions of indistinct and baffled human forms. We are ants whose ant-hill has been kicked and mutilated. The will to live and the instinct to rebuild react more swiftly than our thoughts; and in the pandemonium and seeming confusion of our initial reactions we are already beginning to rebuild—in spite of ourselves.

But human beings are perhaps more stubborn and less intelligent than the ants. We accept under protest much of what law we now have. We fought centuries of wars before bowing to so comprehensive and logical a thing as *national* law. Today we see all the inconveniences of global law. Surely, we would prefer a veto power, so long as that privilege is reserved for *us;* so long as the weaker and less fortunate are not strong enough to shout us down. Surely, we would prefer to keep our national armies and clutch our own atomic bombs to our bosoms—yet we tell the world that *we* would never tolerate a police state and a dictatorship in our country. How we can possibly build an atomic *national* defense without accepting a police-ruled, dictatorial government, most of us do not attempt to explain. But we cannot avoid this quandary—and already the leaders of the world have turned significantly away from what purely *national* atomic defense would compel. The arguments for the veto and against a world control of atomic weapons will be loud, shrill, and long— from Americans as much as from Russians. That these protests should win in the end would constitute such suicidal folly that it cannot be imagined.

We can see this more clearly by considering—

What happened at Moscow.

When the Big Three agreed upon a UN Atomic Commission, they took the first great and fateful step toward a world control to abolish war—and equally toward ultimate world government. The Atomic Commission (which certainly merits capital letters) must produce specific proposals on the following lines:

"(A) For extending between all nations the exchange of basic scientific information for peaceful ends;

"(B) For control of atomic energy to the extent necessary to ensure its use only for peaceful purposes;

"(C) For the elimination from national armaments of atomic weapons *and of all other major weapons adaptable to mass de-struction;* [italics mine]

"(D) For effective safeguards by way of inspection and other means to protect complying states against the hazards of violations and evasions."

The first thing to be said about this remarkably specific program is that the governments of the Soviet Union, Great Britain, and the United States all accepted it—with its very plain implications—as their pledged objective. This is a joint repudiation of strictly national atomic defense, for any one of the Big Three or for anyone else. Of equally great significance, it is joint acceptance of the principle that atomic "and all other major weapons adaptable to mass destruction" must be removed from national control and national use. Thus the epoch-making goal has been declared and made official. What we have since witnessed has been, for the most part, merely a great deal of inevitable debate and difference of opinion about the correct or most prac-tical *procedures* by which to move toward this goal.

It seems to me that this discussion, in itself, marks a notable progress. At last we have come to grips with the central problem. We are committed to the main tasks of controlling and outlawing atomic weapons and of creating a machinery that can prevent war. Whether or not some of us think that the idea of world government is a "butterfly," how are we going to walk out on this job now? We Americans could do so only by breaking up the United Nations Organization (established on our own soil), or by rendering it so impotent as to be the bitter laughing-stock of the entire world. Should we be in any sense more secure with UN smashed or utterly discredited? And has not this become the identical situation of the Soviet Union, too?

These lines are written early in 1946, and a tremendous number of things can happen before they can reach print. But I think we may safely anticipate certain aspects of Russia's policy in regard to UN and the deliberations of the Atomic Commission. The Russians will make a hard fight to retain their veto in the Security Council as long as possible, and they may manage to retain the veto power for a considerable period—even running into years. The Russians, too, will probably take positions in regard to the proposed atomic inspection system which will be unorthodox, complicated, and provocative of prolonged and controversial discussion. If the Russians accept inspection by a world authority for themselves, they will certainly demand the assurance that it will be extremely rigid in regard to all other nations as well. If the Russians should finally seek to hedge—or should reverse themselves and reject the machinery proposed for inspection at some climactic point in the commission's labors—what then?

It seems to me that the Atomic Commission is bound to have a considerable portion of Russian headaches and Soviet crises, along with a great many others. Serious setbacks are bound to threaten, and likely to happen. But if the Soviets were alone or virtually alone in balking at the commission's chief recommendations for atomic control, what could they possibly gain by walking out or blocking any agreement? The most disastrous and fear-compelling thing that could happen, for the Soviet Union, would be for her to find herself alone and isolated from the great majority of the world's nations. From 1917 to 1941 the Soviet Russians learned all the heavy and crippling inconveniences of national isolation. For Moscow to reject a world atomic control would be to revert to an isolation infinitely more dangerous and precarious than anything the Soviets experienced in the past. Being hardheaded realists, and congenitally distrustful still of the capitalistic nations, the Soviets will battle with great determination—and their customary diplomatic skill—to gain an atomic authority as near as possible to their own prescription and their own preferences. But would it not seem that the Russians have far more to gain by being on the inside looking out, than by being on the outside trying to look in?

It would also be possible, of course, for the Russians to be pushed outside through maladroit policies or actions on the part of the United States and Britain. At various times the Russians have gained little by brusqueness, yet we too have people who say that the only way to handle the Russians is "to tell them where to get off." Some of our military (and congressional) minds seem to think that an ideal formula for getting co-operation from the Russians would be an attitude of "take-it-or-leave-it." You can imagine how far the Russians or the British would get trying "take-it-or-leave-it" with us Americans—and that's exactly how far we could expect to get with the Russians by such tactics. It is one thing to be firmly realistic and to know when to say no. But to hand the Russians (or any of our world neighbors) a tough-minded proposition in an ultimatumlike fashion would be child-ish on the part of United States representatives, and fatal for international co-operation. *A world leader cannot afford to sound or act like a bully.* It was the great merit of Secretary of State Byrnes that he carried no blustering obstreperousness to Moscow. By being fair-minded and by seeking to avoid any discriminations, American diplomacy scored an important success.

I emphasize intentionally these two schools of thought about how to deal with the Russians. Obviously the British and Ameri-cans cannot afford to yield to Moscow on every vital issue, and our governments would get into serious trouble by doing so. But neither can the Anglo-Americans appear to stack the cards or gang up against their Big Three partner. We can never win the support of world opinion except by asking no more of the Soviets than we ourselves are willing to concede or accept. The way to win the Russians to increased international co-operation is through persuasion and example. After that, if the Russians some-times provoke crises by their tendency to overreach themselves, it is *their* situation and standing in the world family, rather than ours, which will inevitably be complicated as a result.

These next four or five years are the period of our mutual decisive trial. We must transform the United Nations into a reality equipped to function in an atomic age. We must lay solid foundations of world law for an eventual world federa-tion. But we cannot have any world organization without Soviet Russia, the world's second strongest and largest power. Without Russia the world is split in two, with each camp arming against the other. This is why the kind of suggestion made by Charles A. Lindbergh on December 17 is subject to serious reservations. Mr. Lindbergh advocated "a world organization backed by military power . . . led by Western peoples who developed modern science with its aviation and its atomic bomb." His emphasis was on "Western" nations alone, and he did not mention Russia at all.

We shall hear much more of this kind of talk. It is suspect because it comes from those who were formerly most ardent isolationists. They would gild over their previous isolationism by advocating a "world" organization which would leave out the Soviet Union's one sixth of the earth's surface. In reality, this would be merely a thinly veiled alliance against Russia. It would split the world in two. Between 1939 and Pearl Harbor in 1941 Mr. Lindbergh gradually and skillfully developed an isolationist thesis which revealed itself as pro-Fascist in certain important respects. Lest this statement should seem exaggerated, I would refer you to my analysis of the Lindbergh speeches in Chapter XVII of *No Other Road to Freedom*. Pertinent quotations from these speeches make instructive reading for Americans today; especially since the Lindbergh who was so remarkably inaccurate in his prophecies and analysis of military and political questions in 1940–41 seems inclined to offer us more prophecies and "solutions." To champion "world" organization, without Russia and as a "Western" monopoly, is to oppose the whole basis of UN and world co-operation. Such an artful proposition may appeal to those who fear or hate the Soviets. But to follow it would be to divide the world against itself, and to make an atomic war the only logical and eventual outcome.

Fortunately the Big Three at Moscow chose the alternative course of co-operation. From this one great fact emerged as of supreme significance. It was demonstrated that neither the Soviets, the British, nor we Americans can afford to dynamite or repudiate a system of worldwide atomic control; that none of the Big Three governments is anxious to take this disastrous step. It was also demonstrated that none of the Big Three desires to take a lone course outside the United Nations Organization. This was redemonstrated by Russia's refusal to take more than a face-saving recess from the Security Council at the height of the Iranian crisis in March, 1946. In the Moscow conference the untenable concept of a "Western" world and an "Eastern" world was rejected. It was rejected because all parties concerned recognized that *a split world cannot possibly hope to dominate safely the split atom.*

Thus UN could launch its fateful experiment in January 1946, and thus the world's nations returned to—

World co-operation directed toward world government.

Why did we come back to a revised and expanded League of Nations? The United States and some fifty other countries did this for one all-compelling reason. In our complex but sharply contracted world *there is no place else to go.*

The peoples and their governments understand clearly that half-a-world is no world at all. They begin to understand that we are compelled to have at the very least a world control of all major weapons of mass destruction because we cannot hope to survive in any other way. Perhaps it is not generally understood as yet, but we are also compelled to eliminate the veto privilege of the few big powers (in the Security Council) because it violates all principles of justice and equality under the law. If, in due time, the Soviet Union cannot see that this kind of equality for peace is essential, then that could work out only to the accentuated discomfort and isolation of the U.S.S.R. Equality under world law is far more essential to our common world welfare than the veto power could be to any of UN's leading members. The United Nations Charter can be no more static and unamendable than the Constitution of the United States. UN must change and grow —and the immediate and early deadline of the atomic bomb should prove more than sufficient to make it do so.

For we have taken a road from which there can be no turning back without certain disaster. The first several milestones in world co-operation are clearly marked. Each of them is another step toward creation of a new world sovereignty; toward the final establishment of a world federation governed by a new world law. Achievement of an outright world government may, of course, require a good many years. But the Declaration of Independence in 1776 led straight to the framing of the U.S. Constitution in 1787. In London in January 1946, a momentous event occurred. The world's nations, in fact, adopted a Declaration of *Interdependence* along with a Constitution of the World. A Declaration of Interdependence is an imposing monument to the progress of mankind's comprehension, to the lifting of man's objectives for self-government.

We are gradually learning that national sovereignty alone is neither wide enough nor strong enough to make our world habitable and safe from atomic doom. We have begun to see the only basis sufficiently broad to provide security for us all. In the 1770's there was no safe future for Massachusetts, Virginia, or any of the other thirteen colonies without merging their restricted sovereignty into one that was much greater—capable of greater protection and greater benefits. Do we see among nations today anything essentially different from this logical action for self-preservation? Today Chicago is physically as near to China as Massachusetts was to Virginia in 1776. Thanks to the marvels of aviation and radio, our world has been amazingly telescoped both in space and time. Thanks to the scourge of centuries of nationalistic wars, earth's sixty and more nations have become no more than so many separate colonies—unsafe and insecure without a higher and unifying common authority. Thanks to atomic weapons, no corner of the globe can hope to live unmolested, to itself alone. What we have invented is the imperative necessity of intimate co-operation; the inescapable urgency for world law and a world sovereignty. The ever-rising spiral of mankind's physical, political, and social relationships has merely reached its penultimate level; and now, thrusting persistently against prejudices and antiquated minds, this spiral of hope and safety evolves toward its ultimate plateau.

We can perceive how thinking has already changed in our dawning age of atomic energy when we note the new emphasis which has crept into language since August 6, 1945. Suddenly the most authoritative and thoughtful of our citizens began to speak of "world law," of "a world sovereignty," of "world government." And these same leaders began to advocate a more direct participation on the part of individual citizens in every land. In Dublin, New Hampshire, a group of prominent Americans met [1] and urged that a World Federal Government should supersede the United Nations Organization. The Dublin declaration

[1] In October 1945.

insisted that the UN Charter "is inadequate and behind the times as a means to promote peace and world order." It urged the "pooling of national external sovereignty by all nations for the common good of mankind."

Does this sound visionary? On the contrary, atomic weapons of mass destruction have made world government a final and absolute necessity. We have already moved a good distance on this road, and circumstance will steadily push us farther. If the United Nations Charter cannot be sufficiently amended and expanded, there are many who believe that a World Assembly of some sort—beyond and above UN—will have to be created soon. The first great and epochal impetus to this idea was given by Foreign Secretary Ernest Bevin of Great Britain in his memorable speech in the House of Commons on November 23, 1945. The final consequences of Mr. Bevin's suggestions are unpredictable, but can scarcely fail to be of great historical importance. This is why we must study carefully—

Mr. Bevin's conception of a World Assembly.

On the day before Mr. Bevin spoke, Anthony Eden, former Foreign Secretary, had urged the abandonment of narrow ideas of national sovereignty. Mr. Bevin developed this hitherto radical idea with remarkable boldness. Thus two leading British statesmen became the first representatives of a major power to speak clearly and boldly for evolution toward an unprecedented world sovereignty and toward world government. To Mr. Bevin, in fact, belongs the honor of first championing the establishment of a World Assembly and of doing so as a responsible official of a great nation.

"I am driven to ask," said Foreign Secretary Bevin, "will law be observed if it is arrived at only by treaty and promises and decisions by governments, as at present arranged? In all the years this has broken down so often. . . . Will the people feel that the law is *their* law if it is derived and enforced by the adoption of past methods, whether League of Nations, concert of Europe, or anything of that kind? . . . Where does the power to make law actually rest? It is not even in this House. . . . It is in the votes of the people. They are sovereign authority.

"It may be interesting to call attention to the development of the United States of America. Originally, when the states came together, they met as states with separate governments. But they soon discovered they had little or no power to enforce their decisions. . . . They then decided—for the purpose of conducting foreign affairs, taxation, defense, and for the regulation of commerce—that they would create a federal body and in that body there would be direct representation of the people. . . . So from the outset the United States drew its power to make laws directly from the people. That is the growth of the United States to the great state which it is today."

With this, Foreign Secretary Bevin launched into his most provocative and supremely significant declarations. "The fact is," he said, "no one ever surrenders sovereignty. *They merge it into a greater sovereignty.* I think if you try to take on too big a thing, like all the things you are building up under the United Nations now, such as education and all the rest of it, your organization may break down. It can only deal with the specific objective that the people feel is necessary for their security."

Then Mr. Bevin took the hurdle which no official leader in the Truman administration has, at this writing, yet taken. He spoke, it seems to me, as a Lincoln or a Woodrow Wilson—were they living in our era—could have been expected to speak. "I feel," he declared, "we are driven relentlessly along this road. We need a new study for the purpose of creating a World Assembly *elected directly from the people of the world as a whole* [italics mine]; who, in fact, make the world law which they, the people, will then accept and be morally bound and willing to carry out. For it will be *from their votes* that the power will have been derived, and it will be *for their direct representatives* to carry it out."

This, you will agree, is a new voice and a new approach. This would mean that you and I would not have to depend upon some U.S. senator who, by seniority rights, happened to be chairman of the Senate's Foreign Relations Committee to cast our vote for enforcing world peace. It would mean that we would not have to depend upon someone whom each succeeding President happened to appoint as chief delegate for the United States. It would mean that you and I, and the voters in every land, would elect our peace-enforcing representatives from a special list of our most highly qualified citizens—for one specific job, to devote his entire attention and career to supervising and improving the peace machinery of a world institution authorized to do nothing except prevent war. Such an American delegate would be responsible not merely to the President or to Congress. He would be directly responsible to the American people who selected him for this one task. Presumably there might be several American delegates, but all chosen by direct elections.

"You may invent all kinds of devices to decide who is the aggressor," Mr. Bevin continued. "But . . . the only repository of faith I have ever been able to find to determine that is the common people. *There has never been a war yet which—if the facts had been put calmly before the ordinary folk—could not have been prevented.* [Italics mine.] The fact is they are kept separated from one another. . . . *The common man, I think, is the great protection against war.*

"The supreme act of government is the horrible duty of deciding matters which affect the life or death of the people. That power rests in this House as far as this country is concerned. *I would merge that power into the greater power of a directly elected World Assembly* in order that the great repositories of destruction and science may be their property, against the misuse of which it is their duty to protect us . . . that they may determine in the ordinary sense whether a country is acting as an aggressor or not."

Foreign Secretary Bevin concluded his striking address by saying: "I am willing to sit with anybody, of any party, of any nation, to try to devise a franchise or a constitution—just as other great countries have done—for a World Assembly . . . with a limited objective—the objective of peace. Once we get to that stage, I believe we shall have taken a great progressive step.

"*In the meantime there must be no weakening of the institution which my Right Honorable Friends built in San Francisco. It must be the prelude to further development.* This must not be considered a substitute for it, but rather a completion or a development of it—so that the benefit of the experience and administration derived in that institution [UN] may be carried to its final end. From the moment you accept that, one phrase goes—and that is 'international law.' That phrase presupposes conflict between nations. It would be replaced by 'world law,' with a moral world force behind it—rather than a law with a world judiciary to interpret it. With a world police to enforce it, with the decision of the people with their own votes resting in their own hands . . . the great world-sovereign, elected Authority, which would hold in its care the destinies of the people of the world."

In such new language as this we have been invited to open our imaginations to an eventual World Assembly dedicated solely to the maintenance of peace. At first contact this may seem a daring or rash suggestion. But in reality it is no more daring or rash than was the decision of the founding fathers, in their day, to shape thirteen isolated colonies into the United States of America. Is there any nation's people on this earth today who would not prefer a far more direct influence upon questions of peace and war? Is there any nation which would stand to lose by direct election of specially selected candidates to a world body occupied only with problems of peace? Why should the question of peace or war—in its broad global aspects—be entrusted to a handful of our citizens primarily because of their party connections or party prominence?

I think we already have a sufficient answer in the uninspiring, and sometimes mediocre, character of the first United States delegation to UN in London. Here America was to play its first great role as a leader in the new postwar world organization. Here the greatest knowledge, authority, tact, and wisdom were urgently needed throughout the American delegation and its alternates. But Henry L. Stimson, one of our most distinguished former Secretaries of State, was not included; nor was Hamilton Fish Armstrong, eminent editor of *Foreign Affairs*. One or more of our ablest former ambassadors were not included. Walter Lippmann, who had invaluable official experience throughout the shaping of the 1919 peace treaties, was not included. None of the most distinguished justices of the U.S. Supreme Court was summoned, nor any of the nation's leading educators. And, because of seniority rules and party priorities, neither the Senate nor the House of Representatives was adequately represented with its best brains.

If the American people had been presented with a list of some thirty of our most distinguished Americans from various qualified walks of life, they could not have failed to elect a more able and creditable list of delegates and alternates. We cannot contribute adequately—or safely—to building a new world if we must continue to rely upon delegates to UN who are picked chiefly because of their party seniority in Congress, or because of their personal domestic influence in the Democratic or the Republican parties. Qualification for a vital role on the world stage is by no means merely equivalent to qualification for being elected to Congress from the Eleventh District. But, until the people demand something a lot better, any President must remain the prisoner of domestic politics in selecting men for a tremendously important international role.

As we stumble along, during these next few years when any major error can have incalculably grave consequences for all of us, we shall gradually become conscious of the fact that world co-operation is a full-time job. In every country we shall find, as various governments soon learned under the League of Nations, that we must develop international specialists; that there must be men outside of strict party politics to maintain a continuity for the voice of America, France, China, and every other country. As we proceed we shall learn that those governments which send the ablest and most gifted delegates to represent them will gain an increasing authority in world affairs. Thus, we in America will be forced to adopt a more adult and much more discerning attitude toward the heavy responsibility of meeting international problems and acting as a world leader.

In this respect we have one piece of inestimable good fortune. You can sum this up in a startling and concise phrase—

United Nations Organization, U.S.A.

We Americans have become the hosts, and our country has become the home, of the greatest political experiment that history has even known. When the delegates in London voted to bring UN to the United States, they did far more than pay a tribute to the power and prestige of our young republic. In truth, Mother Europe and Grandmother Asia bowed to a lusty and much younger nationhood in the Western Hemisphere. But in so doing I think the world's nations rendered us a unique service of which we Americans were in urgent need. By coming to us they brought us out into the world in a manner, and to a degree, which could never have been achieved in any other way.

UN and the U.S.A. are now indissolubly linked. Both physically and spiritually we are living now *in* the United Nations Organization. It will become part of American life, as we have become mingled with the world in a new manner. With this vast new world capital building and growing on American soil, the American people cannot escape the drama of its progress. We cannot ignore its deliberations. Scores of thousands of our citizens, and countless thousands of our teachers, students, and schoolchildren, will flock to this seat of world co-operation. The greatest worldwide decisions will be taken on our native soil. They will no longer come to us under a remote and impersonal Geneva dateline. They will come to us under a familiar American name.

There will no longer be any excuse for American Senators and Congressmen not to be well informed on how UN functions, or how its vital decisions have been reached. Every member of Congress will be able to attend United Nations sessions, observe its debates, and make contact with political leaders from all parts of the world. The world capital can scarcely fail to become a second and higher capital for the American people. When UN fails, its failure must inevitably reflect more upon us than the people of any other nation. Its successes must become increasingly our own successes. Its prestige will become bound ever more closely to the prestige of America. Thus, for the second time in our history the United States becomes the home of a tremendous political and social experiment.

United Nations, U.S.A., means a continuous education in world citizenship and world co-operation for the American people. It means that we shall now become more intimately acquainted with world statesmen and with many of the most distinguished spokesmen and thinkers from all other nations. While they are discovering America, we shall be discovering them. We can provide all of the mechanics and techniques for the construction of the most modern, the most superbly equipped capital that the world has ever seen. We can provide it with unsurpassed aerial communications; with the finest in radio, telegraphic, and other facilities. And once we have played a leading role in creating a complete and amazing world capital in a new place, upon virgin soil, who can imagine that this center of dramatic new endeavor will not become a magnet of attraction and a source of great pride to the American people?

We shall live within easy reach of the greatest political and social adventure of modern times. In all probability, we shall be able to follow all of its most important debates by radio. In many ways the great United Nations radio station will be our own station. From our country it will speak eventually to all the world. All these things, it seems to me, are remarkably constituted to appeal to the enthusiasm of the American people and to kindle their imaginations. UN will be blazing a great new trail, and we Americans especially like people and organizations that blaze trails. We are also a people who want to see for ourselves. This we shall have the opportunity of doing. Because we are more essentially provincial than most European peoples, because the outside world has always seemed so much farther away to most of us, I suspect we shall be much more attracted to this momentous drama than we have imagined.

In this process, developing steadily over the next decade, the idea of world co-operation will become familiar to American minds. The world capital of UN, being in our midst, will make the whole world much closer to us. We shall have to learn that peace is built only one stone at a time. We shall have to become accustomed to setbacks, and resigned to occasional periods of crisis and disillusionment. But the reminder of a sovereignty above all national sovereignties will be fermenting within our borders, and developing as one assembly after another meets. Will world government then seem such a remote and visionary conception to us? I believe that we shall see world government in the process of being born. I believe that Americans are richly endowed to grasp its meaning and to understand its imperative necessity. This, at any rate, is the unique opportunity which now opens within our borders. For the nations of mankind will build until they build world government, or they must relapse into anarchy —the self-destruction of atomic war.

Chapter XX

"THE WORLD'S BEST HOPE"

Far along the world-wide whisper of the south-wind
  rushing warm,
With the standards of the peoples plunging thro' the
  thunder-storm;

Till the war-drum throbbed no longer, and the battle-
  flags were furl'd
In the Parliament of Man, the Federation of the World.
                        Tennyson, *Locksley Hall*

We have spent quite a lot of time on this inventory. I suppose we could have flown around the world in less time. But the trouble is we wouldn't have landed in very many places; and we wouldn't have traveled very far from the airports, nor probably have spent more than a few hours in any one spot. That might be fun, but it's no way to take an inventory.

When you take stock you want to know what's located in which warehouses, and what are the various brands of goods, and where the *popular demand* is running. Then, you also need to know what kind of articles are falling off—and what you've got to do if you wish to be in a fairly sound, and safe, position tomorrow. So we couldn't take a world inventory, slap-dash, while buzzing around the world.

I have a hunch that we passengers usually need to prepare for a round-the-world flight just as much as the pilot and navigator do. The pilot aims for a chain of airfields. What do we aim at? It would take a whole series of guidebooks to get us equipped for looking at the kind of world we propose to explore. If we have time to plan in advance, we'd probably be wise to consult quite a number of source books. But there's another hitch. The trouble is that most of the books are outdated. A *Baedeker* for Berlin or Nagasaki, 1939 edition, might as well be a guidebook for ancient Rome. That's why we were so rash as to try to draft an up-to-date inventory. It can't be absolutely complete, or entirely satisfactory. But I believe we have managed to sort out a major portion of—

The common denominators of our postwar, atomic world.

Perhaps this humming sphere of earth and sea looks considerably smaller than when we started out. Perhaps some of those supposedly strange and foreign nations may now be seen to have more in common with each other, and with us, than we might have imagined. Perhaps the destinies of far-away peoples have merged rather surprisingly, and have also emerged closer and more akin to our own. It may be that some of us will come home to our houses of relative plenty wishing we could do a little more, or give a little more, to help balance things and make them right. Perhaps some of us will also come home in a humbler spirit, wondering why we in America have been so blessed; pondering how we can lift ourselves to the fearful level of our responsibilities; and feeling, in a new sense, the oneness of man with man. For "the earth is ours and the fullness thereof"—but for how long, O Lord, how long?

We have seen certain of the common denominators of our newly contracted world; and if we comprehend them we shall perceive that there is more in them than reflexes of despair and the seething lava of revolt. We shall also perceive that there is in them the bursting promise of new life, the lifted face of opportunity, the slender but persistent voice of an unstilled hope. Within this turbulent human fermentation, inside this turmoil and rising with it, dwell mankind's hopes as well as mankind's fears. And "humanity with all its fears, with all the hopes of future years" is humanity astir; humanity awakened in a new and deeper darkness which *could* precede a new and immeasurably brighter dawn.

We look to Europe and we see the enlarged forces of Socialism or of Communism playing a greater role than ever before. We look to Asia and we hear the nationalism of hundreds of millions of brown and yellow peoples speaking with a new voice, newly insistent. The masses of the New Europe are uttering a protest against past failures or past abuses. The masses of the New Asia direct their protest against the exploitation of imperialism. Both in Europe and in Asia tides of humanity repudiate a feudalism which has kept human beings in misery, near-slavery, or slavery for centuries. They are not demanding the lives of other men. They are merely demanding *Life for themselves*. The Negroes of America can understand this, and most of them have not had very much education. It would be better for the rest of us if we made certain that we, too, understand.

They are asking, asking; in all the world they are asking. Asking for what? They are asking for a decent and a fairer share in the productive wealth of their own countries; for perhaps half or two thirds as much as a majority of Americans have had for many generations. Does it seem radical to you that they should demand perhaps one fourth or one fifth as much in China and Malaya—perhaps one half as much in Greece or Hungary—perhaps four fifths as much in Belgium or France—as George Jones, American, has always taken for granted? Does that seem radical?

Oftentimes they do not speak very precisely. But if you listen, the meaning comes clear. If you look, the meaning has its logic. Oftentimes they do not know the big words. Instead they say: "a better life." But what they are saying is that China, India, and Europe can produce much more, but that *their* portion— *for the most*—was always the least. What they are saying is that they too could produce more, but if more is going to be produced then more should also be distributed—*to them*. They are not yet saying, most of them, that Communism is the only way to do this. . . . They *are* saying: "We know it can be done. We know it can be done, but you can't do it *against* us. We are against anything that is against us. You must do it *with* us. We are Men."

They are saying: "We know your automobiles, and your airplanes, and your motion pictures. We have seen some of your wonderful inventions. We know you will make many more. But are your inventions *for* us, or are they *against* us? The feudal landlords also had wonderful things, and the tax-collectors and the warlords—they had all the weapons on their side. Now you can destroy 500,000,000 people in a single night or two. Now you can make engines of godlike power. Are you going to use them to keep us in dread, and half-starved? Are you going to use these marvelous things only for more power and more profits for the white race? Are you going to use them again in Europe chiefly for more profits for the few? Or will you use your great new inventions for *less profits* for the few, and *more benefits* for the many? Will they be used *for* us, or *against* us? It is we who mine the coal and the copper. It is we who grow the wheat and the rice. It is we who eat little, who feed you—who eat well. Do you count us *in*, our Western friends? Or must we bide our time a little longer, until we count you *out*?"

They are asking, asking. They say it in strange and simple words, in scores of languages and hundreds of dialects. At first, it sounds confused to you and me. But it isn't confused. It is a great and vibrant chorus of humanity's long-dispossessed. And what they, in this ever-rising and ever-widening chorus, say is what Abraham Lincoln also said. . . . Human rights are greater than property rights. They say that the most flagrant of inequalities can no longer be tolerated; that inequality of opportunity spells a condemnation to inequality of man. They say that men and women can live better and warmer than before. They say that the human spirit has not been broken. They say: "War could not destroy us. Peace shall not imprison us." They say that human dignity has not been lost; and because it has not been lost, they say that human dignity will yet burgeon in the light of their new day.

In the Occident and the Orient alike the legions of the outcasts and the betrayed, of the impoverished and the long-suffering, are awakening to a new consciousness of their own strength. In many cases they are being sold down the river again; sometimes by their politicians or by their own war profiteers or by their own slippery Fascists; sometimes for the sake of "strategic security" for the big powers. But the underdogs of East and West have learned to see behind the camouflage of handsome phrases and sonorous future promises. Around the global circuit they are demanding that the earth's powerful should give them a greater chance or a first chance to govern themselves. Whether Korean, Chinese, or Indonesian, whether Yugoslav or Greek, they have waited much too long. And the only freedoms which will still their discontent and rising wrath are such freedoms as they may grasp and hold in their own hands.

By whatever Ism of monarchism, Fascism, imperialism, or even parliamentarianism the old deal was called—or by whatever Ism of Communism, Socialism, or republicanism a newer deal may be called—the have-nots and the still unliberated judge it by what it offers in terms of their daily lives. The glittering colors of any Ism's presentation party dress will not dazzle them for long; nor fill their clamoring stomachs, nor clothe their bodies, nor release within them the realization that at last they are men—free to stand and standing free.

For all these, who are the meek and the disinherited and the downtrodden, any Ism is what any Ism does. And if you are afraid of the Isms, Right or Left, they suspect that it is for your own reasons of privilege—not for theirs. "Why should you be afraid of the Ism?" they ask. "Is it not really that you are afraid of *us*? For what we are demanding begins and ends with an Ism which your churches praise and your leaders make beautiful speeches about. They say it as a very big word—*humanitarianism*. Is it not big enough for little people like ourselves? We want only a better life in a better and a freer world. Is it not that which you also believe in? We do not have to wait forever. We have heard the bells and we thought you rang them. We shall go with whoever will help us ring them louder still."

It seems that the wars and the death and the horror have not been altogether wasted. Out of the torment and the travail a new community of humankind is slowly being born. It seeds and sprouts far down, close to the grimy earth; and those who are closest to the soil first see and feel the fragile green of something new. We may walk too self-confidently. We may listen too little. We may look too high. For there is something which the simpler peoples of this earth have sensed and understand. They sense the coming of a new springtime and a new summer. They sense that the multitude of common men and women now have a long-withheld birthright almost within their grasp. They have learned that literacy brings the hope of freedom and that unity promises new power. Having seen what made others strong, they sense at last what is theirs for the seeking and the serving. Things no longer need to be what they have always been. For theirs, the peoples', is *the ultimate power.*

This has never before happened simultaneously throughout much of Europe and much of Asia, yet it is happening today. It has become the pattern of our times; a prophetic finger pointing at tomorrow and the day after tomorrow. As yet it is more spir-itual than physical, the awakening of millions of human souls. As yet, they talk of their own freedom, their own independence, their own rule through popular elections. But when before have so many hundreds of millions spoken so similar a language? Beneath their separate strivings lies a deep, instinctive recognition of man's common plight, man's common hopes, and man's common fate. And the meaning of this? Is it not that in human terms our shrinking world seeks, by some biological instinct, to knit itself together at the bottom levels rather than in the upper crust? Where there exists the greatest community of need and hope and yearned-for justice, there our future world must surely take its shape. Through how many years or generations does not much matter. What matters chiefly is that the long and patient process of knitting together has begun. What matters greatly is that the world's peoples have begun to comprehend *that they are not alone, and that they need not be alone.* On one side of the earth or another, other peoples are seeking and demanding the same things. No longer are any of them alone. Tomorrow and after tomorrow, they shall be in-evitably less alone.

Are you afraid of this? Ah, but was it not this which in Cromwell's day first opened the doors of greatness to England and her people? Was it not this which stirred the hearts of our American colonists in the 1770's, and so "brought forth upon this continent a new nation, conceived in liberty, and dedicated to the proposition that all men are created equal"? Was it not this which made Thomas Jefferson speak of our republican and representative government as "the world's best hope"? Now, in our time, humanity in its hundreds of millions clamors that all men indeed are created equal. Now the world's masses ask that we extend to them that which we have been so proud to cherish for ourselves. It would probably cost us something in annual profits over the first transition years—if that is what concerns you most. But to fail to hearken and to fail to heed could well cost us the full, colossal bill of our present civilization.

With atomic energy at our fingertips, who would presume to insist that our entire world, if we are intelligent, cannot step forward into an era of prosperity hitherto unknown? What the English and the Americans of yesterday demanded and united to achieve, the peoples of a large proportion of our new world are demanding today. If they do not achieve it before complete unity, then they will find unity—as we found it—in struggling toward their clearly perceived goal. Are we afraid because they want the same things we have been so happy to have? There can no longer remain any monopoly on human freedoms. If freedom and self-government are noble things, why should we be afraid?

For what the world revolution gives us is a unique and unprecedented opportunity to make the peoples of Europe and Asia our allies and our brothers. What the extraordinary social upheavals of our time provide is the practical possibility of transforming, gradually and with clear intent, the majority of earth's peoples into another federation far greater than the thirteen colonies. "The world's best hope" has outgrown the boundaries of our North American continent. At last the blood-soaked road has risen and broadened. The world's best hope now belongs, as of human right it should belong, *to the world.* This is what the peoples of earth, through this war and through its continuing revolution, have been trying to tell us. It would be strange and tragic if they, the largely uneducated and the least privileged, should understand this better than we.

For our choices are not many, but few. Either we shall join in helping lift the peoples of our shrinking world to higher opportunities, or we shall in effect remain standing upon their necks. Either we shall say to them: "We are with you"; or we say to them: "We are against you." Either we shall say: "Humanity is one"; or we shall say: "Humanity is civil war—to our common self-destruction." For a little while longer—but only a little while—the choice is more ours than theirs.

And what the peoples say is perhaps no more important than what we ourselves are saying, or are going to say. Believing in democracy is no different from believing in love or in faith. We cannot believe in love, and keep it to ourselves. The one cannot survive the other. No more, it seems to me, can we in America, Britain, or France believe in democratic government without believing that the opportunity for it belongs as much to every other people as to ourselves. If we believe in a steadily rising standard of living and an expanding general prosperity for ourselves, then these are equally desirable and equally the moral rights of people everywhere. Thus what the world's peoples are demanding are only those things which Washington, Jefferson, and Lincoln saw as the natural rights of human beings. These conceptions were the heart of the American Revolution as today they have become the heart of the World Revolution. If we still believe in the principles of our own revolution, then is it not within our power to make much of the world revolution our own?

Ah, but that depends. That depends upon whether we are big enough in soul and spirit to make the peoples' cause our cause; whether we are big enough to see that humanity cannot be less than one. While we wait and wonder, and while some of us fear, they are taking an invisible poll.

"Whom are you for?" they ask. "Are you for Man?"

And those who understand that to live and to survive means to move forward into a great and incredible new world may still constitute a relatively small minority. But they are an élite, and they are unafraid. Being citizens of the world they reply, with Henry George:

"I am for Man!"

I remember an encounter and a conversation in a strange place and time. Almost everything there was old, yet much that was old was new to me. I could scarcely understand the names of some of those hinterland places, and now I'm no longer certain of the exact place. But it was somewhere in the Orient, in a remote and poverty-ridden village. It may have been in that thatched Indo-Chinese village, where we stopped, beyond Pnom Penh. Or it may have been in the Shan foothills of Burma; or higher up, in China's Yunnan province near Paoshan, along the Burma Road. Right now I can't find the name among the hieroglyphics in my many notebooks. But I remember vividly the old man and what he said.

He was brownish yellow and very old and much wrinkled; clad only in a faded denim jacket and frayed trousers, both of them patched. He had thin tufts of white on his chin, and the dignity of a village patriarch. He was much impressed that I came from a strange, far land called America. Somehow, it seemed, he had heard much talk about America—even in that isolated and primitive place.

"Will the Americans come and help us fight the Japanese?" he asked.

I didn't want to say that, right then, the Americans did not want to come. So I said: "In a little while I think they will come."

"And then," he persisted, "will the Americans help make peace?"

"Yes," I said. "The Americans also want peace. They will help make peace."

"But if we want peace, and you Americans want peace, and all the other peoples want peace," said the little old man, "why do we not make a very great peace? Why don't we make a peace so great it will cover all the world?"

"I think that is what we shall have to try to do," I answered.

The little, brownish yellow old man shook his head with a curious, sudden vigor—as if he were saying: "No, no, no!" From above his thin, creased cheeks his dark eyes bored straight at me, half-angrily, accusingly.

"It is not enough," he declared in a tone of deep reproach. "It is not only that you must try. To try is nothing. We have done that before, young man. Now we must *make* a real peace. . . . We must all make peace—*or we shall all be lost.*"

That was long ago. It now seems strange that it could have been so long ago. That was in another century, in another world . . . before Hiroshima.

Epilogue

Epilogue

"FIFTEEN MINUTES MORE, PLEASE"

I am the things that are, and those that are to be, and those that have been. No one ever lifted my skirts; the fruit which I bore was the sun.

From an inscription on the
Temple of Neith, in Egypt

I hold that man is in the right who is most closely in league with the future.

Henrik Ibsen

So a great amount of gold and many other precious things were provided by the ruler of the land; more wealth than any nation's government had ever set aside to combat the plague or tuberculosis, syphilis or cancer; a far greater wealth than any government had ever expended in so short a time for education or to end the scourge of wars. Never before had any government gambled $2,000,000,000 upon a chance so illusive and uncertain. But the most skilled minds of this and other realms were bent upon their tasks. They labored with an all-absorbing devotion; almost with bated breath. And in less than 2,000 days they had telescoped 2,000 years. Surely, this was the greatest bargain of the ages. For only $2,000,000,000 we had bought the power to unleash an unprecedented cosmic catastrophe.

So we have telescoped a score of centuries, more or less; and, telescoping time, have multiplied man's reach in fashions and degrees as yet immeasurable. But the multiplication of the physical leaves our imaginations numbed, and dwarfs our minds and souls. We have chained ourselves to stratospheric rockets and supersonic speed. Atomic power looms as a Frankenstein monster beyond the poets' dreams and capable of conquering all the earth. At last there exists a universal time-fuse. Its minute hand will tick perhaps for three years—perhaps for four—but not for more than five or seven. The minutes tick away, and the Doomsman's hand rests just above our shoulders. Such is our bargain: "the fruit of the sun"—for death, or for life.

So we are left no choice, save to joust with the Final Darkness; to unite for peace, or be consumed. This is the jest to end all jesting. Why did we, who know so little, seek to pry earth's last and mightiest secret from her breast? But now it's done. The secret's out, and something mightier than a million years waits for a finger-pressure on a button—but our fingers and our hearts and minds are what they were before. And what are five years? When the world is running on atomic time they seem as many minutes; not much more. That is the mockery and the risk of telescoping time. For the minds of men change but slowly from their habitual channels. There is no equivalent of plutonium to endow men's spirits with a vastly higher range.

While we seek to find a greater wisdom, while we slowly discern the quandary of a new world which the split atom may blow to atoms, the time-fuse ticks and ticks. Slowly we begin to hear it. And measuring the desperateness of our task we may well plead: "Just fifteen minutes more, please!" A few more years—a few more minutes—might make all the difference. Even a little more time might spell salvation for us all; a little time for millions of men and women to come awake, and throw their minds and wills into the breach; a little time to bring the meaning of the ultimatum clear.

"Just fifteen minutes more, please!"

But who are we to change the laws of earth and sun? When the bomb was made we fixed the deadline, too. When we made more bombs we made the deadline as immutable as time itself. So we shall have to work with that brief span of time which we ourselves fenced off. It is not atomic fission which now can be forced to operate more slowly. It is human minds which must force themselves to operate much faster. *Now man shall decide how much mankind has learned.* The men and women of our imperiled world have been given one last choice; one final vote. All the evidence is in. We have experienced all that thinking creatures need to learn by. The last two lessons have been the most bloody and ghastly in history. In order to learn and understand, no supposedly civilized people should need more than this.

Between 1914 and 1945 tens of millions of human beings have been destroyed by their fellow creatures. Only a few of them had any understanding of how and why it came about. But among them, here and there, of every race and tongue, were those who caught the vision of a world washed clean. Among them, now and then, were voices which spoke truly to the hearts of all mankind. Among them, too, were many high and noble voices which we never heard. Why did we drown them out? Why do we forget so soon? Ah, but there is still a little time to listen—yes, and a little time in which to learn. Fifteen minutes more?

Well, perhaps five minutes anyway.

The notebook, here by my typewriter, is the first one I used in England in November 1944. The letter, which I copied in it, was written by Major John Simonds. He was a British paratroop officer. In the early morning, before they took off for that gallant but disastrous airborne landing at Arnhem, Major Simonds may have had a premonition. At any rate he understood plainly how very slight his chances were; and there were still a few things he had to say. So, just a few hours before he died, the Major wrote a last letter to his three-year-old stepson. Save for a few phrases I copied it down just as he wrote it:

"At the moment, Klim, you're content to ask 'What's this?' But soon you'll be asking 'Why?' Some time, maybe you'll be asking a lot of questions about this particular job.

"War is a horrible affair, Klim. . . . But peace can be as horrible as war. For we can be separated too by poverty, by disease, by oppression. People can be together, yet be torn apart by these things.

"There are two ways of living. One is full and fine and free and hopeful. With the other there is no freedom, and therefore no hope. The job I am on is the job of opening the door to that first way of living—opening it to peoples of all colors and races. Our enemy, fascism, shuts and bolts that door. . . . To open a door! But it's not much good—it's a waste of lives—if, when we've done the job, we don't stride in through that open door and seize all the opportunities, and use them all with both hands, to the full.

"That's the next job, then—just as important as this one. It'll be a long job, Klim. You'll grow up while it's being done, and you too will be faced by it. Remember that all the sacrifices of this war were made to give *you* an opportunity—and you'll waste those sacrifices unless you summon the courage to take that opportunity. Remember, too, that if you and your generation ever allow that door to close again everything we are setting out to do today [taking off for Arnhem] will be thrown away. . . .

"The cause we fight for now is a common cause. Well, then, it can be the same in peace—if we so organize society that men do work with, instead of against, each other. If we eliminate the conflicts. If we destroy the economic factor which opposes man to man—if we work side by side, for the benefit of all.

"It will be a long job. It will need your courage, Klim."

But it was a different world when Major Simonds warned Klim that the job would be long. Now a great portion of the long job has been telescoped by the atomic deadline. If peace, without a Hiroshima, can be "as horrible as war," then the peace which now confronts us exceeds any nightmare hitherto imagined or devised by man. Yet its very terror and the imminence of its menace tells us that the door has been opened, and that we can and must go through.

Beyond the sunset of this recent war we dwell in a great darkness for the moment. Yet there are brave souls and noble spirits who remind us that the night, too, can be telescoped; that the stars of man's faith and hopes still show the way; that the "fruit of the sun" may yet be harvested and used for the greater glory and the higher purposes of all mankind. Listening, we hear a chorus, faint but growing and rising as the minutes tick. Listening, we hear: *"Awake, and live! We are the understanding. We are the believing. We are the undefeated. Come, you of many nations.* Come, and there shall be one house for many nations, and the earth shall be ours, and the fullness thereof. *Come, for there are but five minutes more—and the night is short, or the night will be forever.* Come, you of every nation. We are on the march. *This way lies the dawn!"*

Is it too much to ask? Too much to hope?

A great multitude, who came before us, have dared to hope and dared to do. Their voices are legion and their names are immortal. And of them all, in such an hour as this, there comes the voice of Tennyson's Ulysses. It seems today as though he were speaking for all humanity. The words are for you and for me and for all mankind. They speak as we must speak. They speak for the dawn:

> The long day wanes; the slow moon climbs; the deep
> Moans round with many voices. Come, my friends,
> 'Tis not too late to seek a newer world.
> Push off, and sitting well in order smite
> The sounding furrows; for my purpose holds
> To sail beyond the sunset, and the baths
> Of all the western stars, until I die.
> It may be that the gulfs will wash us down;
> It may be we shall touch the Happy Isles,
> And see the great Achilles, whom we knew.
> Tho' much is taken, much abides; and tho'
> We are not now that strength which in old days
> Moved earth and heaven, that which we are, we are,—
> One equal temper of heroic hearts,
> Made weak by time and fate, but strong in will
> To strive, to seek, to find, and not to yield.

Yes, " 'tis not too late to seek a newer world."

Index

A NOTE ON THE TYPE

The text of this book was set on the Linotype in Baskerville. Linotype Baskerville is a facsimile cutting from type cast from the original matrices of a face designed by John Baskerville. The original face was the forerunner of the "modern" group of type faces.

John Baskerville (1706–75), of Birmingham, England, a writing-master, with a special renown for cutting inscriptions in stone, began experimenting about 1750 with punch-cutting and making typographical material. It was not until 1757 that he published his first work, a Virgil in royal quarto, with great-primer letters. This was followed by his famous editions of Milton, the Bible, the Book of Common Prayer, and several Latin classic authors. His types, at first criticized as unnecessarily slender, delicate, and feminine, in time were recognized as both distinct and elegant, and his types as well as his printing were greatly admired. Four years after his death Baskerville's widow sold all his punches and matrices to the Société Littéraire-typographique, which used some of the types for the sumptuous Kehl edition of Voltaire's works in seventy volumes.

COMPOSED, PRINTED, AND BOUND BY H. WOLFF, NEW YORK